Applications of Synthetic High Dimensional Data

Marzena Sobczak-Michalowska
University of Economics, Bydgoszcz, Poland

Samarjeet Borah
SMIT, Sikkim Manipal University (SMU), India

Zdzislaw Polkowski
The Karkonosze University of Applied Sciences, Jelenia Góra, Poland

Sambit Kumar Mishra
Gandhi Institute for Education and Technology, Bhubaneswar, India

A volume in the Advances in Data Mining and Database Management (ADMDM) Book Series

IGI Global
PUBLISHER of TIMELY KNOWLEDGE

Published in the United States of America by
IGI Global
Engineering Science Reference (an imprint of IGI Global)
701 E. Chocolate Avenue
Hershey PA, USA 17033
Tel: 717-533-8845
Fax: 717-533-8661
E-mail: cust@igi-global.com
Web site: http://www.igi-global.com

Library of Congress Cataloging-in-Publication Data

Names: Sobczak-Michalowska, Marzena, 1964- editor.
Title: Applications of synthetic high dimensional data / edited by Marzena Sobczak-Michalowska, Samarjeet Borah, Zdzislaw Polkowski, Sambit Mishra.

Description: Hershey, PA : Engineering Science Reference, [2024] | Includes bibliographical references and index. | Summary: "This book will also focus on the idea underlying a synthetic data generation along with synthesizing the main properties of real data by prioritizing their features"-- Provided by publisher.
Identifiers: LCCN 2023054250 (print) | LCCN 2023054251 (ebook) | ISBN 9798369318867 (h/c) | ISBN 9798369318874 (ebook)
Subjects: LCSH: Big data.
Classification: LCC QA76.9.B45 A6686 2024 (print) | LCC QA76.9.B45 (ebook) | DDC 005.7--dc23/eng/20240216
LC record available at https://lccn.loc.gov/2023054250
LC ebook record available at https://lccn.loc.gov/2023054251

This book is published in the IGI Global book series Advances in Data Mining and Database Management (ADMDM) (ISSN: 2327-1981; eISSN: 2327-199X)

British Cataloguing in Publication Data
A Cataloguing in Publication record for this book is available from the British Library.

For electronic access to this publication, please contact: eresources@igi-global.com.

Advances in Data Mining and Database Management (ADMDM) Book Series

ISSN:2327-1981
EISSN:2327-199X

Editor-in-Chief: David Taniar, Monash University, Australia

MISSION

With the large amounts of information available to organizations in today's digital world, there is a need for continual research surrounding emerging methods and tools for collecting, analyzing, and storing data.

The **Advances in Data Mining & Database Management (ADMDM)** series aims to bring together research in information retrieval, data analysis, data warehousing, and related areas in order to become an ideal resource for those working and studying in these fields. IT professionals, software engineers, academicians and upper-level students will find titles within the ADMDM book series particularly useful for staying up-to-date on emerging research, theories, and applications in the fields of data mining and database management.

COVERAGE

- Heterogeneous and Distributed Databases
- Neural Networks
- Data Analysis
- Database Security
- Quantitative Structure–Activity Relationship
- Customer Analytics
- Factor Analysis
- Educational Data Mining
- Predictive Analysis
- Data Mining

IGI Global is currently accepting manuscripts for publication within this series. To submit a proposal for a volume in this series, please contact our Acquisition Editors at Acquisitions@igi-global.com or visit: http://www.igi-global.com/publish/.

The Advances in Data Mining and Database Management (ADMDM) Book Series (ISSN 2327-1981) is published by IGI Global, 701 E. Chocolate Avenue, Hershey, PA 17033-1240, USA, www.igi-global.com. This series is composed of titles available for purchase individually; each title is edited to be contextually exclusive from any other title within the series. For pricing and ordering information please visit http://www.igi-global.com/book-series/advances-data-mining-database-management/37146. Postmaster: Send all address changes to above address.

Titles in this Series

For a list of additional titles in this series, please visit:
http://www.igi-global.com/book-series/advances-data-mining-database-management/37146

Recent Advancements in Multimedia Data Processing and Security Issues, Challenges, and Techniques
Ahmed A. Abd El-Latif (Menoufia University, Egypt & Prince Sultan University, Saudi Arabia) Mudasir Ahmad Wani (Prince Sultan University, Saudi Arabia) Yassine Maleh (Sultan Moulay Slimane University, Morocco) and Mohammed A. El-Affendi (Prince Sultan University, Saud Arabia)
Information Science Reference • © 2023 • 288pp • H/C (ISBN: 9781668472163) • US $300.00

Handbook of Research on the Applications of Neutrosophic Sets Theory and Their Extensions in Education
Said Broumi (Laboratory of Information Processing, Faculty of Science Ben M'Sik, University of Hassan II, Casablanca, Morocco & Regional Center for the Professions of Education and Training (CRMEF), Morocco)
Engineering Science Reference • © 2023 • 365pp • H/C (ISBN: 9781668478363) • US $325.00

Handbook of Research on Driving Socioeconomic Development With Big Data
Zhaohao Sun (Papua New Guinea University of Technology, Papua New Guinea)
Information Science Reference • © 2023 • 421pp • H/C (ISBN: 9781668459591) • US $295.00

Handbook of Research on Data-Driven Mathematical Modeling in Smart Cities
Sabyasachi Pramanik (Haldia Institute of Technology, India) and K. Martin Sagayam (Karunya Institute of Technology and Sciences, India)
Engineering Science Reference • © 2023 • 468pp • H/C (ISBN: 9781668464083) • US $325.00

Advancements in Quantum Blockchain With Real-Time Applications
Mahendra Kumar Shrivas (Department of Personnel and Administrative Reforms (E-Governance), Government of Karnataka, Bangalore, India) Kamal Kant Hiran (Aalborg University, Denmark) Ashok Bhansali (Department of Computer Engineering and Applications, GLA University, Mathura, India) and Ruchi Doshi (Azteca University, Mexico)
Engineering Science Reference • © 2022 • 312pp • H/C (ISBN: 9781668450727) • US $300.00

IGI Global
PUBLISHER of TIMELY KNOWLEDGE

701 East Chocolate Avenue, Hershey, PA 17033, USA
Tel: 717-533-8845 x100 • Fax: 717-533-8661
E-Mail: cust@igi-global.com • www.igi-global.com

Table of Contents

Detailed Table of Contents

It has been observed that regeneration as well as constitution of data within the servers may be more complex. It may be due to sharing and storing the data between several remote locations associated with distributed databases. Similarly, the replication of data can enhance the system performance having more data accessibility features and can minimize the link time to the databases. This chapter focuses on a specific algorithm prioritizing the regeneration and constitution of data dynamically, particularly in distributed databases. The proposed mechanism in this work has been prioritized with adaptive features in the sense that changes in the schema objects with regeneration can replicate in the central scheme. In this mechanism, it has also been intended to accumulate the provisioned techniques of the distributed database management systems as the performance can be analyzed experimentally.

Data visualization is one of the techniques to understand the patterns of data in graphical methods. Data visualization is an effective tool for transforming raw data into actionable insights and facilitating data-driven decision-making. High-dimensional synthetic data are datasets created artificially with an abundance of attributes or aspects. This type of synthetic data is particularly helpful for attempting to assess machine learning algorithms and data analysis techniques in scenarios

communication technologies (ICT) on the economic development of countries, identification of advantages and threats that digitalisation presents to society. According to the structure of the study, the essence and key characteristics of the digital economy concept have been specified; the main indices used to assess digitalization and the impact of ICT on the economic development of countries have been considered; the assessment of digitalisation of countries based on the indices has been carried out. It has been revealed that, despite the variety of methods for calculating indices of digitisation and ICT development, the leading countries have already been determined, and they have not significantly changed their positions, so the international economy continues to move towards the digital future at different rates, which, in turn, determine transformational shifts in economies of countries. The generalization of modern studies has made it possible to detect the advantages and threats (of economic, social, technological, political, and control nature) that digitalization presents. It has been proven that its influence on the development of society is contradictory. Therefore, in order to obtain benefits from the spread of digitalisation, a careful and balanced approach to the introduction of digital technologies in all spheres is necessary, taking into account the specifics of the processes taking place and the specifics of the development of countries, as well as the responsible interaction of states in controlling the spread of digital technologies.

In this chapter, the e-learning training in occupational health is analyzed along with safety on a selected group of employees directly employed by a logistics company and employment generated by temporary work agencies. In addition, attention has been focused on the way periodic and initial training was carried out and the impact of adaptation of knowledge of the course participants. The goal of this chapter is to find the opinions of the participants of e-learning courses, as well as to identify the benefits that affect the acquisition of knowledge in business.

The purpose of this research is to investigate the interaction between intercultural sensitivity, ethnocentrism, and social media use by using structural equality modeling method. To this end, the survey was designed by using intercultural sensitivity, ethnocentrism, and social media data scales available in the literature. The expressions in the survey were translated and re-translated by two foreign language teachers. Then, the two translations obtained were applied to a test group of 20 people, and the most accurate translation was used to collect data by easy sampling method. Data were calculated for verifier factor analysis through SPSS for Windows 22.00 and Amos 22.0 and Cronbach's Alpha. Average variety extracted (AVE) and composite reliability (CR) values were also calculated. In addition, the effects mediated by structural equality modeling were also analyzed in the Amos program using the bootstrap method.

Chapter 7

Breast cancer is a sickness that can affect women when some cells in their breasts grow abnormally. It's a serious problem and is one of the main reasons why women pass away. It's hard to accurately diagnose because it's a complex disease, and treatments and patients vary. Thankfully, there have been important discoveries in how to find and treat breast cancer. Now, about 89 out of every 100 women with breast cancer can survive if they find it early. So, we need a special kind of technology that can find breast cancer when it's just starting and reduce the chance of cancer coming back. Scientists use computer programs called "machine learning" to help find breast cancer in lots of data. The fundamental purpose of this research initiative was to prudently apply feature selection methodologies, while integrating the examination of correlations among input features. These selected significant features were subsequently employed in conjunction with a classification method.

Chapter 8

The purpose of this study is to investigate the impact of military threats on the professional burnout of employees in the organizations that have survived the COVID-19 pandemic and currently are in conditions of uncertainty and rapid digitalization, as well as to make recommendations for developing managers' skills to prevent burnout. The study uses a set of methods of scientific knowledge used in the humanities and social sciences, in particular the method of analysis, the method

to addressing these challenges: the use of high-dimensional synthetic data in the healthcare area. The authors investigate the potentials and uses of synthetic data production through a review of current literature and methodology, providing insights into its role in overcoming data access barriers, fostering innovation, and supporting evidence-based decision making. The chapter outlines significant use cases, such as simulation and prediction research, hypothesis and algorithm testing, epidemiology, health information technology development, teaching and training, public dataset release, and data connecting.

In the areas of neuroscience, medical imaging, and machine learning, the creation of synthetic data for brain scans has become a key approach. This chapter explores the concept and significance of synthetic data generation for brain images. In tasks like brain picture segmentation, disease detection, and image analysis, machine learning models perform better when using synthetic data as a catalyst for data augmentation. A wide range of methods and resources including MRI simulators, 3D modeling software, deep learning frameworks, and medical imaging software are used to create synthetic brain images. To guarantee the validity and applicability of synthetic data, however, ethical issues, data representativeness, and transparency in the generation process continue to be essential factors. Synthetic brain data are becoming more useful and realistic as technology develops, and this has the potential to completely change the fields of neuroscience and medical imaging.

The study is devoted to the determination of trends and transformations in the development of the industrial sector in the conditions of the fourth industrial revolution. The global priorities for ensuring the introduction of Industry 4.0 technologies have been analysed. The dynamics of the value added of industrial production in some countries have been determined. The ratio between the share of

Preface

AN OVERVIEW

In general, to enhance the size and capabilities of large data sources, the accessibility of actual data with well-informed decision-making process is quite important. In many situations, the statistical provisioned control mechanisms generally address the same issue by masking the actual values towards maintaining consistency and security. In this situation, the synthetic data can be used for test and operational data sets and can be maintained algorithmically to minimize the constraints implementing test or operational datasets. In true sense, the mechanisms linked towards generation of synthetic data can be accommodated with privacy, fidelity, and utility. The accuracy of specific inferences from the synthetic data can be assured along with mapping of synthetic distributed records with the actual records. This book will be facilitated with the generalized approaches linked to high dimensional synthetic data.

Where the Topic Fits in the World Today

Synthetic data can be designed provisioning specific accumulated tasks towards determination of requisite constraints required for generation of data. Generally, the accessibility of one data set cannot be imposed on other data sets. But the other data set may offer accessibility with codes to the required data set requesting accessibility. In fact, synthetic data may replicate the set of statistics of the real data and can be generated with the purpose of using it in place of real data. By controlling the data generation process, the adjustment linked to the private information released by synthetic data can be done along with the controlled resemblance to real data. Also, it can enable learning across datasets when the privacy of the data needs to be preserved. This book is not only provisioned with classification mechanisms and implementing synthetic data with minimal dimensionality, but also prioritizes the applicability of machine learning generating synthetic data. This book will help researchers and learners to verify and validate the mechanisms providing some assurance of performance. As there are so many advantages of using synthetic data inclusive of minimizing the constraints associated with regulated data, this book will prioritize various approaches linked to synthetic high dimensional data.

Target Audience

The synthetic data sets can provide the needed quantity and variety. Basically, the most basic requirement for synthetic data generation stems from testing applications, automations, and integrations. Accordingly, the demand is growing for data science testing which sometimes requires test data for machine learning as well as artificial intelligence algorithms. Accordingly, synthetic data generation can be supported on reproduction of the internal mechanisms along with preservation of dependencies on specific pieces of information. This book will also focus on the idea underlying synthetic data generation along with synthesizing the main properties of real data by prioritizing their features.

"Everyday Examples" of How This Is Used in Our Society

(i) The high dimensional synthetic data can enhance the performance of methods on numerous tasks by minimizing the challenges. Today many health care sectors are using synthetic medical data for clinical research. For example, during operation of pseudonymized personal data using different computational methods, the re-identification may remain in risk. So specific mechanisms can be considered to prioritize the synthetic data of individual granularity maintaining data privacy.

(ii) Some insurance companies in the present situations primarily test the synthetic data for predictive analytics to identify the requirements of the customers and predict regarding the services as well as products.

A DESCRIPTION OF THE IMPORTANCE OF EACH OF THE CHAPTERS

Chapter 1: A Novel Approach Towards Regeneration and Constitution of Data Linked to Distributed Databases

Many times, it has been observed that regeneration as well as constitution of data within the servers may be more complex. It may be due to sharing and storing the data between several remote locations associated with distributed databases. Similarly, the replication of data can enhance the system performance having more data accessibility features and can minimize the link time to the databases. In this chapter specific techniques have been prioritized towards regeneration and constitution of data.

Chapter 2: Data Visualization in Large Scale Based on Trained Data

Data visualization is one of the techniques to understand the patterns of data in graphical methods. Data visualization is an effective tool for transforming raw data into actionable insights and facilitating data-driven decision-making. High-dimensional synthetic data are datasets created artificially with an abundance of attributes or aspects. This chapter elaborates on visualizing, Synthetic high-dimensional data for better understanding by common men.

Chapter 3: Deep Machine Learning Towards the Intelligence Level of Man

With deep learning technology, machine learning has shown impressive results. Nonetheless, these techniques frequently use excessive amounts of resources; they demand big datasets, a lot of parameters, and a lot of processing power. In order to develop machine learning models that are efficient with resources, general machine learning techniques have been outlined in this chapter namely deep machine learning.

Chapter 4: Digitalisation and Its Impact on the Development of Society

The research is devoted to the analysis of the essence of the concept of digitalization and its impact on the development of the economy and society. In this chapter, the analysis of approaches to the interpretation of the concept of "digital economy", analysis of approaches and assessments of the impact of digitalization and information and communication technologies (ICT) on the economic development of countries along with identification of advantages and challenges have been focused.

Chapter 5: E-Learning as a Training Concept for Staff

In this chapter, the E-learning training in occupational health has been prioritized along with safety on a selected group of employees. In addition to that attention has been focused on the way periodic and initial training was carried out and the impact of adaptation of knowledge of the course participants. The main intention focused in this chapter is to find out the opinions of the participants of e-learning courses, as well as to identify the benefits that affect the acquisition of adequate knowledge.

Chapter 6: Factor Analysis of Intercultural Sensitivity, Ethnocentrism, Social Media by the Means of Structural Equation Modelling

The main motivation in this chapter is to investigate the interaction between intercultural sensitivity, ethnocentrism, and social media use by using structural equality modeling method. To this end, the survey has been designed by using intercultural sensitivity, ethnocentrism, and social media data scales available in the literature. The expressions in the survey were translated and re-translated by two foreign language teachers. It has been observed that the direct effect of participation in interaction and confidence in interaction variables on ethnocentrism is insignificant, but the indirect effect on social media use is significant.

Chapter 7: Feature Selection Using Correlation Analysis for Accurate Breast Cancer Diagnosis

In this chapter, the fundamental purpose is to apply feature selection methodologies, while integrating the examination of correlations among input features linked towards accuracy in the diagnosis of the disease. These selected significant features have been subsequently employed in conjunction with a classification method aiming towards enhancement of the precision of classification through a comprehensive assessment.

Chapter 8: Managerial Peacemaking Soft Skills Development as a Method of Professional Burnout Prevention and Work-Life Rebalance

The primary intention in this chapter is to investigate the impact of military threats on the professional burnout of employees in the organizations that have survived the COVID-19 pandemic and currently are in conditions of uncertainty and rapid digitalization, as well as to make recommendations for developing managers' skills to prevent burnout. The assessment uses a set of methods of scientific knowledge used in the humanities and social sciences.

Chapter 9: Prospects of Practice-Based Education Implementation for Students of Educational Management Profile

The main motivation of this chapter is to develop a practice-based education model describing possible scenarios of educational and professional internships for students majoring in management at the university level of bachelor`s degree. Also, the study highlights the theoretical and applied aspects of the practice-based education implementation for the management specialists. The main components inherent in the practice-based education model that distinguish it from the traditional process of practice within the framework of the generally accepted educational model have been analyzed. Also, specific innovative approaches have been developed to the areas and profiles of activities choices.

Chapter 10: The Privacy Preserving High Dimensional Synthetic Data Generation and Evaluation in the Healthcare Domain

In the fast-changing environment of healthcare research and technology, there is an increasing demand for varied and vast information. However, issues with data privacy, unavailability, and ethical considerations frequently limit smooth access to true high-dimensional healthcare data. In this chapter, the investigation has been carried out with a viable approach to addressing the challenges, i.e. the use of high-dimensional synthetic data in the health care area. Also, the investigation has been done implementing the synthetic data and overcoming data access barriers and outlining the significant use cases.

Chapter 11: Tools to Create Synthetic Data for Brain Images

In the areas of neuroscience, medical imaging, and machine learning, the creation of synthetic data for brain scans has become a key approach. In this chapter, It explore the concept and significance of synthetic data generation for brain images. In tasks like brain picture segmentation, disease detection, and image analysis, machine learning models perform better when using synthetic data as a catalyst for data augmentation. A wide range of methods and resources, including MRI simulators, 3D modeling software, deep learning frameworks, and medical imaging software, are used to create synthetic brain images. To guarantee the validity and applicability of synthetic data, however, ethical issues, data representativeness, and transparency in the generation process continue to be essential factors. Synthetic brain data are becoming more useful and realistic as technology develops, and this has the potential to completely change the fields of neuroscience and medical imaging.

Chapter 12: Transformation of Industrial Production: The Effects of Digitalization

In this chapter, the determination of trends and transformations in the development of the industrial sector has been prioritized. The global priorities for ensuring the introduction of Industry 4.0 technologies have been analysed. The dynamics of the value added of industrial production in some countries have been determined. The ratio between the share of the value added of industrial production in the gross domestic product and the value added of medium and high-tech production in the section of the ICT subindex in individual countries has been analysed. The leading countries in the development of digitalization and the growth of industrial production have been identified. Also, the main technologies for ensuring the optimization of production lines have been presented.

Chapter 13: To the Question of Design and Manufacture of Special Equipment for Mechanism of Pneumatic Power Receiving Mechanism

In this chapter, the basic technologies of 3D printing, types and structure of 3D printers for designing and manufacturing of special equipment provisioned with synthetic high dimensional data and pneumatic engine have been analyzed and also thoroughly examined. In the experimentation, the main materials for printing, the carbon-bearing materials for FDM printing, along with their characteristics have been considered. Also processing of statistical and synthetic data has been carried out making comparison of the obtained holes with the given nominal values.

CONCLUSION

With the changing environment and limited required resources there is a requirement of basic approaches towards synthesized data. The methods and applications with these data can be the novel approach for changing the old methodologies adopted by traditional techniques to achieve the goal. This book focuses on applicability towards high dimensional synthetic data on making the system as well as organization sustainable through engineering aspects along with modern education and solutions. It also explores concepts and the role of synthetic data along with the recent developments towards making the environment sustainable and relevance to the society. Synthetic data keeps the original data properties and safeguards its business value preserving the quality and structure of data. Accordingly, this book also prioritizes on application of large scaled synthetic data with solutions exploring the mechanisms on the parametric evaluation of specified synthetic data.

Marzena Sobczak-Michalowska
University of Economics, Poland

Samarjeet Borah
Sikkim Manipal University, India

Zdzislaw Polkowski
Karkonosze University, Poland

Sambit Kumar Mishra
Gandhi Institute for Education and Technology, India

Chapter 1
A Novel Approach Towards Regeneration and Constitution of Data Linked to Distributed Databases

Rashmi Rekha Swain
Biju Patnaik University of Technology, India

Sambit Kumar Mishra
Biju Patnaik University of Technology, India

ABSTRACT

It has been observed that regeneration as well as constitution of data within the servers may be more complex. It may be due to sharing and storing the data between several remote locations associated with distributed databases. Similarly, the replication of data can enhance the system performance having more data accessibility features and can minimize the link time to the databases. This chapter focuses on a specific algorithm prioritizing the regeneration and constitution of data dynamically, particularly in distributed databases. The proposed mechanism in this work has been prioritized with adaptive features in the sense that changes in the schema objects with regeneration can replicate in the central scheme. In this mechanism, it has also been intended to accumulate the provisioned techniques of the distributed database management systems as the performance can be analyzed experimentally.

DOI: 10.4018/979-8-3693-1886-7.ch001

1. INTRODUCTION

In every aspect of applications in the real world, decentralization of data may be more preferable, due to diversification of geographical locations. In such situation, it may be required to prioritize the mechanisms of distributed database appearing as single database. In fact, the replica of the data can be easily provisioned along with the restoration even if in applications in remote locations. In practical perspective, it may support in backing up the data with enhanced scalability. In the present situation, particularly the specified mechanism has its own importance in large scaled databases. Accordingly, the methods of accumulation and maintenance of similar set of data in large scale linked to distributed databases can be well adopted.

2. RELATED WORK

Makris et al. (2019) prioritized the challenges by organizing the query process as well as prioritized the quantitative approach of the high computation complexity of spatial queries. Also they considered the specific checkpoints by incorporating the performance and applicability of spatial databases linked with distributed database mechanisms.

In Sharding (n.d.), the process towards distribution of data across multiple machines has been described. Somehow the sharding mechanism focused on the specified linked dataset along with partially loads on the multiple servers with increased capacity. In some cases, it may be essential to enable each machine to process a subset of the overall workload to achieve better efficiency.

Gkamas et al. (2022) observed that somehow performance of MongoDB is 19 to 30% enhanced as compared with Postgre-SQL particularly during insert operation of the queries. By that it may achieve on an average 55% higher throughput. Also as per their research, it has been seen that the relational Postgre-SQL is yielding better performance as compared with MongoDB and also it is quite faster than Postgres-JSON during initiation of selection operation for queries. Somehow it may achieve almost 35% more higher throughput.

Rossman (n.d.) observed that the metrics of the Postgre-SQL database can be probably 4 to 5 times more faster as compared with MongoDB. During the specific application, the performance measurement of the transaction associated with Postgre-SQL may be better with lower latency.

Seghier and Kazar (2021) compared the specific databases i.e. NoSQL databases, Redis, MongoDB as well as Cassandra. According to their research, Redis may be more efficient in reading operations, whereas the MongoDB may be better in its optimum performance linked to the write operations.

Asiminidis et al. (2018) prioritized the performance linked to the experimentations using industrial IoT sensory data. In their research, they have focused on the average response time, jitter, as well as average achieved throughput mainly to measure the performance of the databases to process a query and to record the insertion time.

Plugge et al. (2010) focused on performance evaluation based on response time achieving the throughput within the quantifiable distributed data-stores. In their study they observed that each system can be computed as a stand-alone server with a proper installation of each database management system against the deployment of the distributed clustered servers.

Tomar (2014), while focusing the design principle of the distributed database, observed the necessity of hosting the databases in different sites as the major objective of the distributed database system is to appear as a centralized system to the end users.

Singh and Singh (2015) prioritized the aspects of the design of distributed database cover. Usually, the design of distributed computer systems involves deciding on the assignment of data and programs to the computer network sites, along with the design of the network. The modeling of the conceptual diagram describes the integrated database, i.e. the data used by the applications. The design of the physical schema illustrates the conceptual schema by determining the data storage areas and the appropriate access methods.

Hussain and Khan (2014) focused on the merge replication that permits two or more databases to be synchronized. All changes applied to a database can automatically be transferred to other databases and vice versa. Also it will allow data modifications on the publisher and the subscriber, but also allows offline scenarios i.e., it can allow synchronization to take place automatically between the subscriber and the publisher after a subscriber has been disconnected from an editor for a given period.

Elmasri and Navathe (2016) discussed the stored procedures in their work which automate actions and sometimes may be complex. It is actually a series of SQL statements designated by a name. Once the procedure is created, it can be easy to call it, by its name.

Ramesh et al. (2015) discussed on advanced synchronization wireless algorithm along with synchronization technique in their work. The main intention is to assure data synchronization under the image format between the mobile device database and the server-side database. Particularly this algorithm can easily compare the two images and identify the synchronization of the image.

Diogo et al. (2019) observed that the NoSQL databases can be able to minimize the gaps in relational databases considering the schema-less design, horizontal scaling as well as eventual consistency. Also they evaluated and compared the consistency models which is inferred from the results compared with MongoDB.

Ramzan et al. (2019) address the challenges during the storage of NoSQL databases. The need of security in terms of trust and privacy are the main outcomes that need to be achieved in the future.

3. METHOD OF REGENERATION OF DATA

Sometimes the regeneration of data can be taken as the basic mechanism towards accumulating and maintaining several linked as well as similar databases particularly in the distributed database environment. Accordingly, it can enhance the performance providing more alternative data accessibilities. In general, the accessibility to local database can be easier and efficient compared with remote server as it minimizes the complete large scaled data provisioning complete transparency on data accessibility. In fact, there are several techniques towards regeneration of data particularly in distributed environment. But working with clustered data, consistency should be maintained. As cited in figure-1, when the accessibility of database may be requested by the user to the server, immediately the server initiates the back-end process and communicates the same to the user. So based on the transactions in the remote location, the auto-link can be established between the user process and back-end process.

4. BASIC APPLICABILITY AND CONCEPTUALIZATION

Prioritizing the constriction parameters and regeneration mechanisms, it is required to initiate the pre-requisite tasks towards creation of global schema from several locations. The system in such situation analyzes the databases and allocates the mechanisms based on the local schemes and linking the same to the remote databases. The extraction from the global scheme can be initiated transferring the fragmentation techniques to the central location or the supervisor.

5. RETRIEVAL AND REGENERATION OF GLOBAL SCHEMA

To obtain the optimality on the situation, it is required to minimize the changes in the databases as well as occurrence of transfers within the provisioned locations and average processing time of applications. Actually, it may be assumed that the accessibility of databases is already provisioned, considering the integrated portion of the existing databases. Accordingly, the existing local conceptual schema can be unified towards global conceptual schema. It is understood that the allocation of a

Figure 1. Accessibility of databases provisioned with clustered data

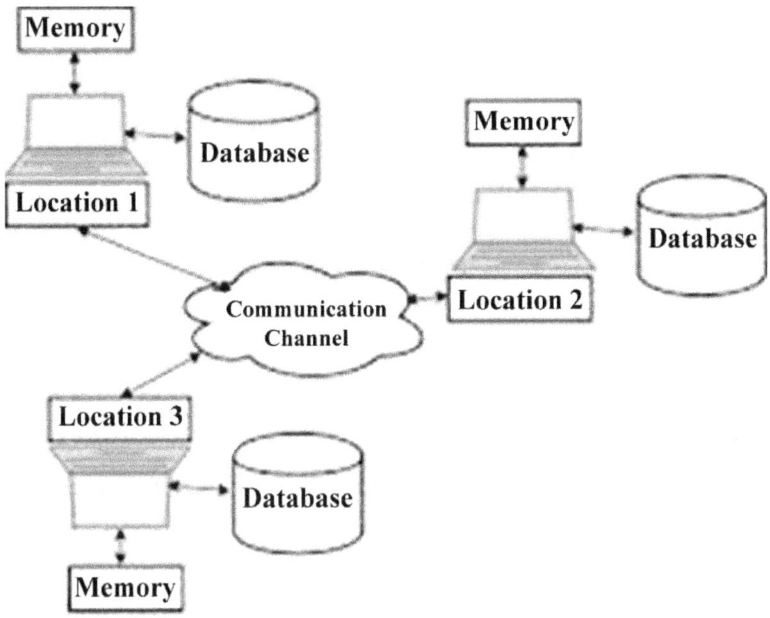

database can be defined in the schematic levels of the architecture prioritizing the physical distribution of data. For example, in the external level, the views can be well distributed in the user locations as shown in figure-2. Similarly, in the conceptual level, the schema can be linked though the allocation by decomposing the structure into the fragmentation pattern and permitting the local schemes to be distributed within the physical locations.

6. STEPS FOR RETRIEVAL AND REGENERATION OF LARGE SCALED DATA FROM DATABASES

Step 1: Initiation and creation of data objects towards extraction from local schema

Step 2: Construct the allocation scheme initiating the interfacing data object

Step 3: Apply the fragmentation mechanism on the data objects

Step 4: Initiate the procedure to accumulate the datasets from server as a part of global Scheme

Step 5: Check the replication of datasets retrieved through global scheme with the central server datasets

Figure 2. Allocation of databases prioritizing schema approach

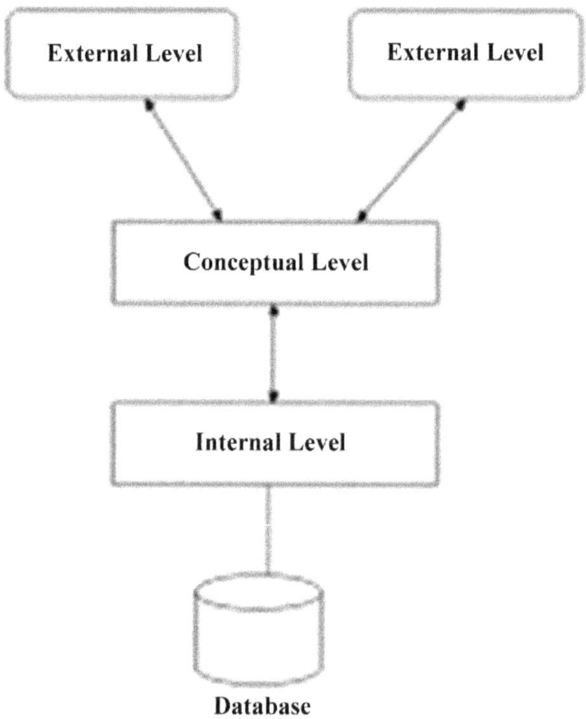

7. PRIORITIZATION OF MULTI AGENT CONCEPT

Generally the techniques associated with multi agent approach are useful to establish the links with other linked agents for sharing the information though not associated with the similar platforms. It can be accomplished observing the commonalities among the datasets within the central server. In this work, prioritization of the datasets has been given in the form of serialization as the datasets can be retrieved through the central database. The complete process is practically based on the communication within the specific nodes where each node executes properly scheduled tasks and linking the intermediary result to accomplish the process. In specific cases, the initiation of the mechanism is accomplished through involvement of the central server.

7.1. Algorithm

The regeneration strategy usually ensures the accuracy and consistency within the data objects as reflected in figure-3. In such situation, being a part and portion of the central database, feasibility is being maintained during modification of datasets

Figure 3. Regeneration strategy with consistency

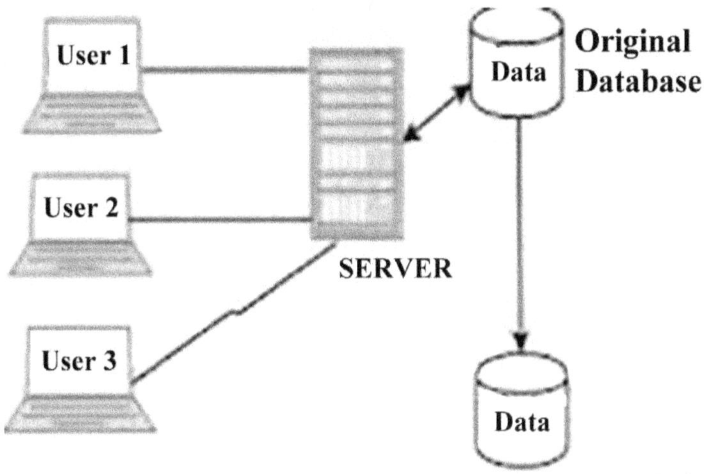

within the central as well as remote databases. Sometimes existence of data objects in the central server may force the central database to append the datasets copied in the existing data object prioritizing the global schema.

Step 1: Initialize the number of locations, q
Step 2: for i=1 to q
initialize loc(i) (prioritizing the individual location)
Step 3: for j=1 to t (t datasets of loc(i))
Co(j)<- datasets of loc(i) (retrieving Co(j) from loc(i) to Central Server
Step 4: if Co(j) exists in Central Server
Create CO Using Select * from Co(j)@loc(i) Union Select * from Co(j)@Central Server else Create CO Using Select * from Co(j)@loc(i)

8. EXPERIMENTAL ANALYSIS

As reflected in Table 1, the simulation has been done with remote databases particularly implementing structured query language in relational database management system. Also, it has been well experimented using the database examples. During analysis it has been seen that the datasets linked to supervisor may evaluate the amount of data objects and can compare each data object of each location with the central server.

In this application, different remote databases have been included and the remote location provisioning the databases can execute specific tasks as required by the central server. As shown in figure-4, the execution time linked to tasks of datasets along with the regeneration time can be computed in the remote locations.

Table 1. Number of locations with dataset accessibility

Number of Locations	4	6
Average time (m.Sec.)	146	218
Execution time (m.Sec.)	0. 245	0.317
Regeneration time (m.Sec.)	236	308

Figure 4. Execution time of queries linked to remote servers

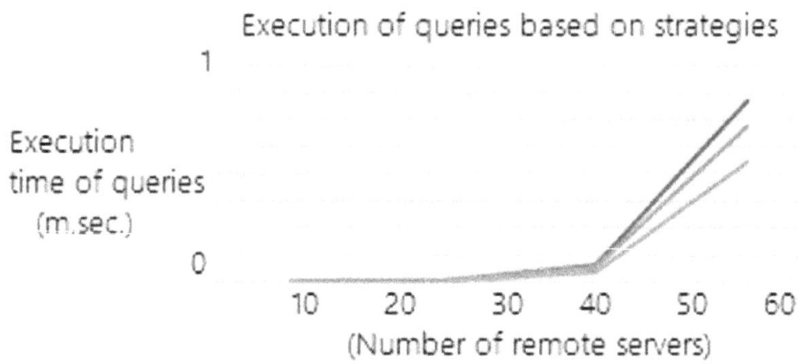

9. DISCUSSION AND FUTURE DIRECTION

In general perspective, the mechanism linked to regeneration of data can build the specified datasets retrieved from the existing databases and extracting schema information. Suppose the provisioned data is accomplished with multiple structures, then the specific techniques can be implemented to analyze the combination frequencies of the provisioned structure. After the formalization, the process can be invoked to generate the corresponding datasets. In this work, it has also been prioritized on the specified workload of the queries. Particularly, to obtain the queries from the datasets along with the result as query plans, the instances may be considered resulting on the queries.

10. CONCLUSION

The regeneration process particularly linked to the distributed database is not only to maintain the replica of the databases but also prioritizes to accumulate optimum availability of data and ensure suitable maintenance. In this experimentation, the specific optimal technique based on remote agent mechanism has been adopted towards extracting the global schema from several schemes existing in the remote locations. Also this mechanism helps to regenerate the global schematic constraints in the central server. The regeneration time as well as the execution time of each task associated with the datasets can be easily computed. Accordingly, the optimality may be achieved as this approach is feasible and the problems linked to the automatic regeneration schemes can be solved in the distributed database.

REFERENCES

Asiminidis, C., Kokkonis, G., & Kontogiannis, S. (2018). Database Systems Performance Evaluation for IoT Applications. *Int. J. Database Manag. Syst.*, *10*(6), 1–14. doi:10.5121/ijdms.2018.10601

Diogo, M., Cabral, B., & Bernardino, J. (2019). Consistency Models of NoSQL Databases. *Future Internet*, *11*(2), 43. doi:10.3390/fi11020043

Elmasri, R., & Navathe, S. (2016). *Fundamentals of database systems*. Pearson.

Gkamas, T., Karaiskos, V., & Kontogiannis, S. (2022). Evaluation of cloud databases as a service for Industrial IoT data. *Proceedings of the 7th International Congress on Information and Communication Technology (ICICT).*

Hussain, A., & Khan, M. N. (2014). Discovering Database Replication Techniques in RDBMS. *International Journal of Database Theory and Application.*, *7*(1), 93–102. doi:10.14257/ijdta.2014.7.1.09

Makris, A., Tserpes, K., Spiliopoulos, G., & Anagnostopoulos, D. (2019). Performance Evaluation of MongoDB and PostgreSQL for spatio-temporal data. *Proceedings of the EDBT/ICDT Workshops.*

Plugge, E., Membrey, P., & Hawkins, T. (2010). *The Definitive Guide to MongoDB: The NoSQL Database for Cloud and Desktop Computing* (1st ed.). Apress. doi:10.1007/978-1-4302-3052-6

Ramesh, U. R., Yogeswari, G., & Tamil, N. (2015). Database Synchronization for Mobile Devices by Using ASWAMD. *National Conference on Computing and Communication-International Journal of Innovative Research in Computer and Communication Engineering*, 3(1).

Ramzan, S., Bajwa, I. S., Kazmi, R., & Amna. (2019). Challenges in NoSQL-Based Distributed Data Storage: A Systematic Literature Review. *Electronics (Basel)*, *8*(5), 488. doi:10.3390/electronics8050488

Rossman, G. (n.d.). *New Benchmarks Show Postgres Dominating MongoDB in Varied Workloads.* Available online: https://www. enterprisedb.com/news/new-benchmarks-show-postgres-dominating-mongodb-varied-workloads

Seghier, N. B., & Kazar, O. (2021). Performance Benchmarking and Comparison of NoSQL Databases: Redis vs. MongoDB vs. Cassandra Using YCSB Tool. *Proceedings of the International Conference on Recent Advances in Mathematics and Informatics (ICRAMI),* 1–6. 10.1109/ICRAMI52622.2021.9585956

Sharding. (n.d.). Available online: https://docs.mongodb.com/manual/sharding/

Singh, I., & Singh, S. (2015). Distributed Database Systems: Principles, Algorithms and Systems. Khanna Book Publishing, Co. (P) Ltd.

Tomar, P. (2014, February). An overview of distributed databases. *International Journal of Information and Computation Technology.*, *4*(2), 207–214.

Chapter 2
Data Visualization in Large Scale Based on Trained Data

S. Suriya
https://orcid.org/0000-0002-2297-4426
SRM Institute of Science and Technology, India

J. Shyamala Devi
https://orcid.org/0000-0002-6265-8380
SRM Institute of Science and Technology, India

R. Agusthiyar
SRM Institute of Science and Technology, India

ABSTRACT

Data visualization is one of the techniques to understand the patterns of data in graphical methods. Data visualization is an effective tool for transforming raw data into actionable insights and facilitating data-driven decision-making. High-dimensional synthetic data are datasets created artificially with an abundance of attributes or aspects. This type of synthetic data is particularly helpful for attempting to assess machine learning algorithms and data analysis techniques in scenarios with a large number of factors. The method can be difficult because of the more complicated nature of high-dimensional data, but it is necessary for a variety of applications, such as testing machine learning algorithms, evaluating data analysis techniques, and exploring model behaviour in high-dimensional spaces. These trained high-dimensional synthetic data are given to the visualization techniques to produce graphical representation and better decision-making models. This chapter elaborates on visualizing synthetic high-dimensional data for better understanding by common men.

DOI: 10.4018/979-8-3693-1886-7.ch002

INTRODUCTION

In our emerging day-to-day technological world dealing with the amount of data increasing, Data refers to Raw facts, observations, measurements, or information collected or recorded from various sources are referred to as data. Text, numbers, images, audio, and other forms of data are all possible. Data without context or meaning is meaningless; it only becomes meaningful when it is processed, organized, and analyzed to extract insights or knowledge. Data, whether small or large, structured or unstructured, serves as the foundation for making sound decisions. Decision-making is the key feature in the process of making serious games that are carried with machine learning algorithms. Through the decision-making process, the level of the user is analyzed, by collecting and monitoring the activities of the learner. After analyzing the user level, the appropriate action is taken to improve the learner.

Big data refers to datasets that are extremely large, complex, and difficult to manage and process with traditional data processing tools and methods. Massive amounts of data are involved in big data, which frequently exceeds the storage and processing capacity of traditional databases and tools. Data is generated, collected, and processed at high rates, frequently in real-time or near real-time. Big data includes a wide range of data types, including structured data (such as databases), unstructured data (such as text and images), and semi-structured data (such as XML or JSON).To effectively manage, store, and analyze big data, specialized technologies such as distributed computing frameworks (e.g., Hadoop), NoSQL databases, and data stream processing systems are frequently required. It's common in fields like social media, e-commerce, IoT (Internet of Things), and scientific research. High-dimensional data are datasets that have a large number of features or dimensions in comparison to the number of observations or data points. To put it another way, high-dimensional data has more variables (columns) than rows.

Large-scale datasets necessitate the use of a combination of data engineering, distributed computing, and data analysis techniques. Specific strategies will be chosen based on the characteristics of the dataset, available computational resources, and the goals of your analysis or application.

LITERATURE REVIEW

Vallejos, C.A. (2019). identifies the drawbacks of the dimensionality reduction techniques now in use, such as t-SNE, pointing out problems with data structure preservation, sensitivity to noise, and processing costs and uses an enhanced nonlinear technique for dimensionality reduction called PHATE (Potential of Heat-diffusion for Affinity-based Transition Embedding), which overcomes the drawbacks of previous approaches.

Tang, L. (2020). Says Effective analysis and visualization of high-dimensional data is hampered by its dimensions. Information loss frequently results from reducing data dimensionality for visualization. - Handling sizable datasets and noise makes analysis more difficult. And proposes PHATE (Potential of Heat Diffusion for Affinity-based Transition Embedding) PHATE uses potential distances to measure global links and encodes local data structures. - Lower-dimensional representations are created by applying multidimensional scaling (MDS), which takes into account both local and global data structures.

Moon, K.R., van Dijk, D., Wang, Z., et al. (2019) identifies High-dimensional data produced by high-throughput technology need visualization tools that can clearly and concisely represent data structure and trends and Presenting PHATE, a new approach to data visualization that may be used to visualize both global and local nonlinear systems. For PHATE to provide meaningful visualizations, there must be an information-geometric distance between each data point.

Li, Y., Chai, Y., Yin, H., et al. (2021) say Classification relies heavily on effective feature extraction, and although dictionary learning techniques perform poorly on high-dimensional datasets that hide discriminative information, deep learning techniques frequently require large amounts of training data and an Adaptive dictionary learning in a low-dimensional space combined with classification-guided optimization yields discriminative low-dimensional features in a unique feature learning framework for high-dimensional data classification.

Sun, E.D., Ma, R., & Zou, J. (2023), in their paper, mention Conventional techniques for dimensionality reduction (DR) result in visual distortions and do not provide means to evaluate their dependability and with the use of DynamicViz, one may create dynamic visuals that are responsive to perturbations in data, which can help identify interpretative errors and optimize DR algorithms by utilizing variance scores.

Yang, Y., Tuong, Z.K., & Yu, D. (2023), when it comes to dimensionality reduction (DR) in biological data visualization, non-expert users sometimes rely on arbitrary parameter values. This might result in visually appealing visualizations that don't correctly represent the data structure. In response to the need for more reliable and data-driven visualization in single-cell genomics, uses a technique presented by Eric D. Sun et al.to summarize the variability of DR and evaluate the dependability of DR visualizations.

Espadoto, M., Martins, R. M., Kerren, A., Hirata, N. S. T., &Telea, A. C. (2021) say that it might be difficult for practitioners to choose the best dimensionality reduction strategy for their unique use cases due to the abundance of available solutions and proposes an extensive analysis of projection methods with quantitative indicators that help practitioners make decisions depending on their own data context. In order to promote transparency and future progress, the methodology and findings are made publicly available. A novel metric reveals previously unrecognized distortion in dimensionality reduction of scRNA-seq data.

Cooley, S. M., Hamilton, T., Aragones, S. D., Ray, J. C. J., & Deeds, E. J. (2022) find due to significant distortion introduced by dimensionality reduction techniques, interpreting and analysing high-dimensional data, especially in single-cell RNA-seq (scRNA-seq), becomes more difficult. In order to address problems with cell type identification, pseudo time ordering, and other analyses, it is necessary to develop new algorithms that can accurately embed high-dimensional data in its true latent dimension. One way to quantify distortion is to introduce a method that compares local neighbourhoods before and after dimensionality reduction.

Nonato, L. G., &Aupetit, M. (2019) in their paper mention that multidimensional projections (MDP) introduce distortions that compromise the reliability of visual patterns, making it difficult for users to appropriately deduce data attributes and to improve the usability of MDP for visual analysis of multidimensional data, develop and execute layout enrichment approaches to limit MDP distortions and disclose additional information not immediately obvious from scatter plots.

Liu, S., Maljovec, D., Wang, B., Bremer, P.-T., & Pascucci, V. (2015). Tells advanced visualization approaches are becoming more and more necessary as massive, complicated, high-dimensional datasets from a variety of sectors continue to be generated. The thorough analysis looks at current developments in high-dimensional data visualization with the goal of assisting data practitioners, generating fresh approaches to visualization, and pointing forth directions for further study in the area.

Working With High Dimensional Data Sets in Large Scale

A high-dimensional large dataset is one with a large number of features or dimensions, which often outnumber the number of data points or observations. Dealing with large, high-dimensional datasets presents unique challenges in data analysis, storage, processing, and visualization. High-dimensional data can be found in various fields, and one common example is gene expression data in genomics. In genomics, researchers often measure the expression levels of thousands of genes across a set of biological samples. Each gene's expression level represents a dimension in the data, and the samples represent data points. This results in high-dimensional gene expression data, which is challenging to analyze and interpret due to its high dimensionality.

Table 1. Features

	Customer_id	Customer_name	Region_id	Region_name	lattitude	longitude	mobile_number	Email_id	Subscription plan	validity	Speed	type of connection	alternate number	year of subscription started	Type of customer
Customer_1															
Customer_2															
Customer_3															
Customer_4															
Customer_5															
Customer_6															
Customer_7															
Customer_8															
Customer_9															
Customer_10															

What Is High Dimensional Data?

High-dimensional data are those in which the number of features (observed variables), O, is close to or greater than the number of observations (or data points), p. Low-dimensional data, on the other hand, has a small number of observations, n. which vastly outnumbers the number of features, O. Wide data is a related concept that refers to data with numerous features regardless of the number of observations (similarly, tall data is frequently used to denote data with a large number of observations). Analyses of high-dimensional data necessitate consideration of potential issues that arise as a result of having more features than observations.

O=Number of Features,
P=Number of Datapoints(Number of Row data)
Consider the following
If (O>P)
Then
Data= High dimensional
Else
Data =Low dimensional

In the above table, there are 14 different features. Here there are various challenges faced for example need to fetch customer_id, customer_name, and Mobile no of the first 100 customers. This is no high dimensional data because needs to fetch 100 details with 3 features, number of features is less than the observation.

For example fetching 200 latitudes along with customer_id,mcustomer_name, and Mobile no for 100 customers is possible. Here number of features is greater than the datapoints.

Figure 1. Features

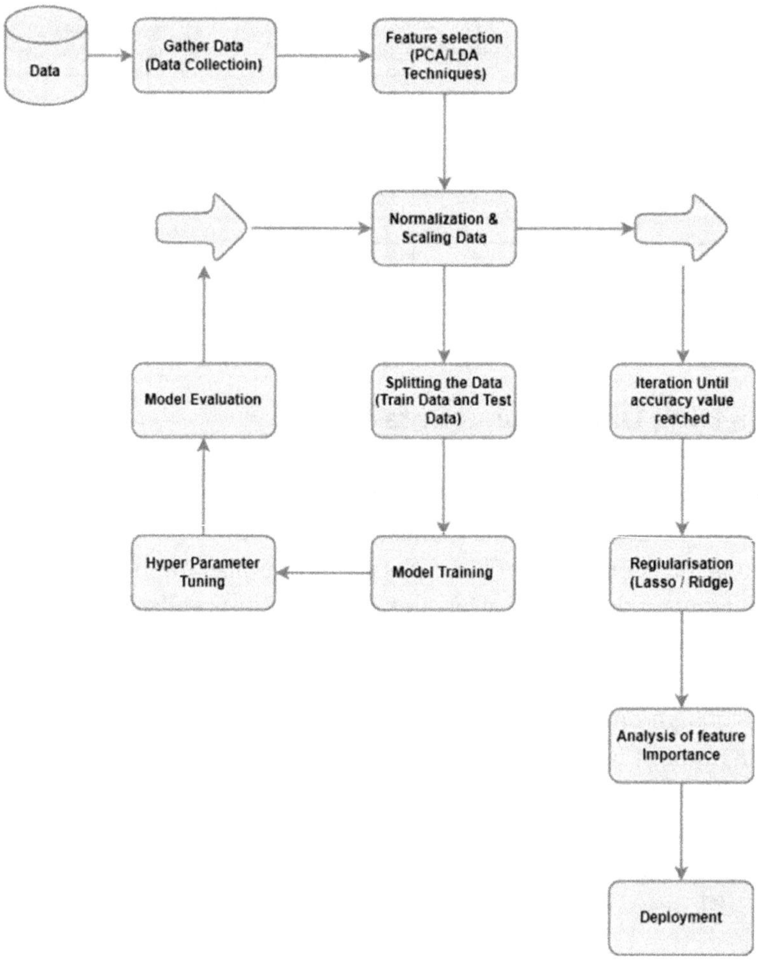

Strategies for Dealing With Large Scale High Dimensional Data

Here are some key considerations and strategies for dealing with large high-dimensional datasets:

Dimensionality Reduction

Dimensionality reduction is a common approach to dealing with high-dimensional data. To reduce the number of dimensions while retaining as much relevant information as possible, techniques such as Principal Component Analysis (PCA), t-Distributed Stochastic Neighbour Embedding (t-SNE), and autoencoders can be used.

Feature Selection

Using feature selection methods, carefully select relevant features. By removing irrelevant or redundant features from the dataset, you can simplify it and improve model performance.

Data Preprocessing

Data preprocessing is critical, especially in large datasets. Handling missing values, scaling and normalizing features, and dealing with outliers are all possible steps.

Data Storage and Administration

Create a solid data storage and management strategy. Consider cloud-based solutions for scalability and use database systems optimized for large datasets (e.g., NoSQL databases).

Visualization

Selectively visualize the data by focusing on specific subsets of features or using dimensionality reduction techniques. Because high-dimensional data can be difficult to visualize directly, consider using 2D or 3D projections or interactive visualizations.

Feature Development

Engage in feature engineering to create new, meaningful features or to transform existing ones in order to reduce dimensionality or capture important information.

Regularisation and Model Selection

Choose algorithms that are robust to high-dimensional data when building predictive models, such as L1 (Lasso) or L2 (Ridge) regularisation.

Cross-Validation

Use cross-validation techniques to effectively evaluate model performance. With imbalanced data, stratified cross-validation can be especially useful.

DATA VISUALIZATION TOOLS

Tableau

Tableau is a powerful and popular data visualization tool that is available in both desktop and web-based versions. It has a simple drag-and-drop interface for creating interactive and visually appealing dashboards.

Features of Tableau

- Tableau's dashboard works with a wide range of data sources, including databases, cloud storage, spreadsheets, web data connectors, and others. It enables users to connect to, extract data from, and analyze data from a variety of platforms.
- Users can use data shaping and cleaning tools to help them prepare their data for analysis. This includes data transformation, missing value handling, and the creation of calculated fields..
- The intuitive drag-and-drop interface of Tableau allows users to create visualizations without extensive coding. To create charts and graphs, simply drag data fields onto the canvas.
- Tableau provides a wide range of customizable visualizations, including bar charts, line charts, scatter plots, heat maps, tree maps, and more. Users can create dynamic and interactive charts to explore their data.
- Dashboards are used to combine multiple visualizations and provide an overview of data. Tableau allows users to design interactive dashboards that facilitate data exploration and decision-making.
- Users can interact with their data by applying filters, actions, and parameters. This interactivity enables dynamic exploration of data and allows for instant insights.
- Tableau includes a powerful calculation engine that enables the creation of calculated fields and custom expressions for complex data transformations and calculations.
- Tableau supports mapping and geospatial analysis, making it suitable for location-based data. Users can create maps and perform geospatial analytics with ease.
- Tableau can integrate with various data sources and platforms, offering connectors and APIs to extend its functionality. It supports data blending for combining data from multiple sources.

- Tableau Server and Tableau Online facilitate the sharing and collaboration of dashboards and reports within an organization. Users can comment, annotate, and subscribe to updates.
- Tableau provides robust security features to protect data, including data source encryption, user authentication, and row-level security to control access to data.
- Tableau dashboards and reports are responsive and can be viewed on various devices, including smartphones and tablets. The Tableau Mobile app enables users to access data on the go.
- Tableau can handle real-time data streaming and visualizations, making it suitable for applications that require up-to-the-minute data analysis.
- Users can automate tasks and processes within Tableau by using scripts and automation tools to save time and improve efficiency.
- Tableau supports integration with machine learning models and AI tools, allowing users to incorporate predictive analytics into their data analysis.
- Tableau has a vibrant user community with forums, training resources, and extensive documentation. Users can find support and resources to enhance their Tableau skills.
- Tableau's versatility and user-friendly features have made it a go-to tool for data visualization and business intelligence in various industries. It empowers organizations to turn data into actionable insights and make informed decisions.

Microsoft Power BI

Microsoft Power BI is a business intelligence application that lets users create interactive reports and dashboards. It works in tandem with other Microsoft products. Microsoft Power BI is a set of business analytics tools and services from Microsoft that allows for data visualisation, analysis, and sharing of insights. It is intended to assist organisations in easily gathering, transforming, analysing, and visualising data from various sources in order to make informed business decisions. Here are some of Microsoft Power BI's key features and aspects:

- Power BI includes a wide range of interactive visualisations, including bar charts, line charts, pie charts, maps, tables, and more. These visualisations are highly customizable to meet the needs of specific data presentation scenarios.
- Power BI has the ability to connect to a wide variety of data sources, including databases, cloud services, spreadsheets, and web services. It can connect to both on-premises and cloud data sources.

- The Power Query Editor in Power BI allows users to transform, clean, and shape data before creating visualisations. This includes data modelling, combining, and manipulating data.
- Using the Power BI Desktop application, users can create data models by defining relationships between tables, creating calculated columns, and adding measures to improve data analysis.
- Power BI creates custom calculations, aggregations, and business logic using the Data Analysis Expressions (DAX) language. DAX functions are similar to Excel functions in that they allow users to create calculated columns and measures.
- Users can build interactive dashboards that combine various visualisations and reports. Dashboards provide a high-level overview of key insights and allow for a consolidated view of data.
- Natural language querying is supported by Power BI, allowing users to ask questions in plain language to retrieve data and generate visualisations.
- To enable predictive analytics and anomaly detection, Power BI integrates with Azure Machine Learning and other machine learning tools.
- Power BI has mobile apps for a variety of platforms, including iOS.

Data Studio by Google

Google Data Studio is a cloud-based tool for creating interactive reports and dashboards that is free to use. It is compatible with Google Analytics and Google Sheets data because it integrates with various Google services.Google Data Studio is a data visualisation and reporting tool that is available for free from Google. It enables users to create interactive and customizable reports and dashboards from a variety of data sources. Here are some of Google Data Studio's key features and aspects:

- Google Data Studio can connect to a variety of data sources via third-party services, including Google Analytics, Google Sheets, Google Ads, Google BigQuery, MySQL, PostgreSQL, and many others. You can combine data from various sources into a single report.
- Data Studio includes a wide range of data visualisation tools, including bar charts, line charts, scatter plots, pie charts, tables, maps, and time series charts. Colours, fonts, and themes can be used to personalise these visualisations.
- Reports and dashboards can be customised to match the user's branding and style. To achieve a consistent look, you can change the fonts, colours, backgrounds, and other visual elements.

- Data Studio's reports and dashboards are interactive. Users can explore data and gain insights directly from the report by using date range controls, dynamic filters, and interactions.
- Multiple users can work on a single report at the same time, making it simple to collaborate on data analysis and visualisation projects. Users can share reports and dashboards, and access permissions can be set.
- Data Studio allows for real-time data updates. You can create reports that automatically refresh to show the most recent data, eliminating the need for manual refreshing.
- Data Studio enables you to combine data from various sources into a single report. This is useful for creating comprehensive dashboards with data from multiple platforms.
- To transform and manipulate your data, you can create calculated fields in Data Studio by using simple formulas or more advanced expressions.
- Reports and dashboards can be embedded into websites or linked to a larger audience. This can be used to share insights with clients, customers, or team members.

QlikView and Qlik Sense

- QlikView and Qlik Sense are data visualization and business intelligence platforms that are known for their associative data model, which enables users to explore data in a variety of ways.
- Qlik Sense is a more recent product that was designed with user-friendliness and self-service analytics in mind. It aspires to be more approachable to a broader audience.
- Drag-and-Drop Interface: Qlik Sense has a drag-and-drop interface that allows users to quickly create visualisations and dashboards. It is more user-friendly for non-technical users.
- Qlik Sense also uses the associative data model, but it has been refined to make it easier for end users to explore and analyse data without the need for complex scripting.Data Connectivity: Qlik Sense provides a variety of data connectors for a variety of data sources, such as cloud services, databases, and flat files.

D3.js

D3.js (Data-Driven Documents) is a JavaScript library that allows you to create custom and interactive data visualizations. It gives you complete control over the visualization design, but programming skills are required.D3.js, an abbreviation for

Data-Driven Documents, is a well-known JavaScript library for creating dynamic and interactive data visualizations in web applications. D3.js, created by Mike Bostock, is a powerful and flexible framework for binding data to the Document Object Model (DOM) and rendering it on a web page as HTML, SVG (Scalable Vector Graphics), or Canvas elements. Here are some of D3.js's key features and aspects:

- D3.js is based on the concept of data binding to web elements. Data can be associated with DOM elements and then used to create dynamic visualisations and interactive graphics.
- D3.js is primarily concerned with SVG, a vector graphics format. SVG enables the development of scalable and resolution-independent visualisations. Using SVG elements, D3 can generate complex charts, maps, and other graphics.
- D3.js offers numerous data manipulation and transformation functions. To meet your visualisation requirements, you can filter, aggregate, and modify data.
- The "data join," which binds data to DOM elements, creates a relationship between the data and the visual elements you create, is one of the core concepts in D3.js.

Plotly

Plotly is a Python library that allows you to create interactive, publication-quality visualizations. It also provides an online dashboard creation platform.Plotly is an open-source data visualisation library for Python, R, and other programming languages that allows you to create interactive, web-based visualisations. It includes a versatile set of tools for creating a wide variety of charts and dashboards, ranging from simple line charts to complex 3D visualisations. Here are some of Plotly's key features and aspects.

- Plotly is an interactive data visualisation company. Charts can be made to respond to user interactions such as hovering, clicking, and zooming. As a result, it's an excellent choice for creating interactive dashboards and reports.
- Plotly is available in a variety of programming languages, including Python, R, JavaScript, and Julia, allowing it to be used by a wide range of data professionals.
- Plotly supports numerous chart types, including scatter plots, bar charts, line charts, heatmaps, 3D surface plots, choropleth maps, and others. These charts can be customised in terms of appearance and behaviour.

- The Dash library from Plotly enables you to create interactive web applications and dashboards by combining Plotly charts and widgets. It's an effective tool for developing data-driven web applications.
- Plotly is capable of handling real-time data streaming and updates.

Plotly is a popular tool for creating interactive data visualisations and dashboards in data science, data analysis, and business intelligence. It's a versatile tool that enables users to effectively communicate data insights and build data-driven applications. Plotly can help you create compelling, interactive data visualisations whether you're a data scientist, analyst, or developer.

Matplotlib

Matplotlib is a popular Python library for creating static, two-dimensional visualizations. For more complex data visualization tasks, it is frequently used in conjunction with other libraries.Matplotlib is a popular and widely used Python data visualisation library. It is an essential tool for data visualisation, data analysis, and scientific computing because it provides a versatile platform for creating static, animated, or interactive plots and charts. Here are some of Matplotlib's key features and aspects:

- Line plots, scatter plots, bar charts, histograms, pie charts, box plots, contour plots, surface plots, and other 2D and 3D visualisations are available in Matplotlib.
- Matplotlib works well with other scientific Python libraries, such as NumPy for numerical computations and Pandas for data manipulation. As a result, it is an extremely effective tool for data analysis and exploration.
- Colours, labels, legends, titles, axis properties, and styles are just a few of the options available to users. You have fine-grained control over how your visualisations appear.
- Matplotlib allows you to create animated visualisations. Animations can be created by updating data or objects in a loop, which is useful for illustrating dynamic processes.
- Matplotlib is intended for the creation of high-quality figures for use in academic papers, presentations, and publications. It supports a variety of file formats and integrates LaTeX for text rendering.
- Matplotlib has a large user community and extensive documentation. There are a plethora of tutorials, books, and examples available to assist users in learning and mastering the library.

- - Matplotlib is actively maintained and receives updates and improvements on a regular basis. New features and improvements are added on a regular basis.
- - The Matplotlib community is alive and well. Forums, mailing lists, and social media channels are available for users to seek assistance and support.
- Matplotlib is a critical component of the Python data science and scientific computing ecosystem, and it is widely used by data scientists, researchers, engineers, and analysts. It is a must-have library for creating static visualisations and is frequently used in conjunction with other Python libraries such as NumPy, SciPy, and Pandas for complex data analysis and visualisation tasks.

Seaborn

Seaborn is a Matplotlib-based Python data visualization library. It offers a high-level interface for producing visually appealing statistical graphics.It is intended to generate visually appealing statistical graphics and is especially well-suited to producing informative and appealing data visualisations. Seaborn makes complex visualisations easier to create, making it a popular choice among data analysts and data scientists.

Here are some of Seaborn's key features and aspects:

- Seaborn offers a high-level interface for producing visually appealing statistical visualisations. It provides users with a simple and intuitive API for creating complex plots with minimal code.
- Seaborn integrates with Pandas DataFrames to enable users to easily create visualisations from data stored in Pandas data structures. This integration makes it easier to manipulate and visualise data.Seaborn includes a number of pre-installed themes and colour palettes that make it simple to create visually appealing and publication-quality plots without requiring extensive customization.

R and the ggplot2 Package

R is a popular programming language for statistical analysis and data visualization. ggplot2 is a R package that allows you to create sophisticated and customizable graphs.

- Grammar of Graphics: ggplot2 is built on the "Grammar of Graphics" framework, which allows for the creation of structured and consistent visualisations. Users can map data to visual elements, layer various plot components, and specify aesthetics and geometric objects.

- ggplot2 allows for extensive customization, including the ability to change titles, labels, legends, scales, colours, and themes. This allows for the creation of highly customised plots.
- By splitting the data into subsets and creating separate plots for each subset, ggplot2 allows you to create small multiples (facet grids). This is especially helpful for visualising relationships between categories.
- Data Exploration: With functions for creating scatter plots, bar plots, histograms, box plots, and more, ggplot2 is well-suited for data exploration.
- ggplot2 is actively developed and continues to evolve with new features and improvements.
- Community and Support: The ggplot2 community is large and active. Documentation, tutorials, and examples are available to help users learn how to create effective data visualisations.
- ggplot2 is well-known for its ability to generate informative and visually appealing data visualisations using a structured and logical approach. It is widely employed.
- Layered Plots: ggplot2 encourages the use of layered plots, in which different visual components (for example, data points, lines, and facets) are added in separate layers. This encourages the development of complex, informative visualisations.
- Faceting: ggplot2 allows you to create small multiples (facet grids) by splitting the data into subsets and plotting each subset separately.

Data Visualisation Types

Data visualisation is a broad field with numerous visualisation types, each designed to convey a specific type of information or insight from data. Here are some examples of common data visualisations:

1. Bar Graphs

Bar charts use rectangular bars of varying lengths or heights to display data. They are frequently used to compare categories or to depict the distribution of a single variable.

Bar graphs, also known as bar charts, are a type of data visualisation that uses rectangular bars to represent data. The length or height of each bar is proportional to the value it represents. Bar graphs are especially useful for comparing data across categories or displaying the distribution of a single categorical variable.

- Comparing Categories: Bar graphs are great for comparing discrete categories or groups, such as sales by product, survey responses by category, or departmental performance metrics.
- Distribution: Bar graphs can also be used to depict the distribution of a single categorical variable, such as the frequency of survey responses.
- The x-axis is typically used to represent categories or labels, while the y-axis is used to represent values. Make sure to label both axes to give the data context.
- Consider whether a vertical or horizontal bar graph is better suited to your data and message.
- To make trends and comparisons more visible, arrange the bars in ascending or descending order based on the data values.
- By stacking bars on top of each other, stacked bar charts allow you to represent multiple variables within each category. This is useful for displaying category composition.

Bar Graph Types:

Vertical Bar Chart: The bars in a vertical bar chart are plotted vertically along the y-axis. The most common kind of bar chart

Horizontal Bar Chart: The bars are plotted horizontally along the x-axis in a horizontal bar chart. When you have long category labels or want to emphasise ranking, these are useful.

2. Line Graphs

Line graphs, also known as line charts, are a type of data visualisation that uses lines to connect data points. They are especially useful for displaying trends, changes over time, or continuous data. Line graphs are widely used in a variety of fields such as business, economics, science, and social sciences. Here are some important characteristics and considerations when working with line graphs:

- Periodic Data: Line graphs are frequently used to visualise time series data, which consists of data points collected over a series of time periods. Each data point represents a value at a particular time.
- Data Points and Lines: Each data point is represented on the graph by a marker (e.g., a dot or a 'x').
- The x-axis is commonly used to represent time (or another continuous variable), while the y-axis is used to represent the values being measured. Both axes' labels provide context for the data.

Figure 2. Bar chart

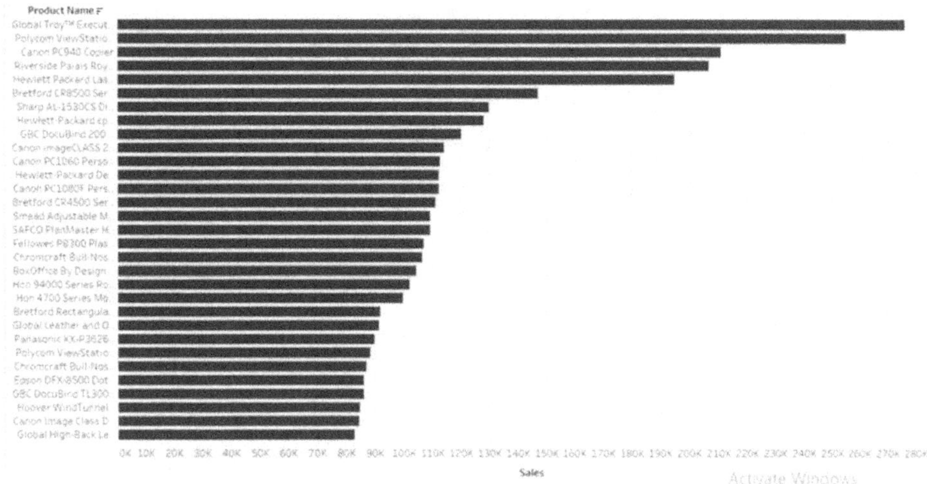

- To compare trends across different variables, line graphs can display multiple lines on the same chart. Each line is frequently distinguished by a distinct colour or pattern.
- To differentiate lines and emphasise data points, customise the style of lines (solid, dashed, etc.) and markers (shape, size).
- Including labels or values at specific data points can help readers interpret the graph by providing additional context.

Data is displayed as a series of data points connected by lines in line charts. They are employed to demonstrate trends, changes over time, or continuous data.

3. Scatter Diagrams

A scatter diagram, also known as a scatter plot or scatter chart, is a data visualization that is used to display individual data points on a two-dimensional graph. Each data point on the graph represents a pair of values from two variables. Scatter diagrams are particularly useful for revealing patterns, trends, and associations between these two variables. Individual data points are represented as dots on a graph, with one variable on the x-axis and another on the y-axis. They are used to demonstrate relationships and correlations between two variables.

Here are the key features and considerations when working with scatter diagrams:

Figure 3. Data points

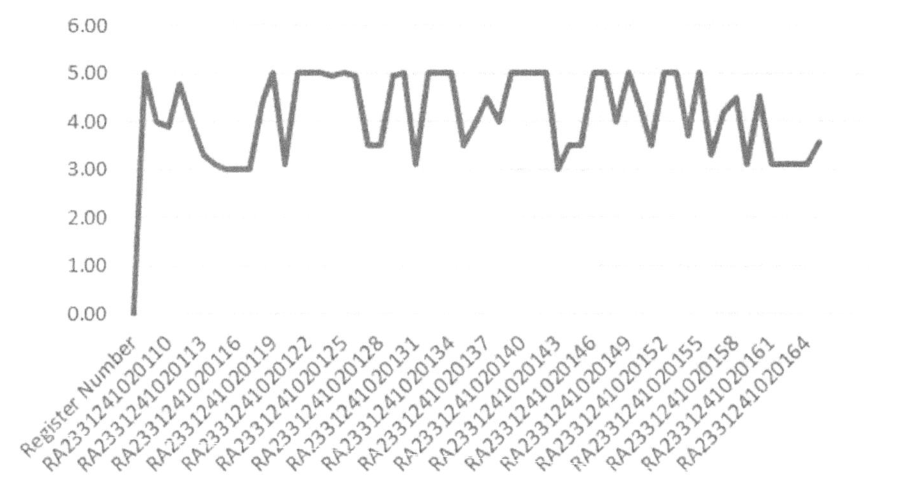

- Scatter diagrams are used to show the relationship of two continuous variables. One variable is plotted horizontally (x-axis), while the other is plotted vertically (y-axis).
- Each data point is represented on the graph as a point, with its position determined by the values of the two variables. The x-coordinate corresponds to the value of one variable, and the y-coordinate corresponds to the value of the other variable.
- Scatter diagrams reveal the distribution of data points and the range of values for both variables. On the graph, you can see how values cluster or disperse.
- You can identify patterns, trends, clusters, outliers, or associations between the two variables by examining the arrangement of data points. Positive correlation, negative correlation, and no correlation are all common patterns.
- Correlation coefficients (e.g., Pearson's correlation coefficient) are frequently used to quantify the relationship between the two variables. These coefficients quantify the strength and direction of the relationship.
- To represent the trend in the data, a line of best fit, also known as a regression line, can be added to the scatter diagram. This line can assist in estimating the relationship between variables and making predictions.
- Colours and markers can be used to distinguish different categories or subsets of data within the scatter plot, making it easier to interpret.

- The axes must be properly scaled to ensure that the data is visually represented accurately. In order to provide context and convey what each variable represents, include axis labels and a title.
- Identify and take into account the presence of outliers or extreme values, which can have an impact on the overall interpretation of the scatter diagram.
- - Analyse the scatter diagram carefully in order to derive meaningful insights and conclusions about the relationship between the two variables. Consider factors such as causality, confounding variables, and data context. Data transformation may be required in some cases to uncover hidden patterns or linear relationships in the scatter plot.
- - Annotations, such as labels or arrows, can be used to draw attention to specific data points or areas of interest.
- Scatter diagrams are commonly used to explore and visualise the relationships between variables in a variety of fields, including statistics, economics, science, anddata analysis. They are an excellent tool for hypothesis testing, data exploration, and comprehending behaviour

4. Tree Maps

A treemap is a data visualisation technique that uses nested rectangles to display hierarchical data. It's an effective way to represent hierarchical structures and how data is classified.

Treemaps are a versatile tool for visualizing hierarchical data, and they offer a unique way to represent complex information in a visually intuitive manner. They can be created using various data visualization tools and libraries, and the choice of color schemes, aspect ratios, and interactive features can greatly influence the effectiveness of the visualization

5. Bubble Chart

A bubble chart is a type of data visualisation that, like a scatter plot, displays data in a two-dimensional coordinate system. A bubble chart, on the other hand, represents each data point not only by a point (or bubble) on the chart, but also by the size and, in some cases, the colour of the bubble. A third quantitative variable is typically encoded by the size of the bubble, making it a three-variable chart.

Bubble charts are an efficient way of communicating complex data with multiple variables, and their visual elements can be customised to improve understanding of data patterns and relationships. They are created with data visualisation tools and

Figure 4. Scatter diagram

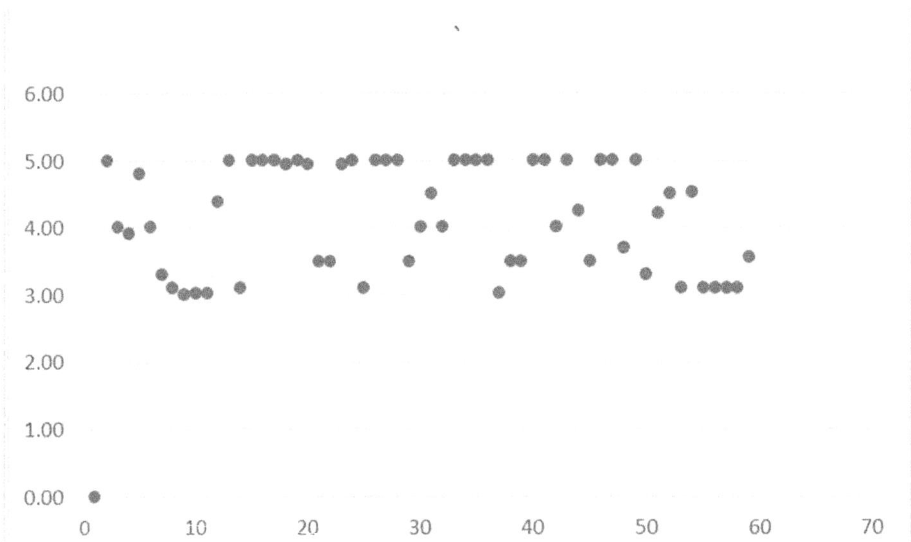

Figure 5. Tree map

Figure 6. Bubble chart

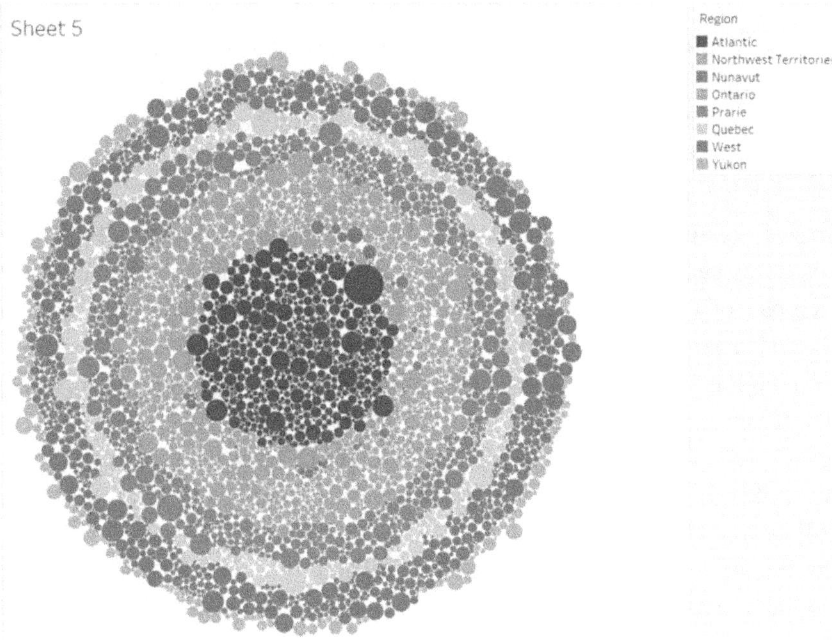

libraries, and the colour schemes, legends, and interactive features can be tailored to the specific data and visualisation objectives.

- Bubble charts represent three variables: two on the X and Y axes and one through the size of the bubbles. As a result, they are well suited to displaying relationships between multiple variables.
- The magnitude of the third variable is represented by the size of each bubble. Larger bubbles represent higher values, while smaller bubbles represent lower values.
- Bubble charts frequently use colour to encode another categorical or quantitative variable in addition to size. Colour can reveal more about the data points, such as categories, groups, or trends.
- Bubble charts are used to reveal data patterns, trends, and relationships. Viewers can quickly grasp the relationships between three variables by examining the position, size, and colour of each bubble.
- Many interactive bubble chart visualisations exist.

High Dimensional Data visualization

1. **A scatterplot matrix (SPLOM):** Is a grid of scatterplots, with each scatterplot displaying the relationship between two variables. While it does not directly visualise high dimensions, it can assist in identifying potential pairwise relationships and patterns.

Grid of Scatterplots: In a Scatterplot Matrix, the variables or features in your dataset are placed on the x and y axes, and a scatterplot in a grid layout is created for each pair of variables. For each variable, the main diagonal typically contains histograms or kernel density plots.

Variable Pairs: The grid size is determined by the number of variables in your dataset. If you have 'n' variables, your grid will be n x n.

Scatterplots: In the matrix, each scatterplot represents the relationship between two variables. It shows how one variable (x-axis) changes in relation to another variable (y-axis).

The diagonal of the matrix is used to display the univariate distributions of each variable. Histograms or kernel density plots can be displayed here to show the distribution of a single variable. Overall, a Scatterplot Matrix is a useful exploratory tool in data analysis, particularly when dealing with medium-sized datasets. It provides an initial overview of variable relationships, allowing you to make informed decisions about subsequent data analysis and modelling steps.

2. **Parallel Coordinates Plot:** Parallel Coordinates Plot is a data visualisation technique used to explore and analyse multivariate data. It is also known as Parallel Coordinates Visualisation or Parallel Coordinate Plots (PCP). It's especially useful for visualising and comprehending high-dimensional datasets with multiple attributes or features per data point. Each dimension is represented as a vertical axis in this type of plot, and data points are connected by lines that show the values of each dimension. The plot can be used to identify patterns, clusters, and relationships.

Coordinates that are parallel Plots are an effective visualisation tool for exploring and comprehending multidimensional data. They are especially useful for tasks such as data exploration, feature selection, and pattern detection in large datasets. Their effectiveness, however, is dependent on the nature of the data and the ability to manage issues such as visual clutter and scaling.

3. **t-Distributed Stochastic Neighbour Embedding (t-SNE):** t-Distributed Stochastic Neighbour Embedding (t-SNE) is a nonlinear dimensionality

reduction technique that can be useful for visualising high-dimensional data. Its goal is to map data points to a lower-dimensional space while keeping neighbourhood relationships intact.

Glyphs and Icons: In some cases, you can represent high-dimensional data with glyphs or icons, where different features are encoded in the size, shape, or colour of the glyphs.

4. **3D Visualisation:** When dimensionality reduction techniques reduce data to three dimensions, you can create 3D scatterplots to explore the data.

Data is typically represented as 3D models in 3D visualisation. These models can be created from scratch using 3D modelling software, or they can be obtained using 3D scanning technologies.

Unlike 2D representations, 3D visualisation allows you to view objects from various angles and perspectives, allowing you to explore objects in greater depth.

Rendering is the process of converting 3D models into 2D images and is essential in 3D visualisation. Rendering software creates realistic or stylized images of 3D scenes using techniques such as ray tracing or rasterization.Textures, such as images or patterns, can be mapped onto the surfaces of 3D models to add realism. This makes objects appear more detailed and textured.

5. **Interactive Visualisation:** Interactive tools and libraries, such as Plotly or Bokeh, allow users to explore high-dimensional data by allowing them to zoom, pan, and select data points interactively.
    - At the heart of interactive visualisation is interactivity. Users can interact with visual elements by clicking, dragging, zooming, filtering, and selecting data points. Changes in the visual representation are triggered by user input.
    - Interactive visualisations respond in real time to user input, allowing users to see immediate changes as a result of their interactions. This dynamic nature of interactivity is required for effective data exploration.
    - Widgets and controls, such as sliders, buttons, checkboxes, and input fields, are frequently used in interactive visualisations to allow users to adjust parameters, apply filters, or change the view.
6. **Density Plots:** Visualising the density of high-dimensional data can reveal clusters and patterns. Techniques such as kernel density estimation can be used for this purpose.Density plots are an important data visualisation and exploratory data analysis tool. They provide a smooth, continuous representation of data

distributions, making it easier to understand and compare different distributions within a dataset.

7. **Projection Techniques:** Techniques such as parallel coordinates projection and hypercube projection aim to project high-dimensional data onto lower-dimensional spaces for easier viewing.Each projection technique has advantages and disadvantages, and the technique used is determined by the characteristics of the data and the goals of the analysis. Projection techniques are useful in data exploration and visualisation because they allow analysts to make high-dimensional data more understandable and interpretable.
8. **Principal Component Analysis (PCA) Plot:** After reducing dimensionality with PCA, you can visualise the data with 2D or 3D plots based on the top principal components. PCA captures the greatest amount of variance in the data, making it an effective visualisation tool.It facilitates data exploration, reduces dimensionality, and can provide insights into data structure. It is frequently used in data analysis, data visualisation, and feature selection as a preprocessing step.
9. **Heatmaps:** Are frequently used to visualise correlation matrices or similarity measures in large amounts of data. They can assist you in comprehending feature relationships and patterns.Heatmaps are useful tools for summarising and presenting data visually, allowing patterns and trends to emerge. When used properly, they can provide insights that would be difficult to discover using other methods of data analysis.
10. **Clustering Based on Hierarchy Dendrogram:** Hierarchical clustering can be used to group data points that are similar. Visualising the hierarchy's dendrogram can reveal how data points cluster.

Techniques for Projection: Techniques such as parallel coordinates projection and hypercube projection aim to project high-dimensional data onto lower-dimensional spaces for easier visualisation.

11. **RadViz (Radial Visualisation):** RadViz is a method for displaying the relationship between features and their influence on data point positions using a circular plot and radial lines.
12. **Feature Importance:** In the field of machine learning and data analysis, feature importance refers to the quantification of the contribution of individual features or variables in a predictive model or dataset to the outcome or target variable. It is used to determine which characteristics are most relevant or influential in making predictions and comprehending the relationship between variables. The importance of features is especially useful for feature selection, model interpretation, and decision-making. There are several techniques for

determining feature importance, and the method chosen is determined by the type of model and the problem at hand. When working with a predictive model, you can visualise feature importance scores to identify the most influential features.

13. **Data Clustering:** Data clustering is a fundamental technique in machine learning and data analysis that involves clustering or subgrouping similar data points or objects based on their inherent similarities or dissimilarities. Clustering's primary goal is to discover patterns, structures, and relationships within data without prior knowledge of the groupings. Clustering is used in a variety of applications, such as customer segmentation, image segmentation, anomaly detection, and others. Group data points with similar characteristics using clustering algorithms such as k-means or DBSCAN. Visualising the clustering results can reveal patterns.

The method used to visualise high-dimensional data is determined by the nature of the data, your objectives, and the insights you seek.

CONCLUSION

In this chapter large-scale dataset has been identified and trained data is visualized using appropriate techniques. This tends users to gain clear knowledge of complex and large data sets that can not be handled by a normal human brain.

REFERENCES

CooleyS. M.HamiltonT.AragonesS. D.RayJ. C. J.DeedsE. J. (2022). A novel metric reveals previously unrecognized distortion in dimensionality reduction of scRNA-seq data. bioRxiv. doi:10.1101/689851

Espadoto, M., Martins, R. M., Kerren, A., Hirata, N. S. T., & Telea, A. C. (2021). Toward a quantitative survey of dimension reduction techniques. *IEEE Transactions on Visualization and Computer Graphics*, *27*(4), 2153–2173. doi:10.1109/TVCG.2019.2944182 PMID:31567092

Li, Y., Chai, Y., Yin, H., & Chen, B. (2021). A novel feature learning framework for high-dimensional data classification. *International Journal of Machine Learning and Cybernetics*, *12*(2), 555–569. doi:10.1007/s13042-020-01188-2

Liu, S., Maljovec, D., Wang, B., Bremer, P.-T., & Pascucci, V. (2015). Visualizing high-dimensional data: Advances in the past decade. *IEEE Transactions on Visualization and Computer Graphics*, *23*(3), 1249–1268. doi:10.1109/TVCG.2016.2640960 PMID:28113321

Moon, K. R., van Dijk, D., Wang, Z., Gigante, S., Burkhardt, D. B., Chen, W. S., Yim, K., Elzen, A., Hirn, M. J., Coifman, R. R., Ivanova, N. B., Wolf, G., & Krishnaswamy, S. (2019). Visualizing structure and transitions in high-dimensional biological data. *Nature Biotechnology*, *37*(12), 1482–1492. doi:10.1038/s41587-019-0336-3 PMID:31796933

Nonato, L. G., & Aupetit, M. (2019). Multidimensional projection for visual analytics: Linking techniques with distortions, tasks, and layout enrichment. *IEEE Transactions on Visualization and Computer Graphics*, *25*(1), 2650–2673. doi:10.1109/TVCG.2018.2846735 PMID:29994258

Sun, E. D., Ma, R., & Zou, J. (2023). Dynamic visualization of high-dimensional data. *Nature Computational Science*, *3*(2), 86–100. doi:10.1038/s43588-022-00380-4 PMID:38177955

Tang, L. (2020). High-dimensional data visualization. *Nature Methods*, *17*(2), 129. doi:10.1038/s41592-020-0750-y PMID:32020095

Vallejos, C. A. (2019). Exploring a world of a thousand dimensions. *Nature Biotechnology*, *37*(12), 1423–1424. doi:10.1038/s41587-019-0330-9 PMID:31796932

Yang, Y., Tuong, Z. K., & Yu, D. (2023). Dimensionality reduction under scrutiny. *Nature Computational Science*, *3*(1), 8–9. doi:10.1038/s43588-022-00383-1 PMID:38177957

Chapter 3
Deep Machine Learning:
Towards the Intelligence Level of Man

Parimal Kumar Giri
Gandhi Institute of Technological Advancement, India

Chandrakant Mallick
Gandhi Institute of Technological Advancement, India

Sambit Kumar Mishra
Gandhi Institute for Education and Technology, India

ABSTRACT

With deep learning technology, machine learning has shown impressive results. Nonetheless, these techniques frequently use excessive amounts of resources; they demand big datasets, a lot of parameters, and a lot of processing power. In order to develop machine learning models that are efficient with resources, the authors have outlined a general machine learning technique in this work that they call deep machine learning. All the methods that initially identify inductive biases and then use those inductive biases to improve the learning efficiency of models come under the umbrella of deep machine learning. Numerous robust machine learning techniques are currently in use, and some of them are highly well-liked precisely because of their efficacy. Deep machine learning, however, is still in its infancy, and much more work remains. The efforts must be focused in order to progress artificial intelligence (AI).

DOI: 10.4018/979-8-3693-1886-7.ch003

1. INTRODUCTION

Over the past few decades, machine learning has advanced remarkably. Machine learning algorithms are capable of learning from data and carrying out a variety of activities that would normally call for human creativity or intelligence (Grigorescu et al., 2020). These elements have made it possible for several innovative applications across numerous fields. Machine learning algorithms, for instance, are capable of producing lifelike portraits, landscapes, and artwork (Brown et al., 2020). Additionally, for a variety of tasks like summarization, translation, and storytelling, they are able to write writings that are cohesive and fluid (Goodfellow et al., 2014). Additionally, they can power autonomous vehicles capable of navigating dynamic and complicated situations. Additionally, machine learning algorithms are so good at board games like Go and Chess that they can even outperform the greatest human players.

However in order to properly train and function, machine learning algorithms also require data and processing capacity. Large and varied data sets are necessary to give them enough instances and feedback to help them teach. Regretfully, these methods are getting close to the boundaries of what can currently be achieved with machine learning technology (Meir et al., 2020). The growing demands on data and model sizes make it harder and harder to improve these applications in terms of intelligence and accuracy. Machine learning models have an insatiable appetite for data; the largest models have close to or over a trillion parameters (Thompson et al., 2020). It's possible that both the data and the model sizes have grown to the highest feasible point.

Furthermore, there's a chance that the machine learning techniques being used now aren't the best, wasting resources. It's possible that a much smaller model can perform as well as or better than a machine learning model for every skill it learns. However, such tiny models are not found by our existing learning technique. This is particularly problematic in the event of insufficient data. The algorithms for multiplying two numbers provide an extreme example: Humans have developed some extremely efficient multiplication algorithms. Furthermore, deep learning models have been developed that have only used examples of proper multiplications to teach them how to multiple. Crucially, deep learning is never able to find the best algorithms. Deep learning can only be applied to extremely resource-hungry, inferior models (Mallick et al., 2023). However, the human mind is able to deduce a multiplication rule from a little

The superiority of human and animal brains over robots in numerous realms of intelligence is one of the reasons we need to advance machine learning technologies. Of course, in certain domains—like chess or calculations—machines can excel at tasks that need for certain knowledge or guidelines. Humans are still superior, though, in other areas like language, art, and social interaction where greater adaptability and inventiveness are needed. People are also able to pick up knowledge from a small number of examples and apply it to novel situations that they have never encountered before. However, in order for machines to learn and generalize beyond their training data, they frequently require large amounts of data and feedback (Giri et al., 2018).

We have developed what is known as powerful machine learning in this chapter. This strategy seeks to get beyond the drawbacks of the existing machine learning techniques, which rely on a lot of data and parameters in order to produce intelligence. Rather than going down this route, we may investigate technologies that allow machines to learn more efficiently. Robust machine learning allows computers to learn new abilities and activities while consuming less data and resources by utilizing their existing knowledge and experience. Robust machine learning enhances machines' creativity and adaptability, bringing them closer to animal or human learners.There are now several approaches available for powerful machine learning. We have attempting to bring them all together less than one heading in this chapter. Despite their apparent differences, seemingly unrelated techniques may share a crucial characteristic: they could all be variations of powerful machine learning.

The intention is to unite these endeavours under a shared vision, so enabling additional initiatives along the same path. Additionally, determining the fundamental conditions that must be met for an activity to be classified as strong machine learning should serve as a guide for these efforts.John Searle's idea of strong artificial intelligence served as the model for deep machine learning. AI can be classified as either strong or weak by Searle. Strong artificial intelligence, according to him, is computer intelligence that functions similarly to that of humans or animals. According to his assertion, only highly advanced artificial intelligence would possess the same capacity to decipher and comprehend the universe as both humans and animals. Similarly, the weak AI—machine intelligence limited to imitating human or animal intelligence-could possibly lead to strong AI was another point he raised.

2. RELATED WORKS

Prior knowledge can help when beginning a machine learning assignment rather than starting from scratch (George Karimpanal & Bouffanais, 2019; Brown et al., 2020; Yuan et al, 2021). Both speed and data requirements for learning may be reduced. There may also be a requirement for reduced processing power. Furthermore, learning a new task may require less parameter for models that start from the beginning if they are pre-trained with prior information. Deep machine learning depends on resources that are already available, while weak machine learning depends on resources that are already known. Smaller models or fewer data required, or both, are the outcome

Table 1. Characteristics of weak vs. deep machine learning

S. No	Characteristics	Weak	Strong
1	Demand on training data sets	large	small
2	Demand on parameters	high	low
3	Inductive biases	scarce	abundant
4	Previous knowledge	scarce	abundant
5	Generality of learning capabilities	High	low
6	Domain of application	broad	narrow
7	Data points	large	small
8	Algorithm	High	low
9	Model-Centric	broad	narrow
10	Data-Centric	scarce	abundant

of the current understanding. Table 1 enumerates the key distinctions between weak and deep machine learning.

How machine learning gets to greater degrees of intelligence distinguishes strong from weak learning. Consider the scenario where we wish to enhance an existing model that currently operates at a specific level. The number of categories that have been classified or the model's total accuracy can be used to gauge the improvement in accuracy. In what way do we accomplish this advance? We are employing a weak machine learning technique if we add additional raw resources, such as more data or parameters in the model. Conversely, a strong machine learning strategy is used if we transfer the information from the prior learning to the current learning in order to make it more effective. Thus, it is easy to define powerful machine learning using words. Strong machine learning is so easily characterized by the resources that are employed: we are using strong machine learning if the main resource is not a raw component (data, parameters), but rather a more refined ingredient, which is previously learned knowledge.

Both humans and animals possess great learning skills from birth. Genes give on the required knowledge; therefore, we inherit strong learning capacities from our ancestors. We can swiftly pick up abilities in a variety of areas, including motor skills, manipulating objects, hunting, avoiding predators, and more, thanks to our prior knowledge. When it comes to studying language, math, and other skills, humans are also proficient. It is obvious that human learning outperforms machine learning. To train a state-of-the-art machine learning model, for instance, a human adult's lifetime exposure to language is only a small portion of the total amount of language. It is possible to say that this understanding of genetics adds strength.

Natural selection has evolved our genes over millions of years, progressively changing them, which is one of the reasons why our genes have tremendous learning capacity. Because evolution by natural selection relies heavily on haphazard mutations that aren't informed by past experiences or feedback, it's an example of weak learning. To create new species and ultimately give rise to human intelligence, many generations of individuals and several mutation experiments were required. Weak learning is what it took to create our strong learning abilities, and this delayed, ineffective method of learning was necessary.

This leads us to the conclusion that it is necessary to integrate weak and powerful machine learning. Robust machine learning is impossible to ignore.The task facing scientists and engineers is to come up with methods for improving machine learning and turning weak models into powerful ones. Two sets of strategies will be needed for these methods: one for weak machine learning knowledge acquisition and the other for strong machine learning knowledge application. Consequently, the engineers must first design the training programs, including the curricula and training procedures. Strong machine learning can start after learning is completed effectively. Strong machine learning is a field of study that develops strategies for making machine learning systems more intelligent learners.

3. DEEP MACHINE LEARNING

Strong machine learning is based on a number of theoretical ideas from cybernetics and machine learning. The idea of inductive biases is one of them. The phrase "inductive bias" in machine learning refers to the presumptions made by a learning algorithm in order to forecast the results of novel inputs. Crucially, learning the optimal output for every potential input requires more than just data alone. Prior knowledge or "beliefs" about the nature of the problem and its solution are necessary for the learning process to function. The term "inductive bias" refers to the prior knowledge or beliefs held by the algorithm.

A machine learning model's propensity to discover particular kinds of correlations between variables is influenced by inductive bias (Giri, P. K., 2020). A linear equation model, for instance, may learn linear correlations between variables well, but not sinusoidal ones. On the other hand, a model composed on sinusoidal equations struggles with linear relationships and has a strong propensity to learn sinusoidal patterns in time series. It is possible to argue that each of these two kinds of models is "biased" toward discovering particular kinds of patterns.

To select a model with the appropriate inductive biases for a given task is to make a well-chosen model selection. Compared to standard deep learning models, convolutional neural networks are more adept at identifying objects in pictures.

This is because the convolutional layers of convolutional models have the proper inductive biases. In a similar vein, transformer models benefit from inductive biases that help them learn to resolve sequential data.

Models with mis-selected inductive biases encounter challenges. Although they need additional parameters and training data, they can frequently also learn tasks for which they are not appropriate. For instance, one only requires numerous linear equations and, thus, many parameters to be evaluated in order to approximate sinusoids using linear equations to any degree of precision. Similar to this, a Fourier Transform, which is a model used to approximate time series using sinusoids, is capable of describing any signal, not only sinusoidal ones.

It is possible to use sinusoidal shapes to describe even rectangular signals; the challenge lies in the need for a large number of parameters in the model. Frequently, the size of the original data and the number of parameters used match. Analogously, objects can be identified from photos by a basic deep learning network without the need for convolution. Nonetheless, in comparison to a model that uses convolution, this one will inevitably need a lot more samples, parameters, and computing time. The resulting models can learn significantly faster and be lot smaller if inductive biases are selected carefully.

One may argue that the state-of-the-art models for language or computer vision are not the best ones. They aren't the best models that will ever be; they're only better than basic neural networks. More effective models with superior inductive biases might be achievable. We merely don't know them. Millions of times more efficient models of language and vision may exist, just like in the multiplication example above. In actuality, less than one gigabyte is needed to store one copy of human DNA. Furthermore, the human brain's extraordinary ability to process language and imagery is a result of this DNA. This suggests that there might be far more powerful inductive biases than anything else.

The next concern is what level of machine learning power can be used to find these more useful inductive biases. Traditionally, human engineers and scientists have introduced inductive biases (such as linear, sinusoidal, convolution, attention in transformer models, etc.) to their models. The foundation of these inductive biases is human insight. Strong machine learning can be defined as a methodology that enables computers to acquire inductive biases on their own without requiring human intervention in their design. Machines extract the real inductive biases from data; humans just specify the parameters under which inductive biases can be learned. As a result, after machine learning has acquired its own inductive biases, it becomes more powerful. Inductive biases are learned by a machine learning method and stored for eventual use in an efficient manner.

4. SEVERAL EXISTING STRONG MACHINE LEARNING TECHNIQUES

Numerous current machine learning techniques fall under the category of "strong machine learning." These techniques start with poor machine learning and then apply the learned skills to get strong machine learning (Giri, P. K., 2017). Stated differently, these methodologies learn inductive biases first, and then employ them. There are probably a ton of other techniques that are not included in this list, which is not comprehensive.

1) **Transfer learning:** By far the most well-liked and widely applied method that possesses the characteristics of robust machine learning is transfer learning. It's also perhaps the simplest type of powerful machine learning. According to Bozinovski & Fulgosi (1976; George Karimpanal & Bouffanais, 2019), transfer learning is predicated on pre-training a deep learning network on a relevant task. A network is pre-trained on a sizable dataset by beginning from scratch, and the parameters of the trained network serve as the basis for the subsequent training task. The parameter state acts as an inductive bias for further learning. A much smaller training sample can typically be used to complete the later task. Stated differently, without first pre-training on a comparable task with copious amounts of data, it would be impossible to successfully train a network from beginning on the later task with minimal amounts of data. Later learning stages will require fewer resources as a result of the transfer of learning from one task to another. Pre-training, or transfer learning, is essential to modern machine learning applications. Pre-trained models are readily accessible and widely employed, for instance in natural language processing (Brown et al., 2020) and computer vision (Yuan et al., 2021). By employing several learning phases, transfer learning allows a model to reach higher intelligence and adaptability levels. The weights and biases that are conveyed serve as inductive biases that are used in further learning.
2) **One-shot learning:** A modelling strategy that aimed to imitate human conceptions was described by Lake et al. (2015). A "concept" of handwritten characters could be learned via its model. This included the brushstrokes required to write a character as well as the way the characters looked. For the most part, writing a character involves using numerous strokes in a certain order and direction. The writing concepts were initially taught to the model using an example of writing systems. Weak machine learning's initial training phase can be described as this. The model then developed a "concept" of writing and was able to pick up new handwritten characters frowith the ability to learn from a single example, the model became far more successful. Thus, the term

"one-shot learning" might be used to describe this strategy. We can refer to this subsequent phase as powerful machine learning. The model learned new characters by using its "concept" of writing as the inductive bias. The authors contended that humans learn and apply concepts in a manner akin to this acquired ability to pick things up quickly. Other researchers were motivated to investigate more one-shot learning techniques by the work of Lake et al. (Fei-Fei et al., 2006; Vinyals et al., 2016; REFs).m whole other writing systems.

3) **Zero-shot learning:** Certain models have the ability to handle novel classes or problems without requiring any further learning, that is, without requiring parameter updates. A model might be taught, for instance, using texts that describe pictures of animals. One example of this would be a model that was not trained on zebras but could identify them if it was taught that they resembled striped horses. This is feasible because the model gained knowledge about how horses look and what it means for an animal to be striped by studying, for instance, tigers. One could argue that the original training on tigers and horses constituted weak machine learning. A good use of previously learned information may be seen in the model's recognition of striped horses in a subsequent application. Even though fresh data are now required for training, the model can still complete novel tasks with just one more data sample. Even in the absence of weight updates, the model's knowledge acts as an inductive bias to identify zebras. In natural language processing and picture classification, zero-short learning is widely used (e.g., Brown et al., 2020).
4) **Guided transfer learning:** One method that increases transfer learning's potential is guided transfer learning. While model parameters are transferred over by classic transfer learning, information about which parameters should be permitted to change and which should better remain unchanged is transferred over through guided transfer learning. A weak machine learning component is also the first step in guided transfer learning, when a group of scout networks is trained on simple tasks and with enough data. Information regarding the parameters that tend to change and those that tend to stay the same in subsequent learning is gathered during this process. Afterwards, this understanding of parameter changeability is applied to new tasks and serves as an inductive bias. For guided transfer learning to be effective, the early scout learning tasks and a subsequent learning task must be related, just like for transfer learning. The amount of data and processing required is further reduced by guided transfer learning than by transfer learning alone. Guided transfer learning pushes standard transfer learning's boundaries wherever they are. When using guided transfer learning, inductive biases become even more pronounced and task-specific than they would with classical transfer learning.

Reducing catastrophic interference (forgetting old information by novel learning) and solving problems based on a mixture of logical operations (OR, AND, XOR) are two tasks that are typically very difficult for deep learning. These are tasks that guided transfer learning has been shown to help with (Nikolić, 2023).

5) **Few-shot learning:** Gathering and annotating a large amount of data for training can be difficult, costly, and time-consuming in many real-world situations. When there are insufficient data points available for a classification assignment, a model built with fewer data points can be useful. Models using the few shot learning (FSL) (Bartunov and Vetrov, 2018) and occasionally low-shot learning (LSL) techniques are fed extremely little data. Few-shot techniques seek to generate accurate predictions with models trained on less data, in contrast to the conventional approach of using large amounts of data for model learning. Humans can frequently pick up new ideas or skills from a small number of instances. Few-shot learning makes an effort to replicate this capacity for quick learning, which in some ways moves AI models closer to being intelligent like humans.
6) **Deep transfer learning (DTL):** The process of efficiently applying previously acquired model knowledge to a new task with little additional training or fine-tuning is known as transfer learning. Moreover, although academics are making great efforts to improve it, the typical DL model still requires a lot of processing resources, such a server with GPU support. Therefore, to overcome this issue, Deep Transfer Learning (DTL), a DL-based transfer learning method, may be useful. A DL model is taught via transfer learning, a two-stage process that includes pre-training and fine-tuning phases where the model is trained on the intended task. Although the majority of recent research focuses on supervised learning, there may be an increase in interest in the ability of deep neural networks to transmit knowledge in unsupervised or semi-supervised learning.
7) **Deep reinforcement learning (DRL):** Compared to other methods, reinforcement learning handles the sequential decision-making problem in a different way. Reinforcement learning aims to learn optimal action sequences by interacting with the environment, which is commonly known as a policy. Agents can learn the right actions in a virtual world by integrating neural networks and reinforcement learning architecture through deep reinforcement learning (DRL). Furthermore, the field in DRL uses Deep Q-Networks, Double DQN, Bi-directional Learning, Monte Carlo Control, etc. (Junwei, H. et al., 2018).

5. GENERALITY VERSUS SPECIFICITY TRADE-OFF

Each and every inductive bias has a trade-off. Only in a specific domain do inductive biases improve machine learning performance. Essentially, inductive biases complicate matters by making it more difficult to excel in unrelated fields. For example, a convolutional network performs well in computer vision but struggles miserably with word sequences in natural languages. Inductive biases make learning in one area more successful at the expense of learning in other domains. The specificity that the inductive biases provide for fast learning and the generality that a machine learning algorithm can learn in principle have to be traded off as a result. A model with stronger inductive biases might be more specialized, which allows it to be used for a smaller range of issues.

For instance, we might focus a model on even more specialized vision issues in addition to computer vision. A machine learning system might, for instance, grow proficient at identifying just animals or handwritten letters. certain more specialized models get even better at learning inside certain domains, but they struggle even more to learn outside of them—for example, to recognize vehicles in pictures. The learning domain becomes smaller as one's capacity to learn within a certain topic increases. Stated differently, a clear trade-off exists between the range of issues that a particular strong machine learning algorithm can solve and the learning capability of strong machine learning, which is characterized by high specificity.

Consider a human-made model, E = mc2, which is a single equation describing a particular property of the cosmos, as an extreme example of specificity. This formula is a straightforward "model" with just one parameter, c. The model can, in theory, be used for several universes with various light speeds. One can "train" the model to estimate energy (E) given mass (m) in any of these universes. The only parameter that the model needs to learn is c, which is the speed of light in that world. Therefore, it might only take one data point containing E and m to identify the parameter c, allowing the model to accurately determine the energies for a brand-new universe. An excellent illustration of domain specificity is provided by this model, which can only learn one thing—the conversion of mass to energy—but it can do so very well—from a single data point. Only this particular issue can be solved using this model; it cannot be used for anything else. Instead of being developed via sophisticated machine learning, this "model" was produced by human insight—specifically, Albert Einstein's insight—which is a powerful brain learning mechanism.

However, the well-known Einstein's equation shows how severe specialization always results in an extreme lack of generalization as well as an extreme learning efficiency. In machine learning, the no-free-lunch theorem is connected to this trade-off between generality and specificity (Adam et al., 2019). There isn't a single optimal learning algorithm that can excel at solving every possible problem, according to the no-free-lunch theorem. The performance of various algorithms is dependent on the properties of the data and the problem, and each method has its own advantages and disadvantages. This suggests that there will always be a trade-off between specificity and generality: an algorithm that excels in one area will inevitably struggle in another. To attain high learning efficiency in terms of data and model sizes, deep machine learning models must forgo generality in favour of specificity.

6. DEEP MACHINE LEARNING AND HUMAN INTELLIGENCE

Developing more potent machine learning methods is one way to build AI that is intelligent like humans (Mallick et al. 2023). These methods need to mimic how both people and animals learn. Living things are excellent learners; they can pick up new ideas fast, extrapolate from a single experience, and adjust to unfamiliar circumstances with little help or information. We will probably need to strengthen the current machine learning models in order to get machines to perform similarly (Ardila et al, 2016). With fewer parameters and data, they ought to be able to learn tasks similar to those performed by humans and animals.

We can take inspiration for these advancements from the way that human brains are made up of specialized modules that are all tuned for different tasks. About 46 distinct regions make up the cerebral cortex, each of which is specialized for a certain task that affects language, vision, motor commands, and other processes (Strotzer, 2009). It's likely that each of these categories is a strong learner and can pick up knowledge from modest amounts of data. Our brain modules become even more specialized as we grow and learn after birth. We so also lose some generality as a result. Babies are able to learn more freely than adults can. However, given their subsequent specializations, adults are better learners than infants.The inductive biases that humans are predisposed to are likely what distinguish human intelligence from that of animals. The total number of brain regions, the general interconnectedness between those regions, and the learning principles that govern our postnatal learning are examples of inductive biases (Kawachi 2017).

Therefore, the approach to AI's human intelligence should involve not only adding more modules but also using powerful machine learning techniques to teach those modules to acquire knowledge in their respective fields. As part of mechanisms for the successful implementation of cognitive processes based on the idea of practopoiesis (Nikolić, 2015), we have recently proposed that these modules apply temporary selections of routes (Nikolić, 2023). Because inductive biases can be stored in mechanisms that temporarily open and close routes in addition to neuronal connections, this opens up new possibilities for the use of strong machine learning.

Strong machine learning-based approaches to intelligent machines and artificial general intelligence (AGI)-based approaches draw significant differences (Goertzel, 2014). Achieving human-level intelligence is the goal shared by both strategies. They do, however, provide various approaches to achieving that aim. According to Hutter (2004), AGI places a strong emphasis on finding one or more "general" algorithms that are applicable to any domain and any problem and don't require a lot of specialization. Generality is the fundamental concept of AGI. On the other hand, strong machine learning stresses specialization and requires the creation of efficient, specialized algorithms that are adept in learning particular areas. We could be better off looking for efficient types of strong machine learning rather than trying to create a universal algorithm. The sole "algorithm" that is universally applicable could be a technique for acquiring inductive biases for the several specialized modules of strong machine learning. Perhaps what AGI is searching for is this theoretical generic approach to specialization learning (Giri et al., 2016).

7. DEEP MACHINE LEARNING

Deep machine learning techniques are undoubtedly a good way to advance AI development. Deep learning is always dependent on weak machine learning (more parameters and data) at the outset of problem solving. However, several machine learning techniques that are frequently used in conjunction with deep learning have shown to be effective, as we have seen (Giri et al. 2017). Adding data and parameters to models is still a major source of bad machine learning, which is still applied too heavily in AI today. It's still early days for strong machine learning (Pandey et al. 2021). Weak machine learning has the drawback of having a rapidly finite potential. With respect to computational costs and environmental issues, the models rapidly expand to their largest possible sizes. Additionally, new data production becomes prohibitively expensive as the models rapidly use up all of the training data.

Thus, weak machine learning models can only be advanced to a certain extent by huge firms with ample resources. More compact groups can't compete. Big companies with the means to develop and maintain them, for instance, are the only ones capable of producing extensive language models. It also lowers competition and innovation in the AI space by giving them an unfair advantage over smaller firms. By using fewer parameters and less data, models with stronger machine learning have the potential to be more intelligent and efficient. More people and organizations will be able to engage and help progress AI as a result, levelling the playing field.

The necessity for intelligent robots at the periphery is another reason to reduce the size of models. This is evident in the field of autonomous driving in particular, but also in robotics in general. Large models that are powered by supercomputers outperform little versions that fit under automobile hoods in such robotic tasks. Smaller models that demonstrate the same excellent performance as larger ones are necessary for autonomous driving and robotics in general. Perhaps only powerful machine learning will be able to accomplish this.

Deep machine learning can sometimes be attributed to the lack of data. The ease of access to a big collection of texts kept in electronic format—nearly all of human writing—has made it possible to develop large language models. This effectively utilized another characteristic of language: Due to its extreme compression, language is incredibly effective at storing information. However, images use up a lot more resources inefficiently. For instance, the same story may be told in a language-based tale or a picture-based movie, but the memory requirements may vary by a factor of a million.

The future advancement of artificial intelligence (AI) based on computer vision may be impacted by this strong recall capacity for visuals. The constraints of language are reached significantly later than with the use of images in poor machine learning (Pandey et al. 2019). It would need resources that even the biggest corporations probably cannot afford to build "large vision models," which would produce movies with the same quality and adaptability as language models produce texts. This increases the demand to create robust computer vision machine learning methods. To circumvent these constraints, only robust machine learning may be used.

8. CONCLUSION

Assumptions incorporated into the learning algorithm that facilitate faster learning in a particular domain are known as inductive biases. It is believed that by learning these inductive biases, robots would eventually be able to learn more efficiently with fewer models and less data. In order for robots to learn their own inductive biases, we still need to create new methodologies. We should concentrate on improving the capability for strong machine learning rather than on creating massive, powerful models. There are currently numerous effective machine learning methods in use. Still, further research is required in this area. Deep machine learning is still in its early stages of development. The trade-off between generality and specificity must be considered as we create ever-stronger machine learning algorithms. Proficient learners possess specialization. Combining several specialized learners into a fully functional system with high intelligence is a difficulty that comes with powerful machine learning. The ultimate goal of deep machine learning is to contribute to the development of strong artificial intelligence (AI), or machines that are as intelligent as humans. The concept is that we can develop robots that are capable of learning and reasoning in the same ways as people by giving them the same inductive biases that humans have.

REFERENCES

Adam, S. P., Alexandropoulos, S. A. N., Pardalos, P. M., &Vrahatis, M. N. (2019). No free lunch theorem: A review. *Approximation and optimization: Algorithms, complexity and applications*, 57-82.

Ardila, A., Bernal, B., & Rosselli, M. (2016). How localized are language brain areas? A review of Brodmann areas involvement in oral language. *Archives of Clinical Neuropsychology*, *31*(1), 112–122. doi:10.1093/arclin/acv081 PMID:26663825

Bartunov, S., & Vetrov, D. P. (2018). Few-shot generative modelling with generative matching networks. AISTATS.

Brown, T., Mann, B., Ryder, N., Subbiah, M., Kaplan, J. D., Dhariwal, P., & Amodei, D. (2020). Language models are few-shot learners. *Advances in Neural Information Processing Systems*, *33*, 1877–1901.

Dash, S. K., & Panda, C. K. (2015). An Evolutionary programming based neuro-fuzzy technique for multi-objective generation dispatch with non-smooth characteristic functions. *2nd International Conference on Electronics and Communication Systems, ICECS*, 1663–1674.

Fei-Fei, L., Fergus, R., & Perona, P. (2006). One-shot learning of object categories. *IEEE Transactions on Pattern Analysis and Machine Intelligence*, *28*(4), 594–611. doi:10.1109/TPAMI.2006.79 PMID:16566508

George Karimpanal, T., & Bouffanais, R. (2019). Self-organizing maps for storage and transfer of knowledge in reinforcement learning. *Adaptive Behavior*, *27*(2), 111–126. doi:10.1177/1059712318818568

Giri, P. K., De, S. S., & Dehuri, S. (2016). A Novel Locally and Globally Tuned Biogeography Based Optimization Algorithm. *International Conference on Soft Computing: Theories and Applications (SoCTA)*, 28-30.

Giri, P. K., De, S. S., Dehuri, S., & Cho, S-B. (2017). Locally and Globally Tuned Chaotic Biogeography Based Optimization Algorithm. *International Conference on Information Technology (ICIT2017)*, 28-29.

Giri, P. K., De, S. S., & Dehuri, S. (2018). Adaptive neighbourhood for locally and globally tuned biogeography-based optimization algorithm. *Journal of King Saud University. Computer and Information Sciences*, *33*(4), 453–467. doi:10.1016/j.jksuci.2018.03.013

Giri, P. K., De, S. S., Dehuri, S., & Cho, S.-B. (2020). Biogeography Based Optimization for Mining Rules to Assess Credit Risk. *Intelligent Systems in Accounting. Financial Management*, *28*(1), 35–51.

Goertzel, B. (2014). Artificial general intelligence: Concept, state of the art, and future prospects. *Journal of Artificial General Intelligence*, *5*(1), 1–48. doi:10.2478/jagi-2014-0001

Goodfellow, I., Pouget-Abadie, J., Mirza, M., Xu, B., Warde-Farley, D., Ozair, S., & Bengio, Y. (2014). Generative adversarial nets. *Advances in Neural Information Processing Systems*, 27.

Grigorescu, S., Trasnea, B., Cocias, T., & Macesanu, G. (2020). A survey of deep learning techniques for autonomous driving. *Journal of Field Robotics*, *37*(3), 362–386. doi:10.1002/rob.21918

Hota, P. K., Barisal, A. K., & Dash, S. K. (2009) An artificial neural network method for optimal generation dispatch with multiple fuel options. Journal of the Institution of Engineers (India): Electrical Engineering Division, 90, 3–10.

Hutter, M. (2004). *Universal artificial intelligence: Sequential decisions based on algorithmic probability*. Springer Science & Business Media.

Junwei, H., Dingwen, Z., Gong, C., Nian, L., & Dong, X. (2018). Advanced Deep-Learning Techniques for Salient and Category-Specific Object Detection: A Survey. *IEEE Signal Processing Magazine*, *35*(1), 84–100. doi:10.1109/MSP.2017.2749125

Kaplan, J., McCandlish, S., Henighan, T., Brown, T. B., Chess, B., Child, R., & Amodei, D. (2020). Scaling laws for neural language models. *arXiv preprint arXiv:2001.08361*.

Kawachi, J. (2017). Brodmann areas 17, 18, and 19 in the human brain: An overview. *Brain and nerve= Shinkeikenkyu no shinpo, 69*(4), 397-410.

Lake, B. M., Salakhutdinov, R., & Tenenbaum, J. B. (2015). Human-level concept learning through probabilistic program induction. *Science*, *350*(6266), 1332–1338. doi:10.1126/science.aab3050 PMID:26659050

Mallick, C. K., Giri, P. K., & Mishra, S. N. (2023). A multi-objective LGBBO algorithm for overlapping community detection in a social network analysis. *Malaysian Journal of Computer Science*, *36*(2), 173–192. doi:10.22452/mjcs.vol36no2.4

Mallick, C. K., Giri, P. K., Paikaray, B. K., & Mishra, S. N. (2022). Machine Learning Approaches to Sentiment Analysis in Social Networks. *International Journal of Work Innovation*, *3*(4), 317–337. doi:10.1504/IJWI.2023.128860

Mallick, C. K., Mishra, S. N., Giri, P. K., & Paikaray, B. K. (2023). (in press). A Meta Heuristic Optimization based Deep Learning Model for Fake News Detection in Online Social Networks, Int. *J. of Electronic Security and Digital Forensics.*

Meir, Y., Sardi, S., Hodassman, S., Kisos, K., Ben-Noam, I., Goldental, A., & Kanter, I. (2020). Power-law scaling to assist with key challenges in artificial intelligence. *Scientific Reports, 10*(1), 19628. doi:10.1038/s41598-020-76764-1 PMID:33184422

Nikolić, D. (2015). Practopoiesis: Or how life fosters a mind. *Journal of Theoretical Biology, 373*, 40–61. doi:10.1016/j.jtbi.2015.03.003 PMID:25791287

Nikolić, D. (2023). Where is the mind within the brain? Transient selection of subnetworks by metabotropic receptors and G protein-gated ion channels. *Computational Biology and Chemistry, 103*, 107820. doi:10.1016/j.compbiolchem.2023.107820 PMID:36724606

Nikolić, D., Andrić, D., & Nikolić, V. (2023). Guided Transfer Learning. *arXiv preprint arXiv:2303.16154.*

Pan, S. J., & Yang, Q. (2009). A survey on transfer learning. *IEEE Transactions on Knowledge and Data Engineering, 22*(10), 1345–1359. doi:10.1109/TKDE.2009.191

Pandey, T. N., Giri, P. K., & Jagadev, A. (2019). Classification of Credit Dataset Using Improved Particle Swarm Optimization Tuned Radial Basis Function Neural Networks. *Conference on (BITMDM),* 1–11.

Pandey, T. N., Mahakud, R. R., Patra, B., & Giri, P. K. (2021) Performance of Machine Learning Techniques, before and after COVID-19 on Indian Foreign Exchange Rate. *International Conference on Biologically Inspired Techniques in Many-Criteria Decision Making (BITMDM-2021),* 20-21.

Searle, J. R. (1980). Minds, brains, and programs. *Behavioral and Brain Sciences, 3*(3), 417–424. doi:10.1017/S0140525X00005756

Silver, D., Huang, A., Maddison, C. J., Guez, A., Sifre, L., Van Den Driessche, G., & Hassabis, D. (2016). Mastering the game of Go with deep neural networks and tree search. *Nature, 529*(7587), 484–489. doi:10.1038/nature16961 PMID:26819042

Strotzer, M. (2009). One century of brain mapping using Brodmann areas. *Clinical Neuroradiology, 19*(3), 179–186. doi:10.1007/s00062-009-9002-3 PMID:19727583

Tan, C., Sun, F., Kong, T., Zhang, W., Yang, C., & Liu, C. (2018). A survey on deep transfer learning. *International Conference on artificial neural networks*, 270–279.

Thompson, N. C., Greenewald, K., Lee, K., & Manso, G. F. (2020). The computational limits of deep learning. *arXiv preprint arXiv:2007.05558.*

Vinyals, O., Blundell, C., Lillicrap, T., & Wierstra, D. (2016). Matching networks for one shot learning. *Advances in Neural Information Processing Systems*, 29.

Yuan, L., Chen, D., Chen, Y. L., Codella, N., Dai, X., Gao, J., & Zhang, P. (2021). Florence: A new foundation model for computer vision. *arXiv preprint arXiv:2111.11432*.

Chapter 4
Digitalization and Its Impact on the Development of Society

Viktoriia Khaustova
National Academy of Sciences of Ukrain, Ukraine

Olha Ilyash
National Technical University of Ukraine the Igor Sikorsky Kyiv Polytechnic Institute, Ukraine

Liubov Smoliar
National Technical University of Ukraine the Igor Sikorsky Kyiv Polytechnic Institute, Ukraine

Dmytro Bondarenko
National Technical University of Ukraine the Igor Sikorsky Kyiv Polytechnic Institute, Ukraine

ABSTRACT

The research is devoted to the analysis of the essence of the concept of digitalisation and its impact on the development of the economy and society. The structure of the research consists of three stages: analysis of approaches to the interpretation of the concept of "digital economy" and the main characteristics of this concept, analysis of approaches and assessments of the impact of digitalisation and information and communication technologies (ICT) on the economic development of countries, identification of advantages and threats that digitalisation presents to society. According to the structure of the study, the essence and key characteristics of the digital economy concept have been specified; the main indices used to assess digitalization and the impact of ICT on the economic development of countries have been considered; the assessment of digitalisation of countries based on the indices has been carried out. It has been revealed that, despite the variety of methods for calculating indices of digitisation and ICT development, the leading countries have already been determined, and they have not significantly changed their positions, so the international economy continues to move towards the digital future at different

DOI: 10.4018/979-8-3693-1886-7.ch004

rates, which, in turn, determine transformational shifts in economies of countries. The generalization of modern studies has made it possible to detect the advantages and threats (of economic, social, technological, political, and control nature) that digitalization presents. It has been proven that its influence on the development of society is contradictory. Therefore, in order to obtain benefits from the spread of digitalisation, a careful and balanced approach to the introduction of digital technologies in all spheres is necessary, taking into account the specifics of the processes taking place and the specifics of the development of countries, as well as the responsible interaction of states in controlling the spread of digital technologies.

INTRODUCTION

The modern digital age changes approaches to doing business, ensuring competitiveness, and requirements for the information technologies that are being used. In 2010, the Digital Agenda for Europe was implemented; its main goal was the development of the European economy, aimed at ensuring sustainable socio-economic benefits for the single digital market (Szeles & Simionescu, 2020). In this new environment, digital technologies have had a more significant impact on the economy and society.

Digital tools such as social, mobile, analytical and cloud (SMAC) technologies boost digitalisation (Teubner & Stockhinger, 2020), accelerating not only technological progress but also economic and social progress (Legner et al.,2017). Aström et al. point out that digital technologies play a central role in the creation and the reinforcement of disruptions that take place in society and the levels of industry (Aström et al., 2022). Teubner R.A., Stockhinger J. (Teubner & Stockhinger, 2020) prove that digitalisation refers to the interaction between digital technologies and both the social and the institutional processes converting these technologies into infrastructural technologies and impacting on society and the economy.

Therefore, technology trends emerging as a result of digitalisation, such as IoT (Internet of Things), AI (Artificial Intelligence), data analytics by means of Big Data, and AR (Augmented Reality), not only have a considerable impact on society and the working environment, but also on business operations in industry (Oberzaucher, 2019):

IoT (Internet of Things) is a network of connected devices (sensors) that generates data used to collect, analyse and provide information for making informed decisions. According to Cisco, by 2030, 500 billion devices will be connected to the Internet. The world's ever-increasing Internet connection opens up new opportunities for companies, organizations, governments, and individuals (Figures 1 and 2).

Figure 1. How 2300 executives across 15 countries envision the future. Keys to creating an IoT strategy.
(Oberzaucher, 2019; Khaustova et al., 2022a, 2022b; IDC, 2020)

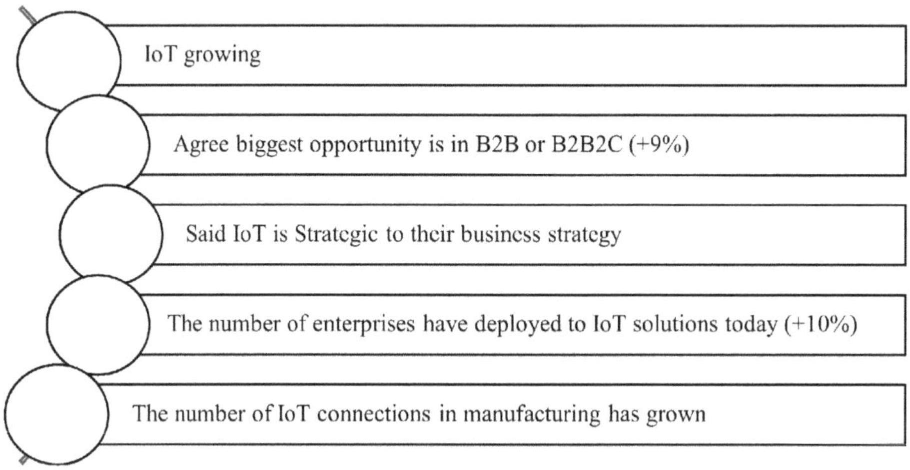

AI (Artificial intelligence) imitates various aspects of human cognition - perception, reasoning, planning and the ability to autonomously perform certain tasks (understanding the language, recognizing objects and sounds, learning and solving problems). Many researchers of the world define AI as the most important technology ever invented. AI-powered digital twin simulations are already implemented in many manufacturing industries. These technologies present unprecedented opportunities to forecast processes and new business strategies.

Big Data. Today, the volume of accumulated data is constantly growing. Big Data are sets of information of such large sizes that traditional methods and approaches cannot be applied to them. Therefore, the leading digital trends of the next decade will concern tools that can analyse and use such data. The world's leading companies are already developing tools and methods for Big Data processing and analysis. Microsoft, SAP, SAS, and Salesforce are leaders in this market.

AR/VR (Augmented/Virtual Reality). AR is the result of introducing any sensory data into the field of perception in order to supplement information about the environment for improving the perception of information. VR is a world created by technical means and transmitted to a person through their senses (sight, hearing, touch, etc.). Currently, VR and AR are one of the most important technological trends that can supplant other technologies and displace conventional mobile communication. Industry has already tested virtual applications in mobile devices for maintenance, operation and training and, in many cases, it is successfully implementing them. In

Figure 2. IoT connected devices installed base worldwide from 2015 to 2025. *(Szeles & Simionescu, 2020)*

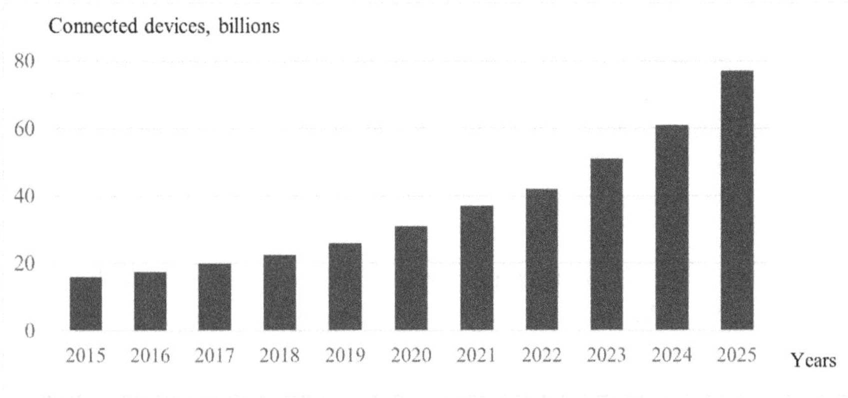

addition, AR and VR applications can be employed as sales tools to increase business success (Oberzaucher, 2019; Khaustova et al., 2022a;Khaustova et al., 2022b).

In fig. 1, there are results of a study into the vision of the future of 2,300 managers in 15 countries and the key factors in creating an IoT strategy. Fig. 2 presents the dynamics of IoT connected devices installed base worldwide from 2015 to 2025.

The information shown in fig. 1 and 2 reflects the steady growth of the role of IoT and digitalisation in the modern world.

The United Nations and the European Commission have identified that today in the countries where ICT is used in a variety of sectors ranging from industry, trade, healthcare, education and transport, in public and private sectors, it contributes to the

Figure 3. The number of articles in WoS Core Collection, devoted to digitalisation in three mature areas of the firm: marketing, management, and finance and accounting *(Calderon-Monge & Ribeiro-Soriano, 2023).*

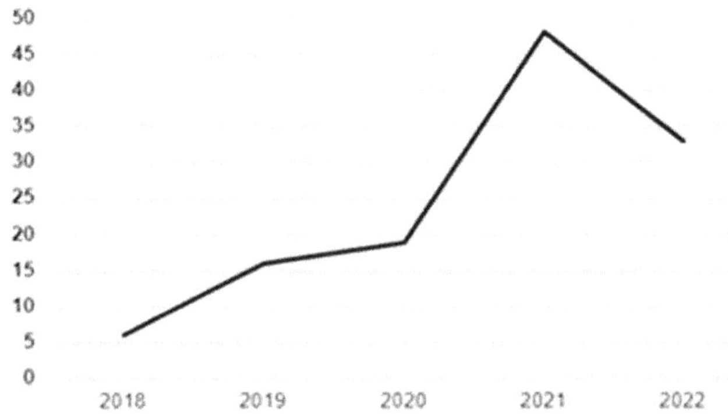

provision of goods and services, the improvement of quality of life of the population and economic development (Gomes et al., 2022).

The impact of digitalisation on the development of the world economy and society was also reflected in the intensification of scientific research in this field. Esther Calderon-Monge and Domingo Ribeiro-Soriano have conducted a systematic review of the literature on digitalisation in three mature areas of the firm: marketing, management, and finance (Calderon-Monge& Ribeiro-Soriano, 2023) and accounting and analysed the dynamics and content of the publications devoted to this issue (Fig. 3).

Fig. 3 shows a significant increase in the number of articles about digitalisation starting from 2018, while in 2022, the number of publications was somewhat smaller (but still large). Such fluctuations can most likely be explained by a shift in focus of research from digitalisation to other areas of the firm. Further observations based on various sources of information will be able to more clearly reveal such trends.

Thus, the rapid spread of digitalisation processes in all spheres of society is a trend that will determine further directions and features of their development. Under these conditions, it is necessary to thoroughly research the state, rates and directions of the development of digitalisation, as well as the impact, the positive and negative consequences that it will have. According to preliminary assessments of scientists and practitioners, the impact of digitalisation has not been fully understood yet, and it can cause major, so far unpredictable and sometimes uncontrollable shifts in all spheres of life.

MAIN FOCUS OF THE ARTICLE

The purpose of the presented research is to generalize theoretical approaches to defining the essence of the digital economy and analyse its impact on the economy and the life of society.

The general structure of the study consists of the following stages: the analysis of approaches to interpreting the concept of "digital economy" and the main characteristics of this concept; the analysis of approaches and assessments of the impact of digitalisation and ICT on the economic development of countries; the identification of advantages and threats that digitalisation presents to society.

PRESENTATION OF THE MAIN RESEARCH MATERIAL

The digital economy is based on the use of technologies of large data sets (Big data), industrial Internet of Things and Internet of Things (IIoT/IoT), cloud

Table 1. The explanation of the essence of the concept of "digital economy"

Institution/Author	Definition
The World Bank (World Bank Group, 2018)	A new paradigm of accelerated economic development based on real-time data exchange.
The OECD (OECD, 2022)	The result of the transformational effects of new technologies of general purpose in the field of information and communications.
The World Economic Forum, the Group of Twenty (Li et al., 2020)	A variety of economic activity, which uses digital knowledge and information as critical factors in production, information and communication technologies, and modern information networks as a virtual space of activity to promote productivity growth.
The Cabinet of Ministers of Ukraine (Cabinet of Ministers of Ukraine, 2018)	Activities in which the main means (factors) of production are digital (electronic, virtual) data, both numbers and texts.
Razumkov Centre (Razumkov Center, 2020)	An economy based on digital computer technologies and information and communication technologies (ICT), but unlike informatization, digital transformation is not limited to the introduction of information technologies, but fundamentally transforms spheres and business processes through the Internet and new digital technologies.
Holoborodko A. (Holoborodko, 2022)	Multifaceted process activity, which is based on the combination of the infrastructure links of a number of flow processes - technological, intellectual and grouping them into a network economy.
Veretiuk S. M.,Pilinskyi V.V. (Veretiuk &Pilinskyi,2016).	The ongoing transformation of all spheres of the economy involving the transfer of all information resources and knowledge to a computer platform.
Kraus N. (Kraus et al., 2018).	An economy, which is based on digital computer technologies and is now increasingly intertwined with the traditional one.
Kindzerskyi Yu. (Kindzerskyi, 2022)	A new stage of the development of productive forces and the economy that is characterized by new properties, trends and laws inherent in the modern historical period. In contrast to the industrial stage of society's development, which is associated with tangible, material means of production, the main factors in production and the development of the digital economy are information and intellectual resources, as well as an intangible product - information, knowledge and their carriers. The driving force behind the development of this stage is science and the implementation of its achievements in business practice.

computing, quantum and NBIC technologies, additive manufacturing, robotics and other end-to-end information technologies and information security technologies (Khaustov&Bondarenko, 2020a; Putsenteilo & Humeniuk, 2018). It includes the digitalisation of production, distribution, exchange and consumption of goods, forms a system of more general processes that determine new patterns of economic functioning and becomes a global concept of the development of a new economy that sets new standards of the quality of life, work and communications in society (Khaustov & Bondarenko, 2020b).

Figure 4. Approaches to the interpretation of the concept of "digital economy" in the scientific literature
(Holoborodko, 2022)

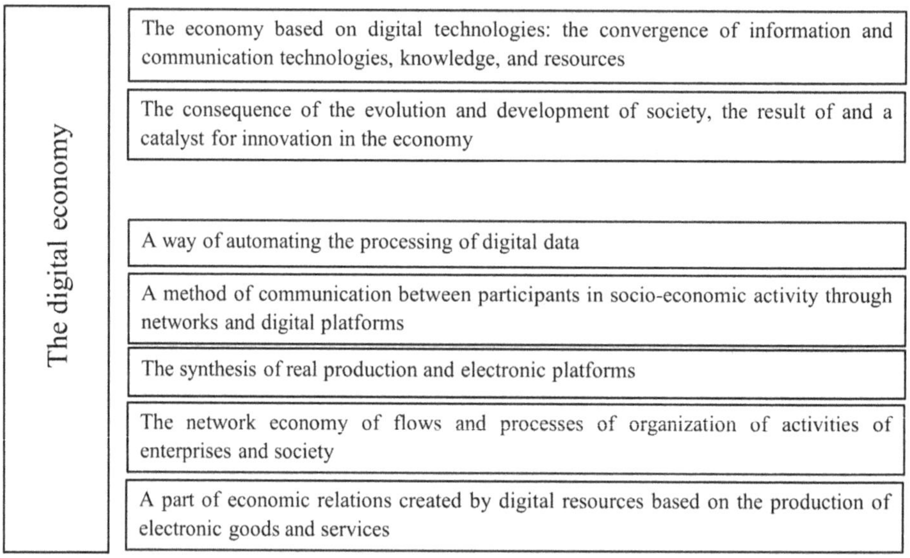

Technological changes occurring within these processes are accompanied by the "fusion" of telecommunications, information and communication technologies (ICT) and innovations, leading to the formation of a new type of economy, which is based on the active implementation and use of digital technologies for storing, processing and transmitting information in all spheres of human activity (Khaustov & Bondarenko, 2020b).

The OECD identifies three main components of the digital economy:

- supporting infrastructure (hardware and software, telecommunications, networks, etc.);
- electronic business or e-business (conducting business activities and any other business processes through computer networks);
- electronic commerce or e-commerce (distribution of goods via the Internet).

Nowadays, in the scientific literature, there are ongoing discussions regarding the interpretation of the category "digital economy". Table 1 shows some of them.

In his work A. Holoborodko conducted a thorough study of approaches to the essence of the concept of "digital economy" (Holoborodko, 2022) existing in the scientific literature and singled out some of them (Fig. 4).

Key characteristics of the digital economy concept include the following:

Table 2. The main indices used to assess digitalisation and the impact of ICT on the economic development of countries

Index	Peculiarities of Calculation	Results
Global Competitiveness Index, GCI	Calculated since 2004 by the World Economic Forum (WEF). Sub-index C - "innovations and improvement factors" is devoted to the innovative component, which includes indicators like competitiveness of companies, compliance of business with modern requirements of companies and innovation potential. However, the GCI can only conditionally be considered an indicator of the development of the digital economy, as it does not fully detail the specific components related to the development of digitalisation.	According to this index, the group of leading countries has not changed much over the past five years. Switzerland, Finland, Israel, the USA, Germany, the Netherlands, Sweden, Japan, Singapore and Denmark take the leading positions not only in terms of the "innovation" indicator, but also according to the index itself.
Global Innovation Index, GII	The GII is the result of global research by the International Business School "INSEAD", Cornell University (the USA) and the World Intellectual Property Organization. The research analyses the level of implementation of innovations in institutions, education, infrastructure and business based on 82 indicators, which form the corresponding ranking. Due to the dynamism of innovation processes, the list of basic indicators is periodically updated and supplemented. The GII indicators cover the components of the innovation sphere and are grouped into two sub-indices: the first one combines 55 indicators characterising the innovation potential of a country and is called the Innovation Input Subindex, the second one comprises 27 indicators, which characterise the scientific and creative results of innovative activity and form the Innovation Output Subindex. The use of the GII to determine the impact of digitalisation on economic development is also quite difficult for practical application due to numerous indicators used in its construction (including those not related to digitalisation), the complexity of their calculations, and limited access to the necessary information.	In 2022, 132 countries of different levels of innovative development were included in this ranking. The USA is the leader in the number of GII innovation indicators, ranking first in the world in 15 out of the 81 indicators, that is two indicators higher than it was in 2021, including: global corporate R&D investors, venture capital investors, the quality of its universities, the quality and impact of its scientific publications (H-index), the number of patents by origin, computer software spending, and the value of corporate intangible asset intensity. The US is followed by Singapore, while China, Hong Kong (China) and Israel shared the 3rd place. The following main changes in the global innovation landscape are identified: a marked shift in the Top 15 innovators this year (the United States, Singapore, Germany and China moved up in the ranking, the latter overtook France, and Canada returned to the Top 15 thanks to increased innovation efficiency); the continued significant development of new innovation hubs in Turkey, India, and to some extent in the Islamic Republic of Iran, while the growth in Vietnam and the Philippines has stalled somewhat; the emergence of signs of innovative growth in Indonesia, Uzbekistan and Pakistan. In this ranking, Ukraine belongs to the group of countries with a level of income below the average (which includes 36 countries). In general, Ukraine takes 57th place in the ranking, and 4th in this group. Ukraine's worst indicators are Market sophistication (102nd place), Institutions (97th) and Infrastructure (82nd).
Networked Readiness Index, NRI	The NRI is developed by the WEF together with the international business school INSEAD and the Samuel Curtis Johnson Graduate School of Management at Cornell University (since 2013) as part of the annual series of reports on the development of an information society in the countries of the world (The Global Information Technology Report). Moreover, it helps to assess the level of the development of an information society in the national economic system. The NRI is calculated as the arithmetic mean of four sub-indices that measure the environment for ICT development, society's readiness to use ICT, the actual use of ICT by the state, business and the population, and the consequences that ICT has in the economy and society. The first three sub-indices are regarded as growth drivers, which are prerequisites for the fourth sub-index – the impact of ICT on society and the economy. These four sub-indices are divided into 10 indices and 53 indicators. The calculation of the NRI is based on quantitative indicators - statistical data of international organizations, as well as on qualitative indicators - the results of an annual comprehensive survey of managers conducted by the WEF in the states that became the objects of the study. 40% of the indicators, which make up the NRI, are quantitative and 60% are qualitative. Based on the results of the research, an annual report is prepared, which also contains detailed profiles of the countries, the characteristics of economic development of each country in terms of the penetration and use of ICT.	In 2022, 131 countries were included in the ranking. The first positions according to the NRI index were taken by the USA, Singapore, Sweden, the Netherlands, Switzerland, Denmark, Finland, Germany, Korea, and Norway. The top ten countries in the NRI 2022 ranking show that developed economies in Europe, America, Asia and the Pacific are the most network-ready in the world. In particular, of the top 25 countries, 17 come from Europe (mainly Northern and Western Europe), four are from East and Southeast Asia (Singapore, the Republic of Korea, China and Japan), two are from Oceania (Australia and New Zealand), and two come from North America (Canada and the USA). As for Ukraine, the values of the main sub-indices and indicators show that the biggest problems of the network economy development in the country are not concentrated in the technological sphere, but in the sphere of managing socio-economic processes, ensuring conditions for free competition, a favourable investment environment and a stable political and legal situation, adequate regulatory and legal support.

continued on following page

Table 2. Continued

Index	Peculiarities of Calculation	Results
Huawei Global Index of NetworkInteraction or Global Connectivity Index, GCI.	The Huawei company proposed the index in 2013 and it reflects the progress of the world's largest countries in the transition to digital technologies. For the first time, the GCI 2020 report presented five key stages of digital transformation for the industry: task efficiency, functional efficiency, system efficiency, organizational efficiency and agility, and ecosystem efficiency and resilience. According to ICT investment, ICT maturity, and digital economic performance, the S-curve groups nations into three clusters: Starters, Adopters, and Frontrunners.	The 2020 research covered 79 countries that generate 95% of global GDP and represent 84% of the world's population. According to this index, the USA, Singapore, Switzerland, Sweden, Denmark, Finland, the Netherlands, Great Britain, Japan, and Norway take the first places in the ranking. In 2020, Ukraine took 52nd place in the ranking. The GCI research found that economies that can increase productivity and digitize through smart connectivity typically have higher gross value added (GVA) per worker or hour worked.
Digital Opportunity Index, DOI	The DOI was measured in 2004-2006 anddetermined ICT capabilities by analysing infrastructure, availability and coverage, quality. The index was evaluated based on 3 sub-indices such as capability, infrastructure and utilization. Since its calculation has been discontinued, it is not available for modern analysis	According to the latest available data (2006), the leaders in this indicator were the Republic of Korea (0.80); Japan (0.77); Denmark (0.76); Iceland (0.74); Singapore (0.72); the Netherlands (0.71); Taiwan (0.71) and Hong Kong (0.70), belonging to China; Sweden (0.70), Great Britain (0.69)
Digital Access Index, DAI	The DAI was developed within the framework of the International Telecommunication Union until 2003 and it was aimed at assessing the access and use of ICT by the citizens of a country. The index was based on four components: infrastructure, accessibility, knowledge and quality, and the actual use of ICT. Like the previous index, it is not available for modern analysis as its calculation has been stopped.	According to the latest available data (2003), the leading countries by this index were Sweden (0.847); Denmark (0.828); Iceland (0.820); the Republic of Korea (0.817); Norway (0.793); the Netherlands (0.792); Hong Kong, China (0.790); Finland (0.786); Taiwan, China (0.786); Canada (0.779); the USA (0.778)
ICT Development Index	TheICT Development Index has been calculated since 2002 by the International Telecommunication Union, a specialized unit of the United Nations in the field of telecommunications, and the index characterises the achievements of the countries of the world in the field of ICT. The index includes 11 indicators based on the assessment of access to ICT, use of ICT and ICT skills, i.e. whether the population of individual states or the population of the world has practical knowledge of these technologies.	The total number of countries included in the ICT development ranking was 176 in 2017. According to the ranking, the top five leading countries in terms of ICT development are Iceland (8.89), Korea (8.85), Switzerland (8.74), Denmark (8.71) and Great Britain (8.65), while Ukraine's score is 5.62. The ranking suggests that the fastest rates of ICT development in 2017 compared to 2013 are observed in Ukraine (excluding other rating positions). In contrast to the previous rankings, Iceland is among the traditional leaders in the introduction of ICT. In 2017, this country even took first place among 176 countries.
Digital Economy and Society Index, DESI	The DESI is calculated as a composite index that summarizes the indicators of the development of digital Europe and tracks the evolution of the EU countries in terms of their digital competitiveness. The databases of the DESI are the databases of Eurostat, the International Telecommunication Union and the United Nations. The DESI consists of five indices characterised by more than 30 indicators. They are: - connectivity, which measures the deployment of broadband infrastructure and its quality, access to fast and ultra-fast broadband services and it is a necessary condition for competitiveness; - human capital and digital skills that measure the skills needed for the effective use of ICT; - use of Internet services, which takes account of various online activities, such as consumption of online content, video calls, as well as online purchases and banking transactions; - integration of digital technology that evaluates the activities of enterprises from the standpoint of ICT implementation, i.e., whether enterprises use electronic invoices, cloud services, whether they carry out electronic sales, etc.; - digital public services that evaluate the level of development of the services of e-government and e-health. Each of the five indices is assigned weight determined by the experts of the European Commission. The first two are considered the basis of the digital economy and society, the weight of each of them is equal to 25%. The use of the Internet and digital public services are estimated at 15%. The experts of the European Commission view the integration of digital technology as one of the most important factors in economic growth, the weight of this index is 20%.	According to the DESI 2022 results, most EU member states are making progress in digital development, but the level of the introduction of key digital technologies such as artificial intelligence and big data to business remains low even among the leading countries. The lack of digital skills, a greater digital divide and increased risks of digital exclusion impede digital development; in addition, more and more services, including essential ones, are moving online. Finland, Denmark, the Netherlands and Sweden continue to be the leaders in the EU. However, most leaders also face digital challenges. This means that the EU generally keeps improving its level of digitalisation, for instance, those Member States that started at lower levels are gradually catching up, increasing the pace. The Member States that are lagging behind such as Italy, Poland and Greece have significantly improved their DESI scores over the past five years and have implemented the indicators on a regular investment basis with the increased political focus on digital technologies supported by European funding. Particular attention in the DESI 2022 report is paid to Russia's invasion of Ukraine, and the emphasis is placed on promoting the implementation of innovative digital, technological and infrastructural solutions based on EU values and principles, strengthening cyber security, and countering disinformation from Russia and Belarus in a resolute way. The initiatives taken at the national level to counter the consequences of the Russian invasion of Ukraine are described in the DESI country-by-country reports.

continued on following page

Table 2. Continued

Index	Peculiarities of Calculation	Results
Digital Evolution Index, DEI	The DEI reflects a country's progress in the development of the digital economy, as well as the level of integration of the global network into the lives of the country's citizens. MasterCard and the Fletcher School of Law and Diplomacy at Tufts University developed the DEI. The DEI is calculated for 60 countries and it evaluates each state using 170 partial indicators describing four sub-indices that determine the pace of digitalisation: - the level of supply (availability of access to the Internet and the degree of infrastructure development); - consumer demand for digital technologies; - the institutional environment (state policy, legislation, resources); - the innovative climate (investments in R&D and in digital start-ups). According to the DEI index, countries are divided into four groups: leading countries that demonstrate high rates of digital development; countries, whose growth rates are slowing down, i.e. those that have demonstrated steady growth for a long period of time, but, at the time of the study, the rate of their development has significantly decreased; promising countries that, despite a relatively low overall level of digitalisation, are at the peak of digital development and demonstrate sustainable growth rates that attract investors; problem countries that have a low level of digital development and low growth rates. In 2017, another sub-index (fifth) was added to the DEI – the level of digital trust or the level of trust in digital innovation.	The ranking of countries by the digital evolution index according to the last published Digital Planet 2017 report showed that the Top 10 countries with the most developed digital economy include Norway, Sweden, Switzerland, Denmark, Finland, Singapore, South Korea, the United Kingdom, Hong Kong, and the United States. Russia ranks 39th, China – 36th.
Digital Adoption Index, DAI	The DAI measures the digital adaptation of countries (the adoption of digital technologies) from the standpoint of three main participants in socio-economic relations within the state: 1) people (society), 2) government and 3) business. The DAI is constructed by the World Bank economists in collaboration with Microsoft. It covers 180 countries on a scale of 0 to 1 and highlights the "level" of digital adoption to maximize coverage and simplify theoretical connections. Each sub-index includes the technologies needed by a particular agent to facilitate development in the digital age: improving productivity and accelerating strong business growth, providing more opportunities and improving people's well-being, and increasing the efficiency and accountability of service delivery for the government. Originally built as a part of World Development Report 2016: Digital Dividends, the DAI has been updated to reflect new data sources and improved methodology. The DAI has certain advantages over existing indicators and indices of digitalisation. First, it reflects the extent to which digital technologies are available and accepted by all key agents in the economy—people, businesses (firms), and governments. Hence, it provides the wider picture of technology diffusion than the existing set of indicators does. Second, it is constructed employing coverage and usage data, based on the information from internal sources in the World Bank database, and, therefore the DAI is more reliable than those digitalisation indices based on perception surveys. The Digital Adoption Index was developed in response to requests from policymakers and government officials. It is intended to serve as a benchmark for measuring the "supply side" of the digital economy and to assist policymakers in developing a nuanced digital strategy to promote digital technologies for different user groups. The methodology used to construct the DAI ensures considerable flexibility to adjust the index of adoption of new digital technologies (e.g. mobile money or Big Data) with the purpose of conducting a thorough review of a disaggregated level (e.g. e-retail DAI or digital ID).	For most countries, two DAI observations are available: that of 2014 (applying updated data and methodology to the year covered in the original DAI dataset) and of 2016 (the latest year available). The leaders of the DAI-2016 ranking are Singapore, Luxembourg, Austria, South Korea, Malta, Germany, the Netherlands, Japan, Estonia, and Sweden. It is interesting that this ranking includes only 3 countries (Singapore, Sweden and South Korea), which are the leaders of the digital competitiveness ranking. For example, the United States, the permanent leader of the digital competitiveness ranking, ended up in 27th place.

continued on following page

Table 2. Continued

Index	Peculiarities of Calculation	Results
Boston Consulting Group, e-Intensity	E-Intensity is designed to determine the impact on society and business. For this purpose, a comprehensive assessment is carried out based on 28 indicators, grouped into three sub-indices. The e-Intensity integral index is calculated as the arithmetic mean of three sub-indices, taking their weighting factors into account: - infrastructure development – reflects the availability and quality of Internet access through the accessibility and speed of mobile and fixed Internet access; its weight in the e-Intensity integrated index is estimated by Boston Consulting Group (BCG) experts at 50%; - online costs – include costs of e-commerce and online advertising; - user activity – is calculated as the weighted average value of the following indicators: activity of enterprises, activity of consumers, and activity of state institutions. The weighting factors of the second and third sub-indices are determined by Boston Consulting Group (BCG) experts at the level of 25% each.	E-Intensity is calculated for 85 countries, including 28 EU member states, most Latin American and Asian countries, and 14 African countries. The first positions in the E-Intensityranking belong to Denmark, Luxembourg and Sweden.
IMD World Digital Competitiveness Index, WDCI	The WDCI was developed by the IMD Swiss business school. The WDCI assesses the extent to which a country develops and uses digital technologies that lead to the transformation of the economy, business and society in general. Digital competitiveness is determined by three main sub-indices of the first level, namely knowledge, technology, readiness for the future. Knowledge, evaluated through talent, education and science, is seen as the basis of digital transformation processes thanks to the discovery, understanding and learning of new technologies. Technology is assessed through the shared content that enables the development of digital technologies (it includes a regulatory framework that ensures compliance with necessaryregulatory norms while stimulating business development and innovation). Readiness for the future is regarded as the level of readiness of the economy for its digital transformation. It requires business flexibility and assumes that firms can transform their business models to take advantage of new opportunities.Readiness also assesses how well IT technologies are integrated into the economy and business processes. Each of the three sub-indices of the first level is evaluated through three indicators, resulting in 9 sub-indices of the second level, which will participate in the final ranking assessment. In the future, this will allow countries to be evaluated not only by the integral index, but also by the sub-indices of the first and second level. A total of 50 indicators are used in the calculation of the WDCI; 30 of them are based on statistical data, and 20 are based on expert assessments made as a result of the survey. All the sub-indices have the same weight in the global digital competitiveness index, namely: 11.1%.	Russia and Ukraine were not included in the 2022 ranking due to limited reliability of data. 64 countries were listed in the 2021 ranking. The leading countries of the WDCI ranking include the USA, Hong Kong, Sweden, Denmark, Singapore, Switzerland, the Netherlands, Taiwan (China), Norway, and the UAE. Ukraine improved its position in the ranking- from 58th in 2020 to 54th in 2021 among 64 rated countries. At the same time, it is necessary to pay attention to the fact that the sub-index scores for the country were: knowledge – 38, technology – 58, future readiness – 58, i.e., in terms of the level of knowledge (the basis of digital transformation), Ukraine is ahead of many countries in the world that overtake it in the ranking. However, Ukraine loses to them in terms of technology and readiness for the future.

continued on following page

Table 2. Continued

Index	Peculiarities of Calculation	Results
The UN Global E-Government Development Index, EGDI	The EGDI measures the readiness and capability of public administrations of a country to use ICT to provide public services to the population and business. The EGDI is defined as an aggregated indicator that assesses the level of ICT use in the interaction of citizens with the government, while the emphasis is placed on the willingness and ability of the government to provide services, and on the readiness of citizens to use those services. The e-government development index according to the UN methodology is calculated as the arithmetic mean of three normalized sub-indices: -telecommunication infrastructure (Telecommunication Infrastructure Index - TII), consisting of five indicators that characterise the development of fixed and cellular communications, the Internet; -human capital (Human Capital Index - HCI), consisting of four indicators that evaluate the literacy of the population, the involvement in education and duration of education; -online services (Online Service Index - OSI), which are evaluated based on the results of a survey of official websites.	Thanks to the development of telecommunication infrastructure and human resources, the average global e-Government Development Index (EGDI) has generally increased, although there is also evidence of an existing digital divide. The lowest EGDI scores are mostly typical of countries in special situations and developing countries. The leaders of the ranking are Denmark, Finland and the Republic of Korea. They are followed by New Zealand, Sweden, Iceland, Australia, Estonia, the Netherlands, the United States, the United Kingdom, Singapore, the United Arab Emirates, Japan and Malta. The number of countries in the group with a very high EGDI (with values between 0.75 and 1.00) increased from 57 to 60, representing a 5 percent rise between 2020 and 2022. These 60 countries are evenly distributed among rating classes VH, V3, V2 and V1. Four countries (Georgia, Peru, Serbia and Ukraine) moved from the group with a high EGDI to the group with a very high EGDI. Ukraine took 46th place in the ranking.
E-Participation Index, EPI	The UN uses the EPI as a supplement to the e-Government Development Index and it examines the quality of the delivery of interactive information services to citizens. The EPI characterises the level of development of active communication services between citizens and the state, while electronic participation means the policy in the field of regulatory and legal frameworks, organizational and institutional conditions and the infrastructure of channels and platforms for participation, i.e., tools. The EPI includes three components: electronic information (e-information) – giving citizens the right to access government information; electronic consultation (e-consulting) – involving citizens in the discussion of public policy issues; electronic decision-making (e-decision-making) - expanding the rights and opportunities of citizens through participation in the joint design of state programs.	Japan, Australia, Estonia, Singapore, the Netherlands, Finland, Great Britain and Northern Ireland, the Republic of Korea, and the United States headed the EPI ranking in 2022. The positions of Ukraine in the ranking have increased. In 2022, the country took 57th place. It is necessary to mention the presence of significant fluctuations in the values of the EPART index in all countries over the past 10 years, which is associated with changes in the algorithms for constructing the index and an increase in the indicators that are included in the calculation.

Source: formed by the authors based on (Rudenko,2021; Matveichuk, 2018; Kovtoniuk, 2017; Voitenko, 2020; Huawei, 2021; E-Ukraine, 2019; DESI, 2022; UE E-Knowledgebase, 2020; Khaustov & Bondarenko, 2021; IMD, 2022a; WIPO, 2022; Network Readiness Index, 2022;Huawei, 2020; ITU, 2022; Knoema, 2021; IMD, 2022b; Statista, 2022).

1. The digital economy is a consequence of and catalyst for a permanent qualitative process of innovative development of socio-economic relations.
2. The digital economy is the convergence of information and communication technologies, knowledge, and resources to obtain additional competences for ensuring competitiveness and increasing the efficiency of enterprises.
3. The digital economy is a network activity of synthesis and integration of digital technologies into traditional economic processes through the creation of unified platforms of interaction (Holoborodko, 2022).

At present, a significant number of various indices have been developed in order to assess digitalisation and the impact of ICT on the economic development of countries. According to the research (Rudenko, 2021), the Global Innovation Index

Table 3. The benefits that digitalisation of the economy brings to society

Benefits
Economic
Ensuring economic growth due to further technical progress
An increase in the level of GDP due to the expansion of opportunities for the development of production and non-production spheres, the formation of new sources of income (including through the creation and implementation of new software products and services)
Creation of a multiplier effect in the development of various spheres of the economy through the inclusion of all production chains in a single information space
A rise in the level of labour productivity in economic sectors
Emergence of new business models and new forms of business that will increase the profitability and competitiveness of business entities
Creation of new opportunities for business development as a result of: ensuring accessibility and promotion of products and services of both public and commercial nature, up to the global scale; the elimination of intermediaries (digitalisation allows manufacturers to arrange the sale of goods or services on their sites, as well as find access to potential customers, whereas consumers get the opportunity to independently choose goods and services on the servers of airlines, hotels, electronic stores, etc.); cost optimization, which involves, first of all, the reduction of the costs of searching for information, transaction costs, the costs of promoting goods and services, the costs of opening and conducting negotiations, etc.; the simplification of management and the acceleration of many main and auxiliary business processes, including by reducing communication time; the shorter reaction time to market changes, the shorter terms of developing products and services and bringing them to the market; better understanding of their consumers and improvement of the quality of products and services; the creation of new products and services, an increase in the flexibility of the offered products and their high adaptability to new expectations or needs of consumers, etc.
Reduction in the level of expenses and, accordingly, the prime cost of goods and services due to more efficient use of existing resources during mass digitalisation, including the reduction of production costs because of the shared use of the infrastructure when employing cloud technologies; saving time, labour and financial costs when transferring relations to a digital format; a low level of expenditure on the production of electronic goods and smaller areas occupied by electronic devices and carriers, etc.
Development of the sharing economy. The new wave of digitalisation will lead to the fact that available resources will find their buyers very quickly
Creation of opportunities to solve the information asymmetry problem thanks to the growth in its availability, which will level the positions of large dominating participants in economic relations and increase the positions of other participants, giving them new opportunities for development
Elimination of geographical barriers to ensuring availability of workers of all (including rare and unique) professions in the global labour market, and the possibility of their involvement in business development both on a regular basis and in other ways
Acceleration of financial transactions through instant global data exchange using the Internet and ICT
Social
Improvement to the quality of life by increasing the level of satisfying specific already known and new needs of people and a rise in the GDP of countries as a result of economic growth
Development of human knowledge and creative abilities and skills that ensure ICT
Reduction (simplification, full or partial replacement) of the share of physical labour used by employees

continued on following page

Table 3. Continued

Benefits
An increase in the individual capacity for successful work and opportunities for self-actualisation due to the use of opportunities provided by digitalisation
Development of digital technologies expands the opportunities of workers in the labour market because of the emergence of new types of activities and new flexible forms of employment, and therefore supports their employment
Ensuring the development of social entrepreneurship through the possibility of job mobility with the involvement of disabled persons or persons with partial capacity to work
Ensuring that persons, who, for various reasons, cannot take an active part in social life, are included in it with the help of digital technologies
Technological
Ensuring further technological progress
Providing a basis for the development of a wide range of new technologies and the introduction of innovations into all spheres of human life (industry, health care, education, science, etc.)
The joint use of information and the lack of competition in the consumption of knowledge and various types of data form the basis of the acceleration of technical progress
Accumulation of a vast array of data opens up new opportunities for their automatic processing and analysis, thus leading to a new level of decision-making in many spheres of life
Synchronization of information flows, the possibility of point-based distribution of data within the framework of the entire business present new opportunities for tracking a large number of chains between suppliers and consumers, as well as conducting intelligent and point pattern analysis.
Political
Digitalisation is becoming an important source of technological dominance and global influence of a number of leading countries on the world stage
Digital technologies provide a broad range of new opportunities to influence the formation of political attitudes and the conduct of political struggle
The Internet and other network mechanisms allow people not only to put into practice certain communication interests in politics, but also constantly improve them, including through the use of the latest data analysis mechanisms
Digital technologies create opportunities for the implementation of innovative tools when performing a full range of tasks in the political sphere, such as online voting and others
Through implementing the latest mechanisms to support people's ability to express their opinions, demands, their will, etc., digital technologies become the basis for managing social tension caused by political actions. For example, in addition to social networks, where various civil positions are articulated, electronic platforms for obtaining people's signatures on messages, declarations and appeals to decision-makers have recently become widespread and now play an important role. The function of consolidating support, in fact, of political and social capital, gives such platforms an additional status in the perception of network users, but more often, instead of putting pressure on the authorities, such platforms become a lightning rod for protest energy, thereby reducing social tension in society

Source: summarized by the authors based on (Khaustov& Bondarenko, 2020a; Khaustov& Bondarenko, 2020b; Razumkov Center, 2020; OECD, 2017; Mutula,2010; Bilyk, 2019; Bodrova, 2019; Negroponte, 1995; Cirillo et al., 2021).

Table 4. Threats and risks that digitalisation of the economy poses to society

Threats and Risks
Economic
A decrease in productivity in the field of production of digital technologies themselves and, in turn, a slowdown in investment in their development
The necessity of re-equipping factories and incurring large initial costs, constantly taking into account dynamic changes in technology and revising the organizational structure of business significantly complicates the conditions for conducting business and ensuring its competitiveness
The mismatch between the expected profits from the development of artificial intelligence and reality. According to Forrester's forecast in 2019, artificial intelligence has been overestimated, in particular, it has been predicted that 10% of companies will return to automated processes that will be carried out with the help of the human factor, because the replacement of humans with artificial intelligence in certain areas of business leads to the loss of customers (due to their preference for human contact)
A rise in the cost of a skilled workforce, which will be inevitably driven by the need to upgrade staff skills and the growing demand for a skilled workforce with the necessary digital skills
The virtual nature of economic relations, which negatively affects a number of risks of their support and control
The lack of physical weight of products, the equivalent of which will be information resources and that poses the risks of errors and manipulations in the estimation of their real value
An increased risk of a rise in the level of inflation in the countries of the world due to the unevenness of socio-economic development as a result of the uneven implementation of digitalisation in various spheres of life
Political
Threats of unlimited influence on public sentiment. New technologies are already being widely used for manipulating the mood and opinions of the population, propaganda, inciting hatred, spreading fakes. The creation of the so-called "simulation of the world" platforms will make it possible to implement contradictory strategies of informational dominance capable of influencing people's emotions, thinking and behaviour
Mounting tension between states for technological dominance. An example of this is the trade war between the USA and China, which began in 2018 and which hides the intense rivalry between the two superpowers striving for global technological dominance
Digitalised social media will increase their influence on public opinion. On the one hand, they can become a "weapon of mass distraction" from important problems. On the other hand, they can also be used to promote (enforce) consensus. Both ways of "social engineering" aimed at promoting a certain point of view can undermine the diversity and pluralism of opinion, which are important prerequisites for the development of innovation, social sustainability and democracy. The so-called "big nudge" mechanisms, based on a combination of Big data and personalized prompts, can be used by both military propaganda and business in commercial "neuromarketing" technologies
Threats of the power concentration in the market and strengthening of monopolies due to easier access to leading technologies
Social
Exacerbation of social contradictions during the mass dismissal of workers, a reduction of the degree of social security as a result of the expansion of the autonomy of participants in the network digital economy, growing social inequality, including due to the existing digital inequality, the transformation of socio-economic subjects into "screws" of technological progress. Lower qualifications of production personnel in the conditions of their transformation into an appendage of digitalised production will lead to the displacement of not only low-skilled, but also medium-skilled labour, and will therefore lead to an increase in the number of unemployed

continued on following page

Table 4. Continued

Threats and Risks
Underestimation of the social and other dimensions of the economic development of individual countries can lead to an increase in the unevenness of their development, digitalisation will become stratified, not homogeneous, as a result of which social tension will rise in a number of countries
Increased polarization in society because of the digital divide, which will arise with ever-increasing inequalities in access to social, economic, educational, cultural and other opportunities due to the unequal access to ICTs. Digital inequality will lead to a decrease in the quality of life (fewer opportunities in all areas of life, worse health care and education), will cause other inequalities, and, at the same time, deepen previous inequalities and, in general, will result in a loss of a country's competitive position in the world economy
Activation of migration processes, especially among those in working professions
Displacement of a number of basic technological processes, scientific and technical innovations and economic relations associated with the social orientation of the economy
Blurring the boundaries between work and private life due to the proliferation of work-from-home opportunities
An increase in the workload due to the need for constant professional development in order to obtain a job
Fiercer price competition in the labour market. On the one hand, workers from the periphery, who have approximately the same level of qualifications as workers from the centre, benefit from price competition because they are willing to receive lower wages for work, but on the other hand, ICTs allow workers from even poorer areas to enter the market (for example, from other countries), which actually unleashes a price war
Increased gender inequality in the labour sphere and in society as a whole, primarily due to the gender-asymmetric reduction in employment brought about by digitalisation. In the report of the World Economic Forum, it was noted that future changes in the field of employment would affect women to a greater extent
Interference in private life due to the introduction of general control over citizens with the help of digital technologies, and mainly technologies of wide data arrays (*Big Data*)
The threat of increased oppression and exploitation of people, false accusations of people due to errors in the work of services such as the "digital police". The concept of the digital police has already been tested by many countries and the same is true for predictive programs aimed at predicting future crimes based on previously recorded ones. Today, such police activity is criticized for the lack of transparency and democratic control, systematic discrimination against certain groups of people and minorities, and a very high rate of false positives
Skewing public attention towards digital transformations and boosting profits, instead of going towards the use of health-preserving technologies and the efficient use of natural resources
Digital autism and hyper information of the environment due to the loss of social skills, which causes the inability to think critically and the development of clip thinking (the perception of the surrounding reality as a sequence of unrelated phenomena, and not as a homogeneous structure that exists as an interconnected system)
The threat of restricting people's freedoms and free choice due to the fact that access to goods and services in the digital economy is increasingly determined by algorithms ("a code"). In an era of digitalisation, there is a danger that algorithmic approaches will be inappropriately transferred from objects to subjects, from robots to people. Such an approach, driven by data and algorithms, overlooks many important qualities of human life, which are difficult to measure and which can be associated with freedom, creativity, culture, human dignity, love, etc. As digitalisation continues to spread, society may become increasingly automated and machine-like, threatening to undermine diversity, innovation, societal resilience, and collective intelligence

continued on following page

Table 4. Continued

Threats and Risks
The threat of uncontrolled influence on people due to neurotechnology. Neurotechnology is capable of controlling people's thoughts, emotions, and decisions, shaping their ideas, memories, and values through computer control. This approach, which can be compared in some ways to hypnosis, carries great potential for being misused and people cannot protect themselves from it. It involves deception, which can be more realistic than deep fakes, and can go so far as to involve people in crimes or accidents against their will. Neuralink has already developed brain chips, and researchers and engineers are working on a human-machine interface (HMI) based on the scattering of nanoparticles in the brain. The aforementioned technological developments not only threaten freedom of thought, but also freedom of will. Concerns have been raised in particular by a number of tech billionaires, who have suggested that reality may be a computer simulation
Threats posed by the Internet of Body (IoB) concept. Thanks to the convenience and efficiency of such innovations, the market for devices that monitor the human body, analyse and store data about it, and sometimes intervene in the work of the body for medical purposes - is growing. Some devices, for example, an artificial pancreas for diabetics, could revolutionize the treatment of the disease, but others can only have the opposite effect, increasing the costs of healthcare, widening social disparities due to access of only financially well-off strata of the population to these benefits. Also, IoB devices can increase the risks of physical harm to users, espionage and exploitation of a person's private data and health data by attackers or they can be used to strengthen the positions of authoritarian regimes through surveillance and control of people by means of these devices. In addition, IoB technologies based on nanoparticles and nanobots are being developed, which can be used in medicine for not only diagnosis and treatment, but also in the future - for gene editing. Given that nanotechnology is still largely unregulated, and that nanoparticles can be ingested through food, water, air, drugs, and vaccines, there is a large pool of risks to humans due to the absence of control, insufficient study and unregulated development of IoB technologies
Technological
A high probability of technological failures and man-made disasters
Threats to the national security of countries, first of all, to their cyber and military-industrial security due to the greater likelihood of criminal interventions of various nature with the use of new digital technologies
The threat of cyber-attacks in all spheres of the economy and for any business entities. According to a report by the World Economic Forum, cyberattacks are among the top five threats to humanity, and cybercrime has increased tenfold in recent years.Cryptocurrency fraud and attacks on virtual values in the blockchain have become new trends. According to some estimates, the volume of investments in cyber defence in 2018 amounted to 96 billion dollars
The threat of artificial intelligence obtaining superintelligent qualities. According to Moore's law, the power of information processing grows exponentially; its speed is constantly accelerating. If these trends continue, it is expected that the computing power of supercomputers will eventually exceed the processing power of the human brain, making control over such a system ("superintelligence") impossible and it may lead to unforeseen problems
Control
Threats of information and digital manipulation and fraudulent operations in the non-production sphere
Threats of the impossibility of controlling financial frauds due to legitimating the use of cryptocurrencies as a form of payments in certain areas of the economy, etc.
Threats of IT companies leaving state control, taxation, etc.

Source: improved by the authors based on (Khaustov& Bondarenko, 2020a; Khaustov& Bondarenko, 2020b; Razumkov Center, 2020; OECD, 2017; Mutula,2010; Bilyk, 2019; Bodrova, 2019; Negroponte, 1995; Cirillo et al., 2021).

(GII) is the most popular and recognizable in the modern world, since the number of mentions when making requests on the sites of the Google search engine on the Internet is 457 million. This is followed by the Digital Adoption Index (DAI) - 191 million mentions, the Digital Evolution Index (DEI), the Digital Economy and Society Index (DESI) and the ICT Development Index, (IDI) - 70.7 million mentions.

Let us take a closer look at the indices used to measure the digitalisation of the economy and its impact on economic development (Table 2).

Thus, despite the variety of methods for calculating international indices that characterise the degree of digitalisation and development of ICT in the countries of the world, the leading countries that do not significantly change their positions have been identified. This confirms the fact that the international economy continues to move towards the digital future at different rates, which, in turn, determine transformational shifts in the national economies of countries and the life of society in general.

However, certain digital gaps between countries are detected, causing concern to governments and specialized organizations, and in order to achieve the goals of sustainable development, they need to develop appropriate programs and strategies aimed at narrowing the gaps. In addition, the analysis of coefficients and sub-indices, which are calculated to determine the indices and construct the rankings, allows us to identify the gaps that hold back the development of countries in the direction of digitalisation.

For instance, the analysis of Ukraine's positions in the considered rankings shows that digitalisation in the country is taking place at a fairly active pace. However, the country's low positions within individual indices prove that there is a need for finding comprehensive solutions for the implementation of the basic components of digital transformation in the government, business, and society. In general, with a fairly high level of knowledge and education in the country, low efficiency of management, insufficient development of technologies and insufficient readiness of the economy for the future and for the acceptance of innovations restrain the development of digitalisation processes and the economic development of the country in particular.

The rapid development of digitalisation is becoming a source not only of new opportunities, but also of serious threats to society, which are recognized by well-known international organizations and scientists too.

The 2019 UNCTAD Digital Economy Report states that the digital revolution is changing our lives and societies at unprecedented speed and on a huge scale, creating both enormous opportunities and tremendous challenges. New technologies can make a substantial contribution to the achievement of sustainable development goals, but obtaining positive results is by no means guaranteed.

The OECD report claims that digital technologies can be disruptive, with future negative impacts on productivity, employment and well-being. Furthermore, they can increase disparities in the level of access to them and use of them and lead to a new digital divide and growing inequality (OECD, 2017). However, at the time when almost half of the world's wealth is concentrated in the hands of 1% of the population, and inequality has reached enormous values, this problem becomes urgent.

The UN also views digitalisation as one of the four main threats to humanity. The World Bank notes that digital technologies are proliferating and digital dividends are not satisfying people's expectations. As noted in (Razumkov Center, 2020), firstly, almost 60% of the world's population still lacks access to the Internet and cannot play a significant role in the digital economy, and secondly, certain benefits of digital technologies are nullified by emerging risks.

Summarizing modern research in the field of digitalisation of the economy allows us to highlight its benefits and threats (tables 3 and 4).

CONCLUSION

Hence, digitalisation is already the objective reality, in which our society will develop. It manifests itself in fundamental transformations that are expressed in the deep penetration of digital technologies into all spheres of life. At the same time, the impact of digitalisation on the further development of society is ambiguous and contradictory, as evidenced by the large number of threats it presents. Therefore, in order to gain benefits from the spread of digitalisation, a careful and balanced approach to the implementation of digital technologies in all spheres is necessary, considering the peculiarities of the processes taking place and the real state and features of the development (economic, political, social, cultural, etc.) of all countries of the world, as well as the responsible interaction of states in the spread of digital technologies and control over these processes.

REFERENCES

Aström, J., Reim, W., & Parida, V. (2022). Value creation and value capture for AI business model innovation: A three–phase process framework. *Review of Managerial Science*, *16*(7), 2111–2133. doi:10.1007/s11846-022-00521-z

Bilyk, O. I. (2019). The influence of the digital economy on reducing the negative consequences of social risk. *Problems of Economics and Management, 4,* 8 – 16. Retrieved from:https://science.lpnu.ua/semi/all-volumes-and-issues/volume-7-number-42-2019/impact-digital-economy-reduction-negative

Bodrova D. V. (2019). Institutional aspects of the digital economy development in Ukraine. *Scholarly notes of V.I. Vernadsky Taurida National University. Series: Economics and Management, 5*(30), 163 – 169. doi:10.32838/2523-4803/69-5-57

Cabinet of Ministers of Ukraine. (2018). On Approval of the Concept of Development of the Digital Economy and Society of Ukraine for 2018-2020 and Approval of the Plan of Measures for its Implementation. *Ordinance of the Cabinet of Ministers of Ukraine*, 67. Retrieved from: https://zakon.rada.gov.ua/laws/show/67$2018$%D1%80

Calderon-Monge, E., & Ribeiro-Soriano, D. (2023). *The role of digitalization in business and management: a systematic literature review. Review of Managerial Science*. doi:10.1007/s11846-023-00647-8

Cirillo, V., Fanti, L., Mina, A., & Ricci, A. (2021). *Digital technologies and firm performance: Industry 4.0 in the Italian economy*. Retrieved from: https://oa.inapp.org/xmlui/handle/20.500.12916/862

DESI - Digital Economy and Society Index. (2022). *Shaping Europe's digital future*. https://digital-strategy.ec.europa.eu/en/library/digital-economy-and-society-index-desi-2022

E-Ukraine. (2019). *Ukraine in international rankings*. Retrieved from:https://eukraine.org.ua/ua/news/ukrayina-v-mizhnarodnih-rejtingah

Gomes, S., Lopes João, M., & Ferreira, L. (2022). The impact of the digital economy on economic growth: The case of OECD countries. *RAM. Revista de Administração Mackenzie, 23*(6), 1–31. doi:10.1590/1678-6971/eramd220029.en

Holoborodko, A. Yu. (2022). The digital economy: Approaches to and features of development. *Bìznes Ìnform, 9*(536), 10–18. doi:10.32983/2222-4459-2022-9-10-18

Huawei. (2020). *Global Connectivity Index. Shaping the New Normal with Intelligent Connectivity*. Retrieved from: Https://Www.Huawei.Com/Minisite/Gci/En/

Huawei. (2021). *Huawei released the seventh annual Global Connectivity Index report: five major stages of the industry's digital transformation*. Retrieved from: https://www.huawei.com/ua/news/ua/2021/20210203

IDC. (2020). Retrieved from:https://www.idc.com/

IMD Business School for Management and Leadership Courses. (2022). *World Competitiveness Ranking*. Retrieved from:https://www.imd.org/centers/wcc/world-competitiveness-center/rankings/world-competitiveness-ranking/

ITU. (2022). *ICT Development Index. Measuring digital development: Facts and Figures.* Retrieved from: https://www.itu.int/en/ITU-D/Statistics/Pages/facts/default.aspx

Khaustov, M. M., & Bondarenko, D. V. (2020a). *Digital technologies of the future in the development of society.* The International Scientific and Practical Conference "Competitiveness and Innovation: Problems of Science and Practice". Kharkiv, Ukraine

Khaustov, M. M., & Bondarenko, D. V. (2020b). *Digitalisation: the achievements and threats to society.* The IX International Scientific and Practical Conference "Science and Practice: Implementation to Modern Society", Manchester, UK. Retrieved from: https://ojs.ukrlogos.in.ua/index.php/interconf/article/view/11577

Khaustov, M. M., & Bondarenko, D. V. (2021). *Assessments of digitalisation and the impact of information and communication technologies on the economic development of countries.* The International Scientific and Practical Conference "Competitiveness and Innovation: Problems of Science and Practice", Kharkiv, Ukraine.

Khaustova, V. Ye., Reshetniak, O. I., & Khaustov, M. M. (2022a). Prospective directions of the development of the IT sphere in the world. *Problèmes Économiques, 1*, 3–19. doi:10.32983/2222-0712-2022-1-3-19

Khaustova, V. Ye., Reshetniak, O. I., Khaustov, M. M., & Zinchenko, V. A. (2022b). Directions of the development of artificial intelligence technologies in ensuring a country's defense capability. *Bìznes Ìnform, 3*(530), 17–26. doi:10.32983/2222-4459-2022-3-17-26

Kindzerskyi, Yu. V. (2022). Genesis and features of the digital economy in the context of prospects for its formation in Ukraine. *Economie & Statistique, 8*, 10–14.

Knoema. (2021). *Digital Evolution Index (DEI).*Retrieved from: https://knoema.com/DEI2020/digital-evolution-index-dei

Kovtoniuk, K. V. (2017). Digitalisation of the world economy as a factor in economic growth. *Scientific Bulletin of Kherson State Universi, 27*(1), 29–33.

Kraus, N. M., Holoborodko, O. P., & Kraus, K. M. (2018). The digital economy: Trends and prospects of avant-garde development. *Efficient Economy, 1.* Retrieved from:http://www.economy.nayka.com.ua/?op=1&z=6047

Legner, C., Eymann, T., Hess, T., Matt, C., Böhmann, T., Drews, P., Mädche, A., Urbach, N., & Ahlemann, F. (2017). Digitalization: Opportunity and challenge for the business and information systems engineering community. *Business & Information Systems Engineering, 59*(4), 301–308. doi:10.1007/s12599-017-0484-2

Li, K., Kim, D. J., Lang, K. R., Kauffman, R. J., & Naldi, M. (2020). How should we understand the digital economy in Asia? Critical assessment and research agenda. *Electronic Commerce Research and Applications*, *44*, 101004. doi:10.1016/j.elerap.2020.101004 PMID:32922241

Matveichuk, L. O. (2018). The digital economy: Theoretical aspects. *Bulletin of Zaporizhzhia National University*, *4*(40), 116–127. doi:10.26661/2414-0287-2018-4-40-18

Mutula Stephen, M. (2010). *Digital Economy Components*. University of Botswana. Retrieved from:https://www.igi-global.com/book/digital-economies-smes-readiness/268

Negroponte, N. (1995). *Being Digital*. Knopf.

Network Readiness Index. (2022). *Network Readiness Index – Benchmarking the Future of the Network Economy.* Retrieved from:https://networkreadinessindex.org/

Oberzaucher, B. (2019). Digitalization as a Megatrend. *Spectrum Now, 39*. Retrieved from:https://www.andritz.com/spectrum-en/latest-issues/issue-39/digitalization-as-a-megatrend

OECD. (2017). *Key Issues for Digital Transformation in the G20.* Report Prepared for a Joint G20 German Presidency. Retrieved from: https://www.oecd.org/g20/key-issues-for-digital-transformation-in-the-g20.pdf

OECD. (2022). Retrieved from: https://www.oecd.org/sti/ieconomy/

Putsenteilo, P.R., & Humeniuk, O.O. (2018) The digital economy as the newest vector of the traditional economy reconstruction. *Innovative Economy, 5-6*, 131 – 143.

Razumkov Center. (2020). *The digital economy: trends, risks and social determinants*. "Zapovit" Publishing House. Retrieved from:https://razumkov.org.ua/uploads/article/2020_digitalization.pdf

Rudenko, M. V. (2021). The analysis of Ukraine's position in global indices of the digital economy. *Economie & Statistique*, *2*, 11–18.

Statista. (2022). *E-Government Development Index (EDGI) leaders 2022*. Retrieved from:https://www.statista.com/statistics/421580/egdi-e-government-development-index-ranking/

Szeles, M. R., & Simionescu, M. (2020). Regional patterns and drivers of the EU digital economy. *Social Indicators Research*, *150*(1), 95–119. doi:10.1007/s11205-020-02287-x

Teubner, R. A., & Stockhinger, J. (2020). Literature review: Understanding information systems strategy in the digital era. *The Journal of Strategic Information Systems, 29*(4), 101642. doi:10.1016/j.jsis.2020.101642

UE E-Knowledgebase. (2020). *E-Participation Index.* Retrieved from: https://publicadministration.un.org/egovkb/en-us/About/Overview/E-Participation-Index

Veretiuk, S. M., & Pilinskyi, V. V. (2016). Determining the priority areas of the digital economy development in Ukraine. *Scientific Notes of the Ukrainian Research Institute of Communications, 2,* 51–58.

Voitenko V. O. (2020). Comparative analysis of the level of digitalisation of the economy of Ukraine in international rankings. *The Strategy of Economic Development of Ukraine, 46,* 23-36.

WIPO - World Intellectual Property Organization. (2022). *Global Innovation Index 2022 – Which are the most innovative countries.* Retrieved from: https://www.wipo.int/global_innovation_index/en/2022/

World Bank Group. (2018). *The digital agenda of the Eurasian Economic Union until 2025: prospects and recommendations.* EEC.

Chapter 5
E-Learning as a Training Concept for Staff

Agnieszka Wierzbicka
Wroclaw University of Economics and Business, Poland

ABSTRACT

In this chapter, the e-learning training in occupational health is analyzed along with safety on a selected group of employees directly employed by a logistics company and employment generated by temporary work agencies. In addition, attention has been focused on the way periodic and initial training was carried out and the impact of adaptation of knowledge of the course participants. The goal of this chapter is to find the opinions of the participants of e-learning courses, as well as to identify the benefits that affect the acquisition of knowledge in business.

1. INTRODUCTION

E-learning, according to the literature on the subject by R. Marciniak (2021), is a form of education characterized by the physical separation of the participants in a course or educational teaching, between which there is asynchronous communication. It is taught through modern technologies and electronic tools that complement traditional teaching processes using computers, smartphones, tablets and the Internet. The main objective of training, e-learning courses is to transfer and deliver information at a distance in the shortest possible time in order to increase work efficiency. Solutions of this type make it possible to complete a course or training without the need for physical presence in the classroom. There are several types of e-learning: school, academic and corporate. From a scientific point of view, there has been a global transformation of business processes, using digital methods in a virtual space

DOI: 10.4018/979-8-3693-1886-7.ch005

(Pietrzyk, 2021). Remote learning systems and training itself create an attractive multimedia environment and simulate traditional training through the possibility to realize practical examples, use presentations, interactive animations, online consultations. All these make it possible for knowledge to be not only transferred economically, but also economically applied in practice and business.

Until now different e-learning services have been available through independent institutions using a Learning Management System (LMS) or provided free of charge by third parties. The role of E-learning is not to replace conventional teaching, but to complement the form of teaching through available technologies (Carliner, Shank, 2016). According to K. Krishnapatria (2020) the use of e-learning in business or education can increase interactivity and cognitive efficiency because it gives learners a high potential to communicate with other learners through available IT tools.

According to the research conducted by (J. Skibska, A. Borzecka, A. Twaróg-Kanus), due to "the changes occurring in the educational and social space the nature of competence requirements is changing". Therefore, it was decided to investigate the approach and the level of acquired knowledge in the field of occupational health and safety, of people trained online and to present the benefits of this type of training in an enterprise.

The goal of this article is to find out the opinions of the participants of e-learning courses, as well as to identify the benefits that affect the acquisition of knowledge in business.

The research concerned a certain group of participants of OHS knowledge trainings in a logistics enterprise. Training in this area was conducted in remote and stationary forms. Through the trainings, it was wanted to examine the opinion of employees and the resulting benefits affecting their acquisition of knowledge in E-learning training. A questionnaire and a knowledge test were used in the research, by means of which the conclusions described in the research results were drawn.

2. REVIEW OF THE LITERATURE

Due to the COVID-19 pandemic, which occurred in Poland in March 2020, enterprises and educational institutions were forced to switch from classroom to online learning through various e-learning platforms. Currently, in Poland, the special treatment of COVID-19 is ending, which from April 1, 2022, appears in the system as an ordinary infectious disease. The departure from the epidemiological status is foreseen before the holiday of 2022, cited as per DGP information, https://serwisy.gazetaprawna.pl/zdrowie/artykuly/8391606/pandemia-koronawirus-covid-19.html (Access April 21, 2020).

The epidemiological situation in the world has contributed to the increased interest in training, courses and on-line educational teaching. This was due to the restriction that was intended to prevent the spread of the Covid-19 virus among the population. Therefore, e-learning has become more and more popular among companies that use available communication tools to train their employees through e-learning platforms and applications such as Teams, ZOOM.

In the subject literature, E-learning is defined as a broad set of applications and processes that enterprises use through the available media and electronic tools to provide vocational education and training for their employees (Alqahtani, Rajkhan 2020). Scientists (Muhammad, Ghalib, Ahmad, Naveed, Shah 2016) found that E-learning is the usage of various technological tools that are based on networks distributed in the network or adapted for education. It is being developed year by year and its advantages more broadly affect learning and training in the remote field, which contribute to the growth of information technology. Advantages such as flexibility, accessibility via the Internet and time saving, individual teaching or reduction of financial expenses are the motives for employers to move away from stationary training or courses to online training (Naveed, Muhammad, Sanober, Qureshi, Shah 2017). According to another author, E-learning serves to improve teaching and learning and is also a good tool for learning and research materials (Nwagwu and Azil, 2016).

E-learning platforms in business education have developed since 1999 and have taken various forms. A large part of the current solutions are based on the use of internet modules that can be accessed on a personal computer, smartphones or tablets (Oduma, Nkem 2019).

E-learning in business is conducted with the help of various types of self-study guides, PowerPoint presentations, recordings of training sessions or multimedia online courses. There are also Teams and ZOOM applications on the market, as well as e-learning platforms with the help of which training and remote learning are carried out. The most frequently used tools by enterprises and educational entities include training, interaction and multimedia platforms. One of such platforms is gamification, it is a tool for training and remote learning that combines game mechanics with learning and accelerates the learning process while improving the memorization process (Rozman, Donath 2019). Educational games are another tool as the most effective forms of education. By creating a game instead of training, you can teach your audience to understand decision-making processes with their consequences and benefits. E-learning games are simply simulations of reality, real processes, activities and events. Another example is video training, which is characterized by a high level of realism and communicates a large amount of knowledge in a short time. According to the literature on the subject of A. Razzaque (2020), one of the available online training solutions is M-learning, which works perfectly on mobile devices, such as smartphones, tablets with Internet access. There are many

M-learning platforms, offering wide opportunities for raising qualifications, but from the organizational perspective, the starting point should be a distance learning system (LMS). The corporate e-learning platform allows you to centralize the know-how of the organization, design engaging training and make it available to employees both in the form of e-learning and m-learning. It is also an opportunity to collect feedback, identify training needs of employees and detect possible competency gaps.

Considering the way of transferring knowledge, research has shown (Sandybayev 2020) that participants of trainings or courses should remember about a very important aspect of direct contact with the trainer. It is understood that E-learning is a modern way of acquiring knowledge through technologies that develop learning processes. Online teaching, however, will not be a complete teacher-student interaction and a lively response to the behavior of both parties during training.

3. RESEARCH METHODOLOGY

In this study, the method of diagnostic survey was used, conducted with the technique of a survey among employees directly employed by a logistics company and temporary employees employed by temporary work agencies (APT). The study was aimed at learning the opinions of the participants of E-learning trainings as well as showing the benefits of changing the model of functioning in business.

All training in the field of occupational health and safety in a logistics company in the period 2020/2022 took place using the E-learning method through the Teams application as well as a PowerPoint presentation sent by e-mail to the participant's e-mail address or stationary, of course, course participants had the option of choosing the training. 114 people have already participated in health and safety training in the period February - April 2022 participated in the research. The early months were not taken into account due to the lack of research.

After each completed training, the respondent (employee) was obliged to complete the knowledge test in electronic form and return it to the e-mail address provided in the message or return it in paper form. An additional activity that had to be performed was filling in the questionnaire, also in electronic and paper form, in order to investigate the benefits of e-learning trainings or their disadvantages. The questionnaire was sent back by 112 people out of 114 and this number of questionnaires was taken into account when conducting the analysis and describing the research conclusions.

The E-learning trainings via the Teams application have been conducted for administrative, office and warehouse employees employed by a logistics company.

Such training lasted up to 4 working hours and was conducted by a OHS Specialist who is employed directly by the logistics company under examination, performing duties in the workplace. Training on the Teams platform was a videoconference presented through a presentation prepared in the LibreOffice Impress program, where all knowledge in the field of occupational health and safety was transferred by a OHSSpecialist in a synchronous (real-time) manner. Training participants met in virtual space and communicated on an ongoing basis with the leader and other participants. After completing the training, the participant was obliged to completing a knowledge test and a survey. The test and survey were in electronic form in the Google Forms application.

The second type of E-learning trainings through the PowerPoint application took place after sending a link with the presentation to the email of the course participant who was employed by a temporary employment agency. Each future employee who wanted to work in the area of a logistics company was obliged to complete a course in occupational health and safety supervised by a logistics company health and safety specialist. The entire health and safety course took place asynchronously (in non-real time) and was made available in the PowerPoint application via a link with access to selected people. The duration of self-study was individual, but the scope of acquiring knowledge was set at 2 hours. The course participants decided for themselves when and at what time they would finish the training and could return to the materials sent many times in order to find the correct answer to the knowledge test. After reading the training materials, at the end of the presentation, a test of knowledge in the field of occupational health and safety as well as short recordings with first aid instructions was made available. Time to return the test and the survey was required for 3 working days from receiving an e-mail with a link to all training material in the field of health and safety. The temporary employment agency was not required to train future employees in the knowledge of health and safety **regulations;** therefore this obligation was imposed on the logistic company under study.

Initial and periodic stationary training sessions took place on the premises of the logistics company's warehouse. During the meeting, the OHS Specialist presented PowerPoint presentations using the Microsoft Stream service on a multimedia projector, where training recordings and short instructional videos on first aid and safety at work were displayed. Such training lasted up to 4 working hours and was also completed with a knowledge test and a paper questionnaire.

The data for the research was taken from the company's file on all participants of the training in the field of occupational health and safety. The research period was February - April 2022. 18 people took part in periodic E-learning training in February and 15 people took part in initial training, while 10 participants took part in periodic stationary training. From March to mid-April, 22 people took part in

Table 1. List of periodic training courses

List of Periodic Training Courses		
Periodic Training	**February**	**March - April**
Stationary		
Warehouseworkers	4	
Office'sworkers	6	
E-learning		
Warehouseworkers	14	10
Office'sworkers	4	12

periodic E-learning trainings and 34 people took part in introductory trainings. 15 people were enrolled in introductory training.

The tables below (Table 1, 2) present the distribution and type of training.

Summarizing the number of people participating in periodic and introductory training from February to April, a total of 114 participants were estimated. Some of the employees were employed directly by a logistics company, and the other were employed by a temporary employment agency for a fixed period, as seasonal workers or for a longer period of time.

In order to learn about the participants' opinions on conducting a new training method in the enterprise and the resulting benefits for the business aspect, an online questionnaire was prepared, which contained the most important questions regarding the method of conducting E-learning trainings / courses (Table 4).

The survey was prepared in one version for all forms of training, because the participants of the stationary course had already had contact with online courses, so

Table 2. List of introductory trainings

Initial Training List		
Initial Training	**February**	**March - April**
Stationary		
Warehouseworkers		15
Office'sworkers		
E-learning		
Warehouseworkers	12	31
Office'sworkers	3	3

Table 3. List of trainers at the turn of February - March 2022

Participants in Health and Safety Awareness Training for the Period February - April 2022	
Employees of a logistics company	55 persons
Temporary agency workers	59persons
Total	114persons

they could freely answer questions about the training – E-learning. An additional tool to check and classify the course participant's knowledge on OHS was a knowledge test with 30 questions, which had to be solved and sent back to the OHS specialist. The test was a kind of a test that verified whether the trainee was concentrating during the training, whether he or she could think independently and make decisions, and whether he or she could easily assimilate the knowledge that was being conveyed at a distance. These are only selected basic criteria, which were taken into consideration in the analysis of the examined purpose of this paper (table 5). Only eight questions were included in the paper because the author did not have permission from the OHS Specialist for more questions to be published.

4. RESULTS

The analysis of the collected responses in the online and paper questionnaire allowed for the identification of the most important and the most crucial opinions about the conducted e-learning training. The knowledge test grade was also taken into account to characterize the participants' approach to the remote form of the courses. In the presented research results, the statistics of E-learning and in-class training courses were also used.

The first analysis showed a large difference in the number of employees participating in occupational health and safety training in the form of stationary and e-learning in the period from February to April. Within 2-3 months, as many as 78% of course participants took part in E-learning trainings and only 22% in stationary trainings. As mentioned earlier, employees had the option to choose by declaring which form of training they prefer when confirming attendance at the training.

The analysis of the survey results showed the following conclusions as to the ranking of the most frequently chosen training methods.

Webinar method is in the first place, as 46% of respondents indicated this method, and the least desirable method is individual meetings with the trainer 2%, while stationary training in the group was indicated by 10% of the respondents. This means that the respondents (employees) change their preferences with regard to the

Table 4. Web survey – outline, Source: own elaboration

Survey
The aim of the survey is to find out the opinions of the participants of E-learning courses and also to show the benefits of changing the business model.
Questions
Question 1. Which teaching method is better for you?
a) Stationary teaching / coursesin group b) Individual meetings with the trainer c) Webinars d) Courses in the E-Learning platform e) Training videos f) Games g) Podcasts
Question 2. Why do you prefer stationary training?
a) I like contact with people
b) Knowledge is absorbed faster
c) No need for internet or computer access
Question 3. What barriers do you see in E-learning training?
a) low level of knowledge of information technology
b) training may be superficial c) lack of concentration on training d) no barrier
Question 4. Was the E-Learning training in OHS comprehensive? Select the answer and enter your comment.
a) Yes
b) No
c) comments
Question 5. What benefits do you see from E-learn training?
a) Comfort and time saving
b) Accessibility from various locations
c) It is possible to adapt the pace of learning to one's own abilities
d) Developing personal IT skills
e) Possibility to consolidate knowledge through easier access to training materials
f) Multi-devicecapability
g) Attractive forms of content presentation - e-learning
Question 6. Is E-learning training the future of business?
a) Yes
b) No
Personal data
1. First name and surname
2. Position
3. Employed by
Signature

Table 5. Knowledge test with selected screening questions

……………………………… ……………., Date ……………..
(Name and surname of trainee)
Health and safety knowledge test
1. The supervision and control authority over working conditions and compliance with labour law is:
a) the State Labour Inspectorate,
b) the Public Prosecutor's Office,
c) the Supreme Chamber of Control
2. The State Sanitary Inspectorate is the body that supervises:
a) Working conditions, compliance with labour law,
b) Hygienic conditions in a broad sense,
c) Machinery and equipment used in work processes.
3. Information on the organisation of computer workstations can be found in:
a) Ordinance of the Minister of Labour and Social Policy on safety and hygiene of work at workplaces equipped with screen monitors
b) Regulation of the Minister of Infrastructure on technical conditions to be met by buildings and their location,
c) Regulation of the Minister of Labour and Social Policy on general health and safety rules
4. The legal act that regulates matters related to labour relations and occupational safety is:
a) Ordinance on general regulations of occupational safety and health,
b) the Labour Code Act
c) the Act on social insurance against accidents at work and occupational diseases
5. An accident at work is defined as:
a) A sudden event occurring at the workplace,
b) A sudden event, caused by an external cause, associated with the work performed, even if it did not result in an injury,
c) A sudden event, caused by an external cause, resulting in an injury at work.
6. The minimum light level at a computer workstation should be:
a) 500 lx,
b) 450 lx,
c) 650 lx,
7. The employment of women in prohibited work is:
a) Absolutely prohibited and constitutes an offence against the rights of the worker,
b) Permitted upon written request of the employee,
c) Permitted for selected works
8. The lateral position is used when:
a) The casualty is breathing but unconscious,
b) When the casualty is conscious and feeling well, but has a broken leg,
c) When there is an obvious spinal injury
Number of points scored Test result:......................
5 - 8 points. - passed
0 - 4 points. - failed
…………………………………….. (signature of Health and Safety Inspector)

prevailing restrictions and indications of population isolation among workplaces. It can be noted that in total E-learning training in a given period is 88% higher than stationary training and individual meetings with trainers in the remaining 12%. As reflected in figure-2, this small number of people still can promote classroom training.

Stationary training also has its advantages, which were indicated in the next analysis and show great interest in the possibility of contact with other people in

Figure 1. Percentage list of people participating in trainings

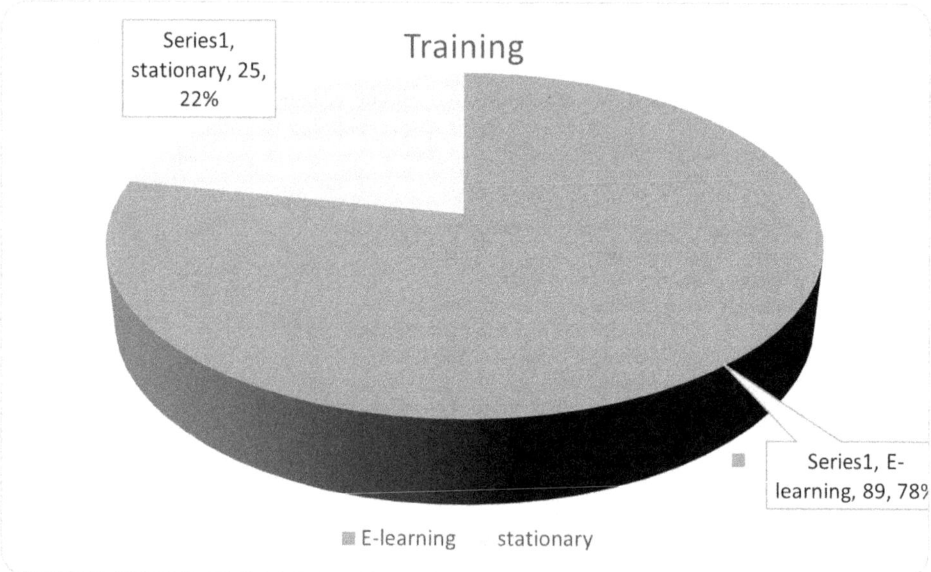

35%, and also do not force emphasis on the need to have access to the Internet and a computer during such training sessions were declared by 59% (Chart 3).

The next analysis touched upon the barriers encountered during E-learning trainings. It is possible that they do not exist among the course participants, because fear of something new is a natural syndrome. In the opinion of the respondents, the greatest fear is the low level of knowledge of information technology in 68%, and the least number of people indicated the barrier as no concentration on training 5%. As many as 15% indicated no barriers, which indicates a fairly large tendency of people willing to learn something new in a different way than before. An important aspect is the approach of course participants to people and the way of conducting E-learning classes, as well as the willingness to participate in something pro-development (Figure 4).

When analyzing the next question from the survey regarding the level of involvement of the trainer and whether the training was comprehensive, the conclusions from the opinions received indicate that the respondents (employees) mentioned several arguments for the above. 82% of them confirmed the complexity of the training, and only 18% indicated negative feelings, which they argued in an unconvincing manner about the erroneous provision of information (Figure 5). One of the repeated accusations was the fact that the amount of materials to be reworked was too large, the other part of the respondents pointed to the too fast pace of classes by the OHSSpecialist.

Figure 2. Training ranking

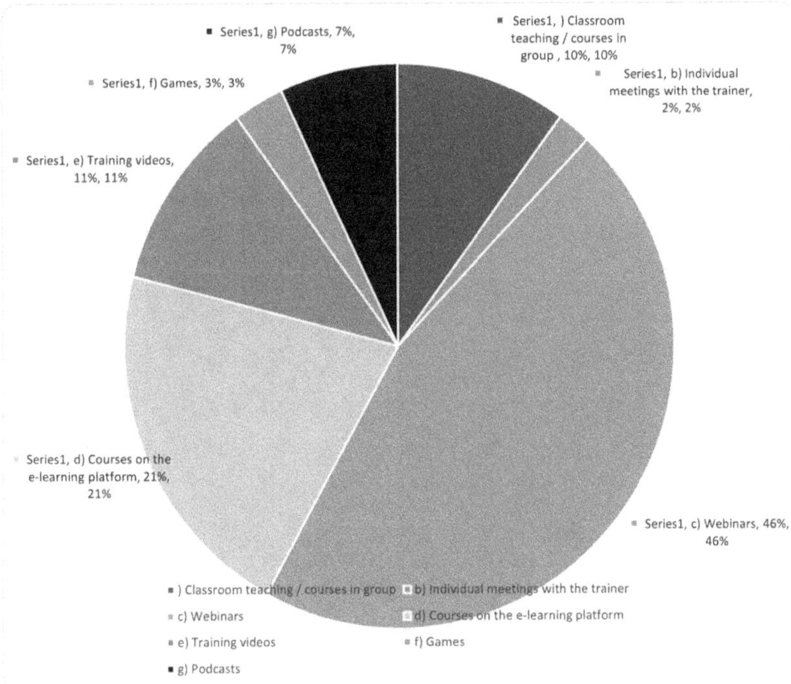

Figure 3. List of strengths of stationary training

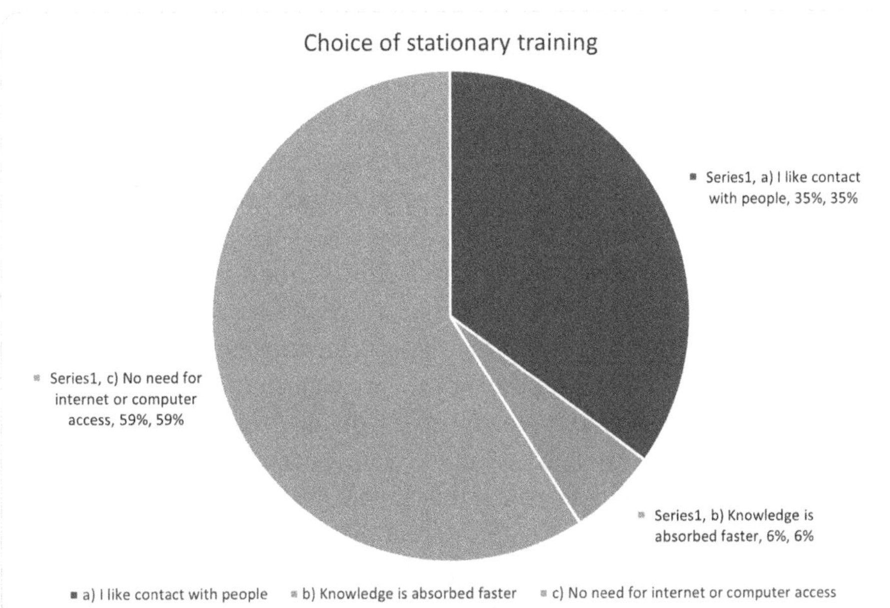

Figure 4. List of e-learning barriers

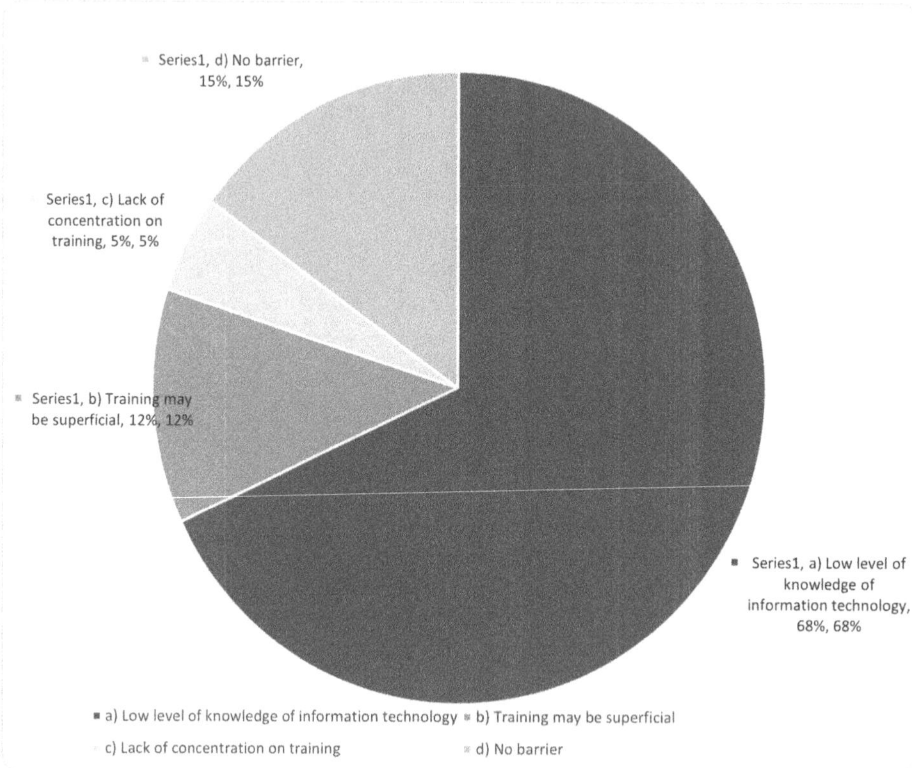

To the positive opinions, respondents indicated that one of the key arguments was the fact that the trainer on the Teams platform was active and conducted the training very vigorously. And here these opinions are very subjective. Some people were disturbed by lively behavior of the trainer, and others it was even suitable. Another positive opinion added that the specialist's knowledge was sufficient to answer the questions asked by the course participants. He had substantive skills and the information in the presentation reflected the most important facts in the field of occupational health and safety. The approach of the trainer to the group was very professional and positive. Some respondents indicated that they have less fear of E-learning classes due to the positive way of conducting such trainings by the trainer. Other responses related to the form of individual learning through the link to the training materials provided. Here, the respondents indicated the time they can devote to learning and the fact that they do not have to participate in an active conversation with the teacher. Another aspect that is highlighted is that you can return to the course several times and take the knowledge test. Alone the training material was extensive, but it was clearly shown through the successive slides of

Figure 5. Comprehensiveness of OHS training

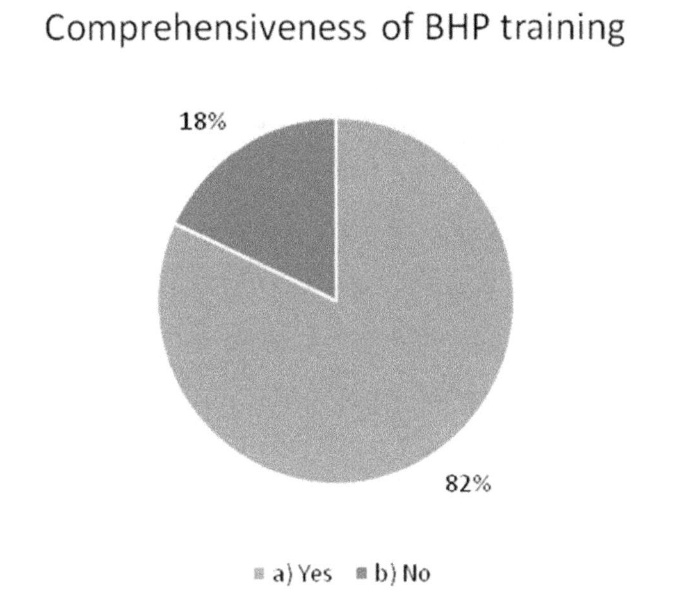

the presentation. The material was comprehensive and all the test questions could be answered.

In another analysis, the research showed that the greatest benefit indicated for employees is the convenience and time savings during the online training in 26%. 1% observing the least benefits in developing IT skills of employees, but here this barrier shows that the opinions of some training participants indicate concerns about the lack of IT knowledge (Figure 6).

The last analysis, of the survey presented the opinion of 90% of respondents (employees) as an endorsement of E-learning in business. This proves that employees are aware of technological changes in running a business, and thus that the development of enterprises and its structures is inevitable in the context of new IT challenges.

The research showed that 100% of the participants of the OHS training passed the knowledge tests. 89 employees passed the test for the maximum number of 8 points, and the rest of the 25 participants passed the 5-6 point test. When analyzing the knowledge tests, it was noticed that the employees had no major problems with solving the test and issues related to it. Most of them were familiar with the general principles of occupational health and safety and were able to indicate the correct answer. The test analysis was to verify whether the training participants are able to solve the test on their own and think creatively when choosing the answer,

Figure 6. Main benefits of e-learning training

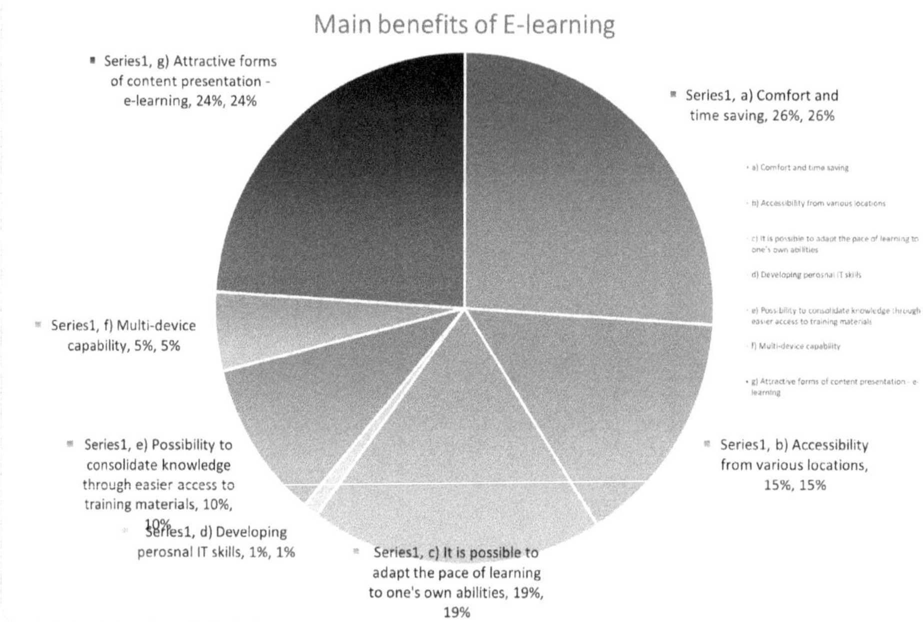

and whether they have self-disciplinary skills in sending the training back for the duration of the test.

The conclusions of the study carried out are as follows.

E-learning methods in the current time of the Covid-19 pandemic may have priority over stationary forms of teaching. This is probably due to the fact that the

Figure 7. The future in business e-learning courses

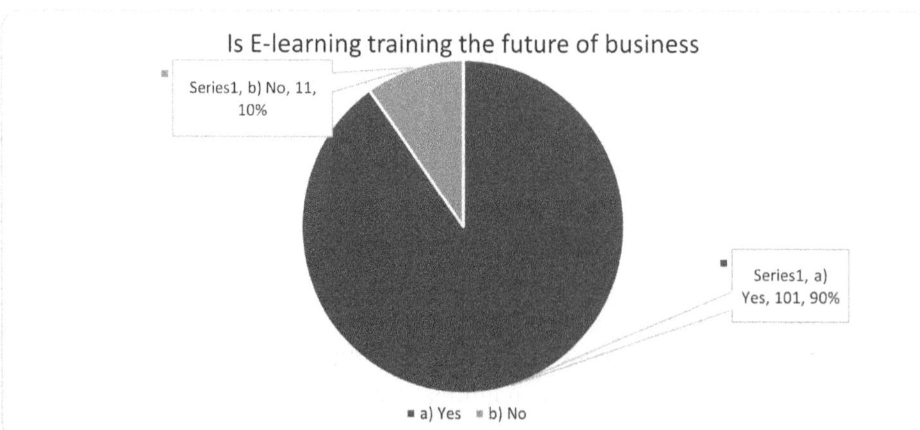

introduced limitations in interpersonal contacts have contributed to the increase in other forms of online learning. The analysis showed that 46% of participants of OHS training in a logistics company showed interest in training in the form of a Webinar, an additional advantage of this form of training is the highest commitment of the training, health and safety specialist, who showed the initiative in the best way to provide key information in the field of OHS. Another important benefit of online training is the possibility of self-study in at any time and place without much pressure from the lecturer. Classes in this form also turned out to be very exhausting and satisfying. The barriers related to technological skills during such training have also decreased. The study also showed interest in stationary training at the level of 12% of the respondents. This method is also still respected by employers due to, for example, individual contact with other people. Summarizing the research and the benefits shown in the analysis, they are the key building blocks for generating and sharing more classes in the form of E-learning in the enterprise.

5. FUTURE RESEARCH

Future research will focus on introducing training methods for office and warehouse workers using mobile devices, i.e. industrial tablets installed in the warehouse and in conference rooms. Training in the form of M-learning in the field of quality as well as stress and emotional management will be used for the research. According to A. Qashou (2021), M-learning is a new knowledge acquisition technique that helps learners to perform educational and training activities with easy access to educational materials without major time or space constraints, using available mobile devices. The usage of communication technology such as smartphones, tablets, small portable PCs or MP3 players towards conduct as well as implementation of various types of courses, study gives us unlimited opportunities to obtain knowledge from various places and in any form (Khan, Radzuan, Alkhunaizan, Mustafa, Khan, 2019). With the use of mobile tools, training on stress and emotion management will be able to take place on the premises of the plant for all comers at a convenient time for them. As you know, stress is an inseparable element of a human being, so one should act in such a way as to minimize its effects in the workplace, which most often lead to "professional burnout", mainly caused by mobbing by superiors or colleagues (Pieniążek, 2016).

6. CONCLUSION

Due to the limitations caused by the outbreak of the COVID-19 virus, companies have decided to temporarily fully or hybrid isolates their employees. For this reason, some companies have abandoned training and stationary courses and adopted the form of remote employee training. Today's technological solutions allow the implementation of such types of solutions as E-learning and M-learning trainings, which create new standards in the film. Let us hope that in the future enterprises will be supported by various forms of online training and will use adapted IT tools. This article discusses the issue of online OHS training and the method of training, which turned out to be a good solution for the employer. The benefits assessed by the training participants indicate the positive aspects of changes in the business, which translate into an increase in the overall satisfaction of the staff. Also, global changes in the trends in running companies and the approach to the modern management of personnel structures contribute to the intensification of processes throughout the organization.

REFERENCES

Alqahtani, A.Y., & Rajkhan, A.A. (2020). E-Learning Critical Success Factors during the COVID-19 Pandemic: A Comprehensive Analysis of E-Learning Managerial Perspectives. *Educ. Sci., 10*, 216. doi:10.3390/educsci10090216,p

Carliner, S., & Shank, P. (2016). *The elearning handbook: past promises, present challenges*. John Wiley & Sons.

COVID-19 wykreślony z systemu. Kiedy koniec pandemii? (n.d.). https://serwisy.gazetaprawna.pl/zdrowie/artykuly/8391606,pandemia-koronawirus-covid-19.html

Khan, R. M. I., Radzuan, N. R. M., Alkhunaizan, A. S., Ghulam, M., & Khan, I. (2019). *The Efficacy of MALL Instruction in Business English Learning*. doi:10.3991/ijim.v13i08.9562

Krishnapatria, K. (2020, June). From 'lockdown' to letdown: Students' perception of e-learning amid the covid-19 outbreak. *ELT in Focus, 3*(1), 1–8. Advance online publication. doi:10.35706/eltinfc.v3i1.3694

Marciniak, R. (2021). *E-learning – projektowanie, realizowanie i ocena*. Wolters Kluwer Polska.

Muhammad, A., Ghalib, M. F. M. D., Ahmad, F., Naveed, Q. N., & Shah, A. (2016). A study to investigate state of ethical development in e-learning. *International Journal of Advanced Computer Science and Applications, 2016*(7), 284–290. doi:10.14569/IJACSA.2016.070436

Naveed, Q. N., Muhammad, A., Sanober, S., Qureshi, M. R. N., & Shah, A. (2017). A mixed method study for investigating critical success factors (CSFs) of e-learning in Saudi Arabian universities. Academic Press.

Nwagwu, L., & Azil, N. (2016). Status of technologies in business education departments of tertiary institutions in Ebonyi State for effective integration of electronic learning. *Brock Journal of Education*, *4*(4), 49–59.

Oduma, Ch. A., & Nkem, O. L. (2019, October). E-learning platforms in business education for skill acquisition. *Nigerian Journal of Business Education*, *6*(2), 106.

Pieniążek M., 2016). Minimalizowanie stresu w miejscu pracy wyznacznikiem bezpieczeństwa. *Nauka – Praktyka – Refleksje, 22*, 339.

Pierwszy przypadek koronawirusa w Polsce. (n.d.). https://www.gov.pl/web/zdrowie/pierwszy-przypadek-koronawirusa-w-polsce

Pietrzyk, S. (2021). Bariery w szkoleniach biznesowych online – raport z badan. *Media i społeczeństwo*, 103.

Qashou, A. (2021). *Education and information technologies*. Springer.

Razzaque, A. (2020). *M-Learning Improves Knowledge Sharing Over e-Learning Platforms to Build Higher Education Students' Social Capital.* doi:10.1177/2158244020926575

Rozman, T., & Donath, L. (2019). The Current State of the Gemification in E-Learning: A Literature Review of Literature Reviews. *Journal of Innovative Business and Management*, 6.

Sandybayev, A. (2020). The Impact of E-Learning Technologies on Student's Motivation: Student Centered Interaction in Business Education. *International Journal of Research in Tourism and Hospitality*, 19.

Skibska, J., Borzęcka, A., & Twaróg-Kanus, A. (2020). Kompetencje diagnostyczne i terapeutyczne w percepcji nauczycieli szkół ogólnodostępnych integracyjnych i specjalnych. *IMPULS, Kraków, 2020*, 21.

Chapter 6
Factor Analysis of the Intercultural Sensitivity, Ethnocentrism, Social Media by the Means of Structural Equation Modelling

Marzena Sobczak-Michalowska
https://orcid.org/0000-0002-4757-0583
WSG University, Poland

Osman Yildirim
https://orcid.org/0000-0003-2282-5997
Istanbul Arel University, Turkey

Laçin Aykil
Istanbul Arel University, Turkey

Olha Ilyash
National Technical University of Ukraine, Ukraine

ABSTRACT

The purpose of this research is to investigate the interaction between intercultural sensitivity, ethnocentrism, and social media use by using structural equality modeling method. To this end, the survey was designed by using intercultural sensitivity, ethnocentrism, and social media data scales available in the literature. The expressions in the survey were translated and re-translated by two foreign language teachers. Then, the two translations obtained were applied to a test group of 20 people, and the most accurate translation was used to collect data by easy sampling method. Data were calculated for verifier factor analysis through SPSS for Windows 22.00 and Amos 22.0 and Cronbach's Alpha. Average variety extracted (AVE) and composite reliability (CR) values were also calculated. In addition, the effects mediated by structural equality modeling were also analyzed in the Amos program using the bootstrap method.

DOI: 10.4018/979-8-3693-1886-7.ch006

INTRODUCTION

The concept of ethnocentrism, first used by William Graham Sumner in 1906, is used quite frequently in the social sciences and especially in the field of psychology (Petrovicova, J.T. and Gibalova, 2014; Bizumic, 2014). Ethnocentrisms is the perception of one's own norms, values, and culture as superior to other cultures, norms and values, and the evaluation in line with this belief. An ethnocentric person positions people who are close to his own values closer to him and people who are far away from his own values as distant to him according to the dimension of differences. In other words, ethnocentrisms is a judgment made by taking one's own culture as a reference point and evaluating other cultures compared to one's own (Başçı, 2017).

The study measured the relationship of intercultural sensitivity to ethnocentrism and social media in line with the structural equality model. In the social media-related section of the study we utilized the "Social Media Experience Scale" developed by Schalkwyk and et. al. (Schwyk, Marin, Ortiz, Rolison, Qayyum, McPortland, Lebowitz, Volkmar and Silverman, 2017). This study examines how adolescents with Autism Spectrum Disorder have difficulty in social communication and make fewer friends than their peers who do not have this disorder, and their interaction with social media. The results showed that 79.6% of respondents used social media and that they were more likely to be in a close friendship relationship than individuals with autism who did not use social media. As a result, whatever its impact on society, social media platforms has gained in popularity and is also beneficial for many adolescents.

As the importance attached to intercultural sensitivity increased in the past years in a multicultural and globalized society, intercultural sensitivity has not yet been fully understood. Guo-Mingand Starosta have stated that the concepts of intercultural sensitivity, intercultural awareness, and intercultural communication competence are misperceived. The confusion of these concepts directly affects the evaluation of intercultural education programs. Intercultural training programs such as emotional training, cognitive training, behavioral training, personal awareness training, cultural consciousness training aims to help them gain understanding and awareness of the cultural differences for participants (Guo-Ming, Starosta, 2000)). The main purpose of this study is to develop and endorse a scale that measures the concept of intercultural sensitivity. 24- intercultural sensitivity items have been created on this scale. The scale has shown high internal consistency with reliability coefficients of 86 and 88 in two separate studies. The result showed that individuals with intercultural sensitivity were not only more careful and empathetic, but also tended to have a high tendency for self-respect and self-monitoring in the process of intercultural communication. The scale is prepared in accordance with reliability, concurrency, and predictive validity (Guo-Ming, Starosta, 2000).

The main tool of the work carried out by Coffrey and et. al. is to learn which element plays the greatest role in influencing intercultural sensitivity. In this study, the "Guo-Mingand Starosta Intercultural Sensitivity Scale" (Guo-Ming, Starosta, 2000) was used. The study also compared intercultural sensitivity according to the time and gender factors. While prior to this study, he contributed significantly to the understanding of the variables that drive intercultural sensitivity as well as the development of the tools used to test this structure, no known study has examined these factors in a comparative way with media channels.

The study assesses technology-mediated communication using both individual and environmental factors in a virtual environment to enhance intercultural sensitivity. In studies on intercultural sensitivity, Olson and Kroeger found that people with overseas experience and foreign language skills were more prone to intercultural sensitivity (Williams, 2005).Guo-Mingand Starostaspecified that intercultural sensitivity ensures respect to the cultural differences of people through education, developing a multicultural mindset and being prepared to contribute as members of a multicultural society. As a result, Guo-Mingand Starostaconcluded that the most valid measurement of intercultural sensitivity is based on emotional elements (Coffey, Kamhawi, Ishwick, Henderson, 2013).

In the study of Kaya, Arslan, Erbaş, Yaşar, Küçükkelepçe (2021), the effect of nursing students' ethnocentrism and moral sensitivity on intercultural sensitivity was discussed. At the end of the study, the fact that nursing students have different cultural backgrounds and deal with patients from different cultural backgrounds showed the effect of ethnocentrism and moral sensitivity on cultural sensitivity. At the same time, it was concluded in the study that senior students were less morally sensitive than other students (Kaya, Arslan, Erbaş, Yaşar and Küçükkelepçe, 2021).

Statistical Analysis

Confirmatory factor analyses of the scales used in the research were performed in the Amos program and Cronbach's Alpha, AVE and CR values were calculated and mediated effects were investigated by structural equality modeling.

Demographic Characteristics

Survey study was conducted with 930 people was carried out between January 2019 and February 2019. However, as a result of the examination, 17 questionnaires were excluded from the evaluation because the filling rate was too low. Thus, the number of participants was determined as 913.

Table 1. Percentage distribution table of demographic characteristics of participants

		Count	Column N %
Cinsiyet	Erkek	326	35,7%
	Kadın	587	64,3%
Yas	20 den az	235	25,7%
	20-25 arası	633	69,3%
	25-30 arası	27	3,0%
	30 ve üzeri	18	2,0%
Bölüm	Adalet/İSG	142	15,6%
	Sağlık bölümleri	417	45,7%
	Muhasebe/banka/işletme	126	13,8%
	Sanat/tasarım	58	6,4%
	Halkal ilişkiler/ Radyo TV	40	4,4%
	Sivil havacılık	106	11,6%
	Diğer	24	2,6%
Kredi	1,5 ve daha az	60	6,6%
	1,6-2,5	443	48,5%
	2,6-3,5	365	40,0%
	3,6 ve üzeri	45	4,9%

Confirmatory Factor Analysis

Confirmatory Factor Analysis (CFA) was investigated with the Amos 22.0 package program and the statistical significance level, degree of freedom and compliance level indices were evaluated with respect to the sample (Bollen, 1989;Fornell and Larcker, 1981; Bagozzi, and Yi, 2012;Schermelleh-Engel, Moosbrugger and Müller, 2003)

The 13-items Emotional Labor Scale (ELS), 6-items Organizational Identification (OI), and 3-items Turnover (CTR) scales together form the measurement model. Since the standard factor loads (FL>0.50) are present in all the items in the applied factor analysis, they are included in the analysis.

CFA analysis was resolved to be valid because CFA analysis test values, ($p<0.05$), x2 (1527,003), x2/DF (3.55) and compliance index values GFI(.905), CFI (.947), SRMR (.0511), RMSEA (.053).

Table 2. Compliance level indices used in CFA analysis

Indexes	Good Fit	Acceptable Fit Limits
$\chi2$ / df	$0 \leq \chi2/df \leq 2$	$2 < \chi2/df \leq 3$
GFI	≥ 0.90	0.85-0.89
CFI	≥ 0.97	≥ 0.95
SRMR	≤ 0.05	$.06 \leq$ SRMR $\leq .08$
RMSEA	≤ 0.05	$.06 \leq$ RMSEA $\leq .08$

Reliability, Combined Reliability, Convergence Validity, Separation Validity, and Described Average Variance Values

In this study, Cronbach's Alpha value is greater than 0.70 and the requirement for composite reliability (CR≥0.70) is provided (Raykov and Marcoulides, 2006).

The indicator of convergence validity is the average variance (AVE) value described. In order for the validity of convergence to be confirmed, the described mean variance must be (AVE≥0.50) (Fornell, Larcker, 1981).

For separation validity, the square root of the AVE values must be greater than the correlation value of the dimension with other dimensions. In this case it can be stated that for each dimensionof the scales used that validity of separation is ensured (Fornell, Larcker, 1981).

Ethnocentrism (ETN, Social Media Use (SMU), Social Media Anxiety (SMA), Respect for Differences (RD), Enjoying Interaction (EI), Attention to Interaction (AI), Participation in Interaction (PI) and Confidence in Interaction (CI) variables used in the research were calculated (Cronbach Alpha>0.80). It can be stated that combined reliability condition is ensured because CR values (CR>0.70) are present for the combined reliability. Since mean for all variables has the variance values described (AVE>0.50), the necessary condition is provided for convergence validity. The square root values of the calculated AVE values are given in parentheses in the table to check at the validity of the separation. All these values were higher than correlation values in that column to where it is recognized that the validity of the separation are provided for all variables.

Structural Equality Model (SEM) and Mediator Variable Effect Research With Amos

Assumptions about SEM were investigated and skewness and Kurtosis values were found to be appropriate and Maximum likelihood method was used (Raykov and

Table 3. Confirmatory factor analysis results for the measurement model

Item		Dimension	Estimate	S. Estimate	C.R.	P
ISS13	<---	PI	1,000	,846		
ISS22	<---	PI	,848	,733	19,359	***
ISS23	<---	PI	,739	,729	19,842	***
ISS8	<---	RD	,747	,746	19,983	***
ISS16	<---	RD	,884	,691	19,212	***
ISS18	<---	RD	1,000	,716		
ISS3	<---	CI	1,000	,753		
ISS4	<---	CI	1,025	,804	22,182	***
ISS5	<---	CI	,938	,718	20,175	***
ISS10	<---	CI	,794	,647	18,205	***
ISS9	<---	EI	1,000	,778		
ISS12	<---	EI	1,415	,795	16,436	***
ISS15	<---	EI	1,377	,761	16,123	***
ISS14	<---	AI	1,000	,807		
ISS17	<---	AI	,983	,696	18,652	***
ETN5	<---	ETN	,567	,795	26,350	***
ETN6	<---	ETN	,692	,742	25,650	***
ETN8	<---	ETN	,618	,717	24,707	***
ETN10	<---	ETN	,534	,711	22,279	***
ETN13	<---	ETN	,702	,693	21,501	***
ETN15	<---	ETN	,829	,657	20,981	***
ETN17	<---	ETN	,957	,778	25,863	***
ETN18	<---	ETN	,960	,733	23,823	***
ETN19	<---	ETN	,987	,766	25,499	***
ETN20	<---	ETN	1,00	,823		
SMU6	<---	SMU	,760	,717	18,857	***
SMU5	<---	SMU	1,021	,711	17,726	***
SMU4	<---	SMU	,939	,712	16,744	***
SMU3	<---	SMU	,976	,655	15,501	***
SMU2	<---	SMU	1,000	,758		
SMU9	<---	SMA	,943	,600	12,362	***
SMU8	<---	SMA	1,000	,867		

***p<0.001 **p<0.01 *p<0.05

Table 5. Correlation, reliability, and separation validity values of the scales used in the research

SCALE		*SD*	*PI*	*RD*	*CI*	*EI*	*AI*	*SMU*	*SMA*	*ETN*
Participation in Interaction (PI)	3,8	,9	**(,771)**							
Respect for Differences (RD)	2,1	,9	-,400**	**(,718)**						
Modelde Confidence in Interaction (CI)	3,6	,9	,444**	-,380**	**(,732)**					
Enjoying Interaction (EI)	3,9	1,0	,260**	-,669**	,348**	**(,777)**				
Attention to Interaction (AI)	4,0	,9	,570**	-,496**	,497**	,352**	**(,753)**			
Social MediaUse (SMU)	2,8	,9	,099**	,134**	,098**	-,202**	,104**	**(,711)**		
Social MediaAnxiety (SMA)	2,8	1,1	-,009	,184**	-,004	-,242**	-,047	,474**	**(,745)**	
Ethnocentrism (ETN)	2,3	,9	-,218**	,580**	-,246**	-,593**	-,327**	,294**	,331**	**(,729)**
Coefficient of Cronbach's Alpha			***.842***	***,801***	***,833***	***,834***	***,800***	***,830***	***,810***	***,910***
Composite Reliability (CR)			***,814***	***,761***	***,822***	***,822***	***,723***	***,836***	***,708***	***,924***
Explained Average Value of Variance (AVE)			***,595***	***,516***	***,537***	***,605***	***,568***	***,506***	***,556***	***,552***

***p<0.001 **p<0.01 *p<0.05

Marcoulides, 2006; Tabachnick and Fidell, 2007; Kline, 2011). The model presented in Figure 1 was tested using path analysis of variables with the help of Amos program 20.0. In addition, sample confidence interval was tested by bootstrapping method instead of Sobel test to investigate the significance of the presented model (Preacher and Hayes 2004, 2008).

Because model test values were x^2 *(22.8235)*,x^2/df*(4.5647) and (p<0.05)*in the path analysis model with observed variables then the model was found to be significant. The compliance index values of the model are GFI(.926), CFI (.941), SRMR (.07029), RMSEA (.0767) within the boundaries of compliance it is understood that the model is valid because. Detailed values for the model parameters are included in the table.

The mediator effect of the Social Media Use (SMU) variable on the Ethnocentrism (ETN) variable of the lower dimensions of cross-cultural awareness to the bootstrap (n=2000) result made for all data (n=913) is included in the table. According to this, respect for Differences (RD), Enjoying Interaction (EI), Attention to Interaction (AI), which have both direct and indirect effects on Ethnocentrism (ETN), are understood

Figure 1. Model of the mediating role of social media anxiety variable in the influence of lower dimensions of intercultural difference to the ethnocentrism variable

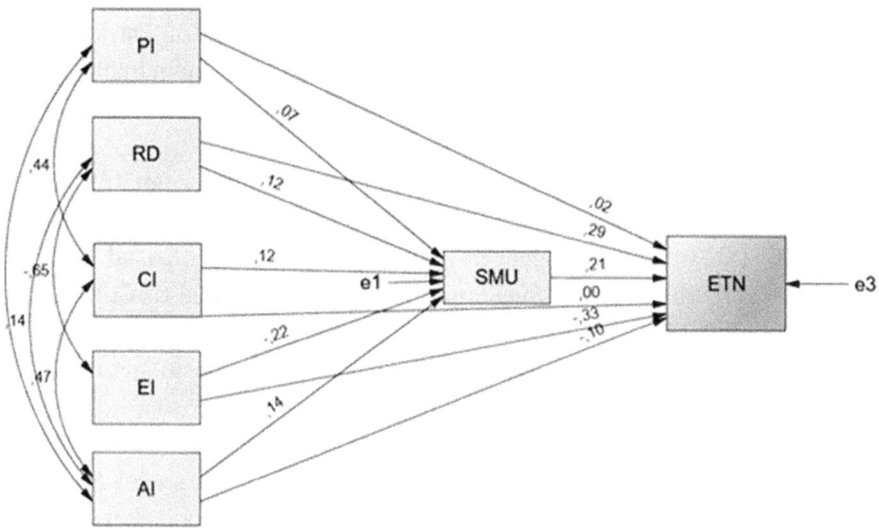

to be social Media Use (SMU) Partial Mediation in relation to Ethnocentrism (ETN). The direct effect of Participation in Interaction (PI) and Confidence in Interaction (CI) on Ethnocentrism (ETN) is insignificant, but the indirect effect of Social Media Use (SMU) on Ethnocentrism (ETN) is significant, so Social Media Use (SMU) is the full mediator of the effect of Participation in Interaction (PI) and Confidence in Interaction (CI) on Ethnocentrism (ETN).

Table 6. Direct and indirect effect values between independent, dependent and mediator variables

Hypothesis	Direct Effect	Direct Effect p	Indirect Effect	Indirect Effect p	Result
PI→SMU→ETN	,021	,499	,014	,048*	Full Mediaton
RD→SMU→ETN	,294	,001**	,025	,003**	Partial Mediaton
CI→SMU→ETN	,000	,967	,023	,002**	Full Mediaton
EI→SMU→ETN	-,291	,001**	-,040	,001**	Partial Mediaton
AI→SMU→ETN	-,094	,012*	,027	,002**	Partial Mediaton

*p<0.05 **p<0.01 PI: Participation in Interaction, RD: Respect for Differences CI: Confidence in Interaction EI: Enjoying Interaction AI: Attention to Interaction ETN: Ethnocentrism, SMU: Social MediaUse

- Direct effect of Participation in Interaction (PI) in the model on Ethnocentrism (ETN) variable (.021) is insignificant, indirect effect on the social Media Use (SMU) variable (.014*) is significant so it is understood that Social Media Use (SMU) has a full mediating role in the influence of Participation in Interaction (PI) on Ethnocentrism (ETN). The participation in Interaction (PI) variable indirectly increases Ethnocentrism (ETN) by positively influencing Social Media Use (SMU).
- Direct effect of Confidence in Interaction (CI) on Ethnocentrism (ETN) in the model (.000) is insignificant, indirect effect on social Media Use (SMU) variable (.023**) is significant so it is understood that the Social Media Use (SMU) variable has a full mediating role in the influence of Confidence in Interaction (CI) on Ethnocentrism (ETN). The Confidence in Interaction (CI) variable indirectly increases Ethnocentrism (ETN) by positively influencing Social Media Use (SMU).
- Direct effect of Respect for Differences (RD) in the model, on Ethnocentrism (ETN) variable (.294) is significant, indirect effect on social Media Use (SMU) variable (.025**) is significant so it is understood that the Social Media Use (SMU) variable has a partial mediating role in the effect of Respect for Differences (RD) variable on Ethnocentrism (ETN). Respect for Differences (RD) indirectly increases the variable Ethnocentrism (ETN) by positively influencing it through variable Social Media Use (SMU).
- Direct effect of Enjoying Interaction (EI) in the model, on Ethnocentrism (ETN) variable (-.294) is significant, its indirect effect on social Media Use (SMU) variable (-.040**) is significant so it is understood that Social Media Use (SMU) has a partial mediating role in the influence of Enjoying Interaction (EI) on Ethnocentrism (ETN). Enjoying Interaction (EI) indirectly reduces the variable Ethnocentrism (ETN) by negatively affecting the variable Social Media Use (SMU).
- Direct effect of Attention to Interaction (AI) on Ethnocentrism (ETN) in the model (-.094) is significant, its indirect effect on social Media Use (SMU) variable (.027**) is significant and it is understood that the Social Media Use (SMU) variable has a partial mediating role in the effect of Attention to Interaction (AI) on Ethnocentrism (ETN) variable. The attention to Interaction (AI) variable indirectly increases Ethnocentrism (ETN) by positively influencing Social Media Use (SMU).

Because model test values were $\boldsymbol{x^2}$ *(26,2842)*, $\boldsymbol{x^2/df}$ *(4,3807) and (p<0.05)* in the path analysis model with observed variables then the model was found to be significant. The compliance index values of the model are ***GFI****(.920)*, ***CFI*** *(.935)*, ***SRMR*** *(,0719)*,

Figure 2. The mediating role model of social media anxiety variable in the influence of intercultural difference sub-dimensions to ethnocentrism variable

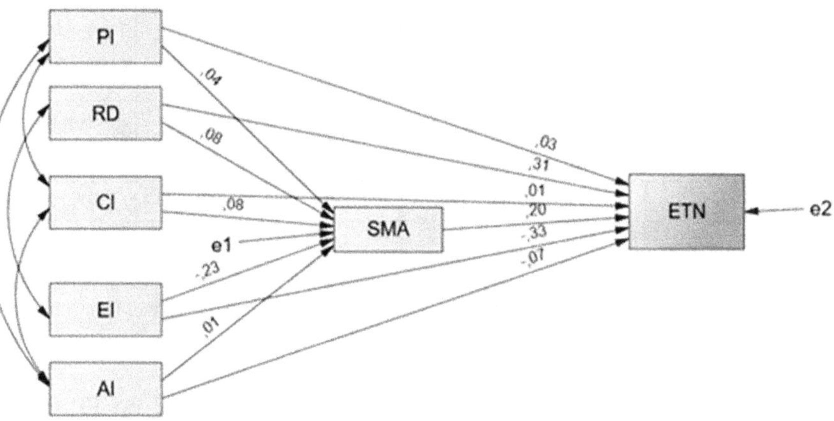

RMSEA *(,0783)* within the boundaries of compliance it is understood that the model is valid because. Detailed values for the model parameters are included in the table.

The mediator effect of the Social Media Anxiety (SMA) variable on the Ethnocentrism (ETN) variable of the lower dimensions of intercultural awareness on the bootstrap (n=2000) result made for all data (n=913) is included in the table. According to this, respect for Differences (RD), Attention to Interaction (AI), Participation in Interaction (PI) and (AI) variables, which have insignificant effect on Ethnocentrism (ETN), are not mediators for social Media Use (SMU) in the effect of Ethnocentrism (ETN). Because the direct effect of Confidence in Interaction (CI) on Ethnocentrism (ETN) is insignificant, the indirect effect of Social Media Anxiety (SMA) on Ethnocentrism (ETN) is significant; Social Media Anxiety (SMA) acts as a full mediator for the effect of Confidence in Interaction (CI) on Ethnocentrism (ETN). Enjoying Interaction (EI), which has both direct and indirect effects on Ethnocentrism (ETN), is understood to be the Social Media Anxiety Partial Mediation (SMA) under the influence of Ethnocentrism (ETN).

- Direct effect of Confidence in Interaction (CI) on Ethnocentrism (ETN) in the model (.008) is insignificant and since indirect effect on social Media Anxiety (SMA) variable (.016**) is significant, it is understood that Social Media Anxiety (SMA) has a full mediating role in the influence of Confidence in Interaction (CI) on Ethnocentrism (ETN). The Confidence in Interaction (CI) variable increases Ethnocentrism (ETN) by positively influencing Social Media Anxiety (SMA).

Table 7. Direct and indirect effect values between independent, dependent and mediator variables

Hypothesis	Direct Effect	Direct Effect p	Indirect Effect	Indirect Effect p	Result
PI→SMA→ETN	,028	,380	,008	,310	Not Mediaton
RD→SMA→ETN	,303	,001**	,016	,067	Not Mediaton
CI→SMA→ETN	,008	,853	,016	,044*	Full Mediaton
EI→SMA→ETN	-,292	,001**	-,039	,001**	Partial Mediaton
AI→SMA→ETN	-,068	,066	,002	781	Not Mediaton

*p<0.05 **p<0.01 PI: Participation in Interaction, RD: Respect for Differences CI: Confidence in Interaction EI: Enjoying Interaction AI: Attention to Interaction ETN: Ethnocentrism, SMA: Social MediaAnxiety

- Direct effect of Enjoying Interaction (EI) in the model on Ethnocentrism (ETN) variable (-.292) is significant, indirect effect of Social Media Anxiety (SMA) on the variable (-.039**) is significant so it is understood that Social Media Anxiety (SMA) has a partial mediating role in the effect of Enjoying Interaction (EI) on Ethnocentrism (ETN). Enjoying Interaction (EI) indirectly reduces the variable Ethnocentrism (ETN) by negatively affecting the variable Social Media Anxiety (SMA).

CONCLUSION

The interplay between intercultural sensitivity, ethnocentrism and social media use has been demonstrated through the structural equality model through this research. To this end, data was collected by research survey using the scales of intercultural sensitivity, ethnocentrism and social media use in the literature. The expressions of the designed questionnaire was translated and re-translated by two foreign language teachers. Then, the two translations obtained were applied to a test group of 20 people, providing linguistic validity for the final version of the survey. Data, were calculated for verifier factor analysis through SPSS for Windows 22.00 and Amos 22.0 and Cronbach's Alpha, average variety extracted (AVE) and composite reliability (CR) values were also calculated. In addition, the effects mediated by structural equality modeling were also analyzed in the Amos program, using the bootstrap method. The mediation effect findings of study revealed by research respectively are as follows;

(1) The use of social media is a partial mediator in the influence of "respect for differences", "enjoying interaction", and "attention to interaction" variables, which have both significant direct and indirect effects on ethnocentrism variable,

(2) The direct effect of "Participation in interaction" and "confidence in interaction" on ethnocentrism is insignificant, but the indirect effect on social media usage is significant. Accordingly, the social media usage variable acts as a full mediator.

REFERENCES

Bagozzi, R., & Yi, Y. (2012). Specification, evaluation and interpretation of structural equation models. *Journal of the Academy of Marketing Science*, *40*(1), 8–34. doi:10.1007/s11747-011-0278-x

Başçı, E. (2017). Küreselleşen Dünyada Etnosentrizm: Üniversite Öğrencileri Üzerine Yapılan Bir Saha Araştırması. *International Journal of Academic Value Studies*, *3*(16), 286–293.

Bizumic, B. (2014). Who Contained the Concept of Ethnocentrism? A Brief Report. *Journal of Social and Political Psychology*, *2*(1), 3–10. doi:10.5964/jspp.v2i1.264

Bollen, K. A. (1989). *Structural equations with latent variables*. Wiley. doi:10.1002/9781118619179

Coffey, A. J., Kamhawi, R., Fishwick, P., & Julie Henderson, J. (2013). New Media Environments' Comparative Effects Upon Intercultural Sensitivity: A Five-Dimensional Analysis. *International Journal of Intercultural Relations*, *37*(5), 605–627. doi:10.1016/j.ijintrel.2013.06.006

Fornell, C., & Larcker, D. F. (1981). Evaluating structural equation models with unobservable variables and measurement error. *JMR, Journal of Marketing Research*, *18*(1), 39–50. doi:10.1177/002224378101800104

Guo-Ming, C., & William Starosta, J., J.W. (2000). The Development and Validation of the Intercultural Sensitivity Scale. *Annual Meeting of the National Communication Association*, 86.

Kaya, Y., Arslan, S., Erbaş, A., Yaşar, B. N., & Küçükkelepçe, G. E. (2021). The Effect of Ethnocentrism and oral Sensitivity on Intercultural Sensitivity in Nursing Students, Descriptive Cross-Sectional Research Study. *Nurse Education Today*, *2021*(100), 1–7. doi:10.1016/j.nedt.2021.104867 PMID:33740704

Kline, R. B. (2011). *Principles and practice of structural equation modeling* (3rd ed.). Guilford Press.

Petrovicova, J. T., & Gibalova, M. (2014). Measurement of Consumer Ethnocentrism of Slovak Consumers. *International Review of Management and Marketing, 4*(4), 247-258.

Preacher, K. J., & Hayes, A. F. (2008). Asymptotic and resampling strategies for assessing and comparing indirect effects in multiple mediator models. *Behavior Research Methods, 40*(3), 879–891. doi:10.3758/BRM.40.3.879 PMID:18697684

Raykov, T., & Marcoulides, G. A. (2006). On Multilevel Reliability Estimation From the Perspective of Structural Equation Modeling. *Structural Equation Modeling, 13*(1), 130–141. doi:10.1207/s15328007sem1301_7

Schermelleh-Engel, K., Moosbrugger, H., & Müller, H. (2003). Evaluating TheFit Of Structural Equation Models: Tests Of Significance And Descriptive Goodness-Of- Fit Measures. *Methods of Psychological Research Online, 8*(2), 23–74.

Schwyk, G. I. V., Marin, C. E., Ortiz, M., Rolison, M., Qayyum, Z., McPortland, J. C., Lebowitz, E. R., Volkmar, F. R., & Silverman, W. K. (2017). Social Media Use, Friendship Quality and the Moderating Role of Anxiety in Adolescents with Autism Spectrum Disorder. *Journal of Autism and Developmental Disorders, 47*(9), 2805–2813. doi:10.1007/s10803-017-3201-6 PMID:28616856

Tabachnıck, B. G., & Fidell, L. S. (2007). Using Multivariate Statistics (5th ed.). Pearson Education, Inc.

Williams, T. R. (2005). Exploring the Impact of Study Abroad on Students' Intercultural Communication Skills: Adaptability and Sensitivity. *Journal of Studies in International Education, 9*(4), 356–371. doi:10.1177/1028315305277681

Chapter 7
Feature Selection Using Correlation Analysis for Accurate Breast Cancer Diagnosis

Jasjit Singh
Ambedkar Institute of Technology, India

Deepanshu Goyal
Ambedkar Institute of Technology, India

Apurva Vashist
Ambedkar Institute of Technology, India

ABSTRACT

Breast cancer is a sickness that can affect women when some cells in their breasts grow abnormally. It's a serious problem and is one of the main reasons why women pass away. It's hard to accurately diagnose because it's a complex disease, and treatments and patients vary. Thankfully, there have been important discoveries in how to find and treat breast cancer. Now, about 89 out of every 100 women with breast cancer can survive if they find it early. So, we need a special kind of technology that can find breast cancer when it's just starting and reduce the chance of cancer coming back. Scientists use computer programs called "machine learning" to help find breast cancer in lots of data. The fundamental purpose of this research initiative was to prudently apply feature selection methodologies, while integrating the examination of correlations among input features. These selected significant features were subsequently employed in conjunction with a classification method.

DOI: 10.4018/979-8-3693-1886-7.ch007

INTRODUCTION

Breast cancer remains a significant contributor to female mortality (Libbrecht & Noble, 2015). Despite the potential for early-stage prevention, many women still receive late-stage diagnoses. The incorporation of advanced diagnostic techniques is essential for tailoring personalized care and treatment plans, serving as a valuable tool in managing and reducing the recurrence of cancer.

Extensive research into the diagnosis and treatment of breast cancer is of paramount importance. Based on comprehensive literature reviews and statistical data, cancer claims approximately 7.4 million lives each year worldwide, representing 13% of all global fatalities. Breast cancer is among the top five most commonly diagnosed cancers globally. Its ripple effects extend beyond the patients, significantly impacting their families. Consequently, simplifying the breast cancer diagnostic process and enhancing the decision-making procedures for medical treatment stages is an essential endeavour for healthcare professionals and physicians. Breast cancer occurs in breast cells of the fatty tissues or the fibrous connective tissues within the breast. Breast cancer is a type of tumour that tends to become gradually worse and that grows fast, which leads to death. Breast cancer is more common among females, but it can also occur among males, although rarely. Various factors, such as age and family history, can also contribute to breast cancer risk.

Approximately 5 to 10 percent of breast cancer cases can be attributed to hereditary gene mutations passed down through generations of a family. The most renowned inherited genetic mutations associated with an elevated risk of both breast and ovarian cancer are known as breast cancer gene 1 (BRCA1) and breast cancer gene 2 (BRCA2). If you possess a strong family history of breast cancer or other related cancers, it is advisable to seek consultation with a medical professional. Your doctor may recommend a blood test to identify specific mutations in genes like BRCA or others that may be inherited within your family. Your doctor may then refer you to a genetic counsellor, a specialist who will carefully assess your family's health history and engage in a detailed discussion with you. This discussion will encompass the advantages, drawbacks, and constraints of genetic testing, aiding you in making informed decisions.

Early detection of breast cancer holds significant importance in reducing the mortality rate associated with this devastating disease, aligning with the United Nations' goal of enhancing health and well-being. However, it presents challenges since cancer symptoms can occasionally be atypical. Employing mammogram screenings and conducting self-breast examinations are crucial for identifying early irregularities before the disease progresses. When a lump is discovered during a mammogram screening, it is categorized as either a benign or malignant tumour.

Benign tumours are manageable and less concerning, whereas malignant tumours are highly aggressive in infiltrating nearby tissues.

In recent times, the healthcare industry has increasingly turned to machine learning algorithms for cancer prediction and detection due to their proven effectiveness. Various machine learning techniques leveraging computational methods have streamlined the analysis and classification of cancer. While these methods have achieved success, they have also encountered some limitations in terms of accuracy and efficiency.

To sum it up, breast tumours can be classified into two main categories:

1. Benign tumours, composed of non-cancerous cells, typically harmless unless they exert pressure on adjacent tissues, nerves, or blood vessels.
2. Malignant tumours, consisting of cancerous cells with the ability to invade nearby tissues and potentially spread to other parts of the body, posing a substantial health risk and the potential for fatal consequences.

LITERATURE REVIEW

Libberchi and Nobel (2015) used applications of machine learning. In this review we identify some recurrent challenges associated with this type of analysis and provide general guidelines to help in the practical application of machine learning. The field of machine learning promised to enable computer to assist human in making sense of large complex datasetimbalanced class size (limitation), a common stumbling block in many applications of machine learning to genomes the large imbalance of size or groups. In this dataset we have some problems related to dataset considering 641 datasets in which 1711+ve examples and roughly 300000-ve but a system can't handle this. To overcome this, we used gaussian model which has accuracy of 99.9%.

Mann et al. (2021) approaches to machine learning and deep learning techniques to discuss model transparency and explainability and data privacy that are required to deploy MS-based biomarkers in clinical settings.

AI has become an integral part of the proteomics enterprise. the advances in biomedical data generation, including MS-based proteomics, coupled with breakthroughs in ML and DL for data analytics and integration.

Al-Thanoon et al. (2018) using firefly algorithm with application in gene selection and cancer classification also PSVM (penalized support vector machine), SCAD (smoothly clipped absolute deviation) is both used in this paper to find the most relevant genes with high classification performance.

A firefly algorithm was proposed for determining the tuning parameter and was compared with the classical CV method.

Darwish and Sayed (2022) used Whale optimization algorithm, Grey Wolf optimizer, Flower pollination algorithm, Moth flame optimization in meta-heuristic optimization algorithms-based feature selection for clinical breast cancer diagnosis.

In their research, A. Darwish and G. I. Sayed (2022) conducted a study that involved the utilization of a variety of meta-heuristic optimization algorithms, which included the Whale Optimization Algorithm (WOA), Grey Wolf Optimizer (GWO), Flower Pollination Algorithm (FPA), and Moth Flame Optimization (MFO). Their primary aim was to apply these algorithms for feature selection in the context of clinical breast cancer diagnosis, with a key focus on evaluating and comparing their efficiency.

The outcomes of this investigation are of significant relevance to both medical practitioners and researchers working in this field. The findings have the potential to advance the understanding of clinical breast cancer diagnoses and offer valuable insights that can be applied to data mining and machine learning applications within this specialized domain. Particularly noteworthy are the reported accuracy rates: WOA-98.77%, GWO-96.65%, FPA-96.66%, and MFO-95.32%. These remarkably high accuracy percentages underscore the promise of these algorithms in enhancing the precision of breast cancer diagnosis.

Nicora et al. (2020) approach the methods Clustering, Features Extraction, Feature Transformation to summarize current state of-art in multi-omics data analysis, relevant topics in terms of machine learning approaches through multi omics dataset of breast cancer.

In their research, Nicora et al. (2020) have taken a comprehensive approach, delving into various methodologies encompassing clustering, feature extraction, and feature transformation. Their primary goal is to provide an up-to-date overview of state-of-the-art techniques in multi-omics data analysis, with a specific emphasis on the application of machine learning within the context of multi-omics datasets related to breast cancer.

The field of their research holds the potential for significant advancements through the development of specialized databases designed to store and facilitate the analysis of multi-omics and clinical data, such as Linked Omics. Additionally, it is essential to prioritize the enhancement of usability and reproducibility by devising methods that can be universally applied across different types of omics data. This broader approach has the potential to streamline and enhance the efficiency and reliability of research in the realm of multi-omics analysis in breast cancer and related fields.

N. Biswas and S. Chakrabarti (2020) employed an innovative artificial intelligence-based system biology approach for the comprehensive analysis of multi-omics data in the context of cancer research. The core methodology of their study involved leveraging artificial intelligence techniques, with a particular focus on the application of Support Vector Machines (SVM) for multi-omics data analysis. SVM, a powerful classification algorithm, was utilized to establish a linear hyperplane for effective data classification and pattern recognition.

Furthermore, the research team incorporated unsupervised machine learning methods, such as autoencoders, to address the challenge of handling large-scale multi-omics datasets.

This research endeavour yielded remarkable results, manifesting in a diverse array of algorithms meticulously tailored to the pursuit of precision oncology. The outcomes were indeed impressive, with the Support Vector Machine achieving an outstanding accuracy rate of 92.5%, the Random Forest algorithm delivering a commendable 84.6% accuracy, and the Autoencoder demonstrating a noteworthy accuracy of 85.5%.

YM-Sobhan Zadeh et al. (2021) used a machine learning approach for feature selection in biological applications. The method used in the study involves a two-step process, combining genetic algorithms and the World Competitive Contest (WCC) algorithm for gene or feature selection

1. Two-Step Approach: The study employs a two-step technique for feature selection. In the first step, a genetic algorithm is used to reduce the overall number of genes or features under consideration. Genetic algorithms are often used for optimization problems and can be used to find a subset of relevant genes or features.
2. Second Step - WCC Algorithm: After the initial reduction by the genetic algorithm, the WCC algorithm is applied to select the optimal subset of features from the reduced set. The WCC algorithm is known for its competitive selection process.
3. Performance Results: The study reports the accuracy of the two algorithms used in the feature selection process. The genetic algorithm achieves an accuracy of 87.3%, while the WCC algorithm achieves a higher accuracy of 89.1%.
4. Conclusion: The findings of the study suggest that this two-step technique, combining genetic algorithms and the WCC algorithm, can potentially yield better results for feature selection in biological applications compared to a single-step approach.

It's important to note that the specific details and context of the study, as well as the dataset and the biological application in question, would be crucial for a more in-depth understanding of the research and its implications. Additionally, the study's publication and availability would be valuable for accessing the full details of the research methodology and results.

S. Azadifer et al. (2022) used a method called 'Graph-Based Relevance Redundancy Gene Selection' for diagnosing cancer, specifically lung cancer dataset. Nowadays, researchers often work with microarray data in molecular biology to aid in cancer diagnosis. One crucial step in this process is selecting the most relevant genes from the microarray data. In this particular study, they employed a gene selection method based on graph theory. This method is innovative because it's the first of its kind to use 'maximum cliques.' By doing so, it improved the efficiency of grouping genes together and reduced the overlap or redundancy between the selected genes.

The results of this study showed promising outcomes. They achieved a classification accuracy of 85.6% using a metric called 'Mi,' 85.05% using the Pearson correlation, and 86.97% using cosine similarity. All of this was done on a lung cancer dataset."

In a study conducted by Isik and Ercan (2017), a novel approach was employed, integrating RNA sequencing (RNA-seq) and Reverse Phase Protein Array (RPPA) data to predict the survival time of cancer patients. This research specifically centered on datasets related to Kidney Renal Clear Cell Carcinoma and Lung Squamous Cell Carcinoma. The primary aim of this study was to identify biomarkers capable of accurately forecasting the potential survival duration of cancer patients by leveraging the combined power of transcriptomics (RNA-seq) and proteomics (RPPA) data. Importantly, the results showcased commendable performance, as the method successfully categorized the survival time classes of cancer patients with an average accuracy ranging from 66% to 78% for these specific datasets.

Kim et al. (2019) conducted a study where they combined RPPA proteomics data with multiple types of biological data to predict survival in breast cancer. They used a method involving pathway analysis to infer the activity of biological pathways. This integrated analysis allowed them to identify disease-related biomarkers that would have remained hidden if they had only looked at individual datasets.

However, it's important to note a limitation of their approach: there was a weak correlation between gene-level data and protein-level data. Interestingly, when they used the RPPA dataset to create a prediction model based on pathways, it performed significantly lower in terms of accuracy compared to a model built using RNA sequencing data.

Nonetheless, their study revealed an important finding: within their analytical framework, RPPA data still proved valuable for predicting the survival of breast cancer patients.

METHODOLOGY

In this paper, an ensemble method is proposed for accurate breast cancer classification, which was made by selecting the appropriate features for processing.

Figure 1. Method for breast cancer feature selection

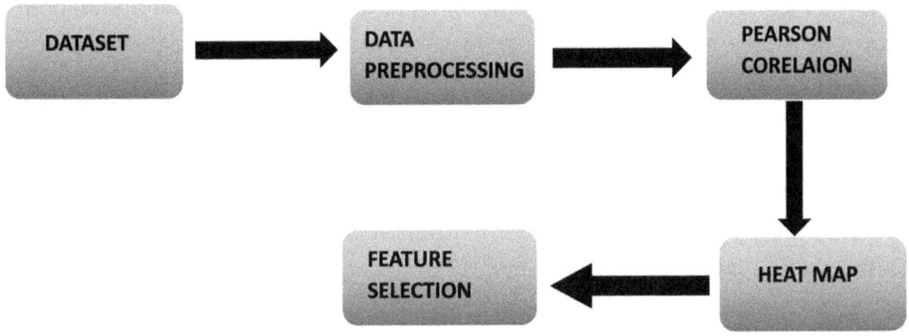

Dataset

This data frame consists of a set of four types of omics and five outcomes for the patients. The omics are:

MU: Whether a somatic mutation (i.e., a mutation that happened after conception) is present for a gene.

CN: Copy number of a part of the genome (i.e., amount of amplification of a part of the genome, this changes between different cells and individuals).

RS: RNA-Seq.

PP: Protein levels.

Size of data set = 705 rows * 1941 columns.

Outcomes of these inputs:

ER (Estrogen Receptor): Estrogen Receptor (ER) is a protein found in various tissues, including female reproductive tissues and some cancer cells. Its primary role is to interact with estrogen hormone. When estrogen binds to these receptors within cells, it can stimulate cell growth, particularly in the context of cancer, such as breast cancer. In cases where cancer cells are estrogen receptor-positive (ER-positive), they rely on estrogen for their growth. Consequently, therapies that block estrogen' s effects on these receptors are commonly used in treating ER-positive breast cancer. This approach aims to inhibit cancer cell growth and improve patient outcomes. Understanding the presence and activity of estrogen receptors is essential for tailoring cancer treatment plans, helping determine if hormonal therapies targeting estrogen are appropriate for a specific patient's cancer.

PR (Progesterone receptor)-PR is indeed an important protein that plays a critical role in various tissues, including the female reproductive system, and its interaction with progesterone can influence cell growth and development. In the context of cancer, identifying whether cancer cells are PR-positive is crucial for determining treatment strategies, as therapies targeting progesterone receptors can be employed to inhibit cancer cell growth and potentially improve patient outcomes. This understanding of receptor status is essential in tailoring precise and effective treatment plans for individuals with PR-positive cancers.

HER2- positive HER2 test result in breast cancer indicates a potential for rapid tumour growth and a higher risk of recurrence. However, this risk can be significantly reduced with the right treatment. Targeted therapies designed to block HER2 can effectively slow down the cancer's progression, improving the prognosis and minimizing the chances of recurrence. It's important for individuals with HER2-positive breast cancer to work closely with their healthcare team to determine the most appropriate treatment plan for their specific case.

Vital status - Vital status is a simple indicator that tells us whether a patient is alive or deceased. It is determined by considering the patient's birth date, the presence or absence of a recorded death date, and whether the patient is marked as 'deceased' in Epic, the medical records system.

Histological cancer subtype- IDC-NST is the most common histological subtype, comprising approximately 40% to 75% of all invasive breast carcinomas. It is characterized by a wide range of morphological variations and clinical behaviours.

Data Preprocessing

Data pre-processing is an essential initial step in constructing accurate models, enhancing data quality, and creating a suitable dataset for modelling. Neglecting pre-processing can lead to significant issues such as data inconsistencies, errors, noise, and missing values, ultimately elevating the risk of model overfitting. To assess the true impact of pre-processing on classification algorithms for breast cancer diagnosis, we systematically compared outcomes with and without pre-processing. In this phase, we explored two distinct feature selection methods, selecting the one that demonstrated superior performance, thus enhancing model accuracy and reliability.

Pearson Correlation

The Pearson correlation coefficient functions as a metric for assessing the relationship between two variables, both of which are measured on interval or ratio scales. This coefficient serves to numerically express the strength of the connection between these two numbers that can keep changing.

Furthermore, this number not only tells us if two things are related, but it also shows exactly how much they are related. What's important is that it doesn't matter what units we use to measure these things, and the number can go from +1, which means they're perfectly related in a positive way, to -1, which means they're perfectly related in a negative way.

Pearson Correlation Formula:

$$r = \frac{n\left(\sum xy\right)-\left(\sum x\right)\left(\sum y\right)}{\sqrt{\left[n\sum x^2-\left(\sum x\right)^2\right]\left[n\sum y^2-\left(\sum y\right)^2\right]}} \tag{1}$$

- "r" stands for the Pearson Coefficient, which tells us how related two things are.
- "n" is the number of pairs of stocks we're looking at.
- "∑xy" is the total of all the products we get by multiplying each pair of stocks.
- "∑x" is the total of all the scores we have for the first thing we're measuring.
- "∑y" is the total of all the scores we have for the second thing we're measuring.
- "∑x2" is the total of all the scores squared for the first thing.
- "∑y2" is the total of all the scores squared for the second thing.

Heat Map

A heat map serves as a two-dimensional portrayal of data, employing a color-coded scheme to depict varying values. It offers a concise visual overview of information distributed across two axes, enabling users to swiftly discern key or pertinent data points. More intricate heat maps facilitate comprehension of intricate data sets.

In essence, a heat map is a means of visually rendering data points within a dataset. All heat maps share a common feature: the utilization of diverse colours or differing intensities of the same hue to symbolize distinct values, conveying potential associations between variables plotted along the x and y axes. Typically, a deeper colour or shade signifies a greater quantity of the represented value within the heat map.

Feature Selection

Feature selection is a method used to make your model work better by choosing the most important data and getting rid of unnecessary information in the dataset. It's like keeping the useful stuff and throwing away the stuff that doesn't really matter.

Genetic Algorithm

The Genetic Algorithm (GA) is a type of Evolutionary Algorithm (EA) that takes its cues from Charles Darwin's theory of natural selection, following the idea of "survival of the fittest." In simpler terms, it mimics how nature Favours the best-adapted individuals, helping in solving problems effectively.

Formula: We start by calculating a fitness value (let's call it "f1") for each person in a group (population). We do this for each person in the group, one by one (j = 1, 2, ... up to n).

$$p_i = f_i \backslash \sum_{j=1}^{n} \quad (2)$$

Next, we add up all these fitness values to get a total sum. Think of it like adding up scores.

$$F = \sum_{j=1}^{n} f_i$$

To decide which person gets selected, we use a formula to calculate the probability of each person being chosen. We'll call this calculated value "k." We repeat this for each person in the group (k = 1, 2, ... up to n).

$$p_k = f_k / \sum_{j=1}^{n} f_i \quad (4)$$

The provided instructions describe the "runner method" within a selection process, which involves choosing a certain number of rotations (N times). Each time this method is applied, a new individual is included in a fresh population.

So, in simpler terms, we're figuring out how fit each person is, adding up their fitness scores, and then using a formula to determine the chance of each person being picked.

RESULT

In Table 1, the utilization of the Pearson correlation method reveals that among the four input factors in the Multi Omics Breast Cancer Dataset (samdemharter/

Table 1. Performance evaluation

S. No.	Correlation Between	Outcome
1	RNA-seq and Copy number	-0.136
2	RNA-seq and Somatic mutation	-0.036
3	RNA-seq and Protein level	-0.004
4	Somatic mutation and Protein level	0.013
5	Copy Number and Protein level	**0.014**
6	Copy number and Somatic mutation	-0.076

brca-multiomics-tcga), namely Copy Number (CN), Protein Level (PP), Somatic Mutation (MU), and RNA Sequencing (RS), the analysis yields the highest level of correlation among these variables.

After conducting a Pearson Correlation analysis, we identified a strong correlation between Copy number and Protein Level. Subsequently, we employed a Genetic Algorithm for feature selection. Following this, we generated a heatmap depicting the relationship between Copy number and Protein Level.

Figure 2. Heat map

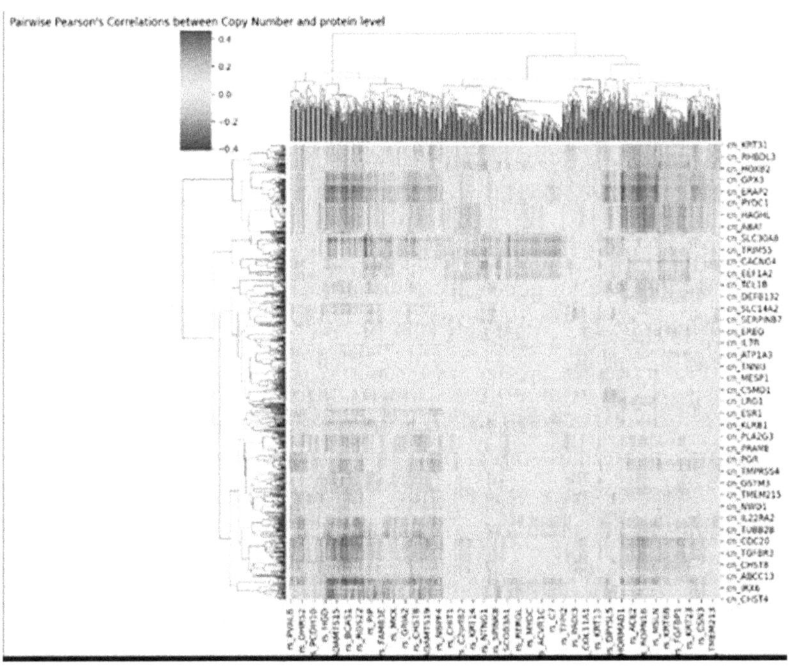

FEATURE SELECTION USING GENETIC ALGORITHM

We applied the genetic algorithm's mathematical formula to the mentioned dataset, resulting in the selection of 705 features related to copy number and 1939 features associated with protein levels.

FUTURE WORK

In our comprehensive research study, we initially utilized Pearson correlation analysis to identify the most significant correlations among Copy Number, Protein Level, RNA-Seq data, and Somatic Mutation. Our analysis revealed that the strongest correlation was observed between Copy Number and Protein Level, with a coefficient of 0.014.

Subsequently, we employed a Genetic Algorithm for feature selection and created a heatmap to visualize these relationships. This step allowed us to pinpoint key features and their interplay.

For future directions in this project, we propose the utilization of advanced optimization techniques such as the Whale Optimization Algorithm and the Grey Wolf Optimizer. These algorithms have the potential to yield improved results, further enhancing the scope and impact of our research.

REFERENCES

Al-Thanoon, Qasim, & Algamal. (2018). *Tuning parameter estimation in SCAD-support vector machine using firefly algorithm with application in gene selection and cancer classification.* doi:10.1016/j.compbiomed.2018.10.034

Azadifar, S., Rostami, M., Berahmand, K., Moradi, P., & Oussama, M. (2022). Graph-based relevancy-redundancy gene selection method for cancer diagnosis. *Computers in Biology and Medicine*, *147*(Aug), 105766. doi:10.1016/j.compbiomed.2022.105766 PMID:35779479

Biswas, N., & Chakrabarti, S. (2020). Artificial intelligence (AI)-based systems biology approaches in multi-omics data analysis of cancer. *Frontiers in Oncology*, *10*(Oct), 588221. Advance online publication. doi:10.3389/fonc.2020.588221 PMID:33154949

Isik, Z., & Ercan, M. E. (2017, October). Integration of RNA-Seq and RPPA data for survival time prediction in cancer patients. *Computers in Biology and Medicine*, *89*, 397–404. doi:10.1016/j.compbiomed.2017.08.028 PMID:28869900

Karimi, M. R., Karimi, A. H., Abolmaali, S., Sadeghi, M., & Schmitz, U. (2020, June). Prospects and challenges of cancer systems medicine: From genes to disease networks. *Briefings Bioinf., 23*(1).

Kim, T. R., Jeong, H.-H., & Sohn, K.-A. (2019, July). Topological integration of RPPA proteomic data with multi-omics data for survival prediction in breast cancer via pathway activity inference. *BMC Medical Genomics, 12*(S5, no. S5), 1–14. doi:10.1186/s12920-019-0511-x PMID:31296204

Libbrecht, M. W., & Noble, W. S. (2015). Machine learning applications in genetics and genomics. *Nature Reviews. Genetics, 16*(6), 321–332. doi:10.1038/nrg3920 PMID:25948244

Mann, M., Kumar, C., Zeng, W.-F., & Strauss, M. T. (2021, August). Artificial intelligence for proteomics and biomarker discovery. *Cell Systems, 12*(8), 759–770. doi:10.1016/j.cels.2021.06.006 PMID:34411543

Masoudi-Sobhanzadeh, Y., Motieghader, H., Omidi, Y., & Masoudi-Nejad, A. (2021, February). A machine learning method based on the genetic and world competitive contests algorithms for selecting genes or features in biological applications. *Scientific Reports, 11*(1), 1–19. doi:10.1038/s41598-021-82796-y PMID:33558580

Chapter 8
Developing Peacemaking Soft Skills of Managers as a Method of Preventing Professional Burnout and Restoring Work-Life Balance:
A Ukrainian Case Study

Liudmyla Ilich
https://orcid.org/0000-0002-8594-1824
Borys Grinchenko Kyiv Metropolitan University, Ukraine

Olena Akilina
https://orcid.org/0000-0001-9968-4921
Borys Grinchenko Kyiv Metropolitan University, Ukraine

ABSTRACT

The purpose of this study is to investigate the impact of military threats on the professional burnout of employees in the organizations that have survived the COVID-19 pandemic and currently are in conditions of uncertainty and rapid digitalization, as well as to make recommendations for developing managers' skills to prevent burnout. The study uses a set of methods of scientific knowledge used in the humanities and social sciences, in particular the method of analysis, the method of synthesis, the method of deduction, the survey diagnostic method, the method of experimental research, which includes the development and testing of e-learning course modules and the method of generalization. All participants were surveyed using Google Forms, and students were tested in the Moodle system. Prior to the full-scale invasion of Ukraine, the problem of professional burnout among employees in local organizations was rather common, but it intensified during the quarantine restrictions caused by the COVID-19 pandemic.

DOI: 10.4018/979-8-3693-1886-7.ch008

METHODS

Research Model/Design (Qualitative, Quantitative, or Mixed Methods)

The study uses a set of methods of scientific knowledge used in the humanities and social sciences, in particular:

- the method of analysis, which allowed to identify the main structural components of the research object and their interrelationships;
- the method of synthesis, which made possible to shape a general picture of the research object and its functioning;
- the method of deduction, which enabled to test hypotheses about the research object;
- the survey diagnostics method, which helped obtain data on the attitude of the research participants to a certain phenomenon;
- the method of experimental research, which included the development and testing of e-learning course content modules, during which data on their effectiveness were collected. These data were obtained using various methods, such as surveys, testing, and tracking student performances;
- the method of generalization, which assisted in shaping general conclusions of the study.

The survey of all participants was conducted using Google Forms, which enabled to automate the data processing. Students were tested in the Moodle system. These tools greatly accelerated the processing of the results and emphasize the feasibility of their application.

Results

This research originates from student microstudies conducted under the guidance of O. Akilina within the framework of the Center for Management Basics at Borys Grinchenko Kyiv Metropolitan University in 2019-2020. These studies were conducted in Kyiv and aimed at identifying the problem of work-life balance among employees of local organizations. This problem was identified in general "...12% of respondents said that work impacts negatively their family relationships, 31.3% clained they lacked time to raise their children, and 24.1% of respondents emphasized that they felt that work creates a gap between them and their families..." (Borys Grinchenko Kyiv Metropolitan University, 2020).

Based on the results of this study, we assumed that the problem of professional burnout should be quite common and has grounds for aggravation within the transition to a remote work format during the COVID-19 quarantine restrictions. Therefore, at the end of 2020, a study was launched to identify the problem of professional burnout among employees of local organizations, which lasted until the beginning of 2022 (Borys Grinchenko Kyiv Metropolitan University, 2022). Our hypothesis was confirmed by the results of this study. According to them, it was clear that the quarantine caused by the COVID-19 pandemic resulted in emergence of additional stress factors that exacerbated the professional burnout of individual employees. In our opinion, it was the inability of local organizations to restructure their work processes properly during the quarantine and make the necessary changes in organizational culture that provoked the increase in employees' burnout. Some respondents confirmed our findings, indicating that they did not have a proper workflow organization and were not provided with adequate technical and psychological support. As a result, about 60% of employees showed symptoms of professional burnout. The most common symptoms were emotional and physical exhaustion, increased irritability, and decreased performance.

After the start of the full-scale invasion of Ukraine, this research was suspended but was renewed in September 2022, when the city life conditions stabilized to some extent. Under such specific conditions a whole new study was launched. We created a new questionnaire and conducted a new survey that covered both the period of quarantine restrictions and the period of large-scale war outbreak. However, we believe that some results of the previous surveys can be used to compare with the results of the new survey, assuming that most of the employees have already returned from evacuation to the city. This assumption is based on the fact that 40.2% of the newly surveyed respondents have been working at their jobs for more than 6 years, and only 18.8% have been working for less than a year. The rest of the respondents have been working from 1 to 6 years, which is 41.1% of their total number.

A total of 112 people aged 21-60 took part in the survey, of whom 38.8% were aged 21-30, and 28.6% were aged 31-40. Due to the mobilization, we were unable to achieve gender balance, so the number of women surveyed is 77.7%. Nevertheless, we have balanced representation of all categories of personnel (managers, professionals, specialists and workers), except for a slightly smaller share of technical executives. The survey also covered employees of all major sectors of the city economy, but the largest share is occupied by the sectors of finance, insurance, wholesale and retail trade, vehicle repair, information and telecommunication. The survey also covers both state-owned and privately owned enterprises in a balanced manner.

In wartime, 70.5% of our respondents work remotely. From the answers of respondents who had experience of remote work in the pre-war period, it is seen that most of the problems they faced during remote work were related to combining personal/family responsibilities with workload (42%), managing time (33.9%), maintaining proper communication with the team (24.1%), maintaining productivity (23.2%), as well as managing technology/communication tools (18.8%) and excessive control by the administration (12.5%). This is in line with the results of our previous survey.

During wartime, these factors underwent partial structural changes. For instance, previous experience of remote work has taught a certain part of employees to find a balance between work and family. Only 32.1% of respondents mentioned the problem of its absence (9.9 percentage points less than in the comparative period). But, in our opinion, the main reason for these changes was the reassessment of values that almost every Ukrainian experienced with the beginning of the active phase of the war.

According to the survey, the problem of time management in the war has worsened by only 0.9 percentage points. This may seem insignificant, but in our opinion, the situation could have deteriorated significantly. Nevertheless, the high level of education of Ukrainian workers, which in social studies is called "over-education" and seen as a certain disadvantage, now makes them capable of learning and acquiring new skills quickly. During the war, this has become especially valuable, as workers have to adapt quickly to new realities. However, air raids and blackouts with limited internet access made time management difficult. Employees were forced to interrupt their work constantly to keep themselves and their loved ones safe. In addition, they did not always have access to necessary resources and tools.

According to our study, during the war in Kyiv, the structure of employment in terms of working hours has changed (Fig. 1).

DEVELOPING PEACEMAKING SOFT SKILLS OF MANAGERS AS A METHOD OF PREVENTING PROFESSIONAL BURNOUT AND RESTORING WORK-LIFE BALANCE: A UKRAINIAN CASE STUDY

The World Health Organization (WHO) defines burnout as "a syndrome conceptualized as resulting from chronic workplace stress that has not been successfully managed" (World Health Organization, 2019). It is also included in the 11th Revision of the International Classification of Diseases (ICD-11) by the WHO. However, burnout is not classified only as a disease or health condition, but also defined as a professional phenomenon characterized by three dimensions:

- "feelings of energy depletion or exhaustion;
- increased mental distance from one's job, or feelings of negativism or cynicism related to one's job;
- reduced professional efficiency" (World Health Organization, 2019).

Burnout leads to a decrease in employees' well-being, loss of working time and productivity, and, as a result, high costs for both employers and society as a whole. Emotional exhaustion is the main component of professional burnout. It is a specific stress-related reaction to the demands made by an organization on its staff, its management and working conditions. In recent years, there has been an increased interest in researching the impact of emotional demands on burnout, especially on emotional exhaustion.

The problems of burnout and emotional exhaustion have been intensified due to the increase in the share of remote work during the COVID-19 pandemic. It was revealed that workers who were socially isolated and lacked support were more likely to be exhausted and suffer from emotional fatigue. In general, it is digitalization that can have a negative impact on the psycho-emotional state of people due to information overload, the spread of false information, the development of digital addiction, social isolation increase, and the growth of cybercrime.

The relevance of the burnout problem for Ukraine within war context is extremely high. The war has caused uncertainty about the future for all Ukrainians, regardless of their place of residence. In its turn, this creates anxiety, fear, apathy and other negative emotions that can lead to burnout. Wartime conditions require considerable emotional cost from people, which resulted in the situation of constant experience stress, anxiety, anger, grief, and other negative emotions. The war has led to significant changes in the operation of many businesses and organizations, that trigger additional stressors such as work overload, changes in working conditions, income instability, etc.

The world has already gained considerable experience in overcoming employee's burnout in military conflict zones. However, this experience does not fully reflect current realities, in particular

- post-COVID society, characterized by increased level of anxiety and depression;
- rapid digitalization, which can lead to additional stress and emotional fatigue;
- the growing risks of global military conflict, including the threat of nuclear conflict, that may result in anxiety, depression and other psycho-emotional disorders.

The Ukrainian experience of getting over burnout in wartime can be useful for the world. It should demonstrate that burnout can be overcome even in extremely difficult circumstances. Also, the Ukrainian experience can provide positive practices for preventing and addressing burnout, which should be directed not only at society as a whole, but also at the local enterprises and organizations.

LITERATURE REVIEW

In scientific circles, Freudenberger (1974) is considered to be the first to mention burnout. This phenomenon was described in more depth and detail by Maslach (1976). She thoroughly described burnout in connection with work in the service sector (Maslach, Jackson, & Leiter, 1997; Maslach, 1982). Maslach, considered burnout as a long-term reaction to chronic emotional and interpersonal stressors at work, which is determined by three dimensions: exhaustion, cynicism and inefficiency (Maslach, Schaufeli, & Leiter, 2001).

In the late 1980s, researchers recognized that burnout could be observed among all categories of employees, as well as among entrepreneurs. In early 2000Schaufeli, Leiter and Maslach(2009) extended the understanding of burnout to various professions. Lubbadeh (2020) argues that the professional burnout syndrome is not limited to social service professions, but extends to other professions, such as bankers and managers. His research traces the evolution of professional burnout, examines the factors and consequences of professional burnout, as well as intervention strategies to reduce or overcome it.

Demerouti, Bakker, Nachreiner, & Schaufeli(2001) proposed the Job Demands-Resources Model (JD-R) in relation to professional burnout and exhaustion. This model was further improved (Bakker, Demerouti, &Euwema, 2005). Researchers have argued that several job resources play a role in buffering the impact on exhaustion of several job demands. Four job demands (e.g., work overload, emotional demands) and 4 job resources (e.g., autonomy, performance feedback) were used to test the central hypothesis that the interaction between (high) demands and (low) resources creates the highest outcome. However, this hypothesis was rejected.

Balancing the emotional demands of work with employees' well-being is a challenge faced by all professions, but for some time research has been inconclusive about the adverse effect of emotional work demands on exhaustion. To address this gap, Hsieh (2014) revised this link and explored the potential additive and interactive effects of job resources, like job control, social support, and rewards.As a result, it was found that when employees are at risk of burnout, the provision of these job resources can ease the workload and reduce work stress. The idea that a high level of job support and fairness in the workplace protects against emotional exhaustion, while high demands, low job control, high workload, low rewards, and job insecurity increase the risk of developing exhaustion is pursued in the research of Aronsson et al. (2017).This approach, with a wide range of factors influencing work, analyzed in relation to specific dimensions of burnout, has expanded the scientific vision of this phenomenon.

Boyas andWind (2009) considered the linkage between employment-based social capital, job stress, and exhaustion among employees of public child welfare agencies. The modeling used in the study indicates that social capital in the form of communication, management support, organizational commitment and trust is significantly related to job stress. But emotional exhaustion is significantly related to age, influence, supervisor support, organizational appealing, and job stress.

Among the large-scale studies of burnout, the results of the study "Burnout in the workplace: A review of data and policy responses in the EU" (Eurofound, 2018). This report examines the extent of workers' exhaustion in the EU based on national surveys. It emphasizes that "over the past 10 years, only a small number of countries have been able to report large cross-sectoral representative studies and data focusing specifically on burnout. These countries include Austria, Belgium, the Czech Republic, Finland, Germany, Estonia, Italy, the Netherlands, Portugal, and the United Kingdom. In other countries, research on burnout has either focused on sectoral and occupational (and therefore often small-scale) studies, or the main cross-sectoral data and research has not directly addressed burnout but has looked at closely related topic areas such as work stress, work intensity and work-related exhaustion" (Eurofound, 2018). The study of professional burnout determinants indicates psychosocial risks. Considerable attention is also paid to high job demands, such as long working hours, intensive work, and busy work schedules. In addition, the authors refer to occupation-specific risks, as well as risks associated with ethical conflicts, value conflicts, role conflicts, unfairness at work, and low rewards. This introduces a social component of burnout that now requires rethinking. In this study, we also drew attention to the authors' identification of another determinant of burnout - the role of management and leadership in terms of human relations.

It is advisable to pay attention to the study of Schaufeli (2018). It provides information that the levels of burnout differ systematically between European countries. «Countries with the highest burnout levels are mainly found in eastern (Poland) and southeastern Europe (Albania, Turkey, and the countries that constituted former Yugoslavia; Slovenia, Croatia, Serbia, Montenegro and Macedonia). Countries with the lowest burnout levels are found in western and northern Europe (the Netherlands, Belgium, Denmark, Norway, Sweden, Finland, and Latvia). The relationship of burnout with economic performance is curvilinear; for countries with lower economic performance the relationship with burnout is stronger than for countries with higher performance…in poorer governed countries with a weak democracy, more corruption, gender inequality, and little integrity the workforce is more burned-out than in better governed countries…» (Schaufeli, 2018).

During the COVID-19 pandemic, researchers revealed that employees who were socially isolated and lacked support experienced symptoms of professional burnout and emotional exhaustion. That is, the pandemic period has exacerbated the problem considered in our study. The study by Sirakaya and Yildirimer (2023) demonstrates that burnout and emotional stress are associated with difficulties in efficient performing professional duties and work commitments, including the particular problem of remote work. Many studies have examined how organizational support systems, adaptation to remote work, and its efficient planning reduce psychological burnout and occupational stress levels, thus improving employees' well-being, including the ones by de Vries, Tummers and Bekkers(2019), Dionisi et al. (2021), Allgood, Jensenand Stritch (2022), Costin, Roman and Balica (2023) and others.

Despite the fact that the problem of remote work was considered in the 1980s, in particular by Kelly (1985), Cross andRaizman (1986), Collins (1986), Hamilton (1987), there were not enough efficient practices for its implementation at the beginning of the pandemic. It should be emphasized that the transition to remote work requires significant adaptations, including the development of new work procedures, the introduction of new management technologies, etc. In their absence, remote workers during the COVID-19 pandemic could experience a loss of control over their work, increased cognitive stress from navigating and implementing the necessary changes, and increased social isolation. Therefore, it is now crucial to expand our awareness of the phenomena that are key for the psychological well-being of employees, including the problem of professional burnout.

The pandemic has highlighted and aggravated another significant factor in the problems of burnout and emotional exhaustion of employees - uncertainty. As noted in «The 2021/2022 Human Development Report: Uncertain times, unsettled lives Shaping our future in a transforming world» «the Covid-19 pandemic and the war in Ukraine are devastating manifestations of today's uncertainty complex. Each exposes limits of – and cracks in – current global governance... The numbers of people reporting negative affect – stress, sadness, anger or worry and experiencing physical pain – have been on the rise for the past decade and have hit a record high ...a trend of increased stress is discernible across the world and across socioeconomic groups» (UNDP, 2022). Uncertainty is expected to undermine people's mental well-being. The Report also mentions the problem of post-traumatic stress disorders, which are common in military conflict zones not only among combatants but also among the civilian population.

The Human Development Report 2023 (UNDP, 2023)aims to comprehend better this challenging reality and explore how to strengthen collective actions. It opens a trilogy of reports framed by three levels of the uncertainty complex. However, already in the 2021/2022 Report, priority areas for investment in innovation, including adaptive peacemaking, social innovation, countering disinformation, etc. were identified to address the above challenges. Adaptive peacemaking involves the ability of society to adapt to changes quickly and efficiently. Peace education practices can help to achieve this by developing people's ability to think critically, analyze information and make decisions in the face of uncertainty. We believe that peace education practices are closely related to all of the above areas, so they need to be actively implemented both globally and locally as an efficient tool for addressing uncertainty to overcome burnout.

Thus, we have enough examples of scientific research on burnout. However, in the current realities of the military conflict in Ukraine, the practices of overcoming burnout at the local level remain insufficiently researched. The local level is more important than the societal level in terms of preventing and overcoming burnout for several reasons. First, at the local level, organizations can better comprehend the needs of their employees and develop measures that will be more effective. Secondly, the local level can be more innovative in its approaches to preventing and addressing burnout. Organizations at the local level have the opportunity to experiment with new ideas and approaches that may be more efficient than traditional approaches. In our opinion, it is necessary to start with the transformation of the organization management on the basis of peace education, which is an important prerequisite for preventing and overcoming employees' burnout. It will help managers develop the skills and values necessary to create a supportive work environment that ensures a healthy work-life balance and support for employees suffering from burnout.

The implementation of these changes should be based on transformational leadership. In her previous studies, O. Akilina (Akilina, Panchenko, &Horozhankina, 2023) examined this process of changes taking an educational institution as an example, but the algorithm applied there can be transferred to a regular organization. A transformational leader has several key tasks to perform: define their own vision of the value and development of peaceful approaches in managing the organization; restructure the organization and rethink the roles of all its employees to make them feel appreciated and involved; focus on shaping social and emotional skills in managers and subordinates; develop partnerships with other organizations and individuals.

Transformational leadership has received considerable attention in modern research. In particular, studies by Wadhawan, Gupta, Kaur andBhardwaj (2022), Hui et al. (2022) have established a significant relationship between transformational leadership and its impact on employees' productivity during the COVID-19 era. The findings of the study by George andVeetil (2023) show that transformational leadership and work-life balance have a positive and significant impact on employees' job satisfaction.

Raza and Qamar (2023) investigated the ways transformational leadership can be used to empower employees, increase their motivation and job satisfaction, and prevent emotional exhaustion.

The readiness of professionals to changes is a prerequisite for their successful implementation in an organization. The study by Stoffers and Mordant-Dols (2015) focuses on the impact of transformational leadership style on the readiness of professionals to changes. It gives us the opportunity to move on to the issue of today's challenges that require managers to update their skills constantly to implement new intellectual tools and efficient practices in their daily management activities.

The researchers Puga Villarreal and Martínez Cerna (2008) have made a theoretical discussion based on the grounded research about the skills that, given the current realities, leaders and managers anywhere in the world should develop, regardless of the specific environment in which they perform their duties. Researchers relate them to mental abilities and personal skills ("soft skills"), which are becoming increasingly popular in managerial training. Researchers state that developing managerial skills helps organizations perform better.

The modern world is evolving rapidly, becoming more dynamic and uncertain. Earlier the success of a manager was determined by the extent to which he or she understood the economic, legal, and technical aspects of the area he or she managed, but nowadays it is also important to have socio-emotional skills, in particular, empathy, emotional intelligence, and resilience. Lemos and Brunstein (2023) contributed to the study of the use of reflection in the work environment, highlighting its use for the development of interpersonal skills. Their study presents procedures for promoting critical reflection using critical incidents, dialogues, and reflective diaries, which can be useful for researchers, managers, consultants, and corporate educators.

Researchers (Barrutia Barreto, Aguilar Ibarra, & Barrutia Barreto, 2024) investigated how managers' communication skills affect the resilience of companies after the pandemic. They found that skills such as leadership, innovation, decision-making, and empathy make companies more resilient. Henderikx and Stoffers (2023) also emphasize the importance of soft skills. They argue (Henderikx, & Stoffers, 2022) that digital transformation requires rethinking of leadership requirements. Digital transformation is disrupting organizations and creating new ways of working. Artificial intelligence can perform routine management tasks, freeing up time for managers to focus on communication skills, coaching, motivation, and empowerment of employees. Communication skills (empathy, humility, honesty, compassion) are becoming increasingly important.

This means that managers who is able to communicate well and understand people's emotions can help their companies survive and thrive even in difficult times. This research is specifically focused on the post-COVID situation and the extremely difficult wartime circumstances in Ukraine, when there is an urgent need to find ways to overcome the problem of professional burnout of employees in organizations by changing traditional management concepts.

During the Russian-Ukrainian war, it has been observed the worsening of team communications (by 6.3 percentage points), maintaining productivity (by 3.6 percentage points), and excessive administrative control (by 0.9 percentage points) in organizations. In open-ended questions, respondents explained these trends by the following factors: an increase in the number of work interruptions due to air raids and

Figure 1. Actual duration of working hours

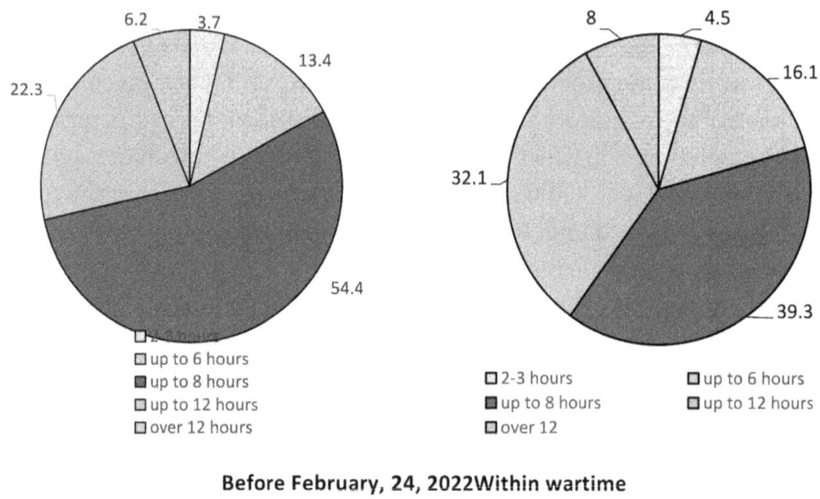

other war-related factors; a decrease in the level of trust between employees due to stress and anxiety caused by the war; and an increase in the workload of employees (longer working hours) in wartime. Increased administrative control may be related to such factors as the need to ensure the security of employees and information, and decrease in employees' motivation, which require to pay more attention to discipline and control by the organization, but is an indirect sign of inefficient and inflexible management of organizations.

The number of people working more than 12 hours increased by 2.6 percentage points, and the number of people working up to 12 hours increased by 9.8 percentage points. At the same time, the number of people working 8 hours a day decreased by 16.1 percentage points. Also, in a separate question, 40.2% of respondents reported an increase in their work responsibilities during wartime. These changes can be explained by the following factors: an increase in the standard working hours for certain professions and employees, in particular, repair and maintenance workers; an increase in the number of jobs requiring long hours, for example, in the healthcare sector; a decrease in labor productivity due to stress and anxiety caused by the war; and violations of labor legislation by some unscrupulous employers.

Meanwhile, the number of part-time workers increased by only 3.6 percentage points. This may be due to the fact that such workers are often students or service workers who cannot work full time due to the lack of demand for their services. Indirectly, this also demonstrates that the Kyiv labor market is still able to maintain its potential and does not have a high level of hidden unemployment.

Thus, we can state that the number of employees working overtime in Kyiv has increased, while the number of those satisfied and dissatisfied with the ratio of wages and working hours is almost evenly distributed (50.9% vs 49.1%). This indicates that there are employees in the city who are willing to work overtime regardless of material motivation. Here again, a reassessment of values is observed: many people have begun to appreciate such things as freedom, independence, and unity more. For them, work for the sake of defeat the Russian aggressor has become more important than material motivation.

The factors of professional burnout syndrome can be divided into two types: organizational and personal. It was organizational factors that we investigated as the root cause. They mainly depend on the organization's workflow and attitude towards employees. As noted above, the inability of organizations to restructure properly their work processes and make the necessary changes in organizational culture in line with changes in the environment of these organizations provokes an increase in the professional burnout level of their employees. That is why our new survey included relevant questions:

1. "Has your company provided employees who worked remotely before or after February 24, 2022 with proper organization of the workflow, its technical support, tasking, time tracking and other procedural issues?" (see Figure 2)

It should be added here that only 58.9% of respondents indicated that their organizations adopted a Regulation on remote work.

2. "Did your company provide its employees with the necessary moral and psychological support, material support (including recovery cost compensation of destroyed housing), assistance in relocating employees and their families, and other types of socially responsible measures related to supporting employees in wartime?" (see Figure 3)

In open-ended questions, employees indicated their expectations for support, including:

– clear task setting;
– training in remote work tools;
– technical support when changing the work format;
– physical security;
– organization of employees and their families relocation;
– payment for mobile Internet;
– assistance in medical treatment;

Figure 2. Organizational support of employees

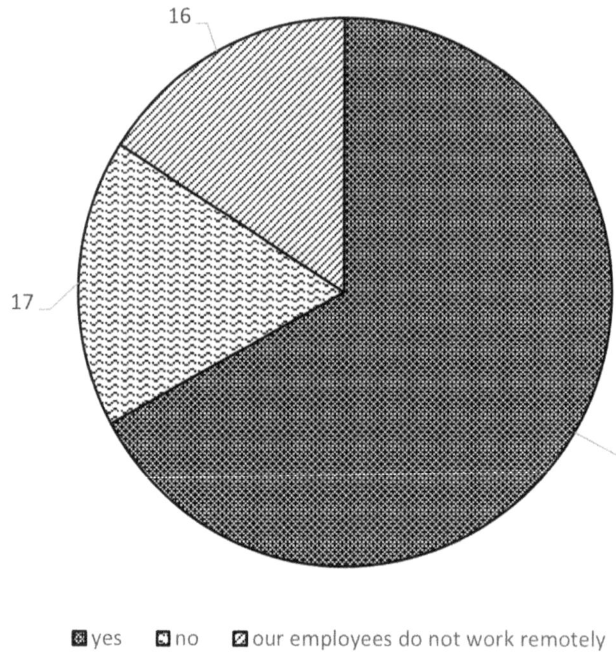

– providing an algorithm of actions in critical situations;
– maintaining the level of salary;
– providing moral and psychological support.

Moreover, the needs for material and moral and psychological support are mentioned by respondents most frequently. Thus, due to the unfavorable organizational factors identified, a significant number of employees have experienced symptoms of professional burnout (see Table 1).

Only 23% of respondents said they did not notice any symptoms. It should also be noted that after the full-scale invasion, there was an increase in the percentage of respondents who experienced all the symptoms. The most significant increases were in the symptoms of emotional and physical exhaustion (by 19.5 percentage points), the emergence and prevalence of negative, pessimistic thoughts (by 16 percentage points), and decline in working capacity (by 9.9 percentage points). The percentage of people who had complicated relationships with their nearest and dearest has not changed, and these are the same people who had these problems before the full-scale invasion. In general, the vast majority of respondents (58.9%) felt worse at work

Figure 3. Availability of socially responsible measures related to support of employees

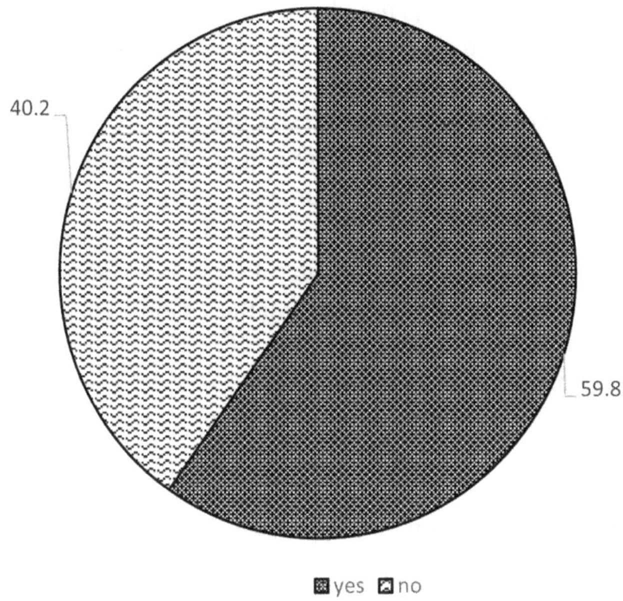

Table 1. Burnout of employees in organizations, Kyiv

Symptoms of Burnout:	A Number of Employees Who Experienced Burnout, %		Deviation in Percentage Points
	Before February 24, 2022	During Full-Scale Military Activities	
Emotional and physical exhaustion	37,5	57	+19,5
Decline in working capacity	25	34,8	+9,9
Existence and prevalence of negative and pessimistic thoughts	17	33	+16
Increased irritability	22,3	28,6	+6,3
Lack of working motivation	21,4	24,1	+2,7
Loss of sense of work	10,7	15,2	+5.5
Complications in relations with families, friends and mates	14,3	14,3	0
Increase in a number of mistakes	7,1	9,8	+2,7

during the war. This is a serious problem that can have negative consequences for labor productivity, employees' health and well-being.

This survey ended with an open-ended question: "What would you like to change about your work in wartime?". The vast majority had one answer, although it was not directly related to the question: "a desire to defeat the enemy and establish a victorious peace". This answer demonstrates that employees in wartime value the victory over the enemy most of all. Despite their own emotional state, Ukrainians are eager to work overtime, sacrifice their personal time and resources for the sake of the common cause.

The rest of answers can be divided into two groups. The first group includes answers related to the expected support from the organization, similar to the above mentioned. Employees want the organization to provide them with safe working conditions; provide them with the necessary material and moral support; and help them adapt to new working conditions. The second group includes answers related to the desire to reduce bureaucracy, the amount of reporting, and excessive administrative control. These responses indicate that employees within wartime want to have less control over their own work (a factor highlighted in most global studies, but unfortunately ignored by Ukrainian management), more freedom and autonomy in their work.

Thus, the results of the study showed that managers of Kyiv organizations lack such skills to address the problem of emotional burnout of their subordinates as:

1. Ability to organize an effective workflow. Managers must be able to create a work environment that promotes employees' productivity and well-being. This includes clearly defining tasks, providing the necessary support and resources, and creating a work-life balance.
2. Ability to identify and respond to burnout risk factors. Managers should be able to recognize factors that can lead to burnout, such as excessive stress, work-life imbalance, and lack of support from the organization. They should be prepared to take actions to address these issues.
3. Ability to provide support and motivation to employees. Managers must be able to create a positive work environment in which employees feel valued and supported. They must be willing to provide moral and material support, as well as help employees develop their skills and careers.

DISCUSSION

International Labor Organization developed a number of materials and recommendations to help organizations ensure the efficient remote work of their staff at the beginning of the COVID-19 pandemic, the. The most useful ones for this research have been identified the following: An employers' guide on managing your workplace during COVID-19 (Tang, 2020) and An Employers' Guide on working from home in response to the outbreak of COVID-19 (ILO, 2020) However, in certain areas of economic activity in Ukraine, in particular in public sector, managers demonstrate little awareness of these issues. This situation is quite typical for countries with poor level of governance, corruption, and low integrity of public and municipal sector officials, which is in line with the findings of the Eurofound (2018) study previously discussed.

After the end of the pandemic-related quarantine, Ukrainian organizations had the opportunity to create a new operating model that would meet the needs of employees in the conditions of uncertainty. However, the full-scale invasion of Russia, accompanied by the bombing of civilian targets and the destruction of utility and energy infrastructure, led to blackouts, and destroyed the traditional employment for many workers in Kyiv. The losses caused by military situation added to the set of the problems caused by the digitalization of workplaces during the pandemic.

The issues of work-life balance and professional burnout in scientific sources are studied mainly from the psychological viewpoint or time management. Accordingly, the recommendations given in them are of the same kind. However, we believe that the core of these problems in the organizations surveyed lies in the unwillingness of employers to make the necessary changes in the organization of work and corporate culture, as well as in numerous violations of labor legislation in the social and labor sphere these days. According to the recommendations of the International Labor Organization (ILO), employers should monitor recommendations provided by national and local authorities, including those related to organization of work; draw up business continuity plans to support employees and their families; introduce flexible work schedules; practice flexible meetings and remote service delivery; change organizational culture, etc.

On supporting fully the idea of the ILO, the following aspects should be taken into account when measuring the productivity of remote workers' labor:

- setting clear goals and deadlines for their achievement and bringing them to employees' attention;
- analysis of tasks and control over the timeline of their implementation;
- replacing the indicator of "time costs" with the indicator of "quantity and quality of tasks completed";
- monitoring the results achievement.

This survey has also confirmed the thesis about numerous violations of labor legislation. Undoubtedly, the above-mentioned violations lead to stress, deterioration of employees' health and generally jeopardize their social security. Most importantly, they cannot have a long-term effect in an organization concerning labor productivity growth. Employees who are provided with 'work-life balance' conditions are more efficient and motivated for the organization, and that is why they should be taken care of. There's no need to talk about human-centeredness here, but just about reasonable selfishness which means one cares and ensures emotional health for organizational efficiency.

We agree with the opinion of the Director of Deloitte Human Capital Advisory Services in Ukraine (Deloitte, 2020),that the current challenges provide "a unique opportunity for companies that can overcome their traditional attitude to people and technology as separate components and combine their capabilities to create synergy...". Managers need to understand "what can happen if they do not offer a workable model of human-technology interaction and do not transform their companies into really social enterprises."

On developing the ideas of The Human Development Report 2023 (UNDP, 2023), the issue of adaptive peacebuilding is of actual importnace. We believe that peace education practices are closely related to all of the above issues, so they need to be actively implemented as an efficient tool to address uncertainty and overcome employees' burnout. According to the authors of the study, the introduction of peace education in organizations should be preceded by certain organizational transformations. In particular, O. Akilina was involved in the development of an indicative algorithm for their implementation (Akilina, Panchenko, &Horozhankina, 2023). We believe that these transformations should start from changes in the organization management system, including the most important ones like the introduction of restorative communication techniques into the organizational communication system; the use of management styles that are relevant to the values of peace education; transformational leadership, which is defined as the ability of a leader to impact the development of peacebuilding skills of his or her subordinates.

Peace education enables managers to develop the skills necessary for efficient management in modern wartime conditions, the lack of which was identified in this study. In order to train qualified managers who are eager to overcome the current challenges of the growing level of staff's burnout in organizations, the authors of this study, within the framework of the EU project (Erasmus+ "Peace education for consolidated and human-centered Europe" (PeaECH)), created content modules that are part of the course "Peace Education in Management and Business", which is taught at the second master's level for managers (including educational managers) and civil servants.

The information basis for the preparation of these training modules was obtained by the authors of the study during an internship at the Higher School of Information Systems Management (ISMA, Riga, Latvia) as part of the PeaECH project, and at

Tallinn University of Technology (TalTech, Estonia) as part of another project. We took into account scientific research relevant to peace education in the Western Balkans. As a result of the study, we have identified the following elements of peace education practices that are appropriate for implementation in Ukraine:

– emphasis on socio-emotional and transformational skills;
– equipping student managers with techniques for recognizing, preventing and resolving destructive violent conflicts;
– special attention to the metacognitive capabilities of students;
– introduction of efficient interactive forms of learning;
– various forms of informal and formal training programs, including mediation;
– development of peacemaking skills training at different educational levels.

Content modules created by the authors of the study: "Development of Managerial Emotional Intelligence" and "Basic Mediation Skills" also take into account the gaps in domestic management identified during the survey of local organizations' employees.

In particular, the content module "Development of Manager's Emotional Intelligence" examines emotional leadership in business; components of emotional intelligence, assessment of emotional intelligence and assessment of managerial potential. Particular attention is paid to the emotional health of the manager and the emotional hygiene of the team. Besides, techniques for developing the manager's emotional intelligence are presented. A special role is given to the issues of emotional burnout and techniques for overcoming stressful situations.

The content module on mediation examines its essence and functions, the stages of the mediation procedure, and the types of mediation depending on the characteristics and stages of conflict development. Special attention is paid to dealing with the interests of the parties to the conflict, finding the root of the conflict and communication tools in addressing the interests.

When creating this training content, we relied on the idea that a manager with a high level of EI should be more sensitive to the needs of their employees and create a work environment promoting their well-being. A manager who can efficiently use mediation assists their employees in resolving conflicts peacefully, which reduces stress and anxiety. Overall, these modules should help managers develop the skills and knowledge necessary to create a safer, healthier and more productive work environment. This, in turn, enables to reduce employees' burnout level in their organizations. These content modules were tested in the educational process of Borys Grinchenko Kyiv Metropolitan University in the first semester of the 2023-2024 academic year and received a positive assessment from students, most of whom have already been working in management positions in their organizations. The students of the modules note that the development of emotional skills is extremely important because it helps to avoid prejudice against colleagues; promotes greater resilience to external and internal challenges; improves communication efficiency and creates trusting relationships in the team. More than half of the students (68%) believe that an organization has high level of employees' engagement if its managers are able to demonstrate empathy.

Specific organizational solutions are beyond the scope of this study, but if an organization has trained managers, the conceptual approach to overcoming employee's burnout should start at the strategic level, which includes:

1. Investing in programs to overcome burnout:
   - discussing with top management the opportunity and necessity of investing resources in mental health support programs;
   - define the expected results of such programs, e.g., increased productivity, reduced staff turnover, improved morale;
   - linking programs to the organization's values and strategic directions.
2. Readiness for systematic work:
   - clear comprehension of the organization's values by all employees;
   - motivation and readiness of HR services to implement programs to prevent burnout, create self-help groups, programs to reduce stress and increase psychological recovery;
   - high level of trust between management and staff;
   - availability of trained managers who are ready to implement changes.

It is the process of discussion and answers to these questions that will help to determine whether the organization is ready to address the problem of burnout and identify specific tactical actions systematically, including: training for HR managers (first aid; development of active listening skills, cognitive empathy, and quality presence) and educational activities (informing employees about chronic stress, coping strategies, ways to overcome stress, breathing programs, body and art therape practices, etc.)

However, the war significantly complicates these organizational decisions for many of the organizations we studied. Limited resources make it problematic to introduce flexible work schedules, shorten working hours, or fund assistance programs. At present, since the beginning of the war, during martial law Ukraine has allowed for an increase in normal working hours to 60 hours per week for employees of certain professions. The second year of active hostilities has depleted the personnel reserve, making it difficult to allocate people for additional tasks.

Unfortunately, some managers formed by the Soviet management system do not realize the seriousness of the burnout problem or do not believe in the efficiency of programs to overcome it. In wartime, the focus of management can also be shifted to other problems, which also leads to underestimation of burnout.

CONCLUSION

Prior to the full-scale invasion of Ukraine, the problem of professional burnout among employees of local organizations was quite common, having become even more acute during the quarantine restrictions caused by the COVID-19 pandemic. The authors of the study revealed that over the wartime period, there have been changes in employees' working hours, as well as in their needs and expectations from the organization. Unfavorable organizational factors have led to an increase in the number of employees experiencing symptoms of professional burnout. The greatest increase is observed in the manifestation of emotional and physical exhaustion symptoms (by 19.5 percentage points), the emergence and prevalence of negative, pessimistic thoughts (by 16 percentage points), and decreased working capacity (by 9.9 percentage points).

Managers of enterprises and organizations in Kyiv lack the skills necessary to address the problem of their subordinates' emotional burnout. Based on the respondents' answers as for the most common problems they encountered while working remotely, one may conclude that managers did not demonstrate the following skills:

1. ***Stress management***. Wartime is a period of increased stress for everyone, including employees. That is why managers need to be able to recognize the signs of employees stress and take preventive measures to avoid emotional burnout.
2. ***Emotional intelligence***. Managers with a high EQ level are always more flexible, versatile, purposeful and efficient, so it is advisable to develop their emotional skills, including the ability to comprehend and interpret their own and other people's emotions, handle them and create favorable atmosphere in the team.
3. ***Team building*** enables to increase the quality and labor productivity, promotes job satisfaction, improves decision-making and communication within the organization, and maximizes the mental abilities, creativity, and responsibility of each employee. In this regard, managers need to be able to demonstrate creativity aimed at combining efforts to achieve the goals of the enterprise as a whole, uniting employees within a unit (department) in order to increase the efficiency of managing subordinates, improving the efficiency of the unit, as well as middle managers in order to accelerate awareness and improve the psychological climate.

4. ***Communicative skills*** relate to the ability to establish and maintain the necessary contacts with colleagues and partners to build a constructive dialogue and interaction. In this context, managers need to develop the ability to change the extent and range of communication, understand and be understood by communication partners, etc.
5. ***Flexibility*** is manifested in the ability to adapt one's own strategy to challenges occurred, i.e. to make managerial decisions in order to achieve the organization goals. It is important for managers to master their flexibility under new conditions, introduce new forms and methods of work, minimizing bureaucracy.

In the course of the study, it is revealed that even if there are unfavorable organizational factors, employees in war conditions are eager to work overtime, sacrifice their personal time and resources for the sake of the common cause, as most of them have reassessed their values. However, without competent managerial support, their burnout level will increase.

Based on the answers to the questions concerning the provision of employees with proper organization of the labor process, necessary moral, psychological and material support, assistance in relocating them and their families, and other types of socially responsible measures, as well as from their responses to the open questions about employees' expectations as for such support, the list of skills that managers lack can be deepened, in particular:

1. Organizational skills and change management. Managers were unable to organize their work efficiently in the context of war. In our opinion, it was advisable to introduce changes in the organization of the work process, provide employees with the necessary machinery and equipment, develop new procedures and rules, and develop effective procedures and mechanisms to support employees. However, as our survey results demonstrate, the Regulation on Remote Work in Organizations was adopted only in every second organization where the respondents work. This indicates a low readiness of managers for changes and their efficient implementation.
2. Social responsibility. During the war, employees are in need of both material and moral support. Managers found it difficult to arrange the required psychological assistance and find the necessary resources to help employees in case of housing loss or relocation. According to the survey, two-thirds of employees received the necessary psychological support from their companies. This is partly due to the fact that not all managers understood the importance of social responsibility and were able to provide it. However, it is also worth noting that since the beginning of the war, most companies and organizations have faced a lack of financial resources for relevant activities.

3. Leadership skills. It was hard for managers to maintain the morale and motivation of their teams. They did not share their vision of the future (or perhaps were unable to shape it), did not provide support and did not help employees adapt to the new conditions. Excessive control by the administration has also become a problem, but it is more likely due to the incompetence of top managers but not middle managers.
4. Mediation skills. Complicated life circumstances related to the war have increased the frequency of conflicts in teams and manifested a weak willingness of managers to resolve conflict situations. That is why we have come to the conclusion that the development of business mediation skills is of extreme importance. Managers need efficient communication with employees under conditions of uncertainty and stress, and obtain restorative communication skills. Managers should be open and transparent, sensitive enough to the requirements and interests of their subordinates, and provide employees with the opportunity to express their thoughts and feelings.

Based on the results of our research, we have concluded that peace education is an efficient tool for addressing the problems of uncertainty and employees' burnout in wartime. This is because peace education involves the development of such skills as emotional intelligence, emotional leadership, and mediation in managers. These skills can help managers become more resilient to emerging challenges and create safer, healthier and more productive work environment, which in turn can reduce the risk of employees' burnout.

Specific results of the testing of the authors' peace education modules at Borys Grinchenko Kyiv Metropolitan University demonstrate that these modules are fairly efficient in training qualified managers capable of overcoming the current challenges of growing staff's burnout in organizations.

The results of the experience can be useful not only in Ukraine but also abroad. They indicate the ways of overcoming the problem of professional burnout of employees in organizations, based on peace education in a post-covid society, in the context of rapid digitalization and under extremely difficult circumstances of the military situation.

REFERENCES

Akilina, O., Panchenko, A., &Horozhankina, A. (2023). Implementation of peacebuilding education in educational institutions of Ukraine. *Continuing Professional Education: Theory and Practice, 4*(77), 7–17. doi:10.28925/1609-8595.2023.4.1

Allgood, M., Jensen, U. T., & Stritch, J. M. (2022). Work-Family Conflict and Burnout Amid COVID-19: Exploring the Mitigating Effects of Instrumental Leadership and Social Belonging. *Review of Public Personnel Administration, 0*(0). Advance online publication. doi:10.1177/0734371X221101308

Aronsson, G., Theorell, T., Grape, T., Hammarström, A., Hogstedt, C., Marteinsdottir, I., Skoog, I., Träskman-Bendz, L., & Hall, C. (2017). A systematic review including meta-analysis of work environment and burnout symptoms. *BMC Public Health, 17*(1), 264. doi:10.1186/s12889-017-4153-7 PMID:28302088

Bakker, A. B., Demerouti, E., & Euwema, M. C. (2005). Job Resources Buffer the Impact of Job Demands on Burnout. *Journal of Occupational Health Psychology, 10*(2), 170–180. doi:10.1037/1076-8998.10.2.170 PMID:15826226

Barrutia Barreto, I., Aguilar Ibarra, A. F., & Barrutia Barreto, A. M. (2024). Soft skills in administrators for the daptation of companies to the new post-pandemic normality. *Sociología y Tecnociencia, 14*(1), 115–134. https://revistas.uva.es/index.php/sociotecno/article/view/6625

Borys Grinchenko Kyiv Metropolitan University, Faculty of Economics and Management, Management Basics Center. (2020). https://surl.li/qezyf

Borys Grinchenko Kyiv Metropolitan University, Faculty of Economics and Management, Management Basics Center. (2022). https://surl.li/pyazu

Boyas, J., & Wind, L. H. (2010). Employment-based social capital, job stress, and employee burnout: A public child welfare employee structural model. *Children and Youth Services Review, 32*(3), 380–388. doi:10.1016/j.childyouth.2009.10.009

Collins, E. G. C. (1986). A company without offices. *Harvard Business Review, 86*(1), 127–136.

Costin, A., Roman, A. F., & Balica, R. S. (2023). Remote work burnout, professional job stress, and employee emotional exhaustion during the COVID-19 pandemic. *Frontiers in Psychology, 14*, 1193854. Advance online publication. doi:10.3389/fpsyg.2023.1193854 PMID:37325768

Cross, T. B., & Raizman, M. (1986). Telecommuting: the future technology of work. Dow Jones-Irwin.

de Vries, H., Tummers, L., & Bekkers, V. (2019). The Benefits of Teleworking in the Public Sector: Reality or Rhetoric? *Review of Public Personnel Administration, 39*(4), 570–593. doi:10.1177/0734371X18760124

Deloitte. (2020). *Returning to work in the future of work Embracing purpose, potential, perspective, and possibility during COVID-19*. https://www2.deloitte.com/ua/en/pages/human-capital/articles/hc-trends-covid-19.html

Demerouti, E., Bakker, A. B., Nachreiner, F., & Schaufeli, W. B. (2001). The job demands-resources model of burnout. *The Journal of Applied Psychology*, *86*(3), 499–512. doi:10.1037/0021-9010.86.3.499 PMID:11419809

Dionisi, T., Sestito, L., Tarli, C., Antonelli, M., Tosoni, A., D'Addio, S., & .... (2021). Risk of burnout and stress in physicians working in a COVID team: A longitudinal survey. int. J. *Clinics and Practice*, *75*, e14755. doi:10.1111/ijcp.147 PMID:34449957

Eurofound. (2018). *Burnout in the workplace: A review of data and policy responses in the EU*. Publications Office of the European Union.

Freudenberger, H. J. (1974). Staff burn-out. *The Journal of Social Issues*, *30*(1), 159–165. doi:10.1111/j.1540-4560.1974.tb00706.x

George, P., & Veetil, S. N. (2023). Ravnotežaposlovnogživota i transformacionoliderstvokaoprediktorizadovoljstvaposlomzaposlenih. *Serbian Journal of Management*, *18*(2), 253–273. doi:10.5937/sjm18-34305

Hamilton, C. (1987). Telecommuting. *The Personnel Journal*, *66*(4), 90–101.

Henderikx, M., & Stoffers, J. (2022). An Exploratory Literature Study into Digital Transformation and Leadership: Toward Future-Proof Middle Managers. *Sustainability (Basel)*, *14*(2), 687. doi:10.3390/su14020687

Henderikx, M., & Stoffers, J. (2023). Digital transformation and middle managers' leadership skills and behavior: A group concept mapping approach. *Frontiers in Psychology*, *14*, 1147002. Advance online publication. doi:10.3389/fpsyg.2023.1147002 PMID:37731886

Hsieh, C.-W. (2014). Burnout Among Public Service Workers: The Role of Emotional Labor Requirements and Job Resources. *Review of Public Personnel Administration*, *34*(4), 379–402. doi:10.1177/0734371X12460554

Hui, S., Hai, F., Yuemeng, G., Weichen, J., Zhi, L., & Junwei, W. (2022). Moderating Effects of Transformational Leadership, Affective Commitment, Job Performance, and Job Insecurity. *Frontiers in Psychology*, *13*, 847147. Advance online publication. doi:10.3389/fpsyg.2022.847147 PMID:35615161

Ilich, L., Akilina, O., & Panchenko, A. (2020). Peculiarities of Implementation of Peace Education in Ukraine. *Education Excellence and Innovation Management: a 2025 Vision to Sustain Economic Development During Global Challenges*, 2198-2206.

ILO. (2020). *An employers' guide on working from home in response to the outbreak of COVID-19.* International Labour Office. https://cutt.ly/8T283oq

Kelly, M. M. (1985). The next workplace revolution: Telecommuting. *Supervisory Management, 30*(10), 3–7.

Lemos, V. A. F., & Brunstein, J. (2023). Fostering soft skills leadership through a critical reflection approach. *Industrial and Commercial Training*, *55*(1), 143–156. doi:10.1108/ICT-01-2022-0001

Lubbadeh, T. (2020). Job Burnout: A General Literature Review. *International Review of Management and Marketing*, *10*(3), 7–15. doi:10.32479/irmm.9398

Maslach, C. (1976). Burn-Out. *Human Behavior*, *5*, 16–22.

Maslach, C. (1982). Understanding Burnout: Definitional Issues in Analyzing a Complex Phenomenon. In W. S. Paine (Ed.), Job Stress and Burnout (pp. 29–40). Academic Press.

Maslach, C., Jackson, S. E., & Leiter, M. P. (1997). Maslach Burnout Inventory. In *Evaluating Stress: A Book of Resources* (3rd ed.). Scarecrow Education.

Maslach, C., Schaufeli, W. B., & Leiter, M. P. (2001). Job burnout. *Annual Review of Psychology*, *52*(1), 397–422. doi:10.1146/annurev.psych.52.1.397 PMID:11148311

Puga Villarreal, J., & Martínez Cerna, L. (2008). Management's competences in global scenarios. *Competenciasdirectivasenescenariosglobalesestudiosgerenciales*, *24*(109), 87–103. doi:10.1016/S0123-5923(08)70054-8

Raza, S. A., & Qamar, S. (2023). Transformational leadership and employee's career satisfaction: Role of psychological empowerment, organisational commitment, and emotional exhaustion. *Asian Academy of Management Journal*, *28*(2), 207–238. doi:10.21315/aamj2023.28.2.8

Schaufeli, W. B. (2018). Burnout in Europe: relations with national economy, governance, and culture. In *Research Unit Occupational & Organizational Psychology and professional learning (internal report)*. KU Leuven.

Schaufeli, W. B., Leiter, M. P., & Maslach, C. (2009). Burnout: 35 years of research and practice. *Career Development International*, *14*(3), 204–220. doi:10.1108/13620430910966406

Sirakaya, Y., & Yildirimer, K. Ş. (2023). Effects of Burnout and Emotional Stress on Social Life in Employees. *Collaborate. Current Science*, *5*(5-9), 76–100. doi:10.5281/zenodo.8312341

Stoffers, J., & Mordant-Dols, A. (2015). Transformational leadership and professionals' willingness to change: A multiple case study in project management organisations. *Human Resource Management Review*, *5*(2), 40–46. doi:10.5923/j.hrmr.20150502.03

Tang, M. T. (2020). An employers' guide on managing your workplace during *COVID-19*. International Labour Office.

UNDP. (2022). *The 2021/2022 Human Development Report: Uncertain times, unsettled lives Shaping our future in a transforming world*. https://hdr.undp.org/content/human-development-report-2021-22

UNDP. (2023). *The Human Development Report 2023*. https://hdr.undp.org/towards-2023-human-development-report

Wadhawan, S., Gupta, N., Kaur, A., & Bhardwaj, A. (2022). Transformational leadership and employee performance amid COVID-19 crisis. *Journal of Information and Optimization. The Sciences*, *43*(6), 1431–1441. doi:10.1080/02522667.2022.2117345

World Health Organization. (2019). *Burn-out an "occupational phenomenon": International Classification of Diseases*. https://surl.li/avahb

Chapter 9
Prospects for the Implementation of Practice-Based Learning for Students of Managerial Profile

Liudmyla Ilich
https://orcid.org/0000-0002-8594-1824
Borys Grinchenko Kyiv Metropolitan University, Ukraine

Igor Yakovenko
https://orcid.org/0000-0003-0723-6377
Borys Grinchenko Kyiv Metropolitan University, Ukraine

Olena Akilina
https://orcid.org/0000-0001-9968-4921
Borys Grinchenko Kyiv Metropolitan University, Ukraine

Alla Panchenko
https://orcid.org/0000-0002-4757-0583
Borys Grinchenko Kyiv Metropolitan University, Ukraine

Marzena Sobczak-Michalowska
https://orcid.org/0000-0002-9533-8316
WSG University, Poland

ABSTRACT

The purpose of the study is to highlight the theoretical and practical aspects of implementing practice-oriented training of management students and to develop a descriptive model of internship based on innovative approaches. The study highlights the theoretical and applied aspects of the practice-based education implementation for management specialists. Achieving the study goal contributed to the use of several methods of scientific knowledge, in particular theoretical (analysis, synthesis, induction, deduction), empirical methods (observation, questionnaires, surveys), the method of

DOI: 10.4018/979-8-3693-1886-7.ch009

experimental work, as well as tabular and graphical methods. The basic parameters of the practice-based education model were substantiated and determined. They provide the student`s participation in educational and professional internship, performing official duties during one academic year. The main components inherent in the practice-based education model that distinguish it from the traditional process of practice within the framework of the generally accepted educational model were analyzed.

INTRODUCTION

The modern university educational process requires the establishment and observance of a reasonable learning structure: 1) academic theoretical education; 2) education at the university whose work is grounded on developing interactive methods, case-method, situational and estimated and analytical tasks; 3) industrial practice. The two latter develop a base for practice-based education which role as an obligatory component of educational process in higher school has recently increased substantially. Educational reform in universities training managers has intensified the innovative efforts to implement practice-based education. However, because of the lack of relevant experience and efficient models adjusted, higher educational establishments faced up to the series of organizational and methodological challenges which prevented from successful spreading of this experience.

According to the authors, the introduction of a practice-based education model, which provides for the student to stay in office and perform their duties for a long period of time, should be identified as a component called educational and professional internship (EPI). So far, the relevant practice does not have sufficient methodological justification and needs to be studied by scientists, practitioners and institutions that ensure the development of modern models in the educational process. The growing demands for the modern management specialists training require the use of innovative dual education practices. There is a reel need to introduce a new model of training, where the practice-oriented component acquires a fundamentally new quality.

LITERATURE REVIEW

The term Practice-Based Education (PBE) concerning higher educational establishments is used in the study by Sheehan and Higgs (2013); it means preparing alumni for fulfillment practical tasks, challenges, goals which are relevant to the sphere of their professional activity. Practice-Based Education is actualized according to the educational program which sets goals, strategies, criteria of estimation interaction and preparation for practice. This form of education combines three kinds of trainings: local (social), training through experience (at a workplace) and professional training.

The work by a group of scholars (Higgs et al. 2012) is grounded on collective vision, research, knowledge and experience of profound scientists in the sphere of professional education and training. Their study represents different viewpoints and critical assessment of this important trend in higher education, alongside with consideration the strategy of implementing the demanding and motivational way of education, teaching, and developing educational programs.

In medical and pharmaceutical education and training as well as in those concerning pedagogy, practice-based education has long been used. Among the relevant works should be mentioned those of Ilich (2017), Chuenjitwongsa, Oliver, and Bullock (2018), Epsteinand, and Hundert (2002), Edelbring, Dahlgren, and WieglebEdström (2018), Conroy, Hulme, and Menter (2013), Greenberg, Putman, and Walsh (2014).

Project-based education model was proposed by the scholar Morgan (1983). Project-based way was identified as "...an activity in which students develop understanding of topic through involvement in actual problem or issue and notes models of project work whereas they bear a responsibility for arrangement of the whole educational process". The idea was supported by other scholars, Cardona, Velez, and Tobon (2016), in particular, who proved that model of practice-based education grounded on project-based platform promoted education efficiency with the use of application sociological survey and correlation analysis methods.

The practice of strategic management spreading with the help of games became popular in the world (Knotts, and Keys 1997). Managerial games are applied in educational processes assisting students to integrate functional knowledge into business sphere, as well as provide with practical awareness of strategical management. Managerial games give the valuable experience in development teamwork skills. The tactics chosen by the instructor is significant for success, considering the fact that the teaching game-oriented courses require more skills than those focused on lectures or specific issue.

Salasa et al. (2017) consider the simulation-based training (SBT) to be the best approach for management education, and in an effort to guide and encourage its appropriate use they provide several practical guidelines regarding best implementation of simulation-based training in the classroom.

The issue of management modeling, games and simulation-based education occurred in the works of Adobor, and Daneshfar (2006), Bell, Kanar, and Kozlowski (2008), Lean et al. (2006).

Educational technologies implementation which spread rapidly requires professionalism and manager willingness to introduce innovative informational technologies. Thus, according to Stupak (2020), use of e-based resources (WebQuest, e-quizzes and online games) in higher education may provide both the development of professional skills and those concerning gaining online environment use experience. She proposes the use of interactive online-games grounded on online-platform Goosechase. Glowacki, Kriukova, and Avshenyuk (2018) shares her viewpoint and regards gamification as innovative approach in higher education. The researchers analyzed the use of gamification in higher educational establishments of Poland and Ukraine, as well as studied the efficiency of Kahoot application as one of gamification technologies. At the same time appeared the following set of social risks: new social policies in the sphere of higher education, digitalization of education, spread of clip-thinking and internet-addiction among students.

The results of Baker Oam (2017) study has the great value for practice. It reviews education and training provision in Australia through a contextualisation of the Australian Qualification Framework (AQF) with work-based learning (WBL) pedagogy to determine how it can improve students learning results. According to the scientist, the application of effective WBL approaches has the potential to create a much larger flow of learners from experiential and vocational backgrounds into undergraduate programmes and onto higher education programmes using a consistent and effective pedagogy. Considering active on-the-job training opportunities, students, teachers, and business managers recognize that the demand for on-the-job training will be higher.

Another practice-based model which has great scientific and practical interest - problem-based learning (PBL). According to the model teachers should educate students how to research and create relying on natural instincts. It was realized in practice in the 1960s in McMaster University (official website, as of March 15, 2021) for the first time, then it was applied in Monash University (official website, as of March 15, 2021) for Bachelor of Medicine program and aimed at arranging the educational process to encourage students to think and make conclusions based on practical experience. Later this approach was applied to other specialties, including Math, Law, Pedagogy etc.

Billett (2001) proposed complete practical model which was well explained in theory and studies to manage work-based learning. His book publication made WBL mature model, as the scientist presented the way to a new level of complexity in approaches to learning and work. That promoted the creation of a lifelong learning concept.

Among Ukrainian scientists who were involved in relevant studies should be mentioned Gorbenko (2015). She identified four approaches to practice-based education:

1) educational, productive and internship practice organization for students to obtain real professional skills according to their profile.
2) career guided educational technologies which implementation enable students to shape personal characteristics that have actual importance for future professional activity, as well as knowledge, skills and experience securing qualitative professional duties performance according to the profile.
3) creating professional employment innovative forms for students to solve actual scientific, practical, productive, and exploratory work according to the profile.
4) designing conditions for learning, obtaining skills and experience aimed to shape student's motivation to acquire professional skills during the time of studying at the university.

Dolzhenkovet al. (2020) emphasizes the necessity of practice-based education dominance while preparing education managers. Her study stresses the need to use the information-factual base of reasonably expected situations in the future education managers learning, since it promotes the development of higher education recipients' abilities, the creation of conditions for their active, fruitful educational and cognitive activities and provide creative use of organizational forms and methods.

A hypothesis implies that a future managers' training is more successful if a practice-based education is implemented. A study by Prescott et al (2021) found a negative effect of practice-based education on academic achievement. The authors concluded that teachers and administration had failed to create a practice-based education model that would provide beneficial effects. Therefore, our research is dedicated to solving this problem. Proposed approach to practice-oriented education should be effective in the presence of such a component as holding office and performing official duties for a sufficiently long period of time. It is also important to choose the right optimal scenario educational and professional internships (EPI).

Therefore, students at the final stage of training should work in one of the positions provided by the specialty educational and professional internships (EPI) program. Based on the results of the students` work, they should be given the opinion of the EPI base commission on the compliance of his training level.

The purpose of the paper is to develop a practice-based education model and to describe possible scenarios of educational and professional internships (EPI) for students majoring in 073 "Management" at the university level of bachelor`s degree.

Table 1. Questionnaire for an intern at the start of EPI.

1.	Which of the business activity directions in the organization may you be interested in? (variants: 1- have no interest, 2- have little interest, 3- may be of interest but I have lack of experience in this work, 4- have some interest, 5- have a lot of interest
2.	Have you prepared a coursework, a paper or a project for a contest on one of the directions proposed? 1 – never prepared, 2- a paper for practical course (seminar), 3- in the process of preparing, 4- prepared a coursework or a project work for a contest, 5- is the theme of my qualification Bachelor's thesis
3.	What does your scientific head at the university department think? 1- objects to the directions chosen, 2- has not come up with the decision, 3- is eager to accept the idea of the training base organization, 4- advises on the choice, 5- emphasizes the choice of the direction
4.	Would you like to focus on one of the profiles (directions) after having passed all the stages of the profile? 1 – no, I would rather pass all stages of EPI equally well by all the directions, 2- I need some time to get familiar with the specificity of training base organization, 3- I have a wish but I do not select the direction among the several ones, 4- I am determined but need some advice, 5- I clearly determined
5.	Would you like to focus on project approach? 1 – No, I would pass all EPI stages equally well in all directions, 2- No, I have chosen the option focusing on one direction, 3- I need some time to get familiar with specificity of training base organization, 4 – I have the wish but I so not select the specific project, I consider several options, 5- I am clearly defined.

Table 2. Questionnaire for a representative of the EPI base organization for an intern

1.	Which of the directions should be given more attention while arranging EPI? 1 – I cannot define, 2- I can recommend only if I consult with the university representative, 3 – I can define the priority direction for the organization, 4 – I accept the direction chosen, 5- I recommend another direction
2.	Is it a good idea for an intern to plan equally all directions or would it be best to focus on one and study it deeply? 1 – I consider passing all stages equally without assigning the specific one, 2- the final decision should be made after two months of EPI, 3- I can recommend without emphasizing, 4- the direction should be identified specifically, 5- I consider identifying two and more directions
3.	Do you recommend the project approach for practical part of EPI? 1- No, organization is not into such projects, 2- Possible, if it is developed in cooperation with the university, 3- The choice is based on intern's training results after one's cooperation with organization employees, 4- I can offer a chance to participate in a specific project, 5 – Yes, I can offer the participation in several projects
4.	What are the chances of granting authority to an intern of EPI? 1- I can offer the training in organization subdivision without any powers, 2- The interns' powers depend on their skills and knowledge, 3 - empowering is considered but needs consulting at the organization, 4- decision is made, 5- The intern is empowered with some responsibilities and duties

Methods

Research Model/Design (Qualitative, Quantitative, or Mixed Methods)

The research is based on the mixed method, it comprises quantitative and qualitative data. According to the research objectives, the survey has been chosen as a quantitative method of the empirical research.

The authors developed a survey-based approach to the most reasonable solution to the choice of internship model. Before internship start such questionnaires are responded by both an intern and a representative who supervises the training from the organization which will be a base of EPI (Table 1).

The further questionnaire is proposed to be responded with the participation of representatives of EPI base organization which will supervise the intern (table 2).

The intern and a supervisor from the organization give one of the five possible responds while being questioned.

After receiving the questionnaire results and considering interests of all parties the constituent meeting is held in the presence of managers from the EPI base, from the university, as well as the future intern in order to adopt the EPI model. It is important to evaluate the results of the EPI and form a conclusion about the students` readiness to work in the chosen specialty. To achieve this the estimate commission is arranged:

1. Head of EOT;
2. Head from the university department;
3. Supervisor from the subdivision organization the intern trains;
4. Representative of the staff or trade union;
5. Representative of the organization executives.

Each member of assemble answers the questionnaire with the following question:

Is the intern`s level sufficient to perform professional duties in accordance with the acquired specialty?

Options: 1 – No, the level of knowledge and preparation does not correspond to the requirements for this occupation, 2 – after obtaining the qualification the person needs EPI training for several time before applying for the post on trial, 3 – the person may be applied for the low rank post according to organization chart, 4 – in general the person meets the requirements and may be employed for some posts, but non-managerial position, 5 - Yes, it is relevant to the requirements of the specialty and may apply for any post.

The evaluation commission conclusions have an advisory nature on the assignment of the relevant educational qualification and are officially submitted to the examination commission, where the bachelor's qualification work is defended.

The application of comparison, classification, systematization methods allowed to compare the new model of practice of training specialists in management introduction as a component of dual education with existing practices of training specialists in other fields; to identify the advantages and disadvantages of using different EPI scenarios for training.

Methods of diagnosis and experiment helped to determine the factors of the new model of practice-oriented internship, the development of stages of its implementation.

After going through each stage of EPI training students were offered to evaluate the matching level of their knowledge and skills to the post they were employed while performing EPI tasks. Block "Current level" was made for defining the present level of skills obtained and had 5-grade scale. Block "Necessary level" was made for assessing the skills specific workplace required.

Data Analysis

Future managers survey was performed in both - the paper questionnaires and Google Forms. It made possible to do manual and automated processing of the received data. It should be stressed that automated one significantly speeds up the result processing that indicates the feasibility of using Google Forms.

EPI covers four stages of production practice: specialty, project, management, and internship. Such sequence is explained by the following.

The main task of the first stage (duration 4 weeks) is to work out in a specific unit and at a specific workplace all the details and nuances of the selected task for which the project solution should be prepared. Upon completion of this stage, the intern should know the specifics of the chosen area, its features of implementation at the enterprise; understand the potential and have a vision of ways to solve problems; be ready to participate in the task implementation.

At the next stage, student chooses together with the enterprise and the university leaders the project that meets the needs of the base and the interests of its management, coincides with the profile of the university tutor`s research interests, and, what is very important, is interesting for the student and is based on his experience of coursework and his researches. After 14 weeks of EPI student should get acquainted with the work of the practice base. Minimum a week student should have practice in departments of different directions; determine the most urgent tasks for the further enterprise activity and choose the direction to implement the project; "defend" own choice regarding the direction and subject of the project.

The key is the third stage - management, where is the implementation of a qualitatively new form – EPI. The student works at the position as an intern and within 13 weeks directly performs the task defined in the previous stages. The project carries out practical work - development and necessary decision making. An intern gains the skills of assignments creation, generalization of propositions made by co-executors, prepares the agenda for the assembly, monitors the realization of decisions made. An intern is directly responsible for all the above mentioned tasks under the control of the supervisors.

The final stage is the practice completion and writing a bachelor's project.

Results

Each of the stages in the proposed EPI model enables students to form all necessary integral and occupational skills which are provided in the standard of higher education for the specialty 073 "Management".

To achieve the successful results of training and provide with new knowledge and practical skills, students are allocated to the profound organizations and executive authorities.

The first year of experimental work reveals that in further program and methodical EPI materials should be individualized and focused on the branch of business which is training base organization is specialized in (production of goods and services, culture, education, local authorities etc.). Furthermore, a specific attention should be given to the following: a degree of specific subdivisions attachment to implementing the tasks set, the level of specific subdivisions self-sufficiency in decision-making process, ratio of the decisions previously made to prompt decisions, responsibility and consequences of the decisions made etc.

The obtained results confirmed the right choice of the chosen EPI direction. The majority of experiment participants showed such skills as communicative (mastering the culture of speech, advanced IT technologies, interpersonal communication etc.), learning (ability to gain new knowledge and apply it in practice), socio-economic (knowledge of economic behavior, which enables to participate effectively and meaningfully in production processes) and management (readiness for decision-making, ability to assess the situation properly, identify and consider most of subjective factors, cope with new and unexpected situations).

Moreover, the interns demonstrated sufficient level of the following skills: psychological (awareness of main principles and categories, general and social psychology, psychology of personality that provide shaping the ability to improve constantly own performance), analytical and diagnostical (skills to collect, develop, analyze and generalize the information and present results), subject-matter (awareness of theoretical foundations of the work performed, ability to apply acquired knowledge in production and social activity, perform main professional and methodical functions) and technological (functional knowledge and technological activity skills aimed at developing professional competences, quick adaptation to new labour conditions skills, information about production objects and technological processes).

Research skills (mastering scientific thinking, ability to observe and analyze, make assumptions, process the results of scientific observations within the frame of the work performed) were evaluated at high level by 43,8% of respondents, although such skills are not required to a great extent at those workplaces where the respondents worked (which is also confirmed by the results of second block of a questionnaire).

At the same time mismatching between workplaces requirements and legal and regulatory skills (awareness of legal and regulatory basis in the professional activity sphere) was revealed, which confirms the lack of theoretical training in educational program for managers.

Figure 1. The interns results of subjective own matching skills evaluation

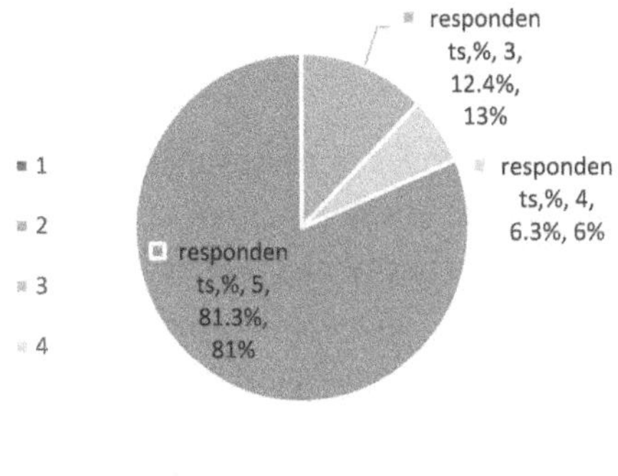

Communicative skills

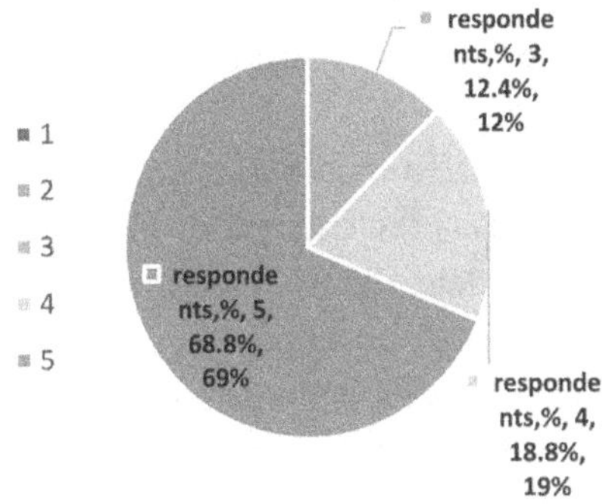

Learning skills

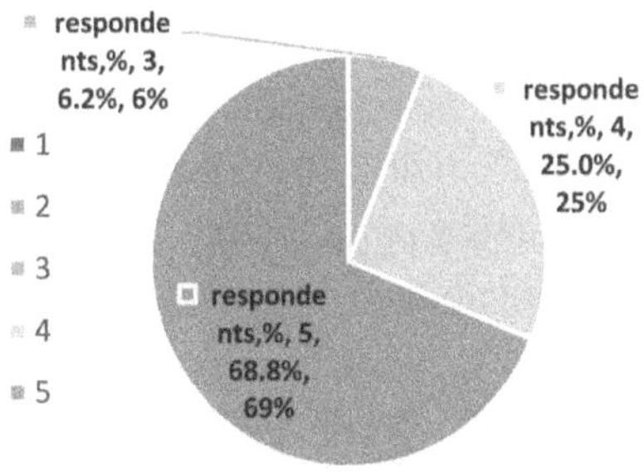

Management skills

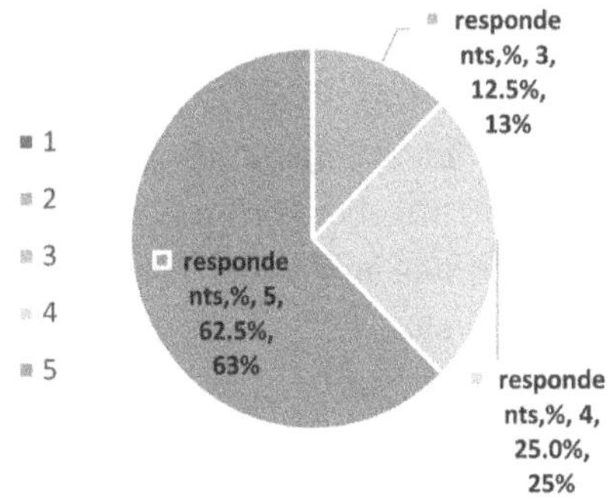

Socio-economic skills

DISCUSSION

Educational and professional internships is a new model of practice-based education centered on the factors that shape the peculiar features of this model and differentiate it from traditional educational models.

In the authors' viewpoint, the following factors can be identified:

a) "actual workplace", i.e. student`s independent performance of an employee's job duties during extended period (minimum three months at one workplace);

b) after adaptation period the specific areas of activity the intern will be responsible for should be determined. All production targets should be clearly defined as well as job duties, plan of work duly approved, responsibilities concerning the task set;

c) the intern obtains individual assignment which includes the introduction of innovative steps, project development beneficial for the enterprise, and real programs of best practices implementation.

The intern should take all steps – from choosing the assignment subject to making decisions at the enterprise. These steps also include development of technical task and mandate, the list of co-performers selection and harmonization, an interim and a final versions preparation of the decision project, analytical report concerning efficiency of the actions and the package of supporting documents. On completion the practice term the intern should report own proposals at the meeting with employers and argue the necessity of specific decision. Finally, the intern should provide the plan of this decision implementation and its execution monitoring;

d) organizational tasks defined in guidance and training documents, in particular:

- terms of EPI training at the final year of bachelor's course;
- clear regulation of interim reports: periodicity, the form of report, members of the commissions with obligatory participation of EPI base and university representatives, requirements and reporting procedure etc.;
- authority of the Department of the university and the intern's university supervisor concerning their effect on setting and changes of assignments defined with specific nature of EPI base enterprise.

The key point of EPI is shaping the intern's post specialization, its direction and profile of activity, duties and responsibilities, individual assignment, the level of authority for decision-making.

The main challenging points in EPI system of future managers concern activity directions they cover. Several alternative scenarios are worth considering. Each of them has its own advantages and disadvantages (Table 3).

CONCLUSION

Universities face up the complicated choice: which of the scenarios is better to select to provide the efficiency of future specialist's preparation. To the authors' mind, the optimal variant is to develop a model which combines all three scenarios in different ratios.

EPI program is divided into stages, each of them include the following three components:

Table 3. Advantages and drawbacks of different EPI scenarios implementation for professional managers' preparation

Scenario	Advantage	Drawback
A) the intern goes through all the main directions and the units that take care of these directions	- participation in the processes of all main business activity operation; - possibility to shape the balanced conclusion concerning all spheres of activity; - managerial experience which requires monitoring all activity trends; - opportunity to choose the activity for further practical or scientific activity which match the appeals or skills of an intern.	- inability to focus on specific directions because of the time limit; - presence of several supervisors with various dimensions; - necessity to communicate with a wide circle of specialists that prevents from researching the experience deeply; - limited opportunities resulted from timing which enable to undergo the full-value way from situation analysis to participation in decision-making process.
B) an intern is focused on the one chosen direction, undergoes all stages available, mastering particular specialization	- deep studying of the specific direction, gaining systematical experience and skills; - relevant experience of teamwork; - opportunity to introduce own real ideas; - more systematical way of studying the environment for chosen direction: market infrastructure, competitors, stakeholders, consumers	- lack of practical skills and relevant work experience as for the directions chosen; - inability to make complex estimate of business activity, efficiency of its work, appropriate management level; - insufficient level of contact with executives and managers, in particular, those who supervise other directions; - the risk of narrow specialization, EPI may not correspond with the future occupational directions in practice
C) an intern is concentrated on preparation of specific project which provides implementing the set of measures, new development models, changes in organization strategy, particularly, its place in competitive environment	- gaining experience in implementing new technologies, development, decisions; - experience of innovative solutions, best practice realization; - skills of the team shaping and the team work, coordination of the teamwork; - managerial and leadership skills obtaining; - experience in planning, justification of managerial decisions, project monitoring	- narrowing of activity on other projects limits the gaining wider experience of economic processes in practice; - lack of opportunities to gain experience of routine everyday practical work in other subdivisions; - interaction with rather narrow circle of specialists which are employed in project team work; - comparatively short time of practice in organization which is less than the term of the project duration

- EPI in several profile subdivisions which provide gaining practical qualification according to the direction;
- choosing the base subdivision where the intern will work;
- choosing the project to participate in which is implemented on the EPI base.

As for the time ratios, we apply the following approaches. The general term of EPI is seven and a half months from September,10, to May,1. Up to May,1 organizational and instructional work is held at the university. From May,1 to June, 10 time is set aside to prepare the Bachelor's thesis. Two months is necessary time for each of the components. In general obligatory program by three components comprises six months. One and a half month is the time provided for individual additional component to the intern who independently may lengthen the time for the component (EPI scenario) desired.

It is necessary to make decision as for the choice of the one of three variants as the leading and to obtain additional individual time period for its executing up to one and a half month before EPI starts. Preparation period should be arranged: to define the workstation, supervisors, develop plan and find out the convincing arguments for the chosen EPI model. As a rule, it is hard to make such choice by all sides – intern, university and organization supervisors.

The authors have developed an approach based on the questionnaire for the most reasonable solving the problem. Before the internship start, the intern and the enterprise (organization) representative who is responsible for this internship, pass a parallel questionnaire.

Author Contributions

In 2020 the Department of Management at BorysGrinchenko Kyiv University started experimental realization of the model of educational and professional internships for four-year students of specialty 073 "Management" (Bachelor's stage of higher education as for educational and occupational program "Management of organization"). The authors of the article belong to the support group of specialty 073 "Management". The head of the department of management is Dr. Prof. Lyudmila Ilyich. The guarantor of the professional educational program "Management of Organizations", whose students were involved in the experiment, is Ph.D., Assoc. Prof.Olena Akilina. The developers of the EPI program and its organizers are Ph.D., Assoc. Prof. Ihor Yakovenko and Ph.D., Assoc. Prof. Olena Akilina. The authors of the article, in particular Ph.D., Assoc. Prof. AllaPanchenko, supervised the students during the experiment.

Ethical Issues

We should emphasize that during the research the most important principles of ethical behavior, which are admitted by scientific community, have been followed: – voluntary participation and safety of the research: students take a voluntary part in the research, the participants can leave the research at any stage without any consequences; – anonymity: the survey of participants is carried out anonymously, so the researcher and anyone who can read the survey results can't identify the answers of a certain participant.

REFERENCES

Adobor, H., & Daneshfar, A. (2006). Management simulations: Determining their effectiveness. *Journal of Management Development*, *25*(2), 151–168. doi:10.1108/02621710610645135

Bell, B. S., Kanar, A. M., & Kozlowski, S. W. J. (2008). Current issues and future directions in simulation-based training in North America. *International Journal of Human Resource Management*, *19*(8), 1416–1434. doi:10.1080/09585190802200173

Billett, S. R. (2001). *Learning in the workplace: Strategies for effective practice*. Allen and Unwin.

Cardona, S., Velez, J., & Tobon, S. (2016). Contribution of socio-formative assessment to academic performance in an undergraduate program. *Educar*, *52*(2), 423–447. doi:10.5565/rev/educar.763

Chuenjitwongsa, S., Oliver, R. G., & Bullock, A. D. (2018). Competence, competency-based education, and undergraduate dental education: A discussion paper. *European Journal of Dental Education*, *22*(1), 1–8. doi:10.1111/eje.12213 PMID:27246501

Conroy, J., Hulme, M., & Menter, I. (2013). Developing a 'clinical' model for teacher education. *Journal of Education for Teaching*, *39*(5), 557–573. doi:10.1080/02607476.2013.836339

Dolzhenkov, O., Chernenko, N., Ruchkina, M., & Sakaliuk, O. (2020). Practice-oriented training as a means of professionalisation of future education managers. *Scientific bulletin of South Ukrainian National Pedagogical University named after K. D. Ushynsky*, *1*(130), 66–72. doi:10.24195/2617-6688-2020-1-9

Edelbring, S., Dahlgren, M. A., & Wiegleb Edström, D. (2018). Characteristics of two questionnaires used to assess interprofessional learning: Psychometrics and expert panel evaluations. *BMC Medical Education*, *40*(18), 40. doi:10.1186/s12909-018-1153-y PMID:29554898

Epstein, R. M., & Hundert, E. M. (2002). Defining and assessing professional competence. *Journal of the American Medical Association*, *287*(2), 226–235. doi:10.1001/jama.287.2.226 PMID:11779266

Glowacki, J., Kriukova, Y., & Avshenyuk, N. (2018). Gamification in higher education: Experience of Poland and Ukraine. *Advanced Education*, *5*(10), 105–110. doi:10.20535/2410-8286.151143

Greenberg, J., Putman, H., & Walsh, K. (2014). *Training our future teachers: Classroom management*. National Council on Teacher Quality. https://files.eric.ed.gov/fulltext/ED556312.pdf

Higgs, J., Barnett, R., Billett, S., Hutchings, M., & Trede, F. (2012). *Practice-Based Education. Perspectives and Strategies*. SensePublishers. doi:10.1007/978-94-6209-128-3

Horbenko, H. (2015). Practice-oriented learning of bachelors of advertising and public relations. *Continuing Professional Education: Theory and Practice,* (4), 64-69. http://npo.kubg.edu.ua/article/view/183566

Ilich, L. (2017). *Drivers of global labor market development. In International Relations 2017: Current issues of world economy and politics: Proceedings of 17th International Scientific Conference (December 1–2, 2017)*. EKONÓM. https://surl.li/cktqv

Knotts, U. S. Jr, & Keys, J. B. (1997). Teaching strategic management with a business game. *Simulation & Gaming*, *28*(4), 377–395. doi:10.1177/1046878197284004

Lean, J., Moizer, J., Towler, M., & Abbey, C. (2006). Simulations and Games: Use and Barriers in Higher Education. *Active Learning in Higher Education*, *7*(3), 227–242. doi:10.1177/1469787406069056

Morgan, A. (1983). Theoretical Aspects of Project-Based Learning in Higher Education. *British Journal of Educational Technology*, *14*(1), 66–78. doi:10.1111/j.1467-8535.1983.tb00450.x

Oam, B. (2017). Work Based Learning: A learning strategy in support of the Australian Qualifications Framework. *Journal of Work-Applied Management*, *9*(1), 70–82. doi:10.1108/JWAM-04-2017-0008

Prescott, P., Gjerde, K. P., & Rice, J. L. (2021). Analyzing mandatory college internships: Academic effects and implications for curricular design. *Studies in Higher Education, 46*(11), 2444–2459. doi:10.1080/03075079.2020.1723531

Salasa, E., Wildman, J. L., & Piccolo, R. F. (2017). Using Simulation-Based Training to Enhance Management. *Academy of Management Learning & Education, 8*(4), 559–573. Advance online publication. doi:10.5465/amle.8.4.zqr559

Sheehan, D., & Higgs, J. (2013). *Practice-Based Education. In Realising Exemplary Practice-Based Education. Practice, Education, Work and Society*. SensePublishers. doi:10.1007/978-94-6209-188-7_2

Stupak, O. (2020). Educational technologies in training future managers. *Advanced Education, 7*(15), 97–104. doi:10.20535/2410-8286.200229

Chapter 10
The Privacy-Preserving High-Dimensional Synthetic Data Generation and Evaluation in the Healthcare Domain

Chandrakant Mallick
Gandhi Institute of Technological Advancement, India

Parimal Kumar Giri
Gandhi Institute of Technological Advancement, India

Bijay Kumar Paikaray
Siksha 'O' Anusandhan University, India

ABSTRACT

In the fast-changing environment of healthcare research and technology, there is an increasing demand for varied and vast information. However, issues with data privacy, unavailability, and ethical considerations frequently limit smooth access to true high-dimensional healthcare data. This research investigates a viable approach to addressing these challenges: the use of high-dimensional synthetic data in the healthcare area. The authors investigate the potentials and uses of synthetic data production through a review of current literature and methodology, providing insights into its role in overcoming data access barriers, fostering innovation, and supporting evidence-based decision making. The chapter outlines significant use cases, such as simulation and prediction research, hypothesis and algorithm testing, epidemiology, health information technology development, teaching and training, public dataset release, and data connecting.

DOI: 10.4018/979-8-3693-1886-7.ch010

1. INTRODUCTION

Synthetic data, defined by the US Census Bureau as micro data records created through statistical modeling, enhances data utility without compromising privacy and confidentiality, enhancing the utility of sensitive information (Philpott, 2017). Synthetic high-dimensional data is critical to a wide range of data science applications. Its relevance stems from the difficulties connected with gathering, disseminating, and analyzing real-world high-dimensional datasets, which frequently contain sensitive or limited information. By creating synthetic data, researchers and practitioners may address privacy issues, ethical constraints, and data limits while correctly capturing the complex structures and patterns seen in high-dimensional settings. This enables the creation, testing, and improvement of algorithms and models in a variety of disciplines, including healthcare, finance, genomics, cyber security, and others, eventually driving innovation and breakthroughs in data-driven research and applications (Giuffrè & Shung, 2023). Synthetic data addresses the challenges of obtaining and using real-world high-dimensional datasets by offering an alternative that addresses several limitations associated with genuine data sources, including cyber security, ultimately fostering innovation and advancements in data-driven research and applications (Wang et al., 2024). Real-world high-dimensional datasets frequently contain sensitive information, making them difficult to distribute or access openly. Synthetic data creation enables academics to construct privacy-preserving replacements that maintain statistical features and trends while concealing sensitive information. This allows for cooperation and experimentation without compromising privacy (James et al., 2021).

Obtaining vast and diverse real-world, high-dimensional datasets can be difficult or expensive. Synthetic data provides a solution by allowing researchers to simulate numerous scenarios and data distributions, resulting in varied datasets that accurately represent the complexity of the target domain. This is especially useful in cases where legitimate data is scarce or unavailable (Xu et al., 2021). In some sectors, ethical constraints may limit the use of real-world data, particularly if it contains personal or sensitive information. Synthetic data production helps to bypass ethical limitations by developing false datasets that mimic the features of actual data, allowing researchers to undertake experiments and analyses without ethical issues (Hao et al., 2024). Developing and testing algorithms on real-world high-dimensional datasets might be difficult owing to the aforementioned concerns. Synthetic data enables controlled trials, giving researchers the ability to evaluate algorithmic performance under a variety of scenarios without depending on potentially sensitive or restricted real-world data (Hoag, 2008).

Synthetic data is a useful technique for enhancing existing datasets. By creating extra synthetic samples, researchers may increase the size and variety of their datasets, improving the resilience and generalization capabilities of machine learning models trained on these augmented datasets (Fawaz et al., 2018). Thus, synthetic data is a diverse and powerful resource that strikes a balance between the requirement for genuine, high-dimensional data and the difficulties involved with getting and utilizing actual datasets. It promotes data science innovation, research, and experimentation while adhering to privacy and ethical guidelines.

Synthetic data, in various forms like textual, media-based, and tabular formats, is used in various domains and applications. Machine learning models enhance natural language understanding systems from synthetic data. Synthetic data overcomes privacy concerns, enables robust training, and facilitates resource-intensive applications.

1.1 Real Data Vs Synthetic Data

Table 1. Distinction between actual and synthetic data

Characteristics	Real Data	Synthetic Data
Source	Gathered from real world	Generated from digital environment
Creation	Occurs in the real-world instances	Fabricated to imitate real data properties
Origin	Directly derived from the real-world occurrences	Crafted without reliance on specific real-world events
Collection Methods	Sensors, devices, online surveys	Algorithms, simulations, statistical modeling
Variability	Reflects natural variations	Controlled variability based on modeling choices
Privacy	May contain sensitive or private information	Can be designed to preserve privacy through generation techniques
Accessibility	Availability depends on real-world occurrences	Easily generated making it readily accessible form model training
Applicability	Commonly used for real-world analysis and decision making	Valuable for scenario where real data is scare, sensitive, impractical to obtain

1.2 Types of Synthetic Data

Synthetic data, which is designed to protect sensitive information while keeping statistical aspects from the original dataset, is classified into three categories.

Fully Synthetic Data is fully fabricated, with no elements from the actual data, and privacy-protected series produced at random using estimated density functions of characteristics in the genuine data. This strategy, which employs techniques such as bootstrap methods and repeated imputations, provides robust privacy protection while depending entirely on the accuracy of the synthetic data.

Partially Synthetic Data substitutes just the values of chosen sensitive characteristics with synthetic counterparts, ensuring privacy in freshly created data, particularly for attributes that are at high risk of exposure. Multiple imputation and model-based approaches are frequently used in this approach, which is especially beneficial for dealing with missing values in actual data.

Hybrid Synthetic Data, which combines real and synthetic data, picks records from both sources for each random record in real data. While it provides advantages in privacy protection and utility over the other two varieties, it comes at the expense of additional memory and processing time.

1.3 Challenges in Healthcare Data Access

Synthetic data refers to datasets in various forms and levels, with some arguing it should only refer to fabricated data without original records, while others, particularly in census and statistics, acknowledge a more diverse sub-classification (Siwicki, 2020).

Synthetic data, a technology based on Artificial Intelligence, presents challenges such as difficulty in generating, inconsistencies, bias, and potential issues with real data validation. Its flexibility may also hinder acceptance of its validity by users, and the intricate task of replicating essential features may lead to complexity. Some of the pressing challenges are:

Data Privacy Concerns: Healthcare data privacy is crucial due to sensitive information, such as medical histories and treatments. Balancing research and innovation with individual privacy is a challenge. Regulatory frameworks like HIPAA address these concerns, emphasizing robust security measures and ethical considerations in handling healthcare information.The use of synthetic high-dimensional data in medical research and imaging is an effective technique for addressing issues such as privacy concerns, data scarcity, and the need for various datasets. Real-world medical datasets frequently contain sensitive patient information, making them difficult to distribute or analyze without breaking privacy laws (Chen et al., 2021). Researchers can use synthetic high-dimensional data to create privacy-preserving alternatives that maintain the statistical properties of actual patient data. This facilitates collaborative research and algorithm development while maintaining patient anonymity (Khalid et al., 2023).

Data Unavailability: Data unavailability in healthcare is a significant challenge due to the dispersion of data across systems, incompatibility between EHR systems, proprietary formats, and silos, and outdated technologies. This fragmented landscape hinders holistic patient health understanding and advancements in research, treatment, and healthcare innovation.Synthetic data is needed in healthcare due to limited availability of real-world sensor-driven datasets and time-consuming, costly human activity data collection. It can provide initial testing, validate new techniques, augment small labeled datasets, and improve model accuracy in limited real-world data availability (Khalid et al., 2023).

Ethical Considerations: Healthcare data ethics involve privacy, consent, and responsible use. It's crucial to protect patient autonomy and confidentiality, with transparent consent mechanisms. Balancing medical knowledge with privacy is essential, and data usage beyond its intended purpose can lead to bias or discrimination. Ensuring data security is crucial, and continuous ethical guidelines and governance frameworks are essential. The authors in (Char, Abràmoff, & Feudtner, 2020) presented a novel model for identifying ethical concerns in machine learning healthcareapplications, highlighting key questions and considerations, aiding systematic appraisals and interdisciplinary collaboration among stakeholders.

1.4 Growing Demand for Synthetic Data in Healthcare Research

The growing demand for synthetic data in healthcare research is driven by privacy and security concerns, fragmentation, and inaccessibility of real-world data. It offers a privacy-preserving alternative and allows researchers to experiment without compromising patient data confidentiality. This makes synthetic data an essential resource for innovative and ethical research in the rapidly evolving healthcare landscape. Synthetic health data can address privacy concerns in biomedical research and healthcare applications, with modern data generation methods demonstrating significant potential (Yan et al., 2022). The increasing demand for synthetic data in healthcare research is driven by challenges like data privacy, unavailability, and ethical considerations. Synthetic data offers a privacy-preserving alternative, providing high-dimensional datasets that enhance research capabilities. It also allows researchers to navigate ethical considerations and privacy issues, fostering innovation and supporting evidence-based decision-making while respecting ethical principles.

This article (Wang, Myles, & Tucker, 2021) discusses the use of electronic healthcare record data for disease risk factors, treatment effectiveness, and service planning. It proposes a framework for generating and evaluating synthetic data, focusing on cross-sectional healthcare data. The framework preserves ground truth data while ensuring privacy, and uses synthetic datasets modeled on the Indian liver patient dataset and UK primary care dataset.Synthetic data is a privacy-preserving, comprehensive, and ethical solution for healthcare research, ensuring patient confidentiality, facilitating innovation, and supporting evidence-based decision-making.The text in (Abouelmehdi, Beni-Hessane, & Khaloufi, 2018) discussed the risks and new technologies for big health data security, focusing on privacy issues in healthcare. It discusses laws, regulations, and techniques used to ensure patient privacy, while identifying limitations in existing approaches.

The rest of the chapter is organized as follows: Section 2 provides a brief literature review on high-dimensional synthetic data generation in healthcare, highlighting its role in overcoming data access barriers, fostering innovation, and supporting research and policymaking. Section 3 provides various synthetic data generation techniques, use cases for synthetic data in healthcare research, its adaptability and application in various fields such as simulation, prediction, epidemiology, health information technology development, teaching, and data connecting. Section 4 provides the proposed framework that combines privacy-preserving algorithms with specialized methodologies for high-dimensional synthetic data generation in the healthcare industry, covering data gathering, preprocessing, synthetic data production, and detailed assessment. Section 5 concludes the chapter with future direction of the work.

2. LITERATURE REVIEW

The increasing focus on data privacy has led to the adoption of synthetic data as a method for preserving privacy while maintaining statistical relevance. This data is effective in conducting privacy-conscious experiments and overcoming data unavailability and fragmentation issues. This survey explores the transformative potential of synthetic data in healthcare research and analytics. This study by (Hernandez et al., 2022) provides a pioneering exploration of Synthetic Data Generation (STDG) approaches in healthcare, focusing on privacy preservation. It examines Generative Adversarial Networks (GANs) and their implications for research. This is the first initiative to scrutinize STDG methodologies in healthcare, encompassing data augmentation and privacy preservation.

Donaldson and Lohr define "privacy" as the activity of remaining hidden from public view, without any inherent negative implications (Lohr & Donaldson, 1994). Authors in (Foraker et al., 2020) discussed privacy violations, identifying threats like identity, attribute, and membership disclosures. Attack models include linkage, homogeneity, background knowledge, skewness, and similarity attacks. These techniques allow adversaries to compromise privacy by disclosing sensitive information about individuals in the data.

McLachlan et al. (2016) examined re-identification concerns in de-personalized Electronic Healthcare Records (EHRs) and proposes the Realistic Synthetic EHR (RS-EHR) as a safe alternative. The article offers the CoMSER technique, which uses Clinical Practice Guidelines (CPGs) and Health Incidence Statistics (HIS) to build realistic RS-EHR without accessing genuine EHRs. The strategy entails formalizing CPGs, including HIS-based limitations, and leveraging domain expertise, resulting in a possible solution to secondary EHR privacy problems.

The authors in (Choi, et al., 2017) investigated the privacy problems while accessing electronic health record (EHR) data and offers medGAN, a novel technique that uses Generative Adversarial Networks to build realistic synthetic patient records. The work shows medGAN's performance through trials on distribution statistics, predictive modeling tasks, and medical expert evaluations, demonstrating its ability to reduce privacy hazards connected with actual EHR data. The suggested method solves collaborative usage issues, opening up a viable pathway for safe and accessible synthetic EHR data sharing in medical research.

The study (Beaulieu-Jones, et al., 2019) explored the use of deep neural networks to generate synthetic participants from the SPRINT trial, ensuring privacy and enabling secondary analyses. The approach, which uses differential privacy, allows for reproducible investigations of clinical datasets while preserving participant confidentiality, offering promising implications for data sharing in clinical research. The study (Abay et al., 2019) analyzes existing synthetic data generation techniques and introduces a novel approach that combines deep learning with privacy cost analysis to generate differentially private synthetic datasets with heightened data utility. This method outperforms state-of-the-art techniques and is accessible for implementation in diverse applications requiring privacy-preserving data release.

The work (Yale et al., 2020) develops metrics to measure the quality of synthetic health data for education and research. They create an end-to-end workflow using generative adversarial network (GAN) method, HealthGAN, which creates privacy-preserving synthetic health data. The workflow meets privacy specifications and is used by external users without de-identification. HealthGAN provides the best privacy and footprint, while maintaining resemblance and utility. Two case studies demonstrate its effectiveness in classroom and research settings. The study (Dash et al., 2020) proposed a workflow for generating synthetic medical data that preserves privacy while maintaining utility. It addresses the longitudinal nature of medical data and incorporates static covariates like age and gender. The workflow shows higher resemblance and utility compared to benchmarks, emphasizing covariate stratification. This approach opens avenues for healthcare research.

The authors in (Wang, Myles, & Tucker, 2021) propose a framework for generating and evaluating synthetic healthcare data, focusing on cross-sectional data. It aims to preserve ground truth data complexities while ensuring privacy. The framework is applied to synthetic datasets like the Indian liver patient dataset and UK primary care dataset, filling a gap in literature.

Goncalves et al. in (Goncalves et al., 2020) evaluated synthetic data generation methods for medical data, comparing probabilistic, classification-based, and generative neural networks. They introduced metrics for evaluating dataset quality, data utility, and privacy, and highlighted their potential for accelerating research in medicine and cancer.

Dahmen and Cook's (2019) introduced SynSys, a machine learning-based method for generating synthetic data. Utilizing hidden Markov models and regression algorithms, SynSys produces more realistic data than other methods, potentially advancing smart home data testing and improvement.

3. BACKGROUNDS

3.1 Methods of Synthetic Data Generation

Synthetic high-dimensional data is critical for developing medical research and imaging because it addresses privacy concerns, augments restricted datasets, simulates varied circumstances, and enables collaborative initiatives. It offers a realistic alternative for academics to build and test breakthrough algorithms while adhering to ethical and privacy concerns in the healthcare area. Various synthetic data creation techniques are used to mimic the statistical properties of real-world datasets while protecting sensitive information. Some popular strategies include the following (Yale et al., 2020) (Lu, Wang, & Wei, 2023) (Murtaza, et al., 2023) (Rodriguez-Almeida et al., 2022) (Rajotte et al., 2022).

i) Statistical Methods

Descriptive statistics include summarizing and duplicating important statistical variables from the original dataset, such as mean, median, and variance.

Probability Distributions: Models the distribution of variables in the original data using probability distributions (e.g., Gaussian, Poisson), and then generates synthetic samples appropriately.

ii) Generative Adversarial Networks (GANs)

Generative Models: GANs are made up of a generator and a discriminator network. The generator generates synthetic data, whereas the discriminator separates actual and synthetic data. The interplay between them improves the quality of synthetic data (Osuala et al., 2021).

iii) Variational Auto Encoders (VAE)

Latent Variable Models (VAEs) discover the underlying structure of data by translating it to a lower-dimensional latent space. Synthetic data is created by sampling from this space and recreating the original features.

iv) Differential Privacy Techniques

Noise Injection adds properly adjusted noise to the original data to avoid individual identification while maintaining general statistical trends.

v) Copula-Based Models

Joint Distribution Modeling: Using copulas to capture the dependence structure between variables, synthetic data with realistic inter-variable interactions may be generated.

vi) Bootstrap Resampling

Resampling techniques include random sampling with replacement from the original dataset, resulting in synthetic datasets with statistical features similar to the real data.

vii) Data Morphing and Transformation

Data Transformation: Applying different transformations (e.g., linear or nonlinear transformations) to the original data results in synthetic datasets with altered but statistically equivalent properties.

viii) Bayesian Networks

Probabilistic Graphical Models: Uses Bayesian networks (Mallick, Giri, and Mishra, 2023) to describe the probabilistic dependencies between variables, allowing for the creation of synthetic data with realistic inter-variable interactions.

ix) Federated Learning

Decentralized Model Training: Trains models using numerous data sources without transferring raw data. Aggregated models are then utilized to create synthetic data using the statistical properties of the original datasets.

x) Rule-Based Approaches

Heuristic Rules: Uses domain-specific rules and heuristics to create synthetic data that is consistent with the known qualities and relationships in the original dataset (Giri et al., 2020)

These approaches are suitable for a variety of applications, with the choice determined by considerations such as the nature of the data, privacy restrictions, and the specific statistical qualities to be kept.

4. THE PROPOSED FRAMEWORK

This section presents a thorough approach for generating privacy-preserving high-dimensional synthetic data in the health care area. Our method strives to fulfill the important need to protect sensitive health-related information while also allowing for the use of synthetic data in a variety of applications. The technique is systematic, with important steps including data gathering, preprocessing, synthetic data production, and detailed assessment. Our methodology strives to strike a compromise between privacy assurance and synthetic data usefulness by methodically combining privacy-preserving algorithms and specialized methodologies intended for high-dimensional datasets. The framework for the proposed methodology is presented in Figure 1. The following textprovide a deep study of each stage, explaining the numerous methods needed to attain.

4.1. Data Collection

4.1.1 Source of Data

We obtained high-dimensional health care data from a variety of sources, including electronic health records (EHR), medical imaging archives, patient surveys, and other relevant datasets. The selection method took into account data richness and diversity to guarantee a full representation of health-related information.

4.1.2 Data Privacy Compliance

To comply with tight data privacy rules, particularly in the health care arena (e.g., HIPAA), we created stringent standards for data collection, storage, and processing. Anonymization techniques were used to remove personally identifying information (PII) and replace it with anonymous identifiers.

4.2. Data Preprocessing

4.2.1 Anonymization

The anonymization procedure includes the elimination of personally identifiable information (PII), such as names, addresses, and contact information. To ensure the confidentiality of individual patient information, anonymized IDs were carefully constructed and assigned to each record.

4.2.2 Feature Selection

To minimize dimensionality and improve the efficiency of the synthetic data production process, we used feature selection techniques. Relevant high-dimensional characteristics were selected based on their importance in contributing to total health-related data.

4.2.3 Handling Missing Values

To verify the dataset's completeness, missing values were corrected using appropriate imputation techniques (Mallick et al., 2022). This approach sought to preserve the data's integrity and increase the robustness of future studies.

4.3. Synthetic Data Generation

4.3.1 Privacy-Protecting Algorithms

We used cutting-edge privacy-preserving methods, such as differential privacy, homomorphic encryption, and federated learning, to create synthetic data. These approaches were chosen because they can safeguard individual records while retaining the statistical properties of the original dataset.

4.3.2 High Dimensional Synthesis

Specialized approaches were created to solve the difficulties associated with high-dimensional data creation. The synthesis approach aimed to preserve the complicated correlations and patterns seen in the original health care data.

4.4. Evaluation Metrics

4.4.1 Quality Metrics

To evaluate the quality of the synthetic data, we established criteria for data dispersion, correlation, and usefulness in specific health care applications. These metrics provide a quantifiable assessment of how closely the synthetic data matched the original dataset.

Figure 1. The proposed framework

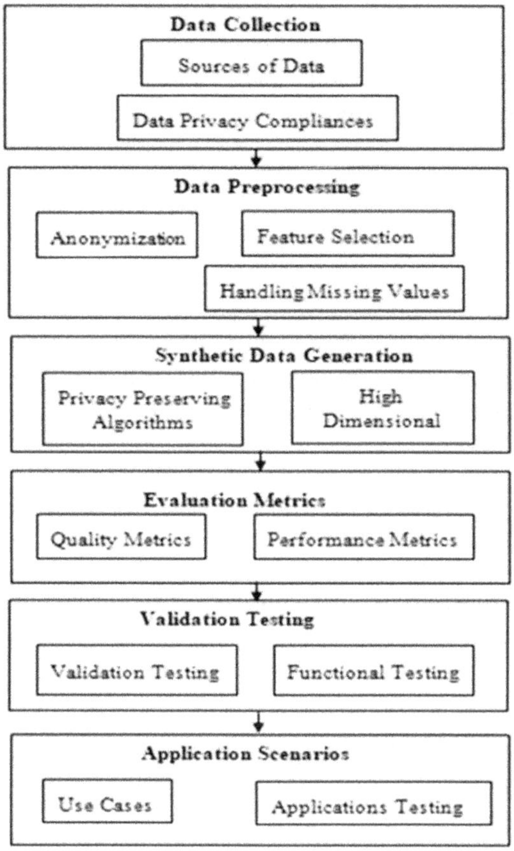

4.4.2 Performance Metrics

Performance criteria including as accuracy, recall, and F1 score were used to assess the success of privacy-preserving synthetic data production. These metrics assessed the model's ability to reliably duplicate important aspects from the original data.

4.5. Validation and Testing

4.5.1 Statistical Validation

The synthetic data was rigorously statistically validated by comparing its attributes to those of the real dataset. This stage guaranteed that the synthetic data properly represented the statistical properties of the health-care data.

4.5.2 Functional Testing

Functional testing entailed determining the acceptability of the synthetic data for various health-care applications. We tested its performance in real-world circumstances to ensure its usefulness for future analyses.

4.6 Application Scenarios

4.6.1 Use Cases

We investigated a wide range of application situations, including machine learning model training, epidemiology investigations, and medical research support. Each use case demonstrated the adaptability and application of privacy-preserving, high-dimensional synthetic data.

4.6.2 Application Testing

The synthetic data's effectiveness was assessed in practical health care applications, with a focus on improving data-driven decision-making and enabling research outcomes.

4.7. Privacy Assurance

4.7.1 Validation Against Standards

To ensure a high level of privacy protection, the suggested approaches were tested against existing privacy-preserving standards and benchmarks. This stage offered assurance about the strength of the privacy-preserving measures used.

4.7.2 Robustness Analysis

A thorough evaluation of the strength of privacy-preserving approaches was carried out, taking into account hypothetical assaults or privacy breaches. This evaluation sought to identify and resolve risks in the suggested technique.

5. CONCLUSION AND FUTURE WORK

The chapter discusses the growing healthcare industry's need for vast information, highlighting challenges like data privacy and ethical considerations, and highlights the potential of synthetic data. It highlights the significant use cases of synthetic data in healthcare research, demonstrating its adaptability and application in various fields such as simulation, prediction, epidemiology, and health information technology development.The work suggested a framework combines privacy-preserving algorithms with specialized methodologies for high-dimensional synthetic data development in the healthcare business, which includes data collection, preprocessing, synthetic data production, and comprehensive assessment.

Future research should focus on the methods produce privacy-preserving high-dimensional synthetic data for the healthcare area. The results will be validated to demonstrate the effectiveness of the proposed strategy in balancing privacy issues with the value of synthetic data.Further research will also focus on improving the methodology, broadening the application fields, and overcoming any constraints discovered during this study. Continuous advancement in privacy-preserving synthetic data creation is critical for furthering data-driven health care research and applications.

REFERENCES

Abay, N. C., Zhou, Y., Kantarcioglu, M., Thuraisingham, B., & Sweeney, L. (2019). Privacy preserving synthetic data release using deep learning. In *Machine Learning and Knowledge Discovery in Databases: European Conference, ECML PKDD 2018, Ireland, Proceedings, Part I 18* (pp. 510-526). 10.1007/978-3-030-10925-7_31

Abouelmehdi, K., Beni-Hessane, A., & Khaloufi, H. (2018). Big healthcare data: Preserving security and privacy. *Journal of Big Data*, *5*(1), 1–18. doi:10.1186/s40537-017-0110-7

Beaulieu-Jones, B. K., Wu, Z. S., Williams, C., Lee, R., Bhavnani, S. P., Byrd, J. B., & Greene, C. S. (2019). Privacy-preserving generative deep neural networks support clinical data sharing. *Circulation: Cardiovascular Quality and Outcomes*, *12*(7), e005122. doi:10.1161/CIRCOUTCOMES.118.005122 PMID:31284738

Char, D. S., Abràmoff, M. D., & Feudtner, C. (2020). Identifying ethical considerations for machine learning healthcare applications. *The American Journal of Bioethics*, *20*(11), 7–17. doi:10.1080/15265161.2020.1819469 PMID:33103967

Chen, R. J., Lu, M. Y., Chen, T. Y., Williamson, D. F., & Mahmood, F. (2021). Synthetic data in machine learning for medicine and healthcare. *Nature Biomedical Engineering*, *5*(6), 493–497. doi:10.1038/s41551-021-00751-8 PMID:34131324

Dahmen, J., & Cook, D. (2019). SynSys: A synthetic data generation system for healthcare applications. *Sensors (Basel), 19*(5), 1181. doi:10.3390/s19051181 PMID:30857130

Dash, S., Yale, A., Guyon, I., & Bennett, K. P. (2020). Medical time-series data generation using generative adversarial networks. In *Artificial Intelligence in Medicine: 18th International Conference on Artificial Intelligence in Medicine, MN, USA, Proceedings 18* (pp. 382-391). 10.1007/978-3-030-59137-3_34

Fawaz, H. I., Forestier, G., Weber, J., Idoumghar, L., & Muller, P. A. (2018). Data augmentation using synthetic data for time series classification with deep residual networks. *arXiv preprint arXiv:1808.02455.*

Foraker, R. E., Yu, S. C., Gupta, A., Michelson, A. P., Pineda Soto, J. A., Colvin, R., Loh, F., Kollef, M. H., Maddox, T., Evanoff, B., Dror, H., Zamstein, N., Lai, A. M., & Payne, P. R. (2020). Spot the difference: Comparing results of analyses from real patient data and synthetic derivatives. *JAMIA Open, 3*(4), 557–566. doi:10.1093/jamiaopen/ooaa060 PMID:33623891

Giri, P. K., De, S. S., Dehuri, S., & Cho, S. B. (2020). Biogeography Based Optimization for Mining Rules to Assess Credit Risk, Journal: Intelligent Systems in Accounting. *Financial Management, 28*(1), 35–51.

Giuffrè, M., & Shung, D. L. (2023). Harnessing the power of synthetic data in healthcare: Innovation, application, and privacy. *NPJ Digital Medicine, 6*(1), 186. doi:10.1038/s41746-023-00927-3 PMID:37813960

Goncalves, A., Ray, P., Soper, B., Stevens, J., Coyle, L., & Sales, A. P. (2020). Generation and evaluation of synthetic patient data. *BMC Medical Research Methodology, 20*(1), 1–40. doi:10.1186/s12874-020-00977-1 PMID:32381039

Hao, S., Han, W., Jiang, T., Li, Y., Wu, H., Zhong, C., . . . Tang, H. (2024). Synthetic Data in AI: Challenges, Applications, and Ethical Implications. *arXiv preprint arXiv:2401.01629.*

Hernandez, M., Epelde, G., Alberdi, A., Cilla, R., & Rankin, D. (2022). Synthetic data generation for tabular health records: A systematic review. *Neurocomputing, 493*, 28–45. doi:10.1016/j.neucom.2022.04.053

Hoag, J. E. (2008). *Synthetic data generation: Theory, techniques and applications.* University of Arkansas.

James, S., Harbron, C., Branson, J., & Sundler, M. (2021). Synthetic data use: Exploring use cases to optimise data utility. *Discover Artificial Intelligence*, *1*(1), 15. doi:10.1007/s44163-021-00016-y

Khalid, N., Qayyum, A., Bilal, M., Al-Fuqaha, A., & Qadir, J. (2023). Privacy-preserving artificial intelligence in healthcare: Techniques and applications. *Computers in Biology and Medicine*, *158*, 106848. doi:10.1016/j.compbiomed.2023.106848 PMID:37044052

Khalid, N., Qayyum, A., Bilal, M., Al-Fuqaha, A., & Qadir, J. (2023). Privacy-preserving artificial intelligence in healthcare: Techniques and applications. *Computers in Biology and Medicine*, *158*, 106848. doi:10.1016/j.compbiomed.2023.106848 PMID:37044052

Lohr, K. N., & Donaldson, M. S. (Eds.). (1994). *Committee on Regional Health Data, Health data in the information age: use, disclosure, and privacy*. National Academies Press.

Lu, Y., Wang, H., & Wei, W. (2023). Machine Learning for Synthetic Data Generation: a Review. *arXiv preprint arXiv:2302.04062*.

Mallick, C. K., Giri, P. K., & Mishra, S. N. (2023). A multi-objective LGBBO algorithm for overlapping community detection in a social network analysis. *Malaysian Journal of Computer Science*, *36*(2), 173–192. doi:10.22452/mjcs.vol36no2.4

Mallick, C. K., Giri, P. K., Paikaray, B. K., & Mishra, S. N. (2022). Machine Learning Approaches to Sentiment Analysis in Social Networks. *International Journal of Work Innovation*, *3*(4), 317–337. doi:10.1504/IJWI.2023.128860

McLachlan, S., Dube, K., & Gallagher, T. (2016). Using the caremap with health incidents statistics for generating the realistic synthetic electronic healthcare record. In IEEE international conference on healthcare informatics (ICHI) (pp. 439-448). doi:10.1109/ICHI.2016.83

Murtaza, H., Ahmed, M., Khan, N. F., Murtaza, G., Zafar, S., & Bano, A. (2023). Synthetic data generation: State of the art in health care domain. *Computer Science Review*, *48*, 100546. doi:10.1016/j.cosrev.2023.100546

Osuala, R., Kushibar, K., Garrucho, L., Linardos, A., Szafranowska, Z., Klein, S., & Lekadir, K. (2021). A review of generative adversarial networks in cancer imaging: New applications, new solutions. *arXiv preprint arXiv:2107.09543*

Philpott, D. (Ed.). (2017). *A guide to federal terms and acronyms*. Bernan Press.

Rajotte, J. F., Bergen, R., Buckeridge, D. L., El Emam, K., Ng, R., & Strome, E. (2022). Synthetic data as an enabler for machine learning applications in medicine. *iScience*, *25*(11), 105331. doi:10.1016/j.isci.2022.105331 PMID:36325058

Rodriguez-Almeida, A. J., Fabelo, H., Ortega, S., Deniz, A., Balea-Fernandez, F. J., Quevedo, E., & Callico, G. M. (2022). Synthetic patient data generation and evaluation in disease prediction using small and imbalanced datasets. *IEEE Journal of Biomedical and Health Informatics*. PMID:35930509

Siwicki, B. (2020). Is synthetic data the key to healthcare clinical and business intelligence? *Healthcare IT News*.

Wang, Z., Myles, P., & Tucker, A. (2021). Generating and evaluating cross-sectional synthetic electronic healthcare data: Preserving data utility and patient privacy. *Computational Intelligence*, *37*(2), 819–851. doi:10.1111/coin.12427

Wang, Z., Draghi, B., Rotalinti, Y., Lunn, D., & Myles, P. (2024). *High-Fidelity Synthetic Data Applications for Data Augmentation*. Academic Press.

Xu, Y., Liu, X., Cao, X., Huang, C., Liu, E., Qian, S., & Zhang, J. (2021). Artificial intelligence: A powerful paradigm for scientific research. *Innovation (Cambridge (Mass.))*, *2*(4), 100179. doi:10.1016/j.xinn.2021.100179 PMID:34877560

Yale, A., Dash, S., Dutta, R., Guyon, I., Pavao, A., & Bennett, K. P. (2020). Generation and evaluation of privacy preserving synthetic health data. *Neurocomputing*, *416*, 244–255. doi:10.1016/j.neucom.2019.12.136

Yan, C., Yan, Y., Wan, Z., Zhang, Z., Omberg, L., Guinney, J., & Malin, B. A. (2022). A multifaceted benchmarking of synthetic electronic health record generation models. *Nature Communications*, *13*(1), 7609. doi:10.1038/s41467-022-35295-1 PMID:36494374

Chapter 11
Tools to Create Synthetic Data for Brain Images

S. Sindhu
https://orcid.org/0000-0002-2133-6377
SRM Institute of Science and Technology, India

N. Vijayalakshmi
SRM Institute of Science and Technology, India

ABSTRACT

In the areas of neuroscience, medical imaging, and machine learning, the creation of synthetic data for brain scans has become a key approach. This chapter explores the concept and significance of synthetic data generation for brain images. In tasks like brain picture segmentation, disease detection, and image analysis, machine learning models perform better when using synthetic data as a catalyst for data augmentation. A wide range of methods and resources including MRI simulators, 3D modeling software, deep learning frameworks, and medical imaging software are used to create synthetic brain images. To guarantee the validity and applicability of synthetic data, however, ethical issues, data representativeness, and transparency in the generation process continue to be essential factors. Synthetic brain data are becoming more useful and realistic as technology develops, and this has the potential to completely change the fields of neuroscience and medical imaging.

1. INTRODUCTION

Image synthetic data is made using computer algorithms or models as opposed to being physically acquired by sensors or cameras and is defined as artificially created images that resemble real-world data. This fake data is frequently used to train, test, and validate algorithms and models in a variety of disciplines, such as computer vision, machine learning, and artificial intelligence.

DOI: 10.4018/979-8-3693-1886-7.ch011

The main programs that were used to create the synthetic brain image dataset are listed in the section that follows. It will go into detail about the most popular tools, including GAN, Simulator, MedIm, MedScribe, and BrainWeb.

However, the image is insufficient to produce the ideal result for the model to train it with a synthetic image dataset. To train the model to exactly generate the projected result with a better level of accuracy, more photos are needed. Building deep learning models for all types of perceptions is the main goal of the Synthetic Date Brain Image Generation effort.

The functions of synthetic image data is as follows:

Data Augmentation: Synthetic data can be used to expand and diversify already-existing datasets. By giving machine learning models more training instances, this can enhance their performance.

Security and privacy: Sometimes, sensitive or private information may be present in real-world data. In order to construct a non-sensitive version of the data while maintaining its statistical features, synthetic data can be employed.

Class imbalance in machine learning datasets can be addressed through the use of synthetic data. The model can learn to distinguish between various classes more effectively by producing synthetic examples of underrepresented classes.

Synthetic data can be useful, but it must accurately reflect the distribution of real-world data and must not include biases or artifacts that could cause over-fitting or poor generalization in models. When utilizing synthetic data in machine learning applications, careful validation and testing are crucial.

Diverse, excellent, and ethically obtained brain image datasets are in high demand in the rapidly developing fields of medical imaging and neuroscience. These datasets are essential for improving it's knowledge of brain anatomy and diseases in addition to being used to train machine learning models and create state-of-the-art image processing techniques. But gathering such data is still a difficult task, frequently hindered by moral issues and restricted access to patient records.

2. USES OF SYNTHETIC IMAGE DATASET

Due of the high cost, only a small amount of real-world data could be acquired. It helps the model receive additional training. It could lead to a deeper knowledge of the dataset's many characteristics. Anyone can use these datasets to train their model correctly and to solve the over-fitting and under-fitting difficulties because they are cleaned and perfectly fit the model without any errors. They will not compromise the findings' privacy.

Synthetic data can be used to establish a baseline for typical behavior, which is helpful for anomaly detection systems. Any difference from this standard might be reported as an abnormality. Data Generation for Rare or Uncommon Scenarios: In some fields, gathering data for unusual or rare scenarios can be difficult or expensive. Examples of these scenarios can be produced using synthetic data for training and testing reasons.

Making a sufficient training dataset is a demanding and time-consuming operation (Brainsuite, n.d.).

In each instance, the photos were to be fed into the model in order to teach it to recognize tissues that would develop in the future at an early stage. The imported photos are more than enough in these circumstances to train the model. The model is made more predictable by the use of synthetic images.

3. DISADVANTAGES OF THE TECHNOLOGY FOR CREATING SYNTHETIC BRAIN IMAGES

Although there are many benefits to using technologies for creating synthetic brain images, there are also disadvantages and restrictions. The following are a few possible disadvantages of artificial brain image generating tools:

Absence of Real-World Variability: The intricate and varied variations seen in real brain imaging may not be adequately captured by synthetic data. This can be particularly restrictive when studying uncommon or rare anatomical or clinical variants.

Data Fidelity: In medical imaging, where high-quality images are necessary for precise diagnosis and treatment planning, the fidelity of synthetic images might not match that of real-world data.

For the objective of training the model to produce better results from the trained dataset, there are many ways to generate synthetic data. This introduction lays the groundwork for a more thorough examination of the synthetic brain image creation tool, it's possible uses, and the implications it may have for the domains of neuroscience, artificial intelligence, and medical imaging. Examining the potential and ramifications of this novel instrument, itfind that it is at the front of revolutionary developments in the field of brain imaging and its vital role in medical and scientific research.

3.1 Generative Model

From a similar statistical sample, it's model creates a synthetic image dataset. Due to its capacity to produce better images with fewer artifacts, Tissue Harmonic Imaging (THI) has experienced significant growth in popularity (Ledig et al., 2017).

Images of uncommon occurrences or edge instances, which may be challenging to capture in real-world data, can be produced using synthetic data. This aids the model's learning about handling peculiar circumstances. The low frame artifacts, sustainability of motion facts, and extraction of the images from the baseline low frame rate in harmonics are problems for tissue harmonic approaches (Islam & Zhang, 2018).

3.2 Procedural Generation

The photos are produced by this algorithmic model using similarities between objects and landscapes. It a method used to create content algorithmically rather than manually, and is utilized in computer graphics, game development, and many other industries. It entails applying mathematical (Betzel et al., 2016) formulas and algorithm ms to create data—such as images, topography, levels, or other content—based on a predetermined set of guidelines or requirements. Numerous applications, such as video games, graphics, simulation, and content production, use procedural generation.

important facets and uses of procedural generation

3.2.1 Terrain Generation

For the purpose of creating realistic and varied terrain for video games, simulations, and virtual worlds, procedural generation is commonly used. Based on a set of parameters, algorithms can produce several types of landscapes, such as mountains, valleys, rivers, and forests.

3.2.2 Level Design

Procedural generation can be used in video game production to create levels, mazes, dungeons, or environments on the fly. This makes levels less of a necessity to be handmade and increases replay ability.

3.2.3 Texture and Asset Generation

To produce textures, 3D models, and other assets, procedural approaches can be used. This lowers the storage requirements for games and enables dynamic visual diversity.

3.2.4 Character and NPC Generation

Procedural generation is used in some games to produce player characters as well as non-playable characters (NPCs), giving each character distinctive abilities, looks, and personalities.

3.3 Rule-Based Generation

To produce the synthetic image data set using the previously established mathematical formulas and procedures. Instead of manually creating or altering photographs, rule-based image production refers to the method of creating images or other visual information using a set of predetermined rules or algorithms. These guidelines and methods outline the proper ways to mix different components, including forms, colors, textures, and patterns, to create an image. Applications for rule-based image generation include computer graphics, visual arts, and generative design (Braun et al., 2021; Tang et al., 2017; Yang et al., 2021). Rule-based picture generation is frequently applied to the creation of procedural textures. Algorithmically generated procedural textures can be used to texture 3D objects, mimic real materials (like marble or wood), or produce abstract patterns.

3.4 Simulation

This simulates the images from fabricated sensor data from the previous study.

The trained image for the deep conservative technique can be created with the help of generative adversarial networks (Yang et al., 2021). This GAN techniques is to understand the relationship between two RF signals and create two related RF signals from noise. This enables us to improve the performance of an ultrasonic application based on deep learning by using the created input-output signal pairs in the training dataset. Conventional techniques, on the other hand, struggle to produce completely original patterns in the dataset because they rely on a finite collection of well-known, straightforward invariance (Parkes et al., 2021). Images with a proper view of the tissues and infected area may be produced by the simulation tool. This kind of simulator is helpful for giving the model the ideal training. For image generation (Faskowitz et al., 2022; Faskowitz et al., 2018; Tang & Bassett, 2018; Witvliet et al., 2021), a variety of simulator tools and software are available, each with unique features and capabilities. The tool it use will rely on unique needs and the kind of image generating it intend to do. While some programs offer greater capabilities for picture generation and editing, certain solutions are more tailored for particular needs.

4. TOOLS FOR CREATING THE SYNTHETIC IMAGE DATASET TO TRAIN THE MODEL

Testing the resistance of computer vision models to hostile attacks can be done using artificial images. Adversarial examples are created to trick models, and a wide range of these instances can be produced using synthetic datasets. Synthetic brain data will likely get better as technology develops, increasing its usefulness as a resource for scientists and professionals working in the disciplines of neuroscience and medical imaging (Murphy et al., 2020). Nevertheless, to ensure that synthetic data is applicable and reliable in real-world circumstances, rigorous validation and careful assessment of its constraints are important. In order to create synthetic datasets for brain image analysis, artificial brain images (Betzel et al., 2020) that closely resemble real brain data must be produced. Without the requirement for actual patient data, these artificial datasets can be useful for developing and assessing machine learning models, testing algorithms, and conducting research. The purpose of this work is to investigate the capacity of various tools to concurrently generate two signals as well as to learn the relationship between two signals and produce synthetic data from random noise. In particular (Stillman et al., 2017), this work introduces the capability to end-to-end train with statistically similar distributions to those of the simulated data, yet with a lower computational burden, to generate meaningful ultrasound linear and nonlinear echo brain tumour images along with their corresponding linear component directly in signal space.

4.1 Generative Adversarial Networks Synthetic Frameworks for Data Generation

To generate synthetic medical images, particularly images of the brain, think about employing frameworks for synthetic data production like Synthetic Data Vault or GANs for Medical Imaging (GanMedIm). The creation of synthetic data has undergone a revolution because to Generative Adversarial Networks (GANs). GANs are made up of two neural networks that compete with one another during training: a discriminator and a generator. While the discriminator seeks to discern between genuine and artificial data, the generator attempts to produce artificial data that is indistinguishable from actual data. It is primarily the goal of this GAN class to develop a machine learning model to produce an unsupervised learning dataset, such as synthetic images, with a focus on generative models for synthetic images. subsequently it became popular in many fields, including text mining, natural language processing, and all other computer vision programs. In 2014, Ian's close pals first mentioned it (Betzel & Bassett, 2017).

Generators and discriminators are two main neural types that can make up a GAN. The data with noise is first entered into the generator network. It aims to produce something that can't be distinguished from actual data. The discriminators can determine whether the sample data provided is real or not, just like a binary classifier. Its major objective is to tell authentic data from fake ones.

The images are produced by the GAN in the following manner:

Figure 1. Workflow of the GAN

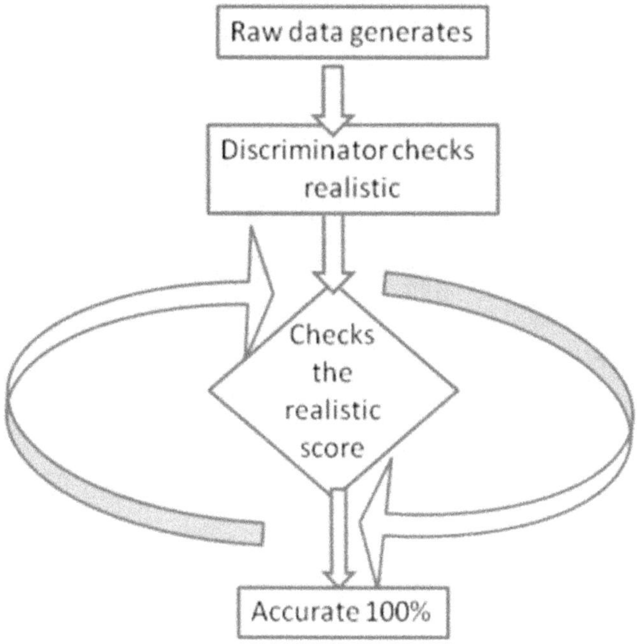

Step 1: The generator will first produce the data. The discriminators examine it to determine its reality.

Step 2: The discriminators always assess how the real and false images differ from the data image.

Step 3: The generators constantly produce fictitious images to educate the discriminators to recognize the similarities or differences between the real and fictitious images.

Step 4: The generator and discriminator both repeat this procedure until the generator generates more accurate data and the discriminator recognizes phony data.

Image generation, image-to-image translation (such as converting sketches into photographs), super-resolution, style transfer, text-to-image synthesis, and other uses for GANs are among their many applications. The development of realistic synthetic data(Figure 1) for a variety of applications has been made possible by GANs, which have made a significant contribution to the field of artificial intelligence.

Consider the noise vector v NP with its generator (g) and discriminator (d). The generated data is denoted by the term g(nd) in equation 1, while the term nd is used to denote the noisy random data. The discriminator sample actual data is denoted as rd(Figure 2), and it then determines the probability that rd may be real data (1)

Figure 2. The VGAN discriminator and general generator architecture are illustrated

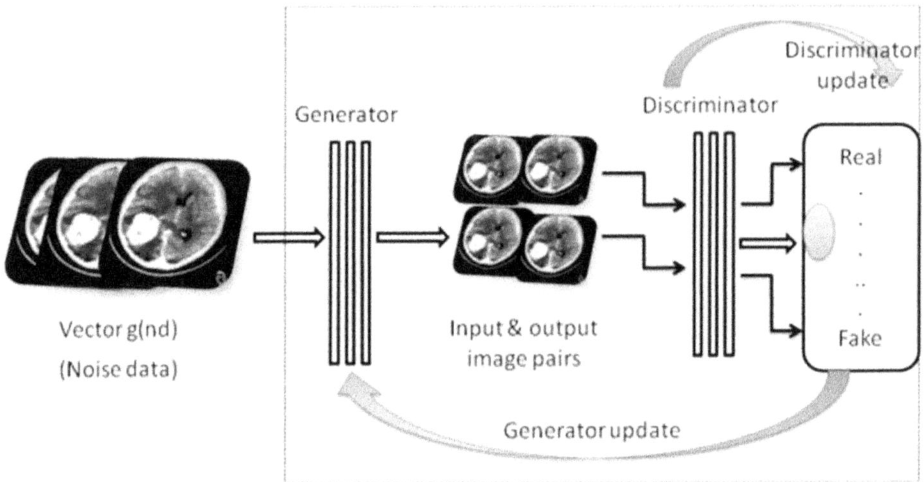

or fake data (0) by calculating the realistic value of a rd. It is indicated as d(rd) or d(g(nd)) after the conclusions.

Following the generation of noisy data that the discriminator can reasonably detect, the generator proceeds to assess the loss function and steer clear of piqued data. Measures the effectiveness of the generator's deception of the discriminator (LossF(g)) in equation 2. Binary cross-entropy loss is a popular option.

$$\text{LossF}(g) = \log(d(g(nd)) \rightarrow \text{equation 1}$$

Measures how successfully the discriminator is able to discern between authentic and fraudulent data.

$$\text{LossF}(d) = [\log(d(rd)) + \log(1 - d(g(nd))] \rightarrow \text{equation 2}$$

It may determine if the data is sufficient to train the model or whether it is under fitting to train the specific model for the prediction process once it has completed the loss function comparability based on the loss function value.

The evaluation of model training on an appropriate dataset is the last step in the GAN approaches. In this instance, the researchers' fixed detection criteria or metrics have been used to adjust the training target. To provide a flawless, realistic dataset for the discriminator, the generator's loss function must first be minimized. To increase the discriminators' ability to distinguish between real data and fake data for the research, reduce or minimize the loss function.

Figure 3. Shown how the resulting nonlinear echo differs from its corresponding linear echo

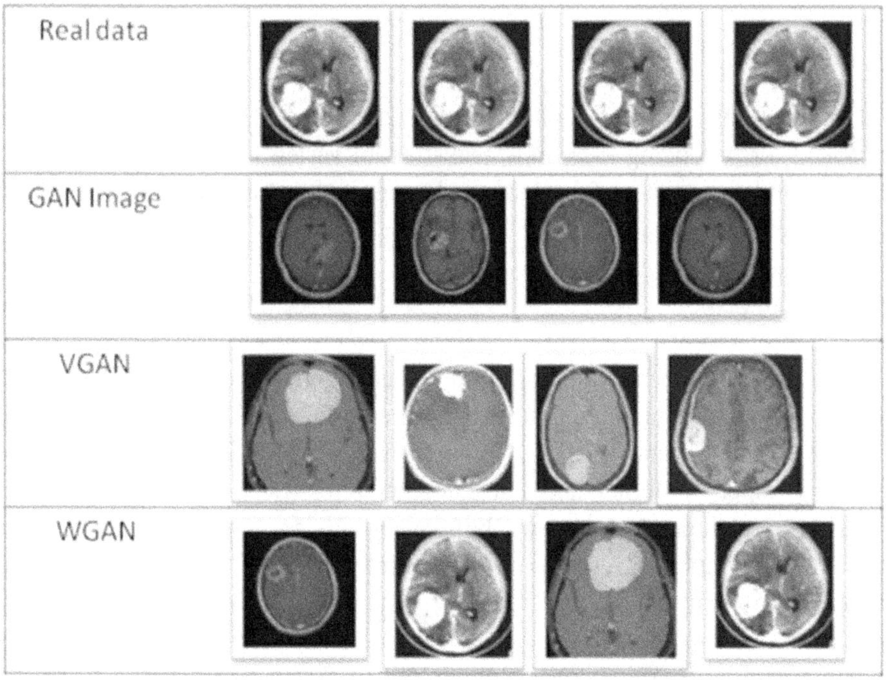

In turn, the training procedure seeks to reduce the loss function for both the generator and discriminator by repeatedly iterating until the generator and discriminator are updated. The discriminator is updated with the back propagation of the loss function during adversarial training, which is the final operation of this generator. The projection of the minimal loss function was then applied to the generator as well. These phases may be continued until they achieve the maximum real data, with its weights changed by the turn.

4.2 NVidia Image Generator Tool

NVIDIA has contributed to the development of GANs, which are widely used for generating synthetic data, including images and other types of data. NVIDIA's research in this area has led to innovations in image synthesis and generation. This is yet another excellent tool for developing the synthetic picture dataset for the datasets related to brain tumors. In 2021, it was developed. It released a lot of tools for creating images. This method aids in producing the various instruments for image creation (Oh et al., 2022). especially in the context of computer vision graphics and deep learning image processing. Here are some notable picture generating tools and technologies from NVIDIA:

(a) StyleGAN (as well as StyleGAN2)

Deep generative models from NVIDIA called StyleGAN and StyleGAN2 are renowned for producing incredibly realistic and varied images, especially faces. The style and appearance of the generated images can be precisely controlled using these models.

(b) NVIDIA NGX

A collection of deep learning tools and technologies known as NVIDIA NGX can be incorporated into numerous programs and services. To enhance the quality of photographs and movies, NGX incorporates capabilities including AI-based denoising, super-resolution, and image augmentation (Sadeghi et al., 2022).

Using this method, the feature will be updated with the current one to provide fresh featured photographs for research and development. This was the external program or application that the photos were used to train for the development of synthetic data. The process for creating the synthetic image data collection is described below.

In step 1(Figure 4), The NGX-generated features and advantages are used to implement the Image features. The NGX is to reduce the noise from the image in the process of de-noising. In the next level, it could develop the image resolution known as super resolution, and finally, it could enhance the image quality from the lower quality. Checking and optimization: In this level, it might be checking whether the performance of the images satisfies the features generated by the NGX tool.

4.3 Three-Dimenssional-Model Rendering Tool

Testing the resistance of computer vision models to hostile attacks can be done using artificial images. Adversarial examples are created to trick models, and a wide range of these instances can be produced using synthetic datasets. In computer graphics and visualization, rendering models are used to convert 3D scene data into 2D or 3D images (Chen et al., 2023; Lei et al., 2022; Papanastasiou et al., 2023; Porter et al., 2023; Sadeghi et al., 2022). This merely entails building the three-dimensional model and turning the finished product into an image or animation. This is a typical activity in many industries, such as product design, computer graphics, architecture, and more.

Figure 4. Overall architecture of the NIVIDIA NGX image generator to extracting the features from the existing dataset

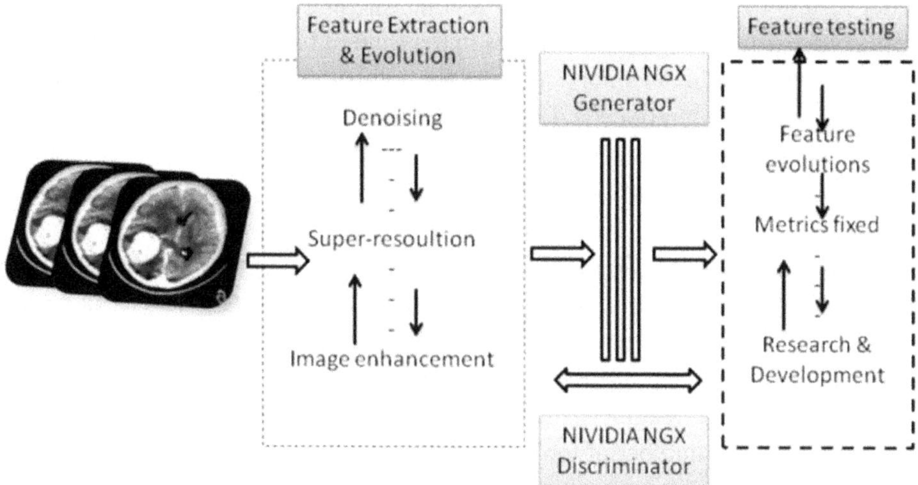

The following list of well-liked 3D model rendering tools:

a) **Blender, a 3D rendering program:** This free and open-source animation 3D modeling program is capable of texturing, picture sculpting, rigging, animation, and video production. Like the Eevee tool, it has its own generating or rendering engine.
b) **3D segmentation and modeling:** Separate the relevant brain structures from the 3D volumetric data. In order to do this, particular physical structures, the cortex, and other areas must be recognized and defined.
c) **Brain segmentation** can be aided by programs like FreeSurfer, FSL (FMRIB Software Library), and SPM (Statistical Parametric Mapping).
d) **Software for 3D Visualization:** Create 3D renderings and visualizations of the segmented brain structures using specialized 3D visualization tools. Popular choices comprise: A flexible open-source software platform for image processing, 3D visualization, and medical imaging informatics is called 3D Slicer. For biomedical imaging, there is a commercial software suite called Amira-Avizo that has potent 3D viewing and analysis features.
e) **BrainSuite:** A collection of software tools with 3D visualization capabilities for analyzing MRI data a 3D rendering. To use rendering techniques inside the 3D visualization program of choice to improve the visual appeal of brain model Realistic representations can be made by adjusting the lighting, shading, and material qualities. To move around, zoom in, and pan to view the brain from different perspectives.

The creation of the 3D brain image dataset using the aforementioned technique is the most helpful in terms of giving each model the best possible training to get better results from the few samples available. Magnetic wavy images in grayscale format were used to capture the images in the field of brain tumors. With the aid of this technique, predictions may be made for both synthetic images of brain tumor cells and non-brain tumor cells. Let's take a quick look at the Brain Suite software and its necessities for the study.

4.3.1 Benefits of BrainSuite in Research

Magnetic resonance imaging (MRI) of the human brain can be processed largely automatically with the help of the open-source software toolkit known as BrainSuite. These tools' main functions include extracting and parameter zing the cerebral cortex's inner and outer surfaces, segmenting and labeling gray and white matter structures, analyzing diffusion imaging data, and processing functional MRI. Additionally, BrainSuite offers a number of tools for engaging and visualizing the data.

The magnetic resonance imaging machine typically captures the image as grayscale; this tool produces the brain images as HSV color-coded data. The name of the peripheral part is likewise labeled on the tool, which also generates the various colors for each segmentation (Lei et al., 2022). The color-coded format may make it easier to distinguish the size and shape of the tissue. The system has no trouble understanding how to outperform the conventional methods.

(i) Processing of MRI Data: T1-weighted, T2-weighted, and diffusion MRI data can all be processed by BrainSuite. It offers resources for organizing and preparing MRI data.
(ii) Brain Segmentation: The software has tools for automatically dividing the brain into different parts and structures, such as the cerebrospinal fluid, the gray matter, and the white matter. For the analyses that come after, accurate segmentation is essential.
(iii) BrainSuite's ability to recreate the cortical surface of the brain enables in-depth examination of the cerebral cortex. This is crucial for mapping the structure and function of the brain.
(iv) Researchers can utilize BrainSuite to quantify cortical thickness, an important parameter for examining the structure of the brain and potential alterations in neurological illnesses. It offers 3D visualization capabilities so that users can explore and investigate brain structures in a three-dimensional space. This aids in understanding complex brain anatomy and spatial relationships.
(v) BrainSuite provides tools for studying the sulci (grooves) and gyri (ridges) on the surface of the brain. Software that facilitates connection analysis enables

Figure 5. The graphical representation of the normal MRI image and BrainSuite tool image

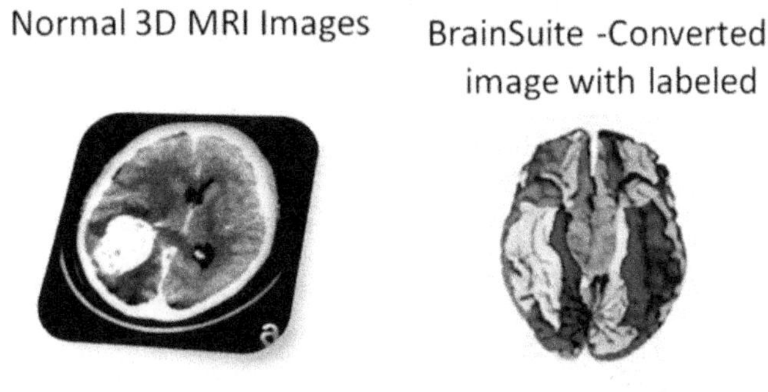

researchers to use diffusion MRI data to look into the connectivity between various brain areas.

(vi) Lesion Analysis: BrainSuite is useful in clinical neuroimaging for locating and analyzing brain lesions since it has lesion analysis and visualization tools. Its usefulness and interoperability with current tools can be improved by integrating it with other neuroimaging software packages and libraries.

4.3.2 How to Use the BrainSuite Tool

The initial step in creating a picture is called cortical surface extraction. At this point, it would be possible to calculate how thick the tissue is covering the organ. Using this tool, the cortical surface of the MRI scans is extracted(Figure 6). The neuroscientific imaging requires this surface computation.

White Matter Tractography: After that, it might follow the white area or space in the brain's MRI data. Understanding how different brain regions are connected is helpful.

In order to compute the real evolution of the MR-signal over time, itaccomplish this by simulating the MRI signal in(Figure 7) each spin in each voxel of the slice volume of the patient model. Itdo this for each time step. After obtaining the k-space, itrebuild the data into the MR-image and image domain.

For this reason, while using the same inputs, such as anatomy, resolution, scan time, SNR, contrast, and artifacts, the output image will be identical to what would be obtained from a real scanner (Brooks & Stamoulis, 2023; Chen et al., 2023; Misiak et al., 2023; Papanastasiou et al., 2023; Song et al., 2019). The simulator is entirely

Figure 6. Democratic view of image generation

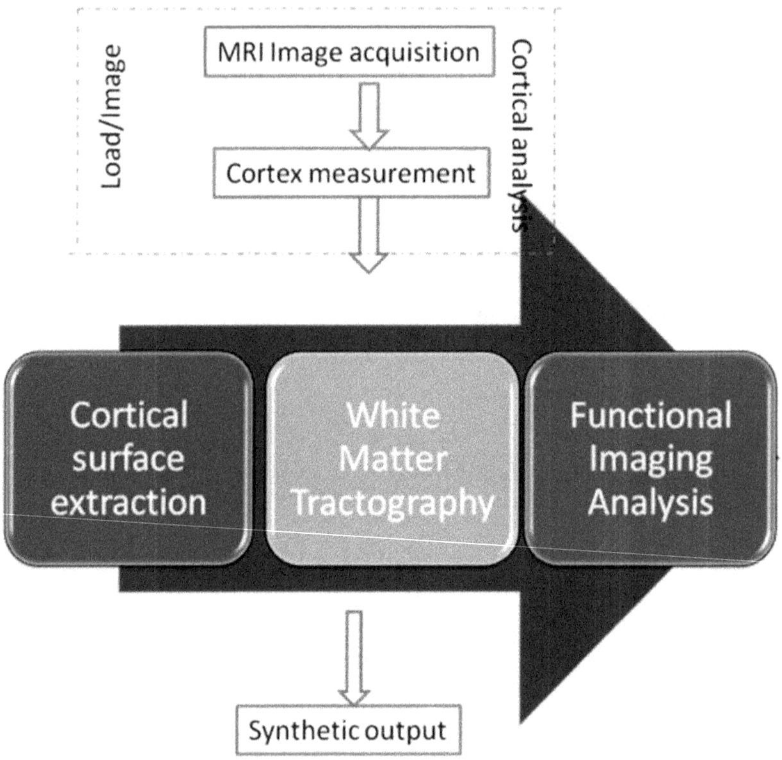

cloud-based, so all it need to use it is a computer with an internet connection. They will receive training and on boarding into the full platform from it's application specialists in the customer success team to assist in getting started with the simulator. The simulator produces the same anticipated outcome as a genuine clinical scanner.

Cortical and Sub cortical Labeling: distinct cortical and sub cortical structures of the brain pictures may be labeled following the identification of the white matter and connections of distinct regions. This section alludes to additional research.

Functional Imaging Analysis: The brain dataset is now prepared for use in studies pertaining to the process of segmentation. Illustration lastly, this application facilitates the exploration and visualization of data in 2D or 3D format.

4.4 Simulators for MRIs

BrainWeb: BrainWeb is a well-liked tool for creating fake MRI scans of the brain. Various tissue types, signal-to-noise ratios, and imaging parameters are available. Additionally, it offers templates for lifelike head phantoms.

Figure 7. BrainSuite image simulator outcome

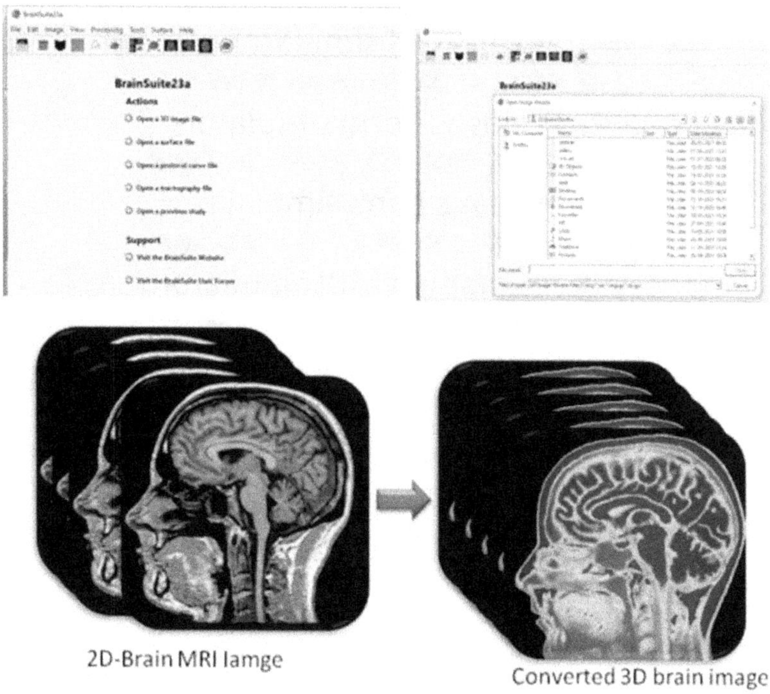

There are a number of software-based evolutions available for MRI simulators(Figure 8) that attempt to replicate the scanning process, but they don't all generate identical images; instead, they each have their own methodology and techniques. These include true MRI simulators, closed-form simulators, and image bank simulators.

(a) True MRI simulator:

This type of simulator, which closely mimics actual MRI image mirroring, is the pinnacle of simulation technology. Like actual scanners, the simulators simply replicate every image straight from the source. The MR signal is calculated by the real simulators for every spin inside each voxel (Brooks & Stamoulis, 2023), for the chosen anatomical volume, and for every pulse sequence time step.

This thorough measurement records the MR signal's evolution during the pulse sequence's application, enabling the creation of K-space (raw data) and the ensuing inverse Fourier transform (or other reconstruction method) to rebuild the MR image. When given the same inputs, parameters, patients, and sequences (Li et al., 2022; Song et al., 2019), a high-quality true MRI simulator should provide images that are

Figure 8. The various types of MRI-based image generating simulators

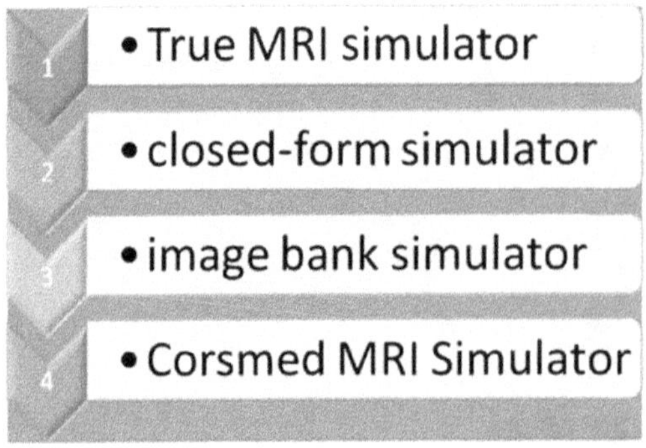

exactly the same as those produced by real scanners. The sole trustworthy choice for instruction and training in operating the scanner, establishing procedures, and making parameter trade-offs is a true MRI simulator.

(b) Closed-form simulator:

This type of simulator—the most authentic kind available—will make an effort to produce surface area-based mathematical estimates for the picture scratches. A few pulsation sequences and elementary physics ideas like analytical expressions could constrain this. In addition to the banking simulator producing photos, it could locate the scram area using surface detection methods (Li et al., 2022). However, compared to other simulation methods, this simulator is quicker (Fouladi et al., 2022). In order to train the model and obtain a better projected value at the training level, the researcher typically needs more data. More data collection is necessary for the processing, according to the experts. When it comes to teaching students how to execute protocols on actual scanners, they fall short.

In order to prepare images for artificial intelligence and other machine analysis, atmospheric correction is a stage in the brain image processing process that clarifies images for seeing and converts the digital signal to surface reflectance. Variable quantities of airborne aerosol particles, such as smoke and dust, deteriorate photos by altering the digital signal and hiding ground details behind haze (Figure 9). However, conversion to surface reflectance eliminates this impact. Surface reflectance estimations from atmospheric correction (AC) enable more reliable, accurate and useful analytics. All optical satellites measuring reflected light in visible to near infrared (VNIR) spectral wavelengths need to have AC.

The MRI simulator uses it's simulation engines and patient models to simulate and create images instead of actually having any images. As a result, when it

Figure 9. Closed form simulated brain image-synthetic data

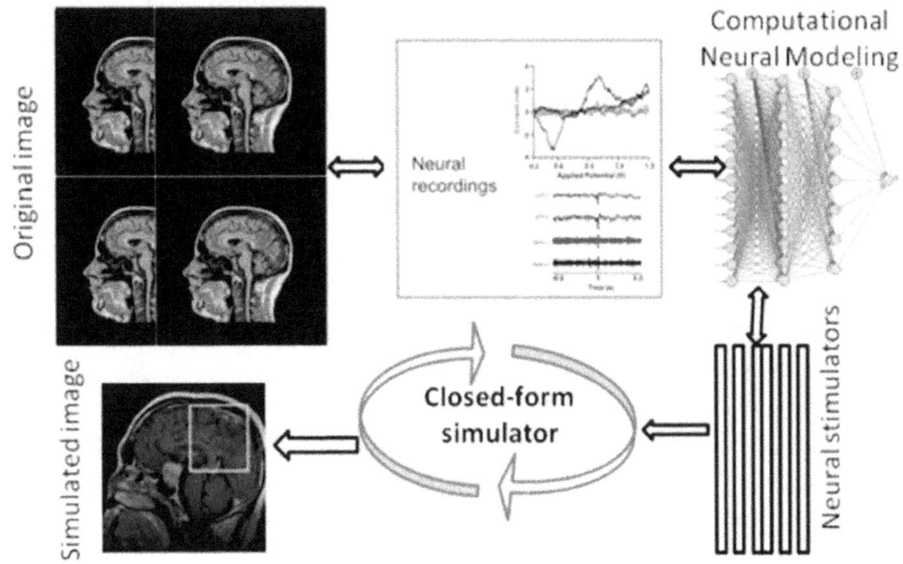

initially use the simulator, there are no pre-made graphics. Instead, it makes use of the simulator to replicate the MR-images. To compute the actual evolution of the MR-signal over time, itsimulate the MRI signal in each spin in each voxel of the slice volume of the patient model. Itdo this for each time step. After obtaining the k-space, itrebuild the data into the MR-image and image domain.

(c) Image bank simulator:

There are two types of image bank simulators: MIPS/MPR-based simulators and pure image bank simulators. These simulators use a variety of gimmicks and strategies to simulate the scanning process using pre-acquired photos (Shukla et al., 2023).

Simulators for pure picture banks feed pre-made images into the interface that closely mimic the images trainees try to make. However, if the database is not indefinitely vast, this strategy may result in wrong brain tumor cell images. In contrast, MIPS/MPR-based simulators use pre-acquired isotropic 3D pictures and generate new slice positions through multi-planar reformatting techniques. Although this method produces precise images, it only addresses the minor and typically less significant portion of the MRI scanning procedure—slice location (Borkar et al., 2023).

The 'end-to-end' image simulations generated by the LSST image simulator confirm the overall LSST system design's scientific performance. Out of 189 CCDs in the LSST focal plane, this color image, which is a composite of three separate frames with various filters, displays one 4Kx4K CCD (13x13 arcminutes of sky). It amounts to barely 2.6 parts per million of the 20,000 square degrees of final sky coverage that LSST will cover.

(d) The Corsmed MRI Simulator:

For a fully trained dataset, the corsmed simulator produces tissue images as arrays with characteristics expressed as binary values, resulting in a more favorable one-to-one experience.

Here (Figure 10) is a simplified explanation of how this process works: Data Acquisition: In MRI, a series of 2D images (slices) are acquired at different depths within the patient's body. These images represent a stack of 2D cross-sectional views. Voxel Data: Each pixel in a 2D image corresponds to a volume element, or voxel, in 3D space. These voxels contain information about the tissue properties, like intensity and location. These methods are commonly used in medical imaging, such as MRI and CT scans, to visualize the data from different angles or perspectives.

Multi-Planar Reformatting (MPR): Users can create multiple perspectives by slicing the 3D volume in different directions (axial, sagittal, coronal, or arbitrary angles), effectively creating 2D images that represent different 3D perspectives. These 2D images are generated on-the-fly by reformatting the 3D data. 3D Rendering: Advanced visualization techniques, such as volume rendering or surface rendering, can be used to generate 3D renderings of the data (Assam et al., 2021; Ferrara et al., 2023; Khairandish et al., 2022; Touqeer et al., 2023; Touqeer et al., 2022). These techniques create 3D images that depict structures as they appear in the 3D volume, providing a more intuitive view of the anatomy or pathology. Interaction: Users can interact with the 3D renderings, adjust the viewing angles, and navigate through the data to examine structures from various perspectives.

The CorsMed has features(Figure 11) such as a wider field of view, a higher matrix resolution setting, higher pixel values, and a higher voxel connection dimension. Several pulse sequences are supported, including high bandwidth, flip angle, balanced steady state free precession, support for gradient method based echo, and too fast inversion recovery.

Its features include slice thickness, slice gaps, number of slices, SNR indicators, SNR monitoring, SAR, and scan percentage will be high.

Figure 10. The CorsMed simulator scratch calculation

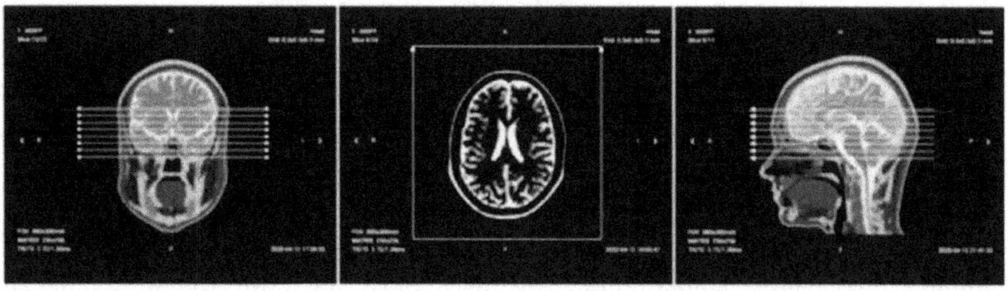

4.5 Tools for DICOM Image Generation

Medical images are typically stored in the DICOM (Digital Imaging and Communications in Medicine) format. There are programs that can produce fake DICOM images with editable information. A common format for medical imaging files, comprising data from several imaging modalities like X-ray, CT, MRI, and ultrasound, is called DICOM (Digital Imaging and Communications in Medicine). Generally, it need specific software or solutions that can create and save medical

Figure 11. Using a single image, the simulator creates many 3D perspectives of the same MRI data

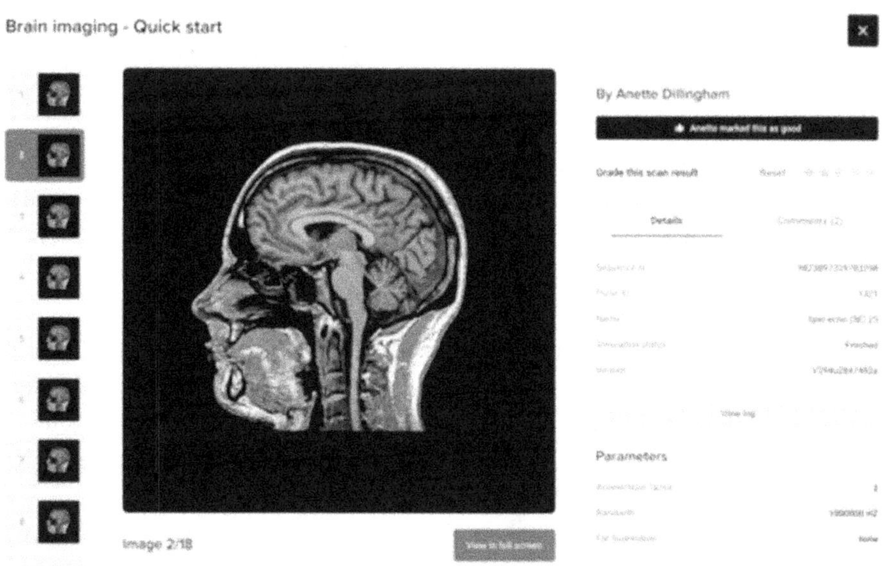

pictures in the DICOM format in order to generate DICOM images. The following libraries and tools can be used to create DICOM images:

DICOM Workstations and PACS Systems: A lot of hospitals are equipped with DICOM workstations that can capture, display, and store medical pictures in the DICOM format, as well as Picture Archiving and Communication Systems (PACS). These systems are used to collect and handle patient imaging data in healthcare settings.

DICOM-Compatible Imaging technologies: MRI, CT, and ultrasound equipment, among other imaging technologies, frequently have the ability to create DICOM images right during the scanning process.

4.5.1 Toolkit Libraries for DICOM

The widely-used open-source DCMTK (DICOM Toolkit) library is used to work with DICOM files. It comes with libraries and command-line tools for generating, modifying, and converting DICOM pictures. GDCM, or Grassroots DICOM, is an open-source library used for DICOM file parsing and generation. From unprocessed data, DICOM images can be produced using it.

a) **Image Editors at DICOM:** OsiriX is an open-source medical picture editor and viewer available for macOS. It is frequently used for education and research, and it facilitates the generation and manipulation of DICOM pictures.
b) **Horos:** Based on OsiriX, Horos is an additional open-source DICOM image viewer and editor for macOS.
c) **DICOM Conversion Tools:** A few programs and tools are available for converting common image formats (such JPEG and TIFF) into DICOM format. DICOM-compliant files can be created from non-DICOM medical images with the help of these programs.
d) **Medical Imaging Simulation Software:** The capacity to create artificial DICOM pictures for training and testing is a common feature of specialized simulation software used in medical education and research.

To preserve the integrity and compatibility of medical imaging data, it's crucial that it follow the DICOM standards and norms when working with DICOM pictures. It can select the best tool or library for creating DICOM images for clinical, scientific, or instructional usage, depending on particular use case (Acharya & Kumar, 2020; Kimberly et al., 2023).

Medical picture annotation for computer vision models necessitates highly-specialized labeling techniques and domain expertise. I've had the chance to work on developing the DICOM annotation tools' capability for several months, and I've written this post to teach it how to utilize various labeling tools on medical volumes to separate things in 3D. Healthcare AI is the focus of Supervisely's DICOM annotation and collaboration platform:

Compatible with both 3D objects and actual DICOM files directly (Pomponio et al., 2020). It shares a comparable user experience, incorporates best practices, and is compatible with ITK Snap, 3D Slicer, and MITK. All need is a browser to use web-based interfaces. The on-premise solution complies with the strictest industry regulations and ensures privacy.

From Figure 12, panel with a really significant instrument Interpolation, a screenshot button, a hotkeys map, layout options, and an operations history are all included. Toolbar for manipulating annotations and switching between planes. Workspace featuring a 3D view and Volume pictures at the planes. tabs listing Figureures, volumes, objects, and their respective settings. Additional interface display settings. It can completely customize the UI. If you're not happy with how the main tabs are arranged by default, it can always switch to the panel variant and rearrange things to liking. This feature alone makes it's solution stand out in terms of usability as it is frequently absent from several web applications.

From Figure 13, Hundreds of slices on various planes can be covered by 3D objects on medical volumes. As a result, their segmentation is exceedingly costly and time-consuming. Only the important slices on various planes can be explicitly identified. On the remaining unlabeled slices, an object can be automatically reconstructed using an interpolation technique. The final interpolation and all hand annotations are shown as a single 3D annotation object that may be edited on any plane and viewed in 3D perspective. If the outcome of the interpolation is not acceptable, it can be reversed, and new intermediate elements can be added and the process repeated for greater precision.

i. Quick Labeling With Engaging AI Support

It takes a lot of effort and time to segment objects across thousands of frames. Because Smart Tool uses a variety of pre-trained neural network (NN) models, it makes it simple to identify the desired object in an image with a few clicks. All it have to do is use a bounding box (bbox) to frame the assumed object.

ii. Windowing and Crosshair Tool

Medical images often contain a multitude of gray levels, whereas typical computer screens are limited to presenting just 256 gray levels. Furthermore, the human eye has constraints in discerning subtle variations in contrast. The Windowing functionality provides a means to modify image contrast, offering not only manual adjustments

Figure 12. Software that resembles the user interface

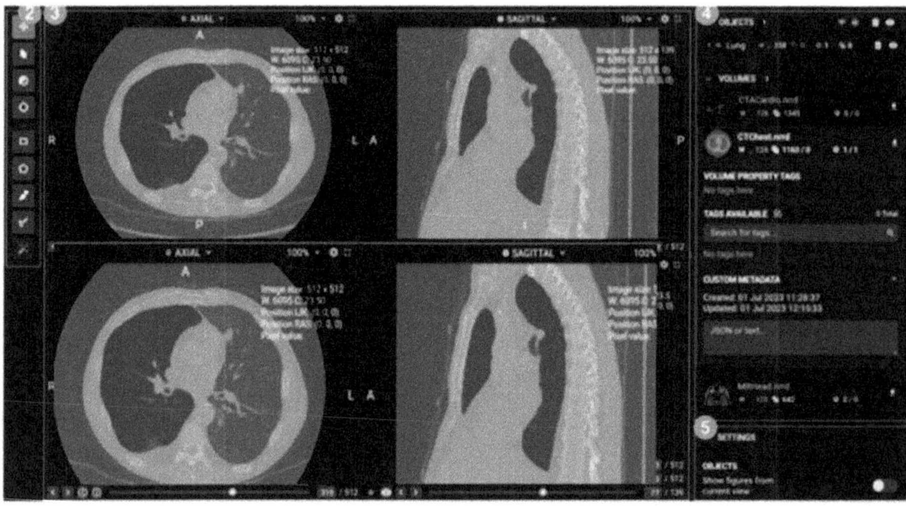

Figure 13. How several cortical points are used to build a 3D MRI brain image

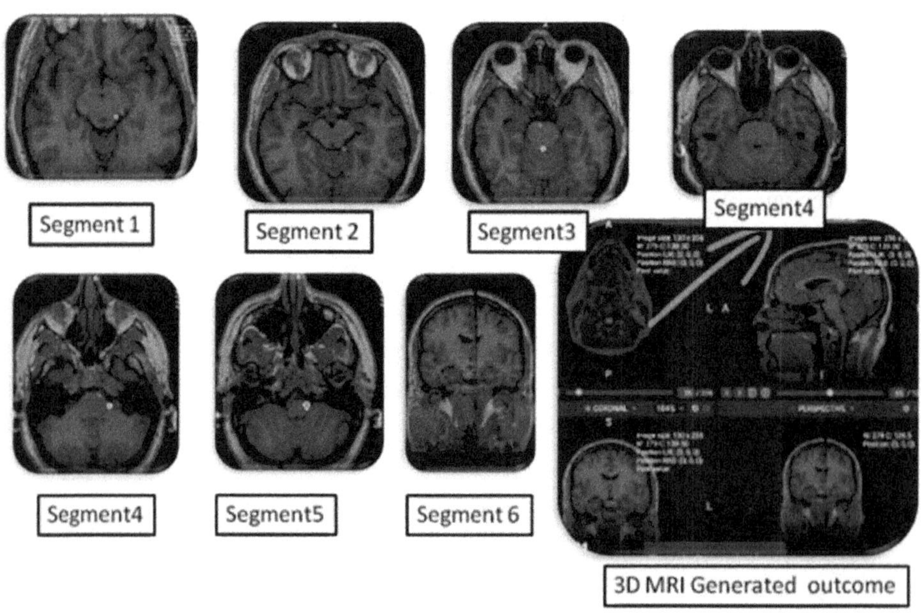

Figure 14. Different automatic reconstruction methods utilizing an interpolation method

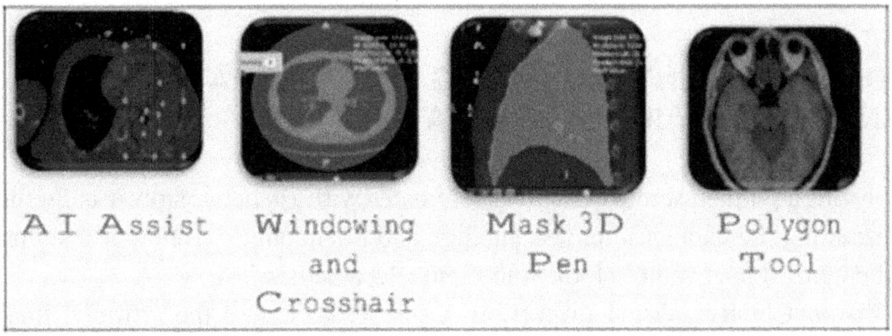

but also a selection of presets. It enables it to refine the presentation of medical images, enhancing the visibility and differentiation of various tissues and structures.

iii. Native Support for Mask 3D

To generate a 3D Figureure that can be altered and rendered on all planes using the volumetric mask, also known as Mask 3D. As itare working with volumetric data, this is the main, most practical, and flexible way to annotate things. It may design and edit Mask 3D for objects using a variety of tools.

iv. Mask 3D: Brush Tool

The Brush Tool is a flexible instrument that allows it to create 3D shape masks and bitmaps, all while adjusting its size in real-time. Additionally, it comes equipped with an "Eraser" feature for effortlessly refining any flaws. When it sketch a bitmap outline, it have the option to fill it using the "Bucket Fill" tool.

v. Polygon Tool

The Polygon Tool is employed for marking polygonal shapes on surfaces when precise detailing isn't necessary. If it simply wants to highlight an object without specifying its boundaries, the Rectangle Tool is a handy choice.

Supervisely apart from other products is its unique structure resembling an operating system. It features numerous Supervisely Apps, which are interactive web-based tools accessible through browser and powered by Python. This structure facilitates the integration of various open-source machine learning tools and neural networks, enhances them with a user-friendly interface, and enables anyone to execute them effortlessly with just a single click.

5. DATA AUGMENTATION USING THE GENERATED SYNTHETIC BRAIN IMAGE DATA SET

Analyzing a synthetic brain image dataset created with a generator tool usually entails determining the data's usefulness, quality, and intended use. Below is a summary of the items it may want to look at in Figure 15 analysis:

Visual Clarity: Visual Inspection: Use eyes to assess the artificial images' quality. Examine whether the images' depictions of gray matter, white matter, and ventricles are similar to actual brain structures.

Noise and Artifacts: Examine the generated images for any inadvertent noise or artifacts, and evaluate the effect they have on the quality of the data.

Diversity and Realism: Actuality: Assess the degree to which the synthetic images, in terms of look, contrast, and anatomical traits, resemble real brain images.

Diversity: Examine the diversity of the dataset. Exist differences between various brain structures, illnesses, imaging modalities, and conditions?

Features of the Data: Entire text Examine the accessibility of the diagnosis, imaging modality, age, gender, and other metadata linked to each image. Examine the properties of the image, including its size, format, and resolution.

The outcome and analysis of a synthetic brain image collection should concentrate on the dataset's diversity, quality, and applicability for particular uses. Together with the possibility of data augmentation and community-based research collaboration, it should also take ethical and legal considerations into account.

6. TRAINING AND VALIDATING THE SYNTHETIC DATASET

Iterative steps are involved in training and validating synthetic datasets; enhancements can be achieved by modifying the dataset and model in response to validation outcomes. The objective is to make sure the synthetic data helps the model perform well on real data by effectively preparing it for the intended job.

The technique used in this study to generate synthetic brain images shows promise for making a big impact in the fields of neuroscience and medical imaging. This tool enhances it's capacity to train and validate machine learning models, test image processing algorithms, and conduct in-depth research by enabling researchers, clinicians, and data scientists to create realistic and diverse brain image datasets. This is achieved by utilizing advanced image synthesis techniques.

Figure 15. Enhancement of data with the help of generated data

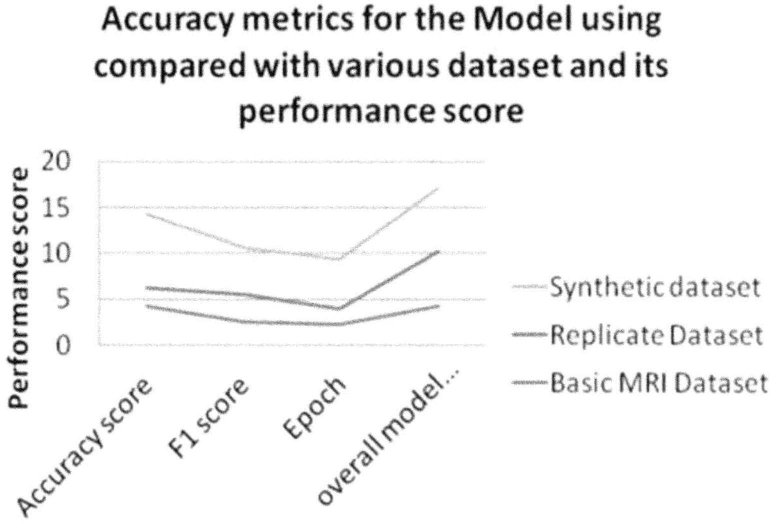

To maximize the model's performance on the synthetic data, adjust the model's hyperparameters, such as learning rates and batch sizes. When a model performs well on synthetic data but badly on actual or unknown data, it is likely overfitting(Table 1). Look for indications of this. Techniques for regularization can be required to reduce overfitting. Compare the model's performance on synthetic data to its performance on real data if it has access to real data for the same task. This aids in evaluating the synthetic data's efficacy.

7. CONCLUSION

In conclusion, the generation of synthetic data for brain images is a valuable approach that holds significant promise for various applications in the field of neuroscience, medical imaging, and machine learning. Synthetic data serves as a versatile tool for overcoming limitations associated with real data, such as privacy concerns, data scarcity, or the need for controlled experiments. The tool for creating synthetic brain images is becoming more and more useful as medical imaging and artificial intelligence develop. It helps researchers and practitioners overcome obstacles like restricted data access, ethical issues, and the requirement for diverse and representative datasets. This technology has the potential to completely transform how itapproach brain imaging, promoting innovation and advancing neuroscience and healthcare

Figure 16. The measurement of training the model performance and validating the model with synthetic image dataset

Training	Validating
Accuracy	Accuracy
Mean squared error	Precision
Dice coefficient	ROC curve (AUC)
Loss Function	F1-score

with additional refining and integration into the larger medical imaging ecosystem. The capacity of the tool to mimic the intricacies of authentic brain scans, along with its ability to customize several factors, has unparalleled prospects for augmenting data, developing algorithms, and enhancing it's comprehension of brain architecture and disorders. Its versatility and flexibility also make it a useful tool for a variety of uses, including academic research, treatment planning, diagnostics, and more.

REFERENCES

Acharya, U. K., & Kumar, S. (2020). Particle swarm optimized texture based histogram equalization (PSOTHE) for MRI brain image enhancement. *Optik (Stuttgart)*, *224*, 165760. doi:10.1016/j.ijleo.2020.165760

Assam, M., Kanwal, H., Farooq, U., Shah, S. K., Mehmood, A., & Choi, G. S. (2021). An efficient classification of MRI brain images. *IEEE Access : Practical Innovations, Open Solutions*, *9*, 33313–33322. doi:10.1109/ACCESS.2021.3061487

Betzel, R. F., Avena-Koenigsberger, A., & Goi, J. (2016). Generative models of the human connectome. *NeuroImage*, *124*, 10541064. doi:10.1016/j.neuroimage.2015.09.041 PMID:26427642

Betzel, R. F., & Bassett, D. S. (2017). Generative models for network neuroscience: Prospects and promise. *Journal of the Royal Society, Interface*, *14*(136), 20170623. doi:10.1098/rsif.2017.0623 PMID:29187640

Betzel, R. F., Byrge, L., Esfahlani, F. Z., & Kennedy, D. P. (2020). Temporal fluctuations in the brain's modular architecture during movie-watching. *NeuroImage*, *213*, 116687. doi:10.1016/j.neuroimage.2020.116687 PMID:32126299

Borkar, P., Wankhede, V. A., Mane, D. T., Limkar, S., Ramesh, J. V. N., & Ajani, S. N. (2023). Deep learning and image processing-based early detection of Alzheimer disease in cognitively normal individuals. *Soft Computing*, 1–23. doi:10.1007/s00500-023-08615-w

Brainsuite. (n.d.). https://brainsuite.org/tutorials/

Braun, U., Harneit, A., Pergola, G., Menara, T., Schäfer, A., Betzel, R. F., Zang, Z., Schweiger, J. I., Zhang, X., Schwarz, K., Chen, J., Blasi, G., Bertolino, A., Durstewitz, D., Pasqualetti, F., Schwarz, E., Meyer-Lindenberg, A., Bassett, D. S., & Tost, H. (2021). Brain network dynamics during working memory are modulated by dopamine and diminished in schizophrenia. *Nature Communications*, *12*(1), 3478. doi:10.1038/s41467-021-23694-9 PMID:34108456

Brooks, S. J., & Stamoulis, C. (2023, June). Generative Models For Large-Scale Simulations Of Connectome Development. In *2023 IEEE International Conference on Acoustics, Speech, and Signal Processing Workshops (ICASSPW)* (pp. 1-5). IEEE. 10.1109/ICASSPW59220.2023.10193544

Chen, X., Ke, P., Huang, Y., Zhou, J., Li, H., Peng, R., Huang, J., Liang, L., Ma, G., Li, X., Ning, Y., Wu, F., & Wu, K. (2023). Discriminative analysis of schizophrenia patients using graph convolutional networks: A combined multimodal MRI and connectomics analysis. *Frontiers in Neuroscience*, *17*, 1140801. doi:10.3389/fnins.2023.1140801 PMID:37090813

Faskowitz, J., Betzel, R. F., & Sporns, O. (2022). Edges in brain networks: Contributions to models of structure and function. *Network Neuroscience (Cambridge, Mass.)*, *6*(1), 1–28. PMID:35350585

Faskowitz, J., Yan, X., Zuo, X. N., & Sporns, O. (2018). Weighted stochastic block models of the human connectome across the life span. *Scientific Reports*, *8*(1), 12997. doi:10.1038/s41598-018-31202-1 PMID:30158553

Ferrara, M., Ahmadian, A., Salashour, S., & Pansera, B. A. (2023). Introduction to the SI "Advances in Operations Research and Machine Learning focused on Pandemic Dynamics". *Operations Research Perspectives, 100287.*

Fouladi, S., Safaei, A. A., Arshad, N. I., Ebadi, M. J., & Ahmadian, A. (2022). The use of artificial neural networks to diagnose Alzheimer's disease from brain images. *Multimedia Tools and Applications*, *81*(26), 37681–37721. doi:10.1007/s11042-022-13506-7

Islam, J., & Zhang, Y. (2018). Brain MRI analysis for Alzheimer's disease diagnosis using an ensemble system of deep convolutional neural networks. *Brain Informatics*, *5*(2), 2. doi:10.1186/s40708-018-0080-3 PMID:29881892

Khairandish, M. O., Sharma, M., Jain, V., Chatterjee, J. M., & Jhanjhi, N. Z. (2022). A hybrid CNN-SVM threshold segmentation approach for tumor detection and classification of MRI brain images. *Ingénierie et Recherche Biomédicale : IRBM = Biomedical Engineering and Research*, *43*(4), 290–299. doi:10.1016/j.irbm.2021.06.003

Kimberly, W. T., Sorby-Adams, A. J., Webb, A. G., Wu, E. X., Beekman, R., Bowry, R., Schiff, S. J., de Havenon, A., Shen, F. X., Sze, G., Schaefer, P., Iglesias, J. E., Rosen, M. S., & Sheth, K. N. (2023). Brain imaging with portable low-field MRI. *Nature Reviews Bioengineering*, *1*(9), 617–630. doi:10.1038/s44222-023-00086-w PMID:37705717

Ledig, C., Theis, L., Huszár, F., Caballero, J., Cunningham, A., Acosta, A., Aitken, A., Tejani, A., Totz, J., & Wang, Z. (2017). Photo-realistic single image super-resolution using a generative adversarial network. *Proceedings of the IEEE conference on computer vision and pattern recognition*, 4681–4690. 10.1109/CVPR.2017.19

Lei, D., Qin, K., Pinaya, W. H., Young, J., Van Amelsvoort, T., Marcelis, M., Donohoe, G., Mothersill, D. O., Corvin, A., Vieira, S., Lui, S., Scarpazza, C., Arango, C., Bullmore, E., Gong, Q., McGuire, P., & Mechelli, A. (2022). Graph convolutional networks reveal network-level functional dysconnectivity in schizophrenia. *Schizophrenia Bulletin*, *48*(4), 881–892. doi:10.1093/schbul/sbac047 PMID:35569019

Li, M. M., Huang, K., & Zitnik, M. (2022). Graph representation learning in biomedicine and healthcare. *Nature Biomedical Engineering*, *6*(12), 1353–1369. doi:10.1038/s41551-022-00942-x PMID:36316368

Misiak, B., Samochowiec, J., Kowalski, K., Gaebel, W., Bassetti, C. L., Chan, A., Gorwood, P., Papiol, S., Dom, G., Volpe, U., Szulc, A., Kurimay, T., Kärkkäinen, H., Decraene, A., Wisse, J., Fiorillo, A., & Falkai, P. (2023). The future of diagnosis in clinical neurosciences: Comparing multiple sclerosis and schizophrenia. *European Psychiatry*, *66*(1), e58. doi:10.1192/j.eurpsy.2023.2432 PMID:37476977

Murphy, A. C., Bertolero, M. A., Papadopoulos, L., Lydon-Staley, D. M., & Bassett, D. S. (2020). Multimodal network dynamics underpinning working memory. *Nature Communications*, *11*(1), 3035. doi:10.1038/s41467-020-15541-0 PMID:32541774

Oh, K. H., Oh, I. S., Tsogt, U., Shen, J., Kim, W. S., Liu, C., ... Chung, Y. C. (2022). Diagnosis of schizophrenia with functional connectome data: A graph-based convolutional neural network approach. *BMC Neuroscience*, *23*(1), 1–11. PMID:34979913

Papanastasiou, G., Dikaios, N., Huang, J., Wang, C., & Yang, G. (2023). *Is attention all you need in medical image analysis? A review.* arXiv preprint arXiv:2307.12775.

Parkes, L., Moore, T. M., Calkins, M. E., Cook, P. A., Cieslak, M., Roalf, D. R., Wolf, D. H., Gur, R. C., Gur, R. E., Satterthwaite, T. D., & Bassett, D. S. (2021). Transdiagnostic dimensions of psychopathology explain individuals' unique deviations from normative neurodevelopment in brain structure. *Translational Psychiatry*, *11*(1), 232. doi:10.1038/s41398-021-01342-6 PMID:33879764

Pomponio, R., Erus, G., Habes, M., Doshi, J., Srinivasan, D., Mamourian, E., Bashyam, V., Nasrallah, I. M., Satterthwaite, T. D., Fan, Y., Launer, L. J., Masters, C. L., Maruff, P., Zhuo, C., Völzke, H., Johnson, S. C., Fripp, J., Koutsouleris, N., Wolf, D. H., ... Davatzikos, C. (2020). Harmonization of large MRI datasets for the analysis of brain imaging patterns throughout the lifespan. *NeuroImage*, *208*, 116450. doi:10.1016/j.neuroimage.2019.116450 PMID:31821869

Porter, A., Fei, S., Damme, K. S., Nusslock, R., Gratton, C., & Mittal, V. A. (2023). A meta-analysis and systematic review of single vs. multimodal neuroimaging techniques in the classification of psychosis. *Molecular Psychiatry*, *28*(8), 1–15. doi:10.1038/s41380-023-02195-9 PMID:37563277

Sadeghi, D., Shoeibi, A., Ghassemi, N., Moridian, P., Khadem, A., Alizadehsani, R., Teshnehlab, M., Gorriz, J. M., Khozeimeh, F., Zhang, Y.-D., Nahavandi, S., & Acharya, U. R. (2022). An overview of artificial intelligence techniques for diagnosis of Schizophrenia based on magnetic resonance imaging modalities: Methods, challenges, and future works. *Computers in Biology and Medicine*, *146*, 105554. doi:10.1016/j.compbiomed.2022.105554 PMID:35569333

Shukla, A., Tiwari, R., & Tiwari, S. (2023). Review on alzheimer disease detection methods: Automatic pipelines and machine learning techniques. *Sci*, *5*(1), 13. doi:10.3390/sci5010013

Song, T. A., Chowdhury, S. R., Yang, F., Jacobs, H., El Fakhri, G., Li, Q., . . . Dutta, J. (2019, April). Graph convolutional neural networks for Alzheimer's disease classification. In *2019 IEEE 16th international symposium on biomedical imaging (ISBI 2019)* (pp. 414-417). IEEE. 10.1109/ISBI.2019.8759531

Stillman, P. E., Wilson, J. D., Denny, M. J., Desmarais, B. A., Bhamidi, S., Cranmer, S. J., & Lu, Z. L. (2017). Statistical modeling of the default mode brain network reveals a segregated highway structure. *Scientific Reports*, *7*(1), 11694. doi:10.1038/s41598-017-09896-6 PMID:28916779

Tang, E., & Bassett, D. S. (2018). Colloquium: Control of dynamics in brain networks. *Reviews of Modern Physics*, *90*(3), 031003. doi:10.1103/RevModPhys.90.031003

Tang, E., Giusti, C., Baum, G. L., Gu, S., Pollock, E., Kahn, A. E., Roalf, D. R., Moore, T. M., Ruparel, K., Gur, R. C., Gur, R. E., Satterthwaite, T. D., & Bassett, D. S. (2017). Developmental increases in white matter network controllability support a growing diversity of brain dynamics. *Nature Communications*, *8*(1), 1252. doi:10.1038/s41467-017-01254-4 PMID:29093441

Touqeer, M., Al Sulaie, S., Lone, S. A., Gunaime, N. M., & Elkotb, M. A. (2023). A Fuzzy parametric model for decision making involving F-OWA operator with unknown weights environment. *Heliyon*, *9*(9), e19969. doi:10.1016/j.heliyon.2023.e19969 PMID:37809988

Touqeer, M., Shaheen, S., Jabeen, T., Al Sulaie, S., Baleanu, D., & Ahmadian, A. (2022). A signed distance based ranking approach with unknown fuzzy priority vectors for medical diagnosis involving interval type-2 trapezoidal pythagorean fuzzy preference relations. *Operations Research Perspectives*, *9*, 100259. doi:10.1016/j.orp.2022.100259

Wilson, J. D., Baybay, M., Sankar, R., Stillman, P., & Popa, A. M. (2021). Analysis of population functional connectivity data via multilayer network embeddings. *Network Science*, *9*(1), 99–122. doi:10.1017/nws.2020.39

Wilson, J. D., Cranmer, S., & Lu, Z. L. (2020). A hierarchical latent space network model for population studies of functional connectivity. *Computational Brain & Behavior*, *3*(4), 384–399. doi:10.1007/s42113-020-00080-0

Witvliet, D., Mulcahy, B., Mitchell, J. K., Meirovitch, Y., Berger, D. R., Wu, Y., Liu, Y., Koh, W. X., Parvathala, R., Holmyard, D., Schalek, R. L., Shavit, N., Chisholm, A. D., Lichtman, J. W., Samuel, A. D. T., & Zhen, M. (2021). Connectomes across development reveal principles of brain maturation. *Nature*, *596*(7871), 257–261. doi:10.1038/s41586-021-03778-8 PMID:34349261

Yang, Y., Qiao, S., Sani, O. G., Sedillo, J. I., Ferrentino, B., Pesaran, B., & Shanechi, M. M. (2021). Modelling and prediction of the dynamic responses of large-scale brain networks during direct electrical stimulation. *Nature Biomedical Engineering*, *5*(4), 324–345. doi:10.1038/s41551-020-00666-w PMID:33526909

Chapter 12
Transformation of Industrial Production:
The Effects of Digitalization

Kravchenko Maryna
https://orcid.org/0000-0001-5405-0159
National Technical University of Ukraine "Igor Sikorsky Kyiv Polytechnic Institute", Ukraine

Olena Trofymenko
National Technical University of Ukraine "Igor Sikorsky Kyiv Polytechnic Institute", Ukraine

Boiarynova Kateryna
National Technical University of Ukraine "Igor Sikorsky Kyiv Polytechnic Institute", Ukraine

Marzena Sobczak-Michalowska
https://orcid.org/0000-0002-4757-0583
WSG University, Poland

Kashuba Svitlana
WSG University, Poland

ABSTRACT

The study is devoted to the determination of trends and transformations in the development of the industrial sector in the conditions of the fourth industrial revolution. The global priorities for ensuring the introduction of Industry 4.0 technologies have been analysed. The dynamics of the value added of industrial production in some countries have been determined. The ratio between the share of the value added of industrial production in the gross domestic product and the value added of medium and high-tech production in the section of the ICT subindex in individual countries has been analysed. The leading countries in the development of digitalization and the growth of industrial production have been identified. The leading global enterprises in the introduction of breakthrough technologies and the prerequisites for the development of Industry 5.0 have been identified. The main technologies for ensuring the optimization of production lines have been presented.

DOI: 10.4018/979-8-3693-1886-7.ch012

INTRODUCTION

Nowadays qualitative and quantitative transformations associated with the implementation of the concept of Industry 4.0 are taking place all over the world. This coordinated initiative mobilizes there source base to accelerate the pace of structural technological transformations, whichwas adopted at the global level in 2014 at theWorld Economic Forum (World Economic Forum, Geneva, Switzerland). The conditions for the development of Industry 4.0 form the system advantages of accelerating the pace of horizontal and vertical integration of production and minimizing the costs of maintaining control systems. At the same time, ensuring the transition to Industry 4.0 involves the modernization of existing industrial systems with innovative technologies that provide sustainable solutions and sustainable production. Therefore, for the past years digital technology at the global level is increasingly appliedin the production processes in leading countries. Technologies in the field of the Internet of Things, Big Data, robotics, blockchain technologies, sensors, artificial intelligence, augmented reality and rapid prototyping technologies transferred to the processing plant industry. Nowadays thanks to innovative technologies in highly developed countries goods are developed, produced and consumed. Moreover, these technologies stimulate the development of new business models, services and form new models of consumer behaviour.

According to the main world priorities, the acceleration achievement goals for sustainable development until 2030 approved at the UN Summit. According to the Voluntary National Review of Sustainable Development Goals in Ukraine (Sustainable development knowledge platform, 2020) great importance attaches to SDG 8 "Decentwork and economic growth", which should become an accelerator of transformations to achieve all goals. Inaddition, another SDG 9 is dedicated to the creation of sustainable infrastructure, promoting inclusive and sustainable industrialization and innovation, which provides relevant infrastructure. In the conditions of Industry 4.0, the development of information and communication (ICT) technologies is the driving force fo rensuringglobaldigitalization, which is important to consider when studying thet ransformational effects of digitalization.

Ofcourse, the development of Industry 4.0 for countries with different stages of industrial development will differ in time and speed of technology implementation. However, given this transitional stage, developing countries are allowed to increase their share of industrialization, implement "smart" (SMART) factories based on digitalization, etc. supporting this development of events inUkraine, it is necessary to predict in details the challenges and opportunities associated withIndustry 4.0, taking into account the current stage of industrial development.That is why,it is important to study the best practices for the development of industrial production based on digitalization at the macro and microlevels, which will allow determining the main transformational effects of digitalization for production processes, and determines the relevance of this research.The purpose of the article is to determine the role of digitization of production for the development of industry based onIndustry 4.0 with a consideration of the main modern effects of its implementation at the macro and microlevels.

BACKGROUND

The formation and development of theconcept of Industry 4.0 were started in 2011 during the opening ceremony of the Hanoverexhibition "HannoverMesse - 2011", where the general director of the German Research Center for Artificial Intelligence, ProfessorWolfgangWalster, announced this definition. In 2011, an initiative groupled by Ch. Grifdstaff (Siemens PLN Software company) defined the principles of Industry 4.0 development as the integration of "cyber-physical systems" into the production process(Kagermann, Lukas, &Wahlster, 2018).The first studies in the field of Industry 4.0, in particular, innovative technologies of a newtype, were conducted in 2015 by M. Herman, T. Pentekand B. Otto(Hermann, Pentek, & Otto, 2016). In the scientific works of L. Smolyar, O. Ilyash, O. Trofymenko and others. (Smoliar, Ilyash, Kolishenko, &Lytvak, 2020;Trofymenko, 2021)was identified and researched the main benchmarks that will ensure an "economic breakthrough" in technological and innovativeareas. Researcher P. Borovsky defines digitalization, Digital-Twins, blockchain and other elementsofIndustry 4.0 as the main elements of the management processat a modern production enterprise and defines their main capabilities to ensure the efficiency of the production process(Borowski, 2021). The practical recommendations ofOlegMykhaylov, the Director of Development of the Ukrainian Academy of Agricultural Sciences (Yurchak, 2018) are significant. It is stated in his scientific works that in order to obtain maximum efficiency in production, adhering to the principles of Industry 4.0, it is necessary for the counter parties of the enterprise that implements Industry 4.0 technologies to implement innovative technologies, which will allow forming the ecosystem of innovations, and this will become possible in the conditions of the strategic synergy of enterprises to transfer production industries to Industry 4.0.However, taking into account the rapidly changing economic environment and the development of breakthrough technologies, in the conditions of the formation of the fourth industrial revolution, the modern issues of ensuring digitization, its components and production effects with the introduction of Industry 4.0 technologies require additional research.

EFFECTS OF BREAKTHROUGH TECHNOLOGIES FOR INDUSTRIAL DEVELOPMENT

TheIndustry 4.0 platform is based on the implementation of artificial intelligence systems in the management of business processes, the development of robotics, cyber technologies, the Internet of Things (IoT), blockchain technologies, SMART factories, cyber-physicalsystems, cloudtechnologies, etc.In the context of ensuring the digitalization of production, one of the main directions is the formation of a cyber-physical system, that is, ensuring the integration of computer and network technologies into the production process, which provides the possibility of controlling automated production in real-time(Hermann, Pentek, &Otto, 2016). The introduction of a cyber-physical system helps speedup the exchange of information in production, which contributes to several positive production effects – increasing speed, minimizing production mistakes and downtime, and increasing production productivity.

The Internet of Things (IoT) is a system of combined computer networks and industrial (production) objects connected tothem with built-in sensors and software for data collection andexchange, with the possibility of remote control and management in an automated mode, without human intervention(Hermann, Pentek, &Otto, 2016). In addition to increasing production efficiency, this technology allows adapting to the situation due to theCOVID-19 pandemic. It is worth mentioning that in the context of cooperating with counterparties, it is convenient to use common internet services. Digitalization is fundamental for constructingSMARTfactories, which involves automated equipment in production with management using ICT. Thanks to this, the minimization of human laborisrealized atSMART factories, because almost all actions are performed autonomously under the control of the sensors of the cyber-physical systems(Hermann, Pentek, &Otto, 2016).

Data and innovative technologies are increasingly used by enterprises in the world's leading countries with a high levelof GDP, which allows ani ncrease in the added value of industrial production. For comparison, the dynamics of the added value of industrial production of individual countries were studied (Fig. 1) such as Poland, Hungary, Latvia, Lithuania, Estonia, Canada, theUnitedKingdom, Germany, France, Turkey, Portugal and Italy. The main countries for comparing the added value of industrial production in these countries were the border countries of Ukraine, similar resource opportunities, countries incooperation with Ukraine in many directions, countrieswith a leading economy, and a highlevelof GDP.Fig. 1 shows that the largest amount of added value of industrial production among those studied is inGermany (905.35 billiondollarsin 2020), and among all countries of theworld, Germanyranks 2nd - afterChina (5771.86 billiondollarsin 2020). Comparedto 2018, the added value of the industry in Germany decreased by morethan 8% in 2020, which is primarily due to the global crisis in connection with the COVID-19 pandemic. A similar trend is observed in other countries.

The UnitedKingdom is in second place interms of the volume of the added value of industrial production among those studied. In the inter-crisis period from 2011 to 2018, the increase in the added value of the industry amounted to more than 12% (upto 551.3 billiondollars), and in 2020, compared to 2019, there was a decline of 11%. Similar dynamics were observed in Italy and Canada, which ranked 3rd and 4th, accordingly, by the volume of the added value of the industry. Considerable progress is observed inTurkey, inaddition, the decrease in added value in 2019 is insignificant - upto 3% andgrowthalreadyin 2020 - by 1%. A similar dynamic is observed in Poland, but the volume of the added value of industrial production is lower than inTurkey - by 42% in 2020 and amounted to 155.9 billiondollars. Ukraine, Portugal, and Hungary are close interms of the volume of the added value of industry – fluctuations in the range from 21 to 43 billiondollars. The leader among these three countries isPortugal, followed by PolandandUkraine. The lowest volume of the added value of industrial production in Latviawas 5.89 billiondollarsin 2020. It can be concluded the expediency research of industrial enterprises in specified leading countries was made to define the implementation of digitization during the production process.

Comparing the level of digitalization processes with the processes of the formation of the added value of industry and, in particular, of medium and high-tech production, 21 countries, in particular the 11 previously identified countries, were graphically depicted with the values of the ICT sub index of the Global Innovation Index (diameter of the circle) in the coordinates of the indicators of the added value of industrial production in % to GDP and the added value of the medium and high-tech production in % to the value of total production (Fig. 2).

Thus, the subindex of information and communicationtechnologies (ICT) of the Global Innovation Index (Global Innovation Index, 2021) characterizes at the country level the overall development of such indicators as ICT availability, ICT use, the level of development of online government services and the development of electronic participation (E - participation). This indicator was chosen as one of the resulting indicators of the state of digitization of various processes in thecountry.

Fig. 2 shows that in 2019 the United Arab Emirates (44%), China (39%), the Czech Republic (32%) and Norway (29%) are the leaders among the research countries in terms of the share of the added value of industrial production in GDP. By share of added value, the average – and high-tech production in the total volume of industrial production, the leaders with a share of more than 50% are Germany (61%), Denmark (58%), Hungary (54%), Sweden (52%), the CzechRepublic (52%) and France (50%). At the sametime, high indicators of the ICT subindex are observed in Germany, the UnitedArabEmirates, Sweden, Norway, Germany, France, and the UnitedKingdom.

Figure 1. Dynamics of the added value of industrial production (including construction) of some countries from 2011 to 2020, billiondollars (in 2015 US dollars)
Source: made by the authors based on data (World Bank, 2022)

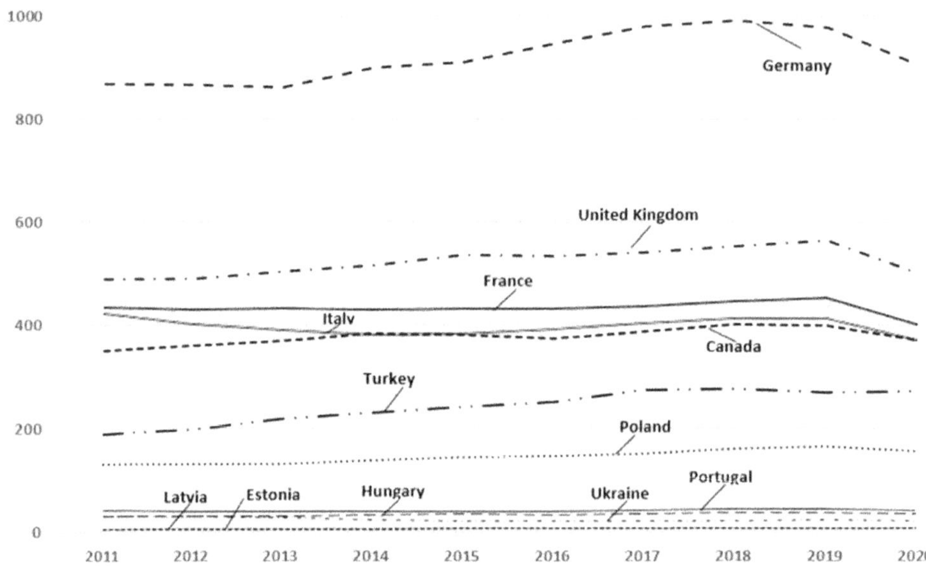

For comparison, Fig. 3 shows specified indicators of the share of the added value of industrial productionin GDP and the share of the added value of the medium and high-tech production in the added value of aggregate productionin 2020. In 2020, as in 2019,Sweden, the United Kingdom, France, Denmark, Germany, the Czech Republic remained the leaders in terms of the indicator of the medium and high-tech production in the added value and had morethan 50% of the added value of medium and high-tech production in the added value of manufacturing, which indicates their high technological development. At the same time, among these leaders according to this indicator, the share of added value of industrial production in WPP exceeded 20% in a few, namely: Germany, CzechRepublic, Hungary, Sweden, Denmark.

The indicators of Ukraine are relatively low, it can be noted that even according to the indicatorsof 2021, Ukraine demonstrates a low position in the main indicators of the ICT infrastructure. Accordingtothe ICT sub-index within theGlobal Innovation Index, Ukraine took 70th place (among 152 countries) with a scoreof 64.9 outof 100 maximum points, which is lower than inRomania, the CzechRepublic, Belarus, Lithuania andPoland. While the top 20 are SouthKorea, GreatBritain, Japan, Denmark, theNetherlands, Estonia, the USA, etc. The rating according to the Network Readiness Index is also indicative. Forexample, in 2021, Ukraine took 53rd place out of an index value of 55.7 and was overtaken by such countries asBrazil, Turkey, Uruguay,

Figure 2. The ratio of the share of the added value of industrial production in GDP and the share of the added value of the medium and high-tech production in the added value of aggregate productionin 2019 in the section of the subindex of information and communication technologies in 2020
Source: made by the authors based on data (World Bank, 2022)

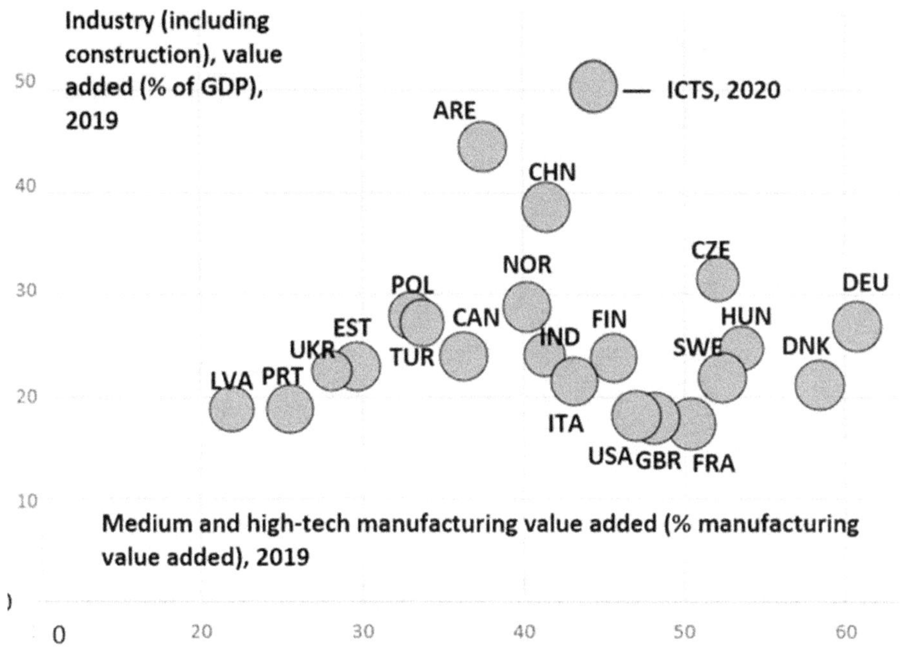

Malaysia, Hungary, and Poland.However, in 2022, the ICT sub-index in Ukraine increased significantly from 58 in 2020 to 74.9 in 2022 and stays in a strong position according to the Global Innovation Index report. This shows that even in the conditions of large-scale military aggression of the Russian Federation in Ukraine, large-scale losses of infrastructure and devastating consequences, thanks to the support of the international community, in particular the development of strongPolish-Ukrainian cooperation and in the areas of support for scientific research and innovation projects, thereis a positive trend in Ukraine dynamics of digitalization and development of innovative technologies of Industry 4.0.

Therefore, in most developed countries, there is a direct relationship between the share of medium and high-tech production and the ICT sub-index. Inaddition, since these are only relative indicators of GDP, it is worth additionally analyzing the absolute indicators of the added value of industrial production (Fig. 1) and thelevelof GDP. And within the limits of absolute indicators, countries with a high share of medium and high-tech production and indicators of digitalization have much higher

Figure 3. The ratio of the share of the added value of industrial production in GDP and the share of the added value of the mediumand high-tech production in the added value of aggregate production in 2020 in the section of the subindex of information and communication technologiesi n 2022
Source: made by the authors based on data (World Bank, 2022)

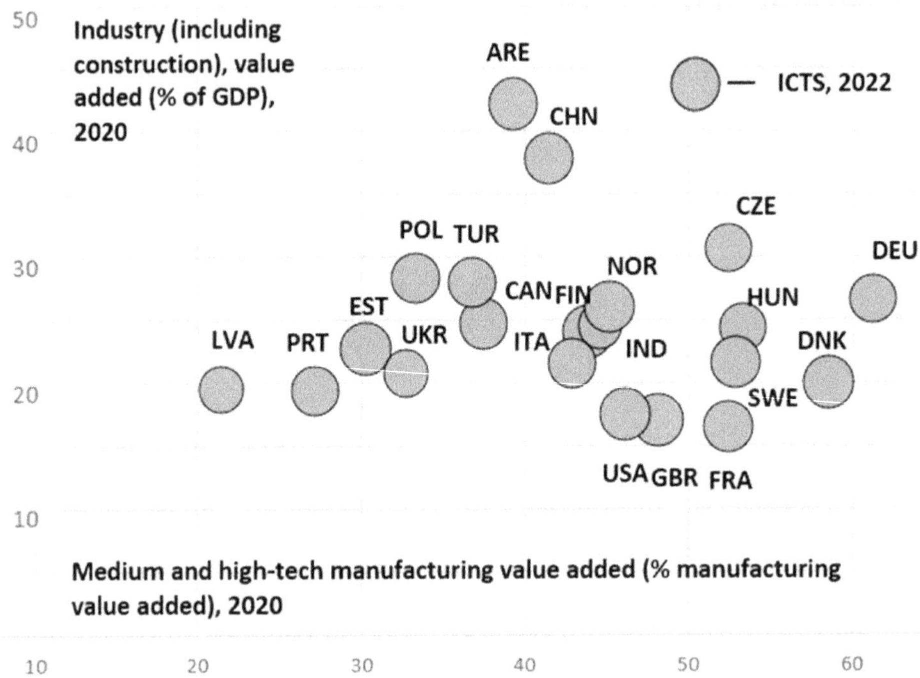

indicators of the added value of industrial production. In general, world industrial production accounts for only 16% ofthe world GDP (Digital economy: trends, risks and social determinants, 2021). With the increase in the number and quality of functioning ofindustrial enterprises in theworld through the introduction of Industry 4.0 technologies, the structure of the economy of most countrieswill change, which will lead to economic growth. Modern flexible methods of product development lead to qualitative changes in production because they allow minimizing "time" indicators that market" (TTM), i.e. increase speed as one of the most important competitive advantages of companies(Starlight, 2021). According to a McKinseystudy, industry leaders are using Industry 4.0 solutions while 39% haveimplemented a nerve center or control tower approach toincrease end-to-end supply chain transparency, and about a quarter have implemented rapid automation programs to stem emerging labor shortages due to COVID-19.

According to a study published by theWorld Economic Forum (Garms, Jansen, Schmitz, Hallerstede, &Tschiesner, 2019), many companies are trying to introduce Industry 4.0 technologies into production, but few manage to do it on a scale that allows for a significant financial and economic effect. At the sametime, the main directions of production transformation are determined by three global technological trends: network integration, intellectualization and flexible automation. It can be noted that these advanced enterprises, which managed to use these trends successfully (according to the study (Garms, Jansen, Schmitz, Hallerstede, &Tschiesner, 2019)), reaching a new level of efficiency, are located in those countries with high indicators of the added value of production and ICT (Fig. 1, Fig. 2). It can be listed the enterprises and the features of their revolutionary innovative technologies, which according to studies (Garms, Jansen, Schmitz, Hallerstede, &Tschiesner, 2019) are called "beacons", that is, leading enterprises in the implementation of Industry 4.0 technology, which should be followed in thetable. 1.

For global and Ukrainian enterprises, the implementation ofIndustry 4.0 technologies is particularly relevant inorder to minimize the negative impact of the global COVID-19 pandemic. On the one hand, this is an opportunity to optimize production processes, on the other hand, it is an opportunity to manage the production process remotely and economically.Among the main global trends, it is possible to note that the market conditions are changing rapidly, the demandis unstable, shifting demand toward developing markets and new start-ups, growing demand for an individual approach, personalization and integration, which determines the value characteristics of the fourth industrial revolution(Wright, 2017), based on which has a modern production line 4.0 built. The production line involves1) optimization of processes using data, in particular, integration of IT technologies for digital management of production efficiency, digital optimization of processes basedon a database, an automated filingsystem; 2) a wide range of digital technologies for workers, in particular, real-time production control, electronic document management and digitization of team tasks and control sheets, online updates and descriptions of new tasksforworkers; 3) an integrated product model from development to production, which provides, in particular, the integration of production data, offline programming of production processes, virtual commissioning, which allows monitoring production, monitoring and quality control from the customer'splace.

Taking into account the technologies of Industry 4.0, the automation of supply systems is carried out based on the robotization of production processes. According to market research of manufacturing companies(Mantec, 2022), it isthe "humanfactor" that is the cause of about 23% of shortages and a decrease in the use of production facilities. Therefore, to ensure positive effects, it is important to develop human capital to ensure Industry 4.0 technologies, and to increase the level of production automation and the use of robotics. According to forecasts(Mantec, 2022), global

Table 1. Examples of enterprises implementing successful practices of implementing breakthrough technologies of Industry 4.0

Country	Enterprise	Technologies of Industry 4.0
Germany	BMW (Regensburg)	A highly developed enterprise, built On the principles of careful production, set a goal to reach a newlevel thanks to the introduction of digital technologies
	PhoenixContact (BadPyrmontandBlomberg)	To meet the growing demands Customers to the individualization of solutions The company introduced a set of new scenarios Use of digital technologies
China	Bosch Automotive (All)	Morethan 30 new scenarios for the use of digital technologies have been implemented To meet the 200% increase in demand
	Danfoss (Tianjin)	The company used Industry 4.0 technologies to improve product quality and reduce costs Expenses taking into account the expectations of customers
	Foxconn Industrial Internet(Shenzhen)	The company decided on a complete reorientation of the business, that is, the transformation from a manufacturer of electronic equipment into a supplier of industrial Internet technologies
	Haier (Qingdao)	Implementation of digital technologies in production inorder to satisfy consumer demand and create a new business model
	Siemens Industrial Automation Products (Chengdu)	The growth of consumer demand caused The need for digital transformations To maintain productquality
CzechRepublic	Procter & Gamble — Rakona(Rakovnik)	The company implements digital technologies, has set itself the task of changing the range of products and plans to continue operating for the next 140 years
France	Schneider Electric (Le Vaudreuil)	The company, which has been inexistence for 50 years, realized the need to implement digital Technologies to remain cost competitiveforthenext 50 years
Italy	Rold (Cerro Maggiore)	The company introduced the concept of digital Production to maintain competitiveness And increasing the volume of products produced
Sweden	Sandvik Coromant (Gimo)	The enterprise introduced digital technologies And intelligent automated systems, Which allows producing of large volumes of products (cuttingtools) from competitive Cost price with minimum lot volumes

Compiled by the authors based on(Garms, Jansen, Schmitz, Hallerstede, &Tschiesner, 2019)

demand in the field of production for breakthrough robotics technologies should grow to 3.7 billion dollars.

One of the breakthrough technologies in the field of robotics is collaborativerobots (cobots) which are automatic devices that can work together with a person to create or manufacture various products(GlobalSpec, 2015). These mechanisms are being improved with the development of Industry 4.0. Automated production lines in combination with breakthrough technologies of Industry 4.0 will make it possible to obtain such positive socio-economic effects as the release of the inefficient lab or force, increase in lab or productivity, acceleration of the period of turn over of current assets of the enterprise, optimization of wages for production personnel, improvement of lab or safety, taking into account the involvement of robots in performing tasks dangerous for people, increasing the speed of various production processes.

CONCLUSION

In conclusion,according to the results of the research, it can be stated that the development of Industry 4.0 is accompanied by the growth of the added value of medium and high-techproduction, and the introduction of digitalization at the macro and microlevels. At the macro level, it is expedient to introduce support for innovative technologies of Industry 4.0 by forming strategies and plans for the development of the economy, taking into account world programs and globalinitiatives, particularly, EU IndustrialStrategy 2021-2024, European initiatives regarding ICT innovations for SME production (I4MC), MarshallPlan 4.0 "Priority measures for the economic redistribution of Wallonia" (Belgium), Program "NewIndustrialFrance", Innovation program Production2030- Strategic innovation program supported by the Swedish Innovation SystemsAgency (Vinnova),National platforminDenmark MADE, Strategy Industry Conectada 4.0, NationalTechnological Cluster "IntelligentFactory" (FabbricaIntelligente) andothers. It is appropriate to take into account the experience of leading enterprises that implement digitalization technologies to improve production efficiency becauseIndustry 4.0 promotes the acceleration of production processes and structural changes in industries for maintaining competitiveness, companies need to accelerate the turnover period of current assets, which is facilitated by digitalization. The main directions of production transformation are determined by three global technological trends such as networkintegration, intellectualization and flexible automation. In particular, highly effective elements of flexible automation are collaborative works, which can become an important first step form odifying the production lines of companies. Thus, it is advisable to implement the best development practices (at the macro level) and the application of Industry 4.0 technologies (at the microlevel) in Ukraine and Poland, which will ensure positive effects associated with the growth of industrial production, the increase in production flexibility and intellectualization of enterprises.

REFERENCES

Borowski, P. (2021). Digitization, digital twins, Blockchain, and Industry 4.0 as elements of management process in enterprises in the energy sector. *Energies*, *14*(7), 1885. doi:10.3390/en14071885

Digitaleconomy: trends, risks and social determinants. (2021). Retrieved from https://razumkov.org.ua/uploads/article/2020_digitalization.pdf

GarmsF.JansenC.SchmitzC.HallerstedeS.TschiesnerA. (2019). Retrieved from https://www.mckinsey.com/industries/advanced-electronics/our-insights/capturing-value-at-scale-in-discrete-manufacturing-with-industry-4-0

Global innovation index. (2021). Retrieved from https://www.globalinnovationindex.org/about-gii

GlobalSpec. (2015). Retrieved from https://insights.globalspec.com/article/621/collaborative-robots-play-nice-on-the-plant-floor

Hermann, M., Pentek, T., & Otto, B. (2016). Design principles for industrie 4.0 scenarios. *2016 49th Hawaii International Conference on System Sciences (HICSS)*. 10.1109/HICSS.2016.488

KagermannH.LukasW.-D.WahlsterW. (2018). Retrieved from https://www.ingenieur.de/technik/fachbereiche/produktion/industrie-40-mit-internet-dinge-weg-4-industriellen-revolution/

Mantec. (2022). Retrieved from https://mantec.org/robotics-manufacturing/

Smoliar, L., Ilyash, O., Kolishenko, R., & Lytvak, T. (2020). Benchmarks of ensuring an «economic breakthrough» of Ukraine in technological and innovative areas. *Innovative Economy*, (5–6), 19–29. doi:10.37332/2309-1533.2020.5-6.3

Starlight. (2021). *TimeToMarket: What it is, Why it's important, and Five Ways to Reduce it*. Retrievedfrom https://www.starlightanalytics.com/article/time-to-market

Sustainable development knowledge platform. (2020). https://sustainabledevelopment.un.org/content/documents/26295VNR_2020_Ukraine_Report.pdf

Trofymenko, O. (2021). Development of a mechanism for implementation of a national innovative policy in the energy sector based on Industry 4.0. *Technology Auditand Production Reserves*, *4*(4(60)), 34–40. doi:10.15587/2706-5448.2021.238959

WorldBank. (2022). Retrievedfrom https://data.worldbank.org/country

Wright, I. (2017). *Human Error is Worse in Manufacturing Compared to Other Sectors*. Retrieved from https://www.engineering.com/story/human-error-is-worse-in-manufacturing-compared-to-other-sectors

YurchakO. (2018). Retrieved from https://industry4-0-ukraine.com.ua/2017/03/06/industry-4-0-%D1%8F%D0%BA-%D1%83%D0%BD%D0%B8%D0%BA%D0%BD%D1%83%D1%82%D0%B8-%D0%BF%D0%BB%D1%83%D1%82%D0%B0%D0%BD%D0%B8%D0%BD%D0%B8-%D1%82%D0%B0-%D0%BE%D0%B1%D1%94%D0%B4%D0%BD%D0%B0/

Chapter 13
To the Question of Design and Manufacturing of Special Equipment for Mechanism of Pneumatic Power Receiving Mechanism

V. M. Orel
WSG University, Poland

Svitlana Kashuba
WSG University, Poland

M. M. Yatsina
Higher Vocational School N°7, Kremenchuk, Ukraine

V. H. Mazur
Higher Vocational School N°7, Kremenchuk, Ukraine

ABSTRACT

In this work, the existing technologies of 3D printing, types, and structure of 3D printers for designing and manufacturing of special equipment for the mechanism of energy recovery with a pneumatic engine were analyzed and thoroughly examined. The main materials for printing are considered, as well as the carbon-bearing materials for FDM printing, and their properties and characteristics are considered in detail. Measurement of the received detail and processing of statistical data is carried out. A comparison of the obtained holes with the given nominal values is made, and the absolute error for external and internal diameters is calculated. It is possible to calculate the roughness of the bar of the delta work and the stress state of the structure under the action of applied forces.

DOI: 10.4018/979-8-3693-1886-7.ch013

INTRODUCTION

In the modern world, the developers of new concepts in automotive industry increasingly deviate from the use of power units, and try to apply combined power systems. Vehicles with such systems are called “Hybrid Cars”.

The main reasons behind the development of a hybrid power plant are reducing the amount of harmful emissions into the atmosphere, which is very important for urban transport. This system allows you to reduce the emission of soot and hydrocarbons by 90%, nitrogen oxides - by 50%. At the same time fuel economy reaches 60%, and acceleration at the start of the movement has increased by 50%. In particular, a pneumatic power plant can be installed on cars that perform various tasks.

In turn, the mechanism of recuperation of the energy of compressed air during braking is a planetary transmission, and a set of related gears.

In the center is a solar gear coupled to four satellites, which are in a fixed position for each other. The element is a carrier, and the teeth of the largest ring gear are connected with the satellites. The design is quite simple mechanically, but its device provides tremendous opportunities for the transmission and summation of torque.

Each element of the planetary transmission is connected to a separate device: it was driven from the internal combustion engine, a sun gear with a compressor, which compresses the compressed air into the receiver, and a ring gear with a pneumatic engine.

It is the ring gear through the gearbox connected with the wheels. As a result, it is possible to have a very flexible connection and a universal division between the internal combustion engine and the pneumatic engine, while the vehicle can perform both parallel and sequential hybrids (Salenko & Yatsina, 2014).

In the process of energy recovery, the energy from the mop, mounted on the driving wheel, in the mode of braking leads to an extension of the charging time of the energy-saving element of the additional power unit. In particular, when using as an additional engine in a hybrid vehicle, the compressed air energy is used by the working chamber of the pneumatic engine for the torque conversion of Mkr, which is transmitted to the driving wheel through a hinge of equal angular velocities (HEAV).

In turn, the inhibitory process leads to the introduction of a recovery mechanism (Hertz, 1973; Salenko & Yatsina, 2012; Yatsina, 2013; Yatsyna & Litvinenko, 2008), which results in recuperation of energy of Erk (Figure 1).

It should be noted that in Figure 1 shows a schematic arrangement of the additional power unit on the driving wheel without a drive from the main propulsion.

Such a design is due to the fact that the alternate drive of the torque from the main and additional propulsion leads to the complication of the design of the transmission and the pivot node of the driving wheel, which, in turn, is complicated by the energy of the compressed air installed on the reel wheel mounted on the drum.

Figure 1. Schematic representation of the design of the driving wheel of a hybrid vehicle with recuperative braking

1. Crank mechanism; 2. Zapf; 3. Elastic wheel; 4. Brake shoe; 5. Brake drum; 6. Recuperator of compressed air energy; 7. Pendant; 8. Cylinders batteries; 9. Pneumomotor; 10. Body of the vehicle

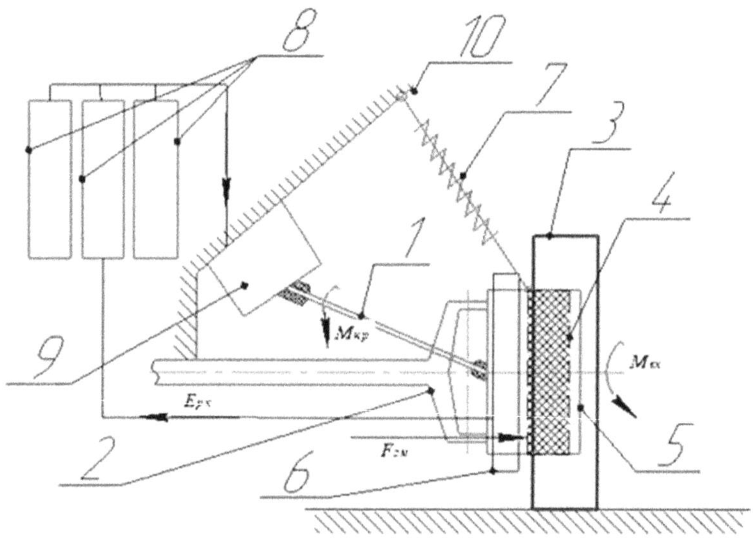

Figure 2. Three-dimensional model of the mechanism of the recuperation of the pneumatic propeller

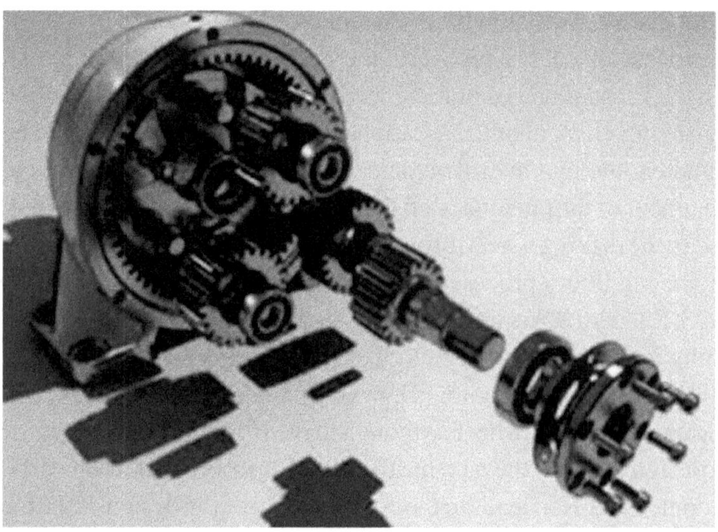

However, the manufacture of special equipment for the mechanism of energy recovery with a pneumatic engine requires new technologies and methods of quality control due to the conditions of operation of this mechanism and the peculiarities of the process of selection of used energy and its redistribution in the compressor-brake system.

STATEMENT OF MATERIAL

Thus, since the beginning of the new millennium, the concept of “3D” has firmly entered into production processes. Industrial 3D printers first appeared in the early 80’s. At that time a cerograph was developed, with the help of which it was possible to create 3D objects from liquid photopolymer plastics. Technology in such equipment is based on the properties of photopolymers - under the influence of a laser, it hardens, acquiring a solid form of plastic.

Another predecessor of the modern 3D printer was the technology of “laser sintering”. The basis for creating volumetric models is a powder of fusible plastic. From the influence of the laser, the plastic melts, and then sintered into a single mass. But in order to prevent the heating of plastic from burning, the inert gas is pumped into the working chamber. The complexity of servicing such equipment does not allow such printers to be used at home.

Consequently, 3D printing is the process of creating three-dimensional objects based on the virtual 3D model. That is, creating a product using a 3D printer means layer-by-stage “cultivation” of a physical object based on its data programmed into a computer. The very special machine, 3D printer, can be completely different sizes, depending on the size of the produced figure (Alberg, 1997).

Therefore, the main objective in designing and manufacturing the elements of the recuperator design of compressed air energy is to carry out mathematical calculations and prediction of the quality of the weaving obtained by the 3D printing method, to conduct a statistical study of the law of the normal distribution of the quality of the printed specimen and to compare the obtained quality data of 3D printing with existing methods of weaving .

In the manufacture of the elements of the design of the recuperator there are various technologies of three-dimensional printing. The difference between them is the way to lay layers of the product. The most common are SLS (selective laser plexus), NRM (imposition of layers of molten materials) and SLA (stereolithography). The most widespread due to the high speed of the construction of objects acquired stereolithography or SLA technology.

Squeezing powder reactants under the action of laser beam is the same SLS - the only technology of 3D printing, which is used in the manufacture of molds, both for metallic and plastic molding. Plastic models have excellent mechanical properties, through which they can be used to produce fully functional products. In SLS technology materials are used close to the properties of the brands of the final product: ceramics, powder plastic, metal, which in turn allows you to create conjugation elements of this construction with a high level of sealing.

It is worth noting that electron-beam smelting is widely used to create metal three-dimensional objects. Unlike them, the EBM-machines generate metal-emitting pulses instead of laser beam for metallurgy. However, this method provides high-quality printing and excellent drawing of small parts of the recuperator, which, with unit production for scientific purposes, not only ensures compliance with the prescribed characteristics, but also reduces the cost of laboratory research of the recovery system of the vehicle.

Some devices allow you to use different materials during one production cycle.

Printing a model from a single material with the stamp of the towers on another, easily soluble material, which allows you to easily remove the supporting structures of the planetary mechanism after the completion of the printing process.

The plastic thread is unwound from the coil and fed into an extruder, equipped with a mechanical drive for filing, a heating element for melting the material and a nozzle through which direct extrusion is carried out. The heating element serves to heat the nozzle, which in turn melt a plastic thread and feeds molten material to the real estate under construction. As a rule, the upper part of the nozzle is cooled by the fan to create a sharp temperature gradient, which is required to ensure smooth flow of material (Alberg, 1997; Russell & Norvig, 2007).

The plastic thread is unwound from the coil and fed into an extruder, equipped with a mechanical drive for filing, a heating element for melting the material and a nozzle through which direct extrusion is carried out. The heating element serves to heat the nozzle, which in turn melt a plastic thread and feeds molten material to the real estate under construction. As a rule, the upper part of the nozzle is cooled by the fan to create a sharp temperature gradient, which is required to ensure smooth flow of material (Alberg, 1997; Russell & Norvig, 2007).

FDM technology can be considered one of the most technologically simple methods of 3D printing. At the heart of the process lies the consistent layering of a thin filament of molten plastic up to the creation of a holistic three-dimensional object. As a consumable material, a plastic thread wound on the coil is used. Occasionally used individual rods of plastic. The standard thread diameter is 1.75 mm or 3 mm. The printing process consists of several stages:

1. Creation or import of a digital three-dimensional model.
2. Processing of the digital model for printing with the addition of structures.
3. Location and orientation of the digital model on the desktop.

4. Slice-cutting of the digital model into separate layers with the conversion of data in the instructions for the printer.
5. If necessary, physical or chemical processing of the finished model.

The next important element is the extruder, that is, the printhead of the printer. These devices can vary in design, but generally have the same basic components:

stretching mechanism for filing the nozzle;

- ◦ Nozzle for slurry and extrusion of molten material;
- ◦ Heating element for heating the nozzle;
- ◦ Propeller mechanism consisting of a gear or screws actuated by an electric motor.

Thus, the electric motor leads the gear movement, carrying the supply of plastic thread to the nozzle (Kalyaev et al., 2007). In the nozzle there is a melting of the filaments with the subsequent extrusion of the viscous material. Extremely important moment is the sharp temperature gradient between the bottom and top of the nozzle - for this purpose and the fan is installed. When passing the threshold of glass transition, the plastic becomes soft, but not viscous, expanding in volume.

If the length of the nozzle (and, as a consequence, the area) of this site is too large, then the total friction coefficient may become unsustainable for pulling out the mechanism. However, the length of the section of the nozzle with the undiluted thread and the length of the site with the molten material are not of particular importance, but the length of the section with plastic at the glass transition temperature should be as short as possible. The most effective solution to this problem is the use of radiators and fans that cool the thread and top of the nozzle. t should be noted that the residence time of the plastic in the molten state should also be minimized, since many thermoplastics lose plasticity after prolonged stay at high temperatures, and formed solid particles can clog the nozzle.

As a rule, such problems do not arise with normal, stable extrusion, because the length of the nozzle is too small. The clogging of the nozzle can occur in the presence of internal inequalities, or in the case of error in the manufacture of threads: the resulting stagnation leads to the gradual formation of grains, which are then captured by the flow of molten plastic and clog the outlet.

In printers using the Cartesian coordinate system, the movement of the platform in the vertical plane is responsible for the vertical positioning of the extruder relative to the platform itself.

Some models also add the movement of the platform on one of the axes in the horizontal plane, which allows you to slightly reduce the size of the device

Figure 3. The quantum delta experimental printer uses an "inverted" design with a movable platform and a stationary extruder

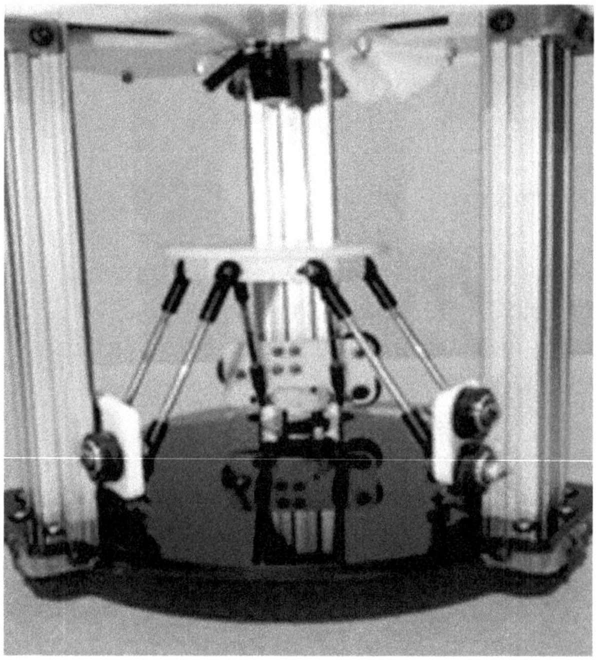

provided the presence of an open case. An example of such printers is the popular 3D Systems Cube

Static platforms (Forsyth, 2004) use the delta-shaped printers ("delta-work") for the manufacture of fastenings of a planetary mechanism whose surfaces are highly accurate and located at different angles to the base. The positioning of the printhead in all three dimensions is carried out solely by the movement of the extruder itself, which is suspended on three manipulators, whose coordinated movement along the vertical guides and moves the head (Figure 3).

Asymmetrically, the motion adjusts the positioning of the extruder horizontally by changing the angle of the manipulator, and symmetrical - vertically. Alternatively, a mobile platform and a stationary extruder may be used.

Before printing, you need to calibrate the platform, that is, eliminating the possible tilt. The calibration mechanisms can be both manual and automatic, depending on the printer model (Figure 4). To measure distance, special templates are used, and in cases of the most simple or homemade designs - just sheets of office paper, whose thickness is approximately equivalent to 100 microns.

Depending on the design, the work platform can be equipped with a removable table. Such a design is used in the manufacture of the body recuperator, which

Figure 4. The perforated worktable of the printer Up! Plus 2

complicate the removal of models from the platform (Tovzhnyansky et al., 2005; Zenkevich & Yushchenko, 2005).

In the case of using perforated tables, such a solution is simply necessary, since the cleaning of the surface is soaked in solvents. Less than a removable table is the possibility of a backlash with sufficient weakness of fasteners or clamps.

A special structure of this type can withstand a strong mechanical impact. Such a plastic belongs to stable groups and if you compare ABS with ordinary polystyrene,

Figure 5. Printed elements of the recovery mechanism using FDM technology

Table 1. ABS characteristics of plastic

Density, g / cm^3	1 - 1,08
Temperature of softening, ° C	90 - 105
Strength at stretching, MPa	35 - 50
Relative elongation,%	10 - 25
Module for flexural bending, GPa	1,5 - 2,4
Charley Shock Strength (with slot), kJ / m^2	10 - 30
Brinell hardness, MPa	90 - 150
Temperature of self-ignition, ° C	395
KPV (bottom) dust-air mixture, g / m^3	16

then it is substantially superior to other analogues in terms of mechanical strength and stiffness. Among other advantages it is possible that this type of plastic can withstand a temperature load of 100 ° C. This consumable material can also be used for electroplating, in the field of vacuum metallization and even for contact adhesion. It is perfect for welding or precision casting. Material has high dimensional stability. The printed objects have a brilliant surface (the luminance level can be adjusted). Among the huge list of advantages can be noted resistance to alkali, lubricants, acids, carbohydrates, fats and even gasoline. However, it is perfectly soluble in acetone, ether, benzene, ethyl chloride, ethylene chloride, aniline and anisol.

The main disadvantage is the sensitivity to the influence of ultraviolet rays and atmospheric precipitation. This material is characterized by a low level of electrical insulation. The cost of a kilo of ABS plastic is about 35 $. However, given that expansion of compressed air significantly reduces its temperature and leads to the condensation of residual moisture, it should be noted that this material virtually does not absorb moisture.

Metal powder is also commonly used in three-dimensional printing. Note that the powder does not necessarily consist of metal. Gold, copper, aluminum or alloy can be used as the starting material. Even ABS plastic can not mimic the glitter of genuine metal, because metal models have higher strength than other types of supplies for 3D printers.

The material with carbon fibers is reinforced by 20% ultra-light and relatively long longitudinal carbon fibers, which gave an exceptionally strong thread for carbon-fiber-reinforced 3D printers. CarbonFil is twice as strong as the HDglass and at the same time 10% more resistant to impact, which is an important property, as the recovery process takes place in the braking mode.

The CarbonFil thread is based on the unique PETG mixture of HD glass and reinforced by 20% ultra-light and relatively long carbon fibers, which gave an

Figure 6. Schematic representation of absolute error

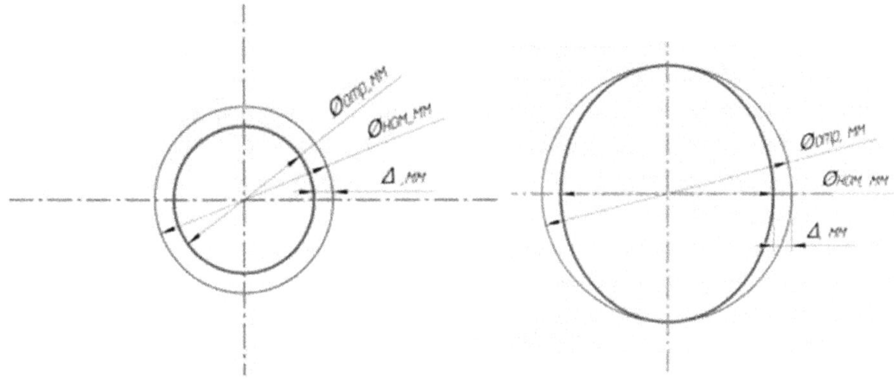

exceptionally strong thread for carbon-fiber-reinforced 3D printers. CarbonFil is twice as strong as the HDglass and at the same time 10% more shock resistant, a great asset for carbon-enhanced fillers (Canessa et al., 2013; Salenko et al., n.d.).

Control measurements and quality analysis of the finished printed part were carried out using an electronic dial caliper. The measurement accuracy of the caliper is 0.01 mm.

When comparing the obtained holes in the part with the given (nominal) values, the calculation of absolute and relative errors of the printing was performed. Absolute error is calculated as the difference between the value obtained and the nominal value (Figure 7), calculated in modulus, measured in millimeters (mm).

$$\Delta = \left| x \text{ received} - x \text{ nominal} \right|$$

The relative error is numerically equal to the absolute measurement error Δ to the true value of the measured value, measured as a percentage (%). The relative error of the formula is calculated:

$$\delta = \left| x \text{ received } x \text{ nominal} \right| \; x \text{ nominal } 100\%$$

or $\delta = \Delta \; x \text{ nominal} \cdot 100\%$

Find the arithmetic mean of the received dimensions for an internal diameter of 6mm:

$$5{,}92 + 5{,}83 = 5{,}87$$

Figure 7. Measurement of dimensions by electronic caliper

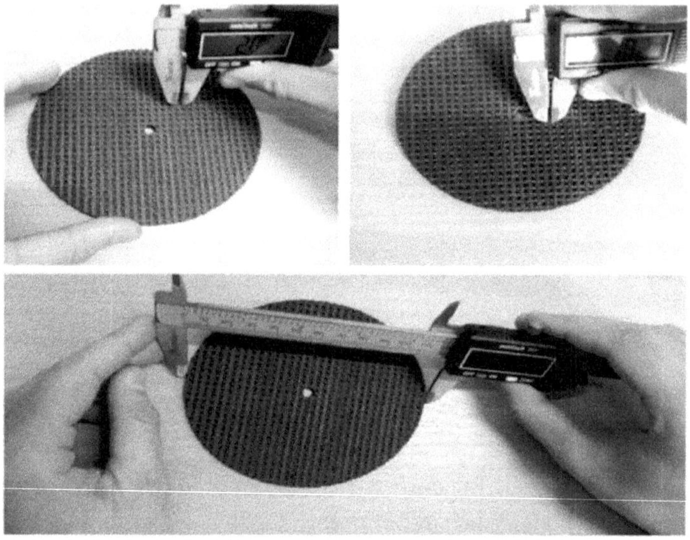

5,83 + 5,51 = 5,67

Static analysis allowed to calculate the stress state of structures under the action of the forces applied to the system of constant time, which makes it possible to assess the strength of the design developed by it under the voltage allowed and to identify the weakest construction sites and make the necessary changes (optimize) the product. Meanwhile, an associative connection is maintained between a three-dimensional model of a product and an estimated finite element model.

Measurement of the outer diameter, hole and thickness of the part, depending on the angle (Figure 8). the received data are recorded in Table 2.

Parametric changes to the output solid-state model are automatically transferred to the net finite-element model.

Table 2. Results of measurements

	Specified Diameters, mm	
Axe	**External Diameter, 120mm**	**Internal Diameter, 6mm**
x	118,78mm;118,62mm	5,51mm
y	119,41mm;118,75mm	5,83mm
z	119,80mm;119,54mm	5,92mm

Figure 8. Schematic representation of measurements of outer diameter

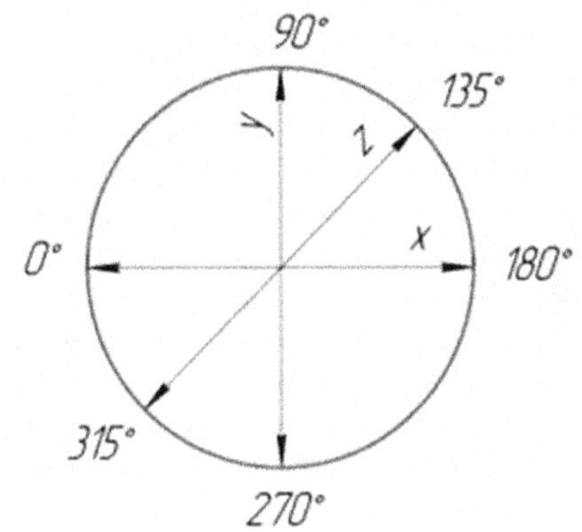

Figure 9. Getting the deflection of the outer diameters

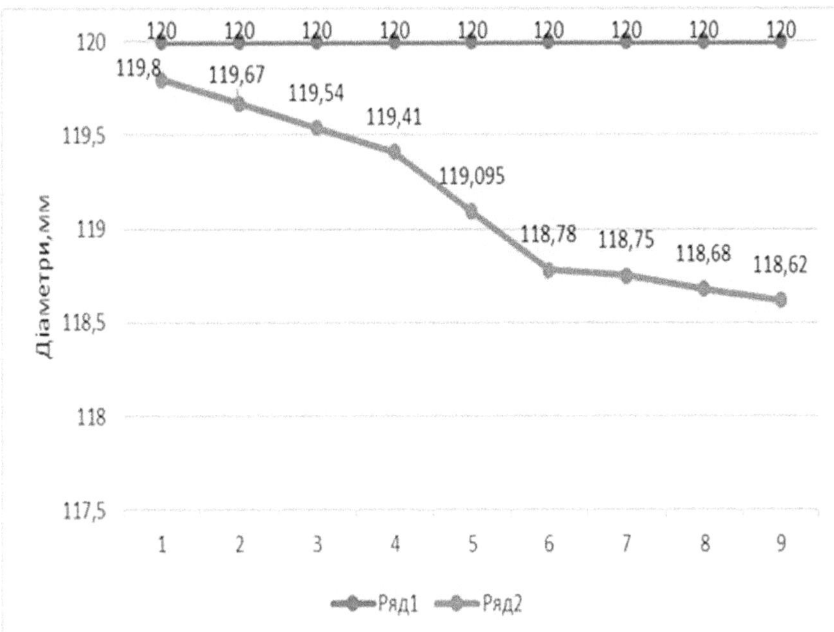

Static analysis gives grounds for:

– take into account geometric nonlinearity;
– to determine the stress-strain state taking into account temperature influences;
– carry out calculations of contact tasks.

Figure 10. Diagram of loadings

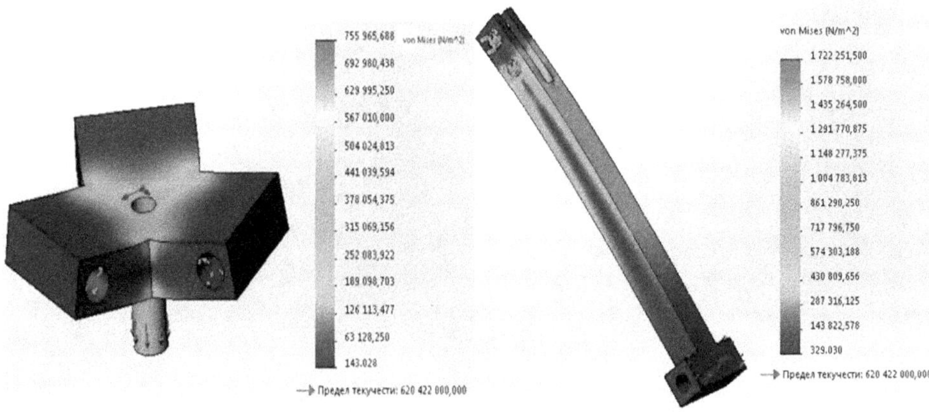

As external loads on the design included force, pressure, rotation, acceleration, cylindrical load, torque, temperature. As fixations can be used full movement restrictions, as well as partial fixation along the axes (in Cartesian, cylindrical and spherical coordinate systems). The main results of static calculations are:

– displacement fields of the design at the calculation points of the finite element grid;
– fields of relative deformation;
– fastening on the axes (in Cartesian, cylindrical and spherical coordinate systems).

The main results of static calculations are:

– displacement fields of the design at the calculation points of the finite element grid;
– fields of relative deformation;–fields of stress components;
– deformation energy;
– hub forces;
– Fields of distribution of the stock factor by voltage in terms of design.

These data are sufficient to predict the behavior of the design and decision making to optimize the geometric shape of the product. All calculations were done using SOLID WORKS SIMULATION. Results of analysis of parts: As a load, the force of 10 N is in force (Figure 10).

Measurement of the received detail and processing of statistical data is carried out. A comparison of the obtained holes with the given nominal values has been made, the absolute error for external and internal diameters is calculated:

Figure 11. The system of lubrication of the pneumatic system of the regenerative mechanism of the pneumatic engine
1. The inlet to the pool cavity; 2. Oil fog; 3. Under the ring cavity with oil emulsion; 4. Working Camera; 5. Oil filter for selection of curtains; 6. Exhaust port for redirection of grease

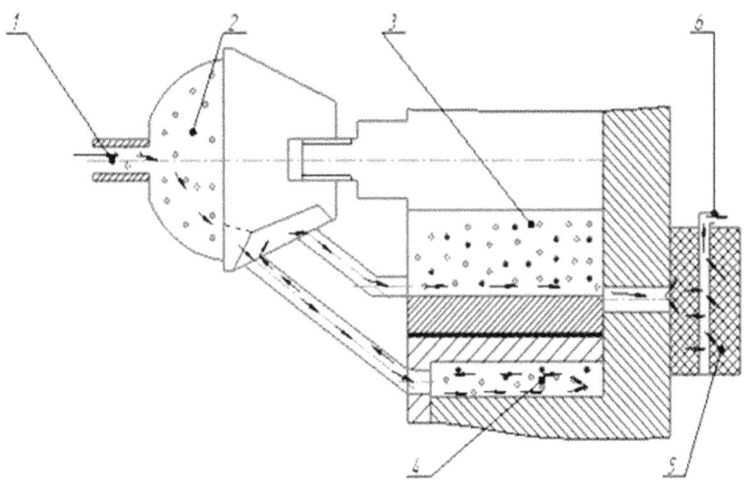

$$\Delta = |118{,}78 - 120| = 1{,}22 \text{ mm};$$

$$\Delta = |118{,}62 - 120| = 1{,}38 \text{ mm}.$$

It is possible to calculate the roughness of the bar of the delta work, calculation of the stress state of the structure under the action of applied forces.

Considering that the lubrication system of the recovery mechanism occurs by redistributing the oil emulsion from the lubrication systems of the pneumatic engine (Figure 11), where the densities between the friction elements performed with 3D printing technology increase, which, in turn, leads to increased energy efficiency and wear the surfaces of the decoration of the recuperator is reduced.

CONCLUSION

Thus, the existing technologies of 3D printing, types and structure of 3D printers for designing and manufacturing of special equipment for the mechanism of energy recovery with a pneumatic engine are analyzed and detailed in detail. The main materials for printing are considered, as well as the carbon-bearing materials for FDM printing, their properties and characteristics are considered in detail. A kinematic analysis of the printer's mechanism for 3D printing of the delta type has been carried out; positioning errors for this type of mechanism have been determined.

The faults of stepping engines and their consequences are determined. Measurement of the received detail and processing of statistical data is carried out. A comparison of the obtained holes with the given nominal values is made, the absolute error for external and internal diameters is calculated. Thus, the manufacture of special equipment for the mechanism of energy recovery with a pneumatic motor through 3D printing enables the use of the material used to reduce the mass of the recuperator, while maintaining the necessary strength of the structural elements.

REFERENCES

Alberg, J. (1997). Splines Theory and Applications. Academic Press.

Canessa, E., Fonda, C., & Zennaro, M. (2013). *Low-cost 3D Printing for Science, Education & Sustainable Development*. http://sdu.ictp.it/3d/book/Low-cost_3D_printing_screen.pdf

Forsyth, D. (2004). *Computer vision*. Modern Approach. Pons, Williams William.

Hertz, E. V. (1973). Dynamic calculation of discrete pneumatic actuators. *Mechanical Engineering*, 17–33.

Kalyaev, I. A., Lochin, V. M., & Makarov, I. M. (2007). *Intelligent Robots*. Machine Building.

Russell, S., & Norvig, P. (2007). *Artificial Intelligence. Modern Approach* (2nd ed.). Academic Press.

Salenko, O. F., & ... (n.d.). On the expediency fusing 3D printing tools to improve the accuracy of static and dynamic studies of lever rotating mechanisms. Bulletin of the Kremenchug National University named after Mikhail Ostrogoradsky, 1(90).

Salenko, O. F., & Yatsina, M. M. (2012). On the possibility of using drives on mobile vehicles with autonomous source International Scientific. *Gabrovo International Conference,* 313-317.

Salenko, O. F., & Yatsina, M. M. (2014). Analysis of dynamics of work of pneumodrive for mobile transport mean with autonomous rower source. *Transactions of Kremenchuk Mikhail Ostrogradsky National University*, *6*(65), 59–62.

Tovzhnyansky, L. L., Grabchenko, A. I., Chernyshov, S. I., Verezub, Y. B., Dobroscok, V. L., Knut, X., & Lierat, F. (2005). *Integrated technologies of accelerated prototyping and manufacturing*. OJSC.

Yatsina, M.M. (2013). Improvement of energy efficiency of a pneumatic engine on the basis of geometrical parameters of elements of a working chamber. Transactions of Kremenchuk Mikhail Ostrogradsky National University, 5(82), 93-97.

Yatsyna, M.M., & Litvinenko, B.Y. (2008). Pneumodyngyon with a circular rotor in mechanotron systems. Transactions of Kremenchuk Mikhail Ostrogradsky National University, 2(49), 68-72.

Zenkevich, S. L., & Yushchenko, A. S. (2005). *Basics of manipulation robot management*. N. E. Bauman.

Compilation of References

Abay, N. C., Zhou, Y., Kantarcioglu, M., Thuraisingham, B., & Sweeney, L. (2019). Privacy preserving synthetic data release using deep learning. In *Machine Learning and Knowledge Discovery in Databases: European Conference, ECML PKDD 2018, Ireland, Proceedings, Part I 18* (pp. 510-526). 10.1007/978-3-030-10925-7_31

Abouelmehdi, K., Beni-Hessane, A., & Khaloufi, H. (2018). Big healthcare data: Preserving security and privacy. *Journal of Big Data*, *5*(1), 1–18. doi:10.1186/s40537-017-0110-7

Acharya, U. K., & Kumar, S. (2020). Particle swarm optimized texture based histogram equalization (PSOTHE) for MRI brain image enhancement. *Optik (Stuttgart)*, *224*, 165760. doi:10.1016/j.ijleo.2020.165760

Adam, S. P., Alexandropoulos, S. A. N., Pardalos, P. M., &Vrahatis, M. N. (2019). No free lunch theorem: A review. *Approximation and optimization: Algorithms, complexity and applications*, 57-82.

Adobor, H., & Daneshfar, A. (2006). Management simulations: Determining their effectiveness. *Journal of Management Development*, *25*(2), 151–168. doi:10.1108/02621710610645135

Akilina, O., Panchenko, A., &Horozhankina, A. (2023). Implementation of peacebuilding education in educational institutions of Ukraine. *Continuing Professional Education: Theory and Practice, 4*(77), 7–17. doi:10.28925/1609-8595.2023.4.1

Alberg, J. (1997). Splines Theory and Applications. Academic Press.

Allgood, M., Jensen, U. T., & Stritch, J. M. (2022). Work-Family Conflict and Burnout Amid COVID-19: Exploring the Mitigating Effects of Instrumental Leadership and Social Belonging. *Review of Public Personnel Administration*, *0*(0). Advance online publication. doi:10.1177/0734371X221101308

Alqahtani, A.Y., & Rajkhan, A.A. (2020). E-Learning Critical Success Factors during the COVID-19 Pandemic: A Comprehensive Analysis of E-Learning Managerial Perspectives. *Educ. Sci., 10*, 216. doi:10.3390/educsci10090216,p

Al-Thanoon, Qasim, & Algamal. (2018). *Tuning parameter estimation in SCAD-support vector machine using firefly algorithm with application in gene selection and cancer classification.* doi:10.1016/j.compbiomed.2018.10.034

Ardila, A., Bernal, B., & Rosselli, M. (2016). How localized are language brain areas? A review of Brodmann areas involvement in oral language. *Archives of Clinical Neuropsychology*, *31*(1), 112–122. doi:10.1093/arclin/acv081 PMID:26663825

Aronsson, G., Theorell, T., Grape, T., Hammarström, A., Hogstedt, C., Marteinsdottir, I., Skoog, I., Träskman-Bendz, L., & Hall, C. (2017). A systematic review including meta-analysis of work environment and burnout symptoms. *BMC Public Health*, *17*(1), 264. doi:10.1186/s12889-017-4153-7 PMID:28302088

Asiminidis, C., Kokkonis, G., & Kontogiannis, S. (2018). Database Systems Performance Evaluation for IoT Applications. *Int. J. Database Manag. Syst.*, *10*(6), 1–14. doi:10.5121/ijdms.2018.10601

Assam, M., Kanwal, H., Farooq, U., Shah, S. K., Mehmood, A., & Choi, G. S. (2021). An efficient classification of MRI brain images. *IEEE Access : Practical Innovations, Open Solutions*, *9*, 33313–33322. doi:10.1109/ACCESS.2021.3061487

Aström, J., Reim, W., & Parida, V. (2022). Value creation and value capture for AI business model innovation: A three–phase process framework. *Review of Managerial Science*, *16*(7), 2111–2133. doi:10.1007/s11846-022-00521-z

Azadifar, S., Rostami, M., Berahmand, K., Moradi, P., & Oussama, M. (2022). Graph-based relevancy-redundancy gene selection method for cancer diagnosis. *Computers in Biology and Medicine*, *147*(Aug), 105766. doi:10.1016/j.compbiomed.2022.105766 PMID:35779479

Bagozzi, R., & Yi, Y. (2012). Specification, evaluation and interpretation of structural equation models. *Journal of the Academy of Marketing Science*, *40*(1), 8–34. doi:10.1007/s11747-011-0278-x

Bakker, A. B., Demerouti, E., & Euwema, M. C. (2005). Job Resources Buffer the Impact of Job Demands on Burnout. *Journal of Occupational Health Psychology*, *10*(2), 170–180. doi:10.1037/1076-8998.10.2.170 PMID:15826226

Barrutia Barreto, I., Aguilar Ibarra, A. F., & Barrutia Barreto, A. M. (2024). Soft skills in administrators for the daptation of companies to the new post-pandemic normality. *Sociología y Tecnociencia*, *14*(1), 115–134. https://revistas.uva.es/index.php/sociotecno/article/view/6625

Bartunov, S., & Vetrov, D. P. (2018). Few-shot generative modelling with generative matching networks. AISTATS.

Başçı, E. (2017). Küreselleşen Dünyada Etnosentrizm: Üniversite Öğrencileri Üzerine Yapılan Bir Saha Araştırması. *International Journal of Academic Value Studies*, *3*(16), 286–293.

Beaulieu-Jones, B. K., Wu, Z. S., Williams, C., Lee, R., Bhavnani, S. P., Byrd, J. B., & Greene, C. S. (2019). Privacy-preserving generative deep neural networks support clinical data sharing. *Circulation: Cardiovascular Quality and Outcomes*, *12*(7), e005122. doi:10.1161/CIRCOUTCOMES.118.005122 PMID:31284738

Bell, B. S., Kanar, A. M., & Kozlowski, S. W. J. (2008). Current issues and future directions in simulation-based training in North America. *International Journal of Human Resource Management*, *19*(8), 1416–1434. doi:10.1080/09585190802200173

Betzel, R. F., Avena-Koenigsberger, A., & Goi, J. (2016). Generative models of the human connectome. *NeuroImage*, *124*, 10541064. doi:10.1016/j.neuroimage.2015.09.041 PMID:26427642

Betzel, R. F., & Bassett, D. S. (2017). Generative models for network neuroscience: Prospects and promise. *Journal of the Royal Society, Interface*, *14*(136), 20170623. doi:10.1098/rsif.2017.0623 PMID:29187640

Betzel, R. F., Byrge, L., Esfahlani, F. Z., & Kennedy, D. P. (2020). Temporal fluctuations in the brain's modular architecture during movie-watching. *NeuroImage*, *213*, 116687. doi:10.1016/j.neuroimage.2020.116687 PMID:32126299

Billett, S. R. (2001). *Learning in the workplace: Strategies for effective practice*. Allen and Unwin.

Bilyk, O. I. (2019). The influence of the digital economy on reducing the negative consequences of social risk. *Problems of Economics and Management, 4,* 8 – 16. Retrieved from:https://science.lpnu.ua/semi/all-volumes-and-issues/volume-7-number-42-2019/impact-digital-economy-reduction-negative

Biswas, N., & Chakrabarti, S. (2020). Artificial intelligence (AI)-based systems biology approaches in multi-omics data analysis of cancer. *Frontiers in Oncology*, *10*(Oct), 588221. Advance online publication. doi:10.3389/fonc.2020.588221 PMID:33154949

Bizumic, B. (2014). Who Contained the Concept of Ethnocentrism? A Brief Report. *Journal of Social and Political Psychology*, *2*(1), 3–10. doi:10.5964/jspp.v2i1.264

Bodrova D. V. (2019). Institutional aspects of the digital economy development in Ukraine. *Scholarly notes of V.I. Vernadsky Taurida National University. Series: Economics and Management, 5*(30), 163 – 169. doi:10.32838/2523-4803/69-5-57

Bollen, K. A. (1989). *Structural equations with latent variables*. Wiley. doi:10.1002/9781118619179

Borkar, P., Wankhede, V. A., Mane, D. T., Limkar, S., Ramesh, J. V. N., & Ajani, S. N. (2023). Deep learning and image processing-based early detection of Alzheimer disease in cognitively normal individuals. *Soft Computing*, 1–23. doi:10.1007/s00500-023-08615-w

Borowski, P. (2021). Digitization, digital twins, Blockchain, and Industry 4.0 as elements of management process in enterprises in the energy sector. *Energies*, *14*(7), 1885. doi:10.3390/en14071885

Borys Grinchenko Kyiv Metropolitan University, Faculty of Economics and Management, Management Basics Center. (2020). https://surl.li/qezyf

Borys Grinchenko Kyiv Metropolitan University, Faculty of Economics and Management, Management Basics Center. (2022). https://surl.li/pyazu

Boyas, J., & Wind, L. H. (2010). Employment-based social capital, job stress, and employee burnout: A public child welfare employee structural model. *Children and Youth Services Review*, *32*(3), 380–388. doi:10.1016/j.childyouth.2009.10.009

Brainsuite. (n.d.). https://brainsuite.org/tutorials/

Braun, U., Harneit, A., Pergola, G., Menara, T., Schäfer, A., Betzel, R. F., Zang, Z., Schweiger, J. I., Zhang, X., Schwarz, K., Chen, J., Blasi, G., Bertolino, A., Durstewitz, D., Pasqualetti, F., Schwarz, E., Meyer-Lindenberg, A., Bassett, D. S., & Tost, H. (2021). Brain network dynamics during working memory are modulated by dopamine and diminished in schizophrenia. *Nature Communications*, *12*(1), 3478. doi:10.1038/s41467-021-23694-9 PMID:34108456

Brooks, S. J., & Stamoulis, C. (2023, June). Generative Models For Large-Scale Simulations Of Connectome Development. In *2023 IEEE International Conference on Acoustics, Speech, and Signal Processing Workshops (ICASSPW)* (pp. 1-5). IEEE. 10.1109/ICASSPW59220.2023.10193544

Brown, T., Mann, B., Ryder, N., Subbiah, M., Kaplan, J. D., Dhariwal, P., & Amodei, D. (2020). Language models are few-shot learners. *Advances in Neural Information Processing Systems*, *33*, 1877–1901.

Cabinet of Ministers of Ukraine. (2018). On Approval of the Concept of Development of the Digital Economy and Society of Ukraine for 2018-2020 and Approval of the Plan of Measures for its Implementation. *Ordinance of the Cabinet of Ministers of Ukraine*, 67. Retrieved from: https://zakon.rada.gov.ua/laws/show/67$2018$%D1%80

Calderon-Monge, E., & Ribeiro-Soriano, D. (2023). *The role of digitalization in business and management: a systematic literature review. Review of Managerial Science*. doi:10.1007/s11846-023-00647-8

Canessa, E., Fonda, C., & Zennaro, M. (2013). *Low-cost 3D Printing for Science, Education & Sustainable Development*. http://sdu.ictp.it/3d/book/Low-cost_3D_printing_screen.pdf

Cardona, S., Velez, J., & Tobon, S. (2016). Contribution of socio-formative assessment to academic performance in an undergraduate program. *Educar*, *52*(2), 423–447. doi:10.5565/rev/educar.763

Carliner, S., & Shank, P. (2016). *The elearning handbook: past promises, present challenges*. John Wiley & Sons.

Char, D. S., Abràmoff, M. D., & Feudtner, C. (2020). Identifying ethical considerations for machine learning healthcare applications. *The American Journal of Bioethics*, *20*(11), 7–17. doi:10.1080/15265161.2020.1819469 PMID:33103967

Chen, R. J., Lu, M. Y., Chen, T. Y., Williamson, D. F., & Mahmood, F. (2021). Synthetic data in machine learning for medicine and healthcare. *Nature Biomedical Engineering*, *5*(6), 493–497. doi:10.1038/s41551-021-00751-8 PMID:34131324

Chen, X., Ke, P., Huang, Y., Zhou, J., Li, H., Peng, R., Huang, J., Liang, L., Ma, G., Li, X., Ning, Y., Wu, F., & Wu, K. (2023). Discriminative analysis of schizophrenia patients using graph convolutional networks: A combined multimodal MRI and connectomics analysis. *Frontiers in Neuroscience*, *17*, 1140801. doi:10.3389/fnins.2023.1140801 PMID:37090813

Chuenjitwongsa, S., Oliver, R. G., & Bullock, A. D. (2018). Competence, competency-based education, and undergraduate dental education: A discussion paper. *European Journal of Dental Education*, *22*(1), 1–8. doi:10.1111/eje.12213 PMID:27246501

Cirillo, V., Fanti, L., Mina, A., & Ricci, A. (2021). *Digital technologies and firm performance: Industry 4.0 in the Italian economy*. Retrieved from: https://oa.inapp.org/xmlui/handle/20.500.12916/862

Coffey, A. J., Kamhawi, R., Fishwick, P., & Julie Henderson, J. (2013). New Media Environments' Comparative Effects Upon Intercultural Sensitivity: A Five-Dimensional Analysis. *International Journal of Intercultural Relations*, *37*(5), 605–627. doi:10.1016/j.ijintrel.2013.06.006

Collins, E. G. C. (1986). A company without offices. *Harvard Business Review*, *86*(1), 127–136.

Conroy, J., Hulme, M., & Menter, I. (2013). Developing a 'clinical' model for teacher education. *Journal of Education for Teaching*, *39*(5), 557–573. doi:10.1080/02607476.2013.836339

CooleyS. M.HamiltonT.AragonesS. D.RayJ. C. J.DeedsE. J. (2022). A novel metric reveals previously unrecognized distortion in dimensionality reduction of scRNA-seq data. bioRxiv. doi:10.1101/689851

Costin, A., Roman, A. F., & Balica, R. S. (2023). Remote work burnout, professional job stress, and employee emotional exhaustion during the COVID-19 pandemic. *Frontiers in Psychology*, *14*, 1193854. Advance online publication. doi:10.3389/fpsyg.2023.1193854 PMID:37325768

COVID-19 wykreślony z systemu. Kiedy koniec pandemii? (n.d.). https://serwisy.gazetaprawna.pl/zdrowie/artykuly/8391606,pandemia-koronawirus-covid-19.html

Cross, T. B., & Raizman, M. (1986). Telecommuting: the future technology of work. Dow Jones-Irwin.

Dahmen, J., & Cook, D. (2019). SynSys: A synthetic data generation system for healthcare applications. *Sensors (Basel)*, *19*(5), 1181. doi:10.3390/s19051181 PMID:30857130

Dash, S. K., & Panda, C. K. (2015). An Evolutionary programming based neuro-fuzzy technique for multi-objective generation dispatch with non-smooth characteristic functions. *2nd International Conference on Electronics and Communication Systems, ICECS*, 1663–1674.

Dash, S., Yale, A., Guyon, I., & Bennett, K. P. (2020). Medical time-series data generation using generative adversarial networks. In *Artificial Intelligence in Medicine: 18th International Conference on Artificial Intelligence in Medicine, MN, USA, Proceedings 18* (pp. 382-391). 10.1007/978-3-030-59137-3_34

De Giri, P. K., S.S., & Dehuri, S. (2016). A Novel Locally and Globally Tuned Biogeography Based Optimization Algorithm. *International Conference on Soft Computing: Theories and Applications (SoCTA)*, 28-30.

De Giri, P. K., S.S., Dehuri, S., & Cho, S-B. (2017). Locally and Globally Tuned Chaotic Biogeography Based Optimization Algorithm. *International Conference on Information Technology (ICIT2017)*, 28-29.

de Vries, H., Tummers, L., & Bekkers, V. (2019). The Benefits of Teleworking in the Public Sector: Reality or Rhetoric? *Review of Public Personnel Administration*, *39*(4), 570–593. doi:10.1177/0734371X18760124

Deloitte. (2020). *Returning to work in the future of work Embracing purpose, potential, perspective, and possibility during COVID-19*. https://www2.deloitte.com/ua/en/pages/human-capital/articles/hc-trends-covid-19.html

Demerouti, E., Bakker, A. B., Nachreiner, F., & Schaufeli, W. B. (2001). The job demands-resources model of burnout. *The Journal of Applied Psychology*, *86*(3), 499–512. doi:10.1037/0021-9010.86.3.499 PMID:11419809

DESI - Digital Economy and Society Index. (2022). *Shaping Europe's digital future*. https://digital-strategy.ec.europa.eu/en/library/digital-economy-and-society-index-desi-2022

Digitaleconomy: trends, risks and social determinants. (2021). Retrieved from https://razumkov.org.ua/uploads/article/2020_digitalization.pdf

Diogo, M., Cabral, B., & Bernardino, J. (2019). Consistency Models of NoSQL Databases. *Future Internet*, *11*(2), 43. doi:10.3390/fi11020043

Dionisi, T., Sestito, L., Tarli, C., Antonelli, M., Tosoni, A., D'Addio, S., & … . (2021). Risk of burnout and stress in physicians working in a COVID team: A longitudinal survey. int. J. *Clinics and Practice*, *75*, e14755. doi:10.1111/ijcp.147 PMID:34449957

Dolzhenkov, O., Chernenko, N., Ruchkina, M., & Sakaliuk, O. (2020). Practice-oriented training as a means of professionalisation of future education managers. *Scientific bulletin of South Ukrainian National Pedagogical University named after K. D. Ushynsky*, *1*(130), 66–72. doi:10.24195/2617-6688-2020-1-9

Edelbring, S., Dahlgren, M. A., & Wiegleb Edström, D. (2018). Characteristics of two questionnaires used to assess interprofessional learning: Psychometrics and expert panel evaluations. *BMC Medical Education*, *40*(18), 40. doi:10.1186/s12909-018-1153-y PMID:29554898

Elmasri, R., & Navathe, S. (2016). *Fundamentals of database systems*. Pearson.

Epstein, R. M., & Hundert, E. M. (2002). Defining and assessing professional competence. *Journal of the American Medical Association*, *287*(2), 226–235. doi:10.1001/jama.287.2.226 PMID:11779266

Espadoto, M., Martins, R. M., Kerren, A., Hirata, N. S. T., & Telea, A. C. (2021). Toward a quantitative survey of dimension reduction techniques. *IEEE Transactions on Visualization and Computer Graphics*, *27*(4), 2153–2173. doi:10.1109/TVCG.2019.2944182 PMID:31567092

E-Ukraine. (2019). *Ukraine in international rankings*. Retrieved from:https://eukraine.org.ua/ua/news/ukrayina-v-mizhnarodnih-rejtingah

Eurofound. (2018). *Burnout in the workplace: A review of data and policy responses in the EU*. Publications Office of the European Union.

Faskowitz, J., Betzel, R. F., & Sporns, O. (2022). Edges in brain networks: Contributions to models of structure and function. *Network Neuroscience (Cambridge, Mass.)*, *6*(1), 1–28. PMID:35350585

Faskowitz, J., Yan, X., Zuo, X. N., & Sporns, O. (2018). Weighted stochastic block models of the human connectome across the life span. *Scientific Reports*, *8*(1), 12997. doi:10.1038/s41598-018-31202-1 PMID:30158553

Fawaz, H. I., Forestier, G., Weber, J., Idoumghar, L., & Muller, P. A. (2018). Data augmentation using synthetic data for time series classification with deep residual networks. *arXiv preprint arXiv:1808.02455.*

Fei-Fei, L., Fergus, R., & Perona, P. (2006). One-shot learning of object categories. *IEEE Transactions on Pattern Analysis and Machine Intelligence*, *28*(4), 594–611. doi:10.1109/TPAMI.2006.79 PMID:16566508

Ferrara, M., Ahmadian, A., Salashour, S., & Pansera, B. A. (2023). Introduction to the SI "Advances in Operations Research and Machine Learning focused on Pandemic Dynamics". *Operations Research Perspectives, 100287.*

Foraker, R. E., Yu, S. C., Gupta, A., Michelson, A. P., Pineda Soto, J. A., Colvin, R., Loh, F., Kollef, M. H., Maddox, T., Evanoff, B., Dror, H., Zamstein, N., Lai, A. M., & Payne, P. R. (2020). Spot the difference: Comparing results of analyses from real patient data and synthetic derivatives. *JAMIA Open*, *3*(4), 557–566. doi:10.1093/jamiaopen/ooaa060 PMID:33623891

Fornell, C., & Larcker, D. F. (1981). Evaluating structural equation models with unobservable variables and measurement error. *JMR, Journal of Marketing Research*, *18*(1), 39–50. doi:10.1177/002224378101800104

Forsyth, D. (2004). *Computer vision. Modern Approach*. Pons, Williams William.

Fouladi, S., Safaei, A. A., Arshad, N. I., Ebadi, M. J., & Ahmadian, A. (2022). The use of artificial neural networks to diagnose Alzheimer's disease from brain images. *Multimedia Tools and Applications*, *81*(26), 37681–37721. doi:10.1007/s11042-022-13506-7

Freudenberger, H. J. (1974). Staff burn-out. *The Journal of Social Issues*, *30*(1), 159–165. doi:10.1111/j.1540-4560.1974.tb00706.x

GarmsF.JansenC.SchmitzC.HallerstedeS.TschiesnerA. (2019). Retrieved from https://www.mckinsey.com/industries/advanced-electronics/our-insights/capturing-value-at-scale-in-discrete-manufacturing-with-industry-4-0

George Karimpanal, T., & Bouffanais, R. (2019). Self-organizing maps for storage and transfer of knowledge in reinforcement learning. *Adaptive Behavior*, *27*(2), 111–126. doi:10.1177/1059712318818568

George, P., & Veetil, S. N. (2023). Ravnotežaposlovnoggživota i transformacionoliderstvokaoprediktorizadovoljstvaposlomzaposlenih. *Serbian Journal of Management*, *18*(2), 253–273. doi:10.5937/sjm18-34305

Giri, P. K., De, S. S., & Dehuri, S. (2018). Adaptive neighbourhood for locally and globally tuned biogeography-based optimization algorithm. *Journal of King Saud University. Computer and Information Sciences*, *33*(4), 453–467. doi:10.1016/j.jksuci.2018.03.013

Giri, P. K., De, S. S., Dehuri, S., & Cho, S. B. (2020). Biogeography Based Optimization for Mining Rules to Assess Credit Risk, Journal: Intelligent Systems in Accounting. *Financial Management*, *28*(1), 35–51.

Giri, P. K., De, S. S., Dehuri, S., & Cho, S.-B. (2020). Biogeography Based Optimization for Mining Rules to Assess Credit Risk. *Intelligent Systems in Accounting. Financial Management*, *28*(1), 35–51.

Giuffrè, M., & Shung, D. L. (2023). Harnessing the power of synthetic data in healthcare: Innovation, application, and privacy. *NPJ Digital Medicine*, *6*(1), 186. doi:10.1038/s41746-023-00927-3 PMID:37813960

Gkamas, T., Karaiskos, V., & Kontogiannis, S. (2022). Evaluation of cloud databases as a service for Industrial IoT data. *Proceedings of the 7th International Congress on Information and Communication Technology (ICICT).*

Global innovation index. (2021). Retrieved from https://www.globalinnovationindex.org/about-gii

GlobalSpec. (2015). Retrieved from https://insights.globalspec.com/article/621/collaborative-robots-play-nice-on-the-plant-floor

Glowacki, J., Kriukova, Y., & Avshenyuk, N. (2018). Gamification in higher education: Experience of Poland and Ukraine. *Advanced Education*, *5*(10), 105–110. doi:10.20535/2410-8286.151143

Goertzel, B. (2014). Artificial general intelligence: Concept, state of the art, and future prospects. *Journal of Artificial General Intelligence*, *5*(1), 1–48. doi:10.2478/jagi-2014-0001

Gomes, S., Lopes João, M., & Ferreira, L. (2022). The impact of the digital economy on economic growth: The case of OECD countries. *RAM. Revista de Administração Mackenzie*, *23*(6), 1–31. doi:10.1590/1678-6971/eramd220029.en

Goncalves, A., Ray, P., Soper, B., Stevens, J., Coyle, L., & Sales, A. P. (2020). Generation and evaluation of synthetic patient data. *BMC Medical Research Methodology*, *20*(1), 1–40. doi:10.1186/s12874-020-00977-1 PMID:32381039

Goodfellow, I., Pouget-Abadie, J., Mirza, M., Xu, B., Warde-Farley, D., Ozair, S., & Bengio, Y. (2014). Generative adversarial nets. *Advances in Neural Information Processing Systems*, 27.

Greenberg, J., Putman, H., & Walsh, K. (2014). *Training our future teachers: Classroom management*. National Council on Teacher Quality. https://files.eric.ed.gov/fulltext/ED556312.pdf

Grigorescu, S., Trasnea, B., Cocias, T., & Macesanu, G. (2020). A survey of deep learning techniques for autonomous driving. *Journal of Field Robotics*, *37*(3), 362–386. doi:10.1002/rob.21918

Guo-Ming, C., & William Starosta, J., J.W. (2000). The Development and Validation of the Intercultural Sensitivity Scale. *Annual Meeting of the National Communication Association*, 86.

Hamilton, C. (1987). Telecommuting. *The Personnel Journal*, *66*(4), 90–101.

Hao, S., Han, W., Jiang, T., Li, Y., Wu, H., Zhong, C., . . . Tang, H. (2024). Synthetic Data in AI: Challenges, Applications, and Ethical Implications. *arXiv preprint arXiv:2401.01629.*

Henderikx, M., & Stoffers, J. (2022). An Exploratory Literature Study into Digital Transformation and Leadership: Toward Future-Proof Middle Managers. *Sustainability (Basel)*, *14*(2), 687. doi:10.3390/su14020687

Henderikx, M., & Stoffers, J. (2023). Digital transformation and middle managers' leadership skills and behavior: A group concept mapping approach. *Frontiers in Psychology*, *14*, 1147002. Advance online publication. doi:10.3389/fpsyg.2023.1147002 PMID:37731886

Hermann, M., Pentek, T., & Otto, B. (2016). Design principles for industrie 4.0 scenarios. *2016 49th Hawaii International Conference on System Sciences (HICSS)*. 10.1109/HICSS.2016.488

Hernandez, M., Epelde, G., Alberdi, A., Cilla, R., & Rankin, D. (2022). Synthetic data generation for tabular health records: A systematic review. *Neurocomputing*, *493*, 28–45. doi:10.1016/j.neucom.2022.04.053

Hertz, E. V. (1973). Dynamic calculation of discrete pneumatic actuators. *Mechanical Engineering*, 17–33.

Higgs, J., Barnett, R., Billett, S., Hutchings, M., & Trede, F. (2012). *Practice-Based Education. Perspectives and Strategies*. SensePublishers. doi:10.1007/978-94-6209-128-3

Hoag, J. E. (2008). *Synthetic data generation: Theory, techniques and applications*. University of Arkansas.

Holoborodko, A. Yu. (2022). The digital economy: Approaches to and features of development. *Bìznes Ìnform*, *9*(536), 10–18. doi:10.32983/2222-4459-2022-9-10-18

Horbenko, H. (2015). Practice-oriented learning of bachelors of advertising and public relations. *Continuing Professional Education: Theory and Practice,* (4), 64-69. http://npo.kubg.edu.ua/article/view/183566

Hota, P. K., Barisal, A. K., & Dash, S. K. (2009) An artificial neural network method for optimal generation dispatch with multiple fuel options. Journal of the Institution of Engineers (India): Electrical Engineering Division, 90, 3–10.

Hsieh, C.-W. (2014). Burnout Among Public Service Workers: The Role of Emotional Labor Requirements and Job Resources. *Review of Public Personnel Administration, 34*(4), 379–402. doi:10.1177/0734371X12460554

Huawei. (2020). *Global Connectivity Index. Shaping the New Normal with Intelligent Connectivity.* Retrieved from: Https://Www.Huawei.Com/Minisite/Gci/En/

Huawei. (2021). *Huawei released the seventh annual Global Connectivity Index report: five major stages of the industry's digital transformation.* Retrieved from: https://www.huawei.com/ua/news/ua/2021/20210203

Hui, S., Hai, F., Yuemeng, G., Weichen, J., Zhi, L., & Junwei, W. (2022). Moderating Effects of Transformational Leadership, Affective Commitment, Job Performance, and Job Insecurity. *Frontiers in Psychology, 13,* 847147. Advance online publication. doi:10.3389/fpsyg.2022.847147 PMID:35615161

Hussain, A., & Khan, M. N. (2014). Discovering Database Replication Techniques in RDBMS. *International Journal of Database Theory and Application., 7*(1), 93–102. doi:10.14257/ijdta.2014.7.1.09

Hutter, M. (2004). *Universal artificial intelligence: Sequential decisions based on algorithmic probability.* Springer Science & Business Media.

IDC. (2020). Retrieved from:https://www.idc.com/

Ilich, L., Akilina, O., & Panchenko, A. (2020). Peculiarities of Implementation of Peace Education in Ukraine. *Education Excellence and Innovation Management: a 2025 Vision to Sustain Economic Development During Global Challenges*, 2198-2206.

Ilich, L. (2017). *Drivers of global labor market development. In International Relations 2017: Current issues of world economy and politics: Proceedings of 17th International Scientific Conference (December 1–2, 2017).* EKONÓM. https://surl.li/cktqv

ILO. (2020). *An employers' guide on working from home in response to the outbreak of COVID-19.* International Labour Office. https://cutt.ly/8T283oq

IMD Business School for Management and Leadership Courses. (2022). *World Competitiveness Ranking.* Retrieved from:https://www.imd.org/centers/wcc/world-competitiveness-center/rankings/world-competitiveness-ranking/

Isik, Z., & Ercan, M. E. (2017, October). Integration of RNA-Seq and RPPA data for survival time prediction in cancer patients. *Computers in Biology and Medicine*, *89*, 397–404. doi:10.1016/j.compbiomed.2017.08.028 PMID:28869900

Islam, J., & Zhang, Y. (2018). Brain MRI analysis for Alzheimer's disease diagnosis using an ensemble system of deep convolutional neural networks. *Brain Informatics*, *5*(2), 2. doi:10.1186/s40708-018-0080-3 PMID:29881892

ITU. (2022). *ICT Development Index. Measuring digital development: Facts and Figures.* Retrieved from: https://www.itu.int/en/ITU-D/Statistics/Pages/facts/default.aspx

James, S., Harbron, C., Branson, J., & Sundler, M. (2021). Synthetic data use: Exploring use cases to optimise data utility. *Discover Artificial Intelligence*, *1*(1), 15. doi:10.1007/s44163-021-00016-y

Junwei, H., Dingwen, Z., Gong, C., Nian, L., & Dong, X. (2018). Advanced Deep-Learning Techniques for Salient and Category-Specific Object Detection: A Survey. *IEEE Signal Processing Magazine*, *35*(1), 84–100. doi:10.1109/MSP.2017.2749125

KagermannH.LukasW.-D.WahlsterW. (2018). Retrieved from https://www.ingenieur.de/technik/fachbereiche/produktion/industrie-40-mit-internet-dinge-weg-4-industriellen-revolution/

Kalyaev, I. A., Lochin, V. M., & Makarov, I. M. (2007). Intelligent Robots. Machine Building.

Kaplan, J., McCandlish, S., Henighan, T., Brown, T. B., Chess, B., Child, R., & Amodei, D. (2020). Scaling laws for neural language models. *arXiv preprint arXiv:2001.08361.*

Karimi, M. R., Karimi, A. H., Abolmaali, S., Sadeghi, M., & Schmitz, U. (2020, June). Prospects and challenges of cancer systems medicine: From genes to disease networks. *Briefings Bioinf.*, *23*(1).

Kawachi, J. (2017). Brodmann areas 17, 18, and 19 in the human brain: An overview. *Brain and nerve= Shinkeikenkyu no shinpo, 69*(4), 397-410.

Kaya, Y., Arslan, S., Erbaş, A., Yaşar, B. N., & Küçükkelepçe, G. E. (2021). The Effect of Ethnocentrism and oral Sensitivity on Intercultural Sensitivity in Nursing Students, Descriptive Cross-Sectional Research Study. *Nurse Education Today*, *2021*(100), 1–7. doi:10.1016/j.nedt.2021.104867 PMID:33740704

Kelly, M. M. (1985). The next workplace revolution: Telecommuting. *Supervisory Management*, *30*(10), 3–7.

Khairandish, M. O., Sharma, M., Jain, V., Chatterjee, J. M., & Jhanjhi, N. Z. (2022). A hybrid CNN-SVM threshold segmentation approach for tumor detection and classification of MRI brain images. *Ingénierie et Recherche Biomédicale : IRBM = Biomedical Engineering and Research*, *43*(4), 290–299. doi:10.1016/j.irbm.2021.06.003

Khalid, N., Qayyum, A., Bilal, M., Al-Fuqaha, A., & Qadir, J. (2023). Privacy-preserving artificial intelligence in healthcare: Techniques and applications. *Computers in Biology and Medicine*, *158*, 106848. doi:10.1016/j.compbiomed.2023.106848 PMID:37044052

Khan, R. M. I., Radzuan, N. R. M., Alkhunaizan, A. S., Ghulam, M., & Khan, I. (2019). *The Efficacy of MALL Instruction in Business English Learning*. doi:10.3991/ijim.v13i08.9562

Khaustov, M. M., & Bondarenko, D. V. (2020a). *Digital technologies of the future in the development of society*. The International Scientific and Practical Conference "Competitiveness and Innovation: Problems of Science and Practice". Kharkiv, Ukraine

Khaustov, M. M., & Bondarenko, D. V. (2020b). *Digitalisation: the achievements and threats to society*. The IX International Scientific and Practical Conference "Science and Practice: Implementation to Modern Society", Manchester, UK. Retrieved from: https://ojs.ukrlogos.in.ua/index.php/interconf/article/view/11577

Khaustov, M. M., & Bondarenko, D. V. (2021). *Assessments of digitalisation and the impact of information and communication technologies on the economic development of countries*. The International Scientific and Practical Conference "Competitiveness and Innovation: Problems of Science and Practice", Kharkiv, Ukraine.

Khaustova, V. Ye., Reshetniak, O. I., & Khaustov, M. M. (2022a). Prospective directions of the development of the IT sphere in the world. *Problèmes Économiques*, *1*, 3–19. doi:10.32983/2222-0712-2022-1-3-19

Khaustova, V. Ye., Reshetniak, O. I., Khaustov, M. M., & Zinchenko, V. A. (2022b). Directions of the development of artificial intelligence technologies in ensuring a country's defense capability. *Bìznes Ìnform*, *3*(530), 17–26. doi:10.32983/2222-4459-2022-3-17-26

Kimberly, W. T., Sorby-Adams, A. J., Webb, A. G., Wu, E. X., Beekman, R., Bowry, R., Schiff, S. J., de Havenon, A., Shen, F. X., Sze, G., Schaefer, P., Iglesias, J. E., Rosen, M. S., & Sheth, K. N. (2023). Brain imaging with portable low-field MRI. *Nature Reviews Bioengineering*, *1*(9), 617–630. doi:10.1038/s44222-023-00086-w PMID:37705717

Kim, T. R., Jeong, H.-H., & Sohn, K.-A. (2019, July). Topological integration of RPPA proteomic data with multi-omics data for survival prediction in breast cancer via pathway activity inference. *BMC Medical Genomics*, *12*(S5, no. S5), 1–14. doi:10.1186/s12920-019-0511-x PMID:31296204

Kindzerskyi, Yu. V. (2022). Genesis and features of the digital economy in the context of prospects for its formation in Ukraine. *Economie & Statistique*, *8*, 10–14.

Kline, R. B. (2011). *Principles and practice of structural equation modeling* (3rd ed.). Guilford Press.

Knoema. (2021). *Digital Evolution Index (DEI)*.Retrieved from: https://knoema.com/DEI2020/digital-evolution-index-dei

Knotts, U. S. Jr, & Keys, J. B. (1997). Teaching strategic management with a business game. *Simulation & Gaming*, *28*(4), 377–395. doi:10.1177/1046878197284004

Kovtoniuk, K. V. (2017). Digitalisation of the world economy as a factor in economic growth. *Scientific Bulletin of Kherson State Universi*, *27*(1), 29–33.

Kraus, N. M., Holoborodko, O. P., & Kraus, K. M. (2018). The digital economy: Trends and prospects of avant-garde development. *Efficient Economy, 1*. Retrieved from:http://www.economy.nayka.com.ua/?op=1&z=6047

Krishnapatria, K. (2020, June). From 'lockdown' to letdown: Students' perception of e-learning amid the covid-19 outbreak. *ELT in Focus*, *3*(1), 1–8. Advance online publication. doi:10.35706/eltinfc.v3i1.3694

Lake, B. M., Salakhutdinov, R., & Tenenbaum, J. B. (2015). Human-level concept learning through probabilistic program induction. *Science*, *350*(6266), 1332–1338. doi:10.1126/science.aab3050 PMID:26659050

Lean, J., Moizer, J., Towler, M., & Abbey, C. (2006). Simulations and Games: Use and Barriers in Higher Education. *Active Learning in Higher Education*, *7*(3), 227–242. doi:10.1177/1469787406069056

Ledig, C., Theis, L., Huszár, F., Caballero, J., Cunningham, A., Acosta, A., Aitken, A., Tejani, A., Totz, J., & Wang, Z. (2017). Photo-realistic single image super-resolution using a generative adversarial network. *Proceedings of the IEEE conference on computer vision and pattern recognition*, 4681–4690. 10.1109/CVPR.2017.19

Legner, C., Eymann, T., Hess, T., Matt, C., Böhmann, T., Drews, P., Mädche, A., Urbach, N., & Ahlemann, F. (2017). Digitalization: Opportunity and challenge for the business and information systems engineering community. *Business & Information Systems Engineering*, *59*(4), 301–308. doi:10.1007/s12599-017-0484-2

Lei, D., Qin, K., Pinaya, W. H., Young, J., Van Amelsvoort, T., Marcelis, M., Donohoe, G., Mothersill, D. O., Corvin, A., Vieira, S., Lui, S., Scarpazza, C., Arango, C., Bullmore, E., Gong, Q., McGuire, P., & Mechelli, A. (2022). Graph convolutional networks reveal network-level functional dysconnectivity in schizophrenia. *Schizophrenia Bulletin*, *48*(4), 881–892. doi:10.1093/schbul/sbac047 PMID:35569019

Lemos, V. A. F., & Brunstein, J. (2023). Fostering soft skills leadership through a critical reflection approach. *Industrial and Commercial Training*, *55*(1), 143–156. doi:10.1108/ICT-01-2022-0001

Libbrecht, M. W., & Noble, W. S. (2015). Machine learning applications in genetics and genomics. *Nature Reviews. Genetics*, *16*(6), 321–332. doi:10.1038/nrg3920 PMID:25948244

Li, K., Kim, D. J., Lang, K. R., Kauffman, R. J., & Naldi, M. (2020). How should we understand the digital economy in Asia? Critical assessment and research agenda. *Electronic Commerce Research and Applications*, *44*, 101004. doi:10.1016/j.elerap.2020.101004 PMID:32922241

Li, M. M., Huang, K., & Zitnik, M. (2022). Graph representation learning in biomedicine and healthcare. *Nature Biomedical Engineering*, *6*(12), 1353–1369. doi:10.1038/s41551-022-00942-x PMID:36316368

Liu, S., Maljovec, D., Wang, B., Bremer, P.-T., & Pascucci, V. (2015). Visualizing high-dimensional data: Advances in the past decade. *IEEE Transactions on Visualization and Computer Graphics*, *23*(3), 1249–1268. doi:10.1109/TVCG.2016.2640960 PMID:28113321

Li, Y., Chai, Y., Yin, H., & Chen, B. (2021). A novel feature learning framework for high-dimensional data classification. *International Journal of Machine Learning and Cybernetics*, *12*(2), 555–569. doi:10.1007/s13042-020-01188-2

Lohr, K. N., & Donaldson, M. S. (Eds.). (1994). *Committee on Regional Health Data, Health data in the information age: use, disclosure, and privacy*. National Academies Press.

Lu, Y., Wang, H., & Wei, W. (2023). Machine Learning for Synthetic Data Generation: a Review. *arXiv preprint arXiv:2302.04062.*

Lubbadeh, T. (2020). Job Burnout: A General Literature Review. *International Review of Management and Marketing*, *10*(3), 7–15. doi:10.32479/irmm.9398

Makris, A., Tserpes, K., Spiliopoulos, G., & Anagnostopoulos, D. (2019). Performance Evaluation of MongoDB and PostgreSQL for spatio-temporal data. *Proceedings of the EDBT/ICDT Workshops.*

Mallick, C. K., Giri, P. K., & Mishra, S. N. (2023). A multi-objective LGBBO algorithm for overlapping community detection in a social network analysis. *Malaysian Journal of Computer Science*, *36*(2), 173–192. doi:10.22452/mjcs.vol36no2.4

Mallick, C. K., Giri, P. K., Paikaray, B. K., & Mishra, S. N. (2022). Machine Learning Approaches to Sentiment Analysis in Social Networks. *International Journal of Work Innovation*, *3*(4), 317–337. doi:10.1504/IJWI.2023.128860

Mallick, C. K., Mishra, S. N., Giri, P. K., & Paikaray, B. K. (2023). (in press). A Meta Heuristic Optimization based Deep Learning Model for Fake News Detection in Online Social Networks, Int. *J. of Electronic Security and Digital Forensics.*

Mann, M., Kumar, C., Zeng, W.-F., & Strauss, M. T. (2021, August). Artificial intelligence for proteomics and biomarker discovery. *Cell Systems*, *12*(8), 759–770. doi:10.1016/j.cels.2021.06.006 PMID:34411543

Mantec. (2022). Retrieved from https://mantec.org/robotics-manufacturing/

Marciniak, R. (2021). *E-learning – projektowanie, realizowanie i ocena*. Wolters Kluwer Polska.

Maslach, C. (1982). Understanding Burnout: Definitional Issues in Analyzing a Complex Phenomenon. In W. S. Paine (Ed.), Job Stress and Burnout (pp. 29–40). Academic Press.

Maslach, C. (1976). Burn-Out. *Human Behavior*, *5*, 16–22.

Maslach, C., Jackson, S. E., & Leiter, M. P. (1997). Maslach Burnout Inventory. In *Evaluating Stress: A Book of Resources* (3rd ed.). Scarecrow Education.

Maslach, C., Schaufeli, W. B., & Leiter, M. P. (2001). Job burnout. *Annual Review of Psychology*, *52*(1), 397–422. doi:10.1146/annurev.psych.52.1.397 PMID:11148311

Masoudi-Sobhanzadeh, Y., Motieghader, H., Omidi, Y., & Masoudi-Nejad, A. (2021, February). A machine learning method based on the genetic and world competitive contests algorithms for selecting genes or features in biological applications. *Scientific Reports*, *11*(1), 1–19. doi:10.1038/s41598-021-82796-y PMID:33558580

Matveichuk, L. O. (2018). The digital economy: Theoretical aspects. *Bulletin of Zaporizhzhia National University*, *4*(40), 116–127. doi:10.26661/2414-0287-2018-4-40-18

McLachlan, S., Dube, K., & Gallagher, T. (2016). Using the caremap with health incidents statistics for generating the realistic synthetic electronic healthcare record. In IEEE international conference on healthcare informatics (ICHI) (pp. 439-448). doi:10.1109/ICHI.2016.83

Meir, Y., Sardi, S., Hodassman, S., Kisos, K., Ben-Noam, I., Goldental, A., & Kanter, I. (2020). Power-law scaling to assist with key challenges in artificial intelligence. *Scientific Reports*, *10*(1), 19628. doi:10.1038/s41598-020-76764-1 PMID:33184422

Misiak, B., Samochowiec, J., Kowalski, K., Gaebel, W., Bassetti, C. L., Chan, A., Gorwood, P., Papiol, S., Dom, G., Volpe, U., Szulc, A., Kurimay, T., Kärkkäinen, H., Decraene, A., Wisse, J., Fiorillo, A., & Falkai, P. (2023). The future of diagnosis in clinical neurosciences: Comparing multiple sclerosis and schizophrenia. *European Psychiatry*, *66*(1), e58. doi:10.1192/j.eurpsy.2023.2432 PMID:37476977

Moon, K. R., van Dijk, D., Wang, Z., Gigante, S., Burkhardt, D. B., Chen, W. S., Yim, K., Elzen, A., Hirn, M. J., Coifman, R. R., Ivanova, N. B., Wolf, G., & Krishnaswamy, S. (2019). Visualizing structure and transitions in high-dimensional biological data. *Nature Biotechnology*, *37*(12), 1482–1492. doi:10.1038/s41587-019-0336-3 PMID:31796933

Morgan, A. (1983). Theoretical Aspects of Project-Based Learning in Higher Education. *British Journal of Educational Technology*, *14*(1), 66–78. doi:10.1111/j.1467-8535.1983.tb00450.x

Muhammad, A., Ghalib, M. F. M. D., Ahmad, F., Naveed, Q. N., & Shah, A. (2016). A study to investigate state of ethical development in e-learning. *International Journal of Advanced Computer Science and Applications*, *2016*(7), 284–290. doi:10.14569/IJACSA.2016.070436

Murphy, A. C., Bertolero, M. A., Papadopoulos, L., Lydon-Staley, D. M., & Bassett, D. S. (2020). Multimodal network dynamics underpinning working memory. *Nature Communications*, *11*(1), 3035. doi:10.1038/s41467-020-15541-0 PMID:32541774

Murtaza, H., Ahmed, M., Khan, N. F., Murtaza, G., Zafar, S., & Bano, A. (2023). Synthetic data generation: State of the art in health care domain. *Computer Science Review*, *48*, 100546. doi:10.1016/j.cosrev.2023.100546

Mutula Stephen, M. (2010). *Digital Economy Components*. University of Botswana. Retrieved from:https://www.igi-global.com/book/digital-economies-smes-readiness/268

Naveed, Q. N., Muhammad, A., Sanober, S., Qureshi, M. R. N., & Shah, A. (2017). A mixed method study for investigating critical success factors (CSFs) of e-learning in Saudi Arabian universities. Academic Press.

Negroponte, N. (1995). *Being Digital.* Knopf.

Network Readiness Index. (2022). *Network Readiness Index – Benchmarking the Future of the Network Economy.* Retrieved from:https://networkreadinessindex.org/

Nikolić, D., Andrić, D., & Nikolić, V. (2023). Guided Transfer Learning. *arXiv preprint arXiv:2303.16154.*

Nikolić, D. (2015). Practopoiesis: Or how life fosters a mind. *Journal of Theoretical Biology, 373*, 40–61. doi:10.1016/j.jtbi.2015.03.003 PMID:25791287

Nikolić, D. (2023). Where is the mind within the brain? Transient selection of subnetworks by metabotropic receptors and G protein-gated ion channels. *Computational Biology and Chemistry, 103*, 107820. doi:10.1016/j.compbiolchem.2023.107820 PMID:36724606

Nonato, L. G., & Aupetit, M. (2019). Multidimensional projection for visual analytics: Linking techniques with distortions, tasks, and layout enrichment. *IEEE Transactions on Visualization and Computer Graphics, 25*(1), 2650–2673. doi:10.1109/TVCG.2018.2846735 PMID:29994258

Nwagwu, L., & Azil, N. (2016). Status of technologies in business education departments of tertiary institutions in Ebonyi State for effective integration of electronic learning. *Brock Journal of Education, 4*(4), 49–59.

Oam, B. (2017). Work Based Learning: A learning strategy in support of the Australian Qualifications Framework. *Journal of Work-Applied Management, 9*(1), 70–82. doi:10.1108/JWAM-04-2017-0008

Oberzaucher, B. (2019). Digitalization as a Megatrend. *Spectrum Now, 39.* Retrieved from:https://www.andritz.com/spectrum-en/latest-issues/issue-39/digitalization-as-a-megatrend

Oduma, Ch. A., & Nkem, O. L. (2019, October). E-learning platforms in business education for skill acquisition. *Nigerian Journal of Business Education, 6*(2), 106.

OECD. (2017). *Key Issues for Digital Transformation in the G20.* Report Prepared for a Joint G20 German Presidency. Retrieved from: https://www.oecd.org/g20/key-issues-for-digital-transformation-in-the-g20.pdf

OECD. (2022). Retrieved from: https://www.oecd.org/sti/ieconomy/

Oh, K. H., Oh, I. S., Tsogt, U., Shen, J., Kim, W. S., Liu, C., ... Chung, Y. C. (2022). Diagnosis of schizophrenia with functional connectome data: A graph-based convolutional neural network approach. *BMC Neuroscience, 23*(1), 1–11. PMID:34979913

Osuala, R., Kushibar, K., Garrucho, L., Linardos, A., Szafranowska, Z., Klein, S., & Lekadir, K. (2021). A review of generative adversarial networks in cancer imaging: New applications, new solutions. *arXiv preprint arXiv:2107.09543*

Pandey, T. N., Giri, P. K., & Jagadev, A. (2019). Classification of Credit Dataset Using Improved Particle Swarm Optimization Tuned Radial Basis Function Neural Networks. *Conference on (BITMDM),* 1–11.

Pandey, T. N., Mahakud, R. R., Patra, B., & Giri, P. K. (2021) Performance of Machine Learning Techniques, before and after COVID-19 on Indian Foreign Exchange Rate. *International Conference on Biologically Inspired Techniques in Many-Criteria Decision Making (BITMDM-2021),* 20-21.

Pan, S. J., & Yang, Q. (2009). A survey on transfer learning. *IEEE Transactions on Knowledge and Data Engineering, 22*(10), 1345–1359. doi:10.1109/TKDE.2009.191

Papanastasiou, G., Dikaios, N., Huang, J., Wang, C., & Yang, G. (2023). *Is attention all you need in medical image analysis? A review.* arXiv preprint arXiv:2307.12775.

Parkes, L., Moore, T. M., Calkins, M. E., Cook, P. A., Cieslak, M., Roalf, D. R., Wolf, D. H., Gur, R. C., Gur, R. E., Satterthwaite, T. D., & Bassett, D. S. (2021). Transdiagnostic dimensions of psychopathology explain individuals' unique deviations from normative neurodevelopment in brain structure. *Translational Psychiatry, 11*(1), 232. doi:10.1038/s41398-021-01342-6 PMID:33879764

Petrovicova, J. T., & Gibalova, M. (2014). Measurement of Consumer Ethnocentrism of Slovak Consumers. *International Review of Management and Marketing, 4*(4), 247-258.

Philpott, D. (Ed.). (2017). *A guide to federal terms and acronyms.* Bernan Press.

Pieniążek M., 2016). Minimalizowanie stresu w miejscu pracy wyznacznikiem bezpieczeństwa. *Nauka – Praktyka – Refleksje, 22,* 339.

Pierwszy przypadek koronawirusa w Polsce. (n.d.). https://www.gov.pl/web/zdrowie/pierwszy-przypadek-koronawirusa-w-polsce

Pietrzyk, S. (2021). Bariery w szkoleniach biznesowych online – raport z badan. *Media i społeczeństwo*, 103.

Plugge, E., Membrey, P., & Hawkins, T. (2010). *The Definitive Guide to MongoDB: The NoSQL Database for Cloud and Desktop Computing* (1st ed.). Apress. doi:10.1007/978-1-4302-3052-6

Pomponio, R., Erus, G., Habes, M., Doshi, J., Srinivasan, D., Mamourian, E., Bashyam, V., Nasrallah, I. M., Satterthwaite, T. D., Fan, Y., Launer, L. J., Masters, C. L., Maruff, P., Zhuo, C., Völzke, H., Johnson, S. C., Fripp, J., Koutsouleris, N., Wolf, D. H., ... Davatzikos, C. (2020). Harmonization of large MRI datasets for the analysis of brain imaging patterns throughout the lifespan. *NeuroImage, 208,* 116450. doi:10.1016/j.neuroimage.2019.116450 PMID:31821869

Porter, A., Fei, S., Damme, K. S., Nusslock, R., Gratton, C., & Mittal, V. A. (2023). A meta-analysis and systematic review of single vs. multimodal neuroimaging techniques in the classification of psychosis. *Molecular Psychiatry, 28*(8), 1–15. doi:10.1038/s41380-023-02195-9 PMID:37563277

Preacher, K. J., & Hayes, A. F. (2008). Asymptotic and resampling strategies for assessing and comparing indirect effects in multiple mediator models. *Behavior Research Methods, 40*(3), 879–891. doi:10.3758/BRM.40.3.879 PMID:18697684

Prescott, P., Gjerde, K. P., & Rice, J. L. (2021). Analyzing mandatory college internships: Academic effects and implications for curricular design. *Studies in Higher Education*, *46*(11), 2444–2459. doi:10.1080/03075079.2020.1723531

Puga Villarreal, J., & Martínez Cerna, L. (2008). Management's competences in global scenarios. *Competenciasdirectivasenescenariosglobalesestudiosgerenciales*, *24*(109), 87–103. doi:10.1016/S0123-5923(08)70054-8

Putsenteilo, P.R., & Humeniuk, O.O. (2018) The digital economy as the newest vector of the traditional economy reconstruction. *Innovative Economy, 5-6*, 131 – 143.

Qashou, A. (2021). *Education and information technologies*. Springer.

Rajotte, J. F., Bergen, R., Buckeridge, D. L., El Emam, K., Ng, R., & Strome, E. (2022). Synthetic data as an enabler for machine learning applications in medicine. *iScience*, *25*(11), 105331. doi:10.1016/j.isci.2022.105331 PMID:36325058

Ramesh, U. R., Yogeswari, G., & Tamil, N. (2015). Database Synchronization for Mobile Devices by Using ASWAMD. *National Conference on Computing and Communication-International Journal of Innovative Research in Computer and Communication Engineering*, 3(1).

Ramzan, S., Bajwa, I. S., Kazmi, R., & Amna. (2019). Challenges in NoSQL-Based Distributed Data Storage: A Systematic Literature Review. *Electronics (Basel)*, *8*(5), 488. doi:10.3390/electronics8050488

Raykov, T., & Marcoulides, G. A. (2006). On Multilevel Reliability Estimation From the Perspective of Structural Equation Modeling. *Structural Equation Modeling*, *13*(1), 130–141. doi:10.1207/s15328007sem1301_7

Raza, S. A., & Qamar, S. (2023). Transformational leadership and employee's career satisfaction: Role of psychological empowerment, organisational commitment, and emotional exhaustion. *Asian Academy of Management Journal*, *28*(2), 207–238. doi:10.21315/aamj2023.28.2.8

Razumkov Center. (2020). *The digital economy: trends, risks and social determinants*. "Zapovit" Publishing House. Retrieved from:https://razumkov.org.ua/uploads/article/2020_digitalization.pdf

Razzaque, A. (2020). *M-Learning Improves Knowledge Sharing Over e-Learning Platforms to Build Higher Education Students' Social Capital*. doi:10.1177/2158244020926575

Rodriguez-Almeida, A. J., Fabelo, H., Ortega, S., Deniz, A., Balea-Fernandez, F. J., Quevedo, E., & Callico, G. M. (2022). Synthetic patient data generation and evaluation in disease prediction using small and imbalanced datasets. *IEEE Journal of Biomedical and Health Informatics*. PMID:35930509

Rossman, G. (n.d.). *New Benchmarks Show Postgres Dominating MongoDB in Varied Workloads*. Available online: https://www. enterprisedb.com/news/new-benchmarks-show-postgres-dominating-mongodb-varied-workloads

Rozman, T., & Donath, L. (2019). The Current State of the Gemification in E-Learning: A Literature Review of Literature Reviews. *Journal of Innovative Business and Management*, 6.

Rudenko, M. V. (2021). The analysis of Ukraine's position in global indices of the digital economy. *Economie & Statistique*, *2*, 11–18.

Russell, S., & Norvig, P. (2007). *Artificial Intelligence. Modern Approach* (2nd ed.). Academic Press.

Sadeghi, D., Shoeibi, A., Ghassemi, N., Moridian, P., Khadem, A., Alizadehsani, R., Teshnehlab, M., Gorriz, J. M., Khozeimeh, F., Zhang, Y.-D., Nahavandi, S., & Acharya, U. R. (2022). An overview of artificial intelligence techniques for diagnosis of Schizophrenia based on magnetic resonance imaging modalities: Methods, challenges, and future works. *Computers in Biology and Medicine*, *146*, 105554. doi:10.1016/j.compbiomed.2022.105554 PMID:35569333

Salasa, E., Wildman, J. L., & Piccolo, R. F. (2017). Using Simulation-Based Training to Enhance Management. *Academy of Management Learning & Education*, *8*(4), 559–573. Advance online publication. doi:10.5465/amle.8.4.zqr559

Salenko, Chencheva, Orel, Pavlyuchenko, & Shchetinin. (n.d.). On the expediency fusing 3D printing tools to improve the accuracy of static and dynamic studies of lever rotating mechanisms. *Bulletin of the Kremenchug National University named after Mikhail Ostrogoradsky, 1*(90).

Salenko, O. F., & Yatsina, M. M. (2012). On the possibility of using drives on mobile vehicles with autonomous source International Scientific. *Gabrovo International Conference,* 313-317.

Salenko, O. F., & Yatsina, M. M. (2014). Analysis of dynamics of work of pneumodrive for mobile transport mean with autonomous rower source. *Transactions of Kremenchuk Mikhail Ostrogradsky National University*, *6*(65), 59–62.

Sandybayev, A. (2020). The Impact of E-Learning Technologies on Student's Motivation: Student Centered Interaction in Business Education. *International Journal of Research in Tourism and Hospitality*, 19.

Schaufeli, W. B. (2018). Burnout in Europe: relations with national economy, governance, and culture. In *Research Unit Occupational & Organizational Psychology and professional learning (internal report)*. KU Leuven.

Schaufeli, W. B., Leiter, M. P., & Maslach, C. (2009). Burnout: 35 years of research and practice. *Career Development International*, *14*(3), 204–220. doi:10.1108/13620430910966406

Schermelleh-Engel, K., Moosbrugger, H., & Müller, H. (2003). Evaluating TheFit Of Structural Equation Models: Tests Of Significance And Descriptive Goodness- Of- Fit Measures. *Methods of Psychological Research Online*, *8*(2), 23–74.

Schwyk, G. I. V., Marin, C. E., Ortiz, M., Rolison, M., Qayyum, Z., McPortland, J. C., Lebowitz, E. R., Volkmar, F. R., & Silverman, W. K. (2017). Social Media Use, Friendship Quality and the Moderating Role of Anxiety in Adolescents with Autism Spectrum Disorder. *Journal of Autism and Developmental Disorders*, *47*(9), 2805–2813. doi:10.1007/s10803-017-3201-6 PMID:28616856

Searle, J. R. (1980). Minds, brains, and programs. *Behavioral and Brain Sciences*, *3*(3), 417–424. doi:10.1017/S0140525X00005756

Seghier, N. B., & Kazar, O. (2021). Performance Benchmarking and Comparison of NoSQL Databases: Redis vs. MongoDB vs. Cassandra Using YCSB Tool. *Proceedings of the International Conference on Recent Advances in Mathematics and Informatics (ICRAMI),* 1–6. 10.1109/ICRAMI52622.2021.9585956

Sharding. (n.d.). Available online: https://docs.mongodb.com/manual/sharding/

Sheehan, D., & Higgs, J. (2013). *Practice-Based Education. In Realising Exemplary Practice-Based Education. Practice, Education, Work and Society*. SensePublishers. doi:10.1007/978-94-6209-188-7_2

Shukla, A., Tiwari, R., & Tiwari, S. (2023). Review on alzheimer disease detection methods: Automatic pipelines and machine learning techniques. *Sci*, *5*(1), 13. doi:10.3390/sci5010013

Silver, D., Huang, A., Maddison, C. J., Guez, A., Sifre, L., Van Den Driessche, G., & Hassabis, D. (2016). Mastering the game of Go with deep neural networks and tree search. *Nature*, *529*(7587), 484–489. doi:10.1038/nature16961 PMID:26819042

Singh, I., & Singh, S. (2015). Distributed Database Systems: Principles, Algorithms and Systems. Khanna Book Publishing, Co. (P) Ltd.

Sirakaya, Y., & Yildirimer, K. Ş. (2023). Effects of Burnout and Emotional Stress on Social Life in Employees.*Collaborate. Current Science*, *5*(5-9), 76–100. doi:10.5281/zenodo.8312341

Siwicki, B. (2020). Is synthetic data the key to healthcare clinical and business intelligence? *Healthcare IT News*.

Skibska, J., Borzęcka, A., & Twaróg-Kanus, A. (2020). Kompetencje diagnostyczne i terapeutyczne w percepcji nauczycieli szkół ogólnodostępnych integracyjnych i specjalnych. *IMPULS, Kraków*, *2020*, 21.

Smoliar, L., Ilyash, O., Kolishenko, R., & Lytvak, T. (2020). Benchmarks of ensuring an «economic breakthrough» of Ukraine in technological and innovative areas. *Innovative Economy*, (5–6), 19–29. doi:10.37332/2309-1533.2020.5-6.3

Song, T. A., Chowdhury, S. R., Yang, F., Jacobs, H., El Fakhri, G., Li, Q., . . . Dutta, J. (2019, April). Graph convolutional neural networks for Alzheimer's disease classification. In *2019 IEEE 16th international symposium on biomedical imaging (ISBI 2019)* (pp. 414-417). IEEE. 10.1109/ISBI.2019.8759531

Starlight. (2021). *TimeToMarket: What it is, Why it's important, and Five Ways to Reduce it.* Retrievedfrom https://www.starlightanalytics.com/article/time-to-market

Statista. (2022). *E-Government Development Index (EDGI) leaders 2022.* Retrieved from:https://www.statista.com/statistics/421580/egdi-e-government-development-index-ranking/

Stillman, P. E., Wilson, J. D., Denny, M. J., Desmarais, B. A., Bhamidi, S., Cranmer, S. J., & Lu, Z. L. (2017). Statistical modeling of the default mode brain network reveals a segregated highway structure. *Scientific Reports*, *7*(1), 11694. doi:10.1038/s41598-017-09896-6 PMID:28916779

Stoffers, J., & Mordant-Dols, A. (2015). Transformational leadership and professionals' willingness to change: A multiple case study in project management organisations. *Human Resource Management Review*, *5*(2), 40–46. doi:10.5923/j.hrmr.20150502.03

Strotzer, M. (2009). One century of brain mapping using Brodmann areas. *Clinical Neuroradiology*, *19*(3), 179–186. doi:10.1007/s00062-009-9002-3 PMID:19727583

Stupak, O. (2020). Educational technologies in training future managers. *Advanced Education*, *7*(15), 97–104. doi:10.20535/2410-8286.200229

Sun, E. D., Ma, R., & Zou, J. (2023). Dynamic visualization of high-dimensional data. *Nature Computational Science*, *3*(2), 86–100. doi:10.1038/s43588-022-00380-4 PMID:38177955

Sustainable development knowledge platform. (2020). https://sustainabledevelopment.un.org/content/documents/26295VNR_2020_Ukraine_Report.pdf

Szeles, M. R., & Simionescu, M. (2020). Regional patterns and drivers of the EU digital economy. *Social Indicators Research*, *150*(1), 95–119. doi:10.1007/s11205-020-02287-x

Tabachnıck, B. G., & Fidell, L. S. (2007). Using Multivariate Statistics (5th ed.). Pearson Education, Inc.

Tan, C., Sun, F., Kong, T., Zhang, W., Yang, C., & Liu, C. (2018). A survey on deep transfer learning. *International Conference on artificial neural networks*, 270–279.

Tang, E., & Bassett, D. S. (2018). Colloquium: Control of dynamics in brain networks. *Reviews of Modern Physics*, *90*(3), 031003. doi:10.1103/RevModPhys.90.031003

Tang, E., Giusti, C., Baum, G. L., Gu, S., Pollock, E., Kahn, A. E., Roalf, D. R., Moore, T. M., Ruparel, K., Gur, R. C., Gur, R. E., Satterthwaite, T. D., & Bassett, D. S. (2017). Developmental increases in white matter network controllability support a growing diversity of brain dynamics. *Nature Communications*, *8*(1), 1252. doi:10.1038/s41467-017-01254-4 PMID:29093441

Tang, L. (2020). High-dimensional data visualization. *Nature Methods*, *17*(2), 129. doi:10.1038/s41592-020-0750-y PMID:32020095

Tang, M. T. (2020). An employers' guide on managing your workplace during *COVID-19*. International Labour Office.

Teubner, R. A., & Stockhinger, J. (2020). Literature review: Understanding information systems strategy in the digital era. *The Journal of Strategic Information Systems*, *29*(4), 101642. doi:10.1016/j.jsis.2020.101642

Thompson, N. C., Greenewald, K., Lee, K., & Manso, G. F. (2020). The computational limits of deep learning. *arXiv preprint arXiv:2007.05558*.

Tomar, P. (2014, February). An overview of distributed databases. *International Journal of Information and Computation Technology.*, *4*(2), 207–214.

Touqeer, M., Al Sulaie, S., Lone, S. A., Gunaime, N. M., & Elkotb, M. A. (2023). A Fuzzy parametric model for decision making involving F-OWA operator with unknown weights environment. *Heliyon*, *9*(9), e19969. doi:10.1016/j.heliyon.2023.e19969 PMID:37809988

Touqeer, M., Shaheen, S., Jabeen, T., Al Sulaie, S., Baleanu, D., & Ahmadian, A. (2022). A signed distance based ranking approach with unknown fuzzy priority vectors for medical diagnosis involving interval type-2 trapezoidal pythagorean fuzzy preference relations. *Operations Research Perspectives*, *9*, 100259. doi:10.1016/j.orp.2022.100259

Tovzhnyansky, L. L., Grabchenko, A. I., Chernyshov, S. I., Verezub, Y. B., Dobroscok, V. L., Knut, X., & Lierat, F. (2005). *Integrated technologies of accelerated prototyping and manufacturing*. OJSC.

Trofymenko, O. (2021). Development of a mechanism for implementation of a national innovative policy in the energy sector based on Industry 4.0. *Technology Auditand Production Reserves*, *4*(4(60)), 34–40. doi:10.15587/2706-5448.2021.238959

UE E-Knowledgebase. (2020). *E-Participation Index*. Retrieved from: https://publicadministration.un.org/egovkb/en-us/About/Overview/E-Participation-Index

UNDP. (2022). *The 2021/2022 Human Development Report: Uncertain times, unsettled lives Shaping our future in a transforming world.* https://hdr.undp.org/content/human-development-report-2021-22

UNDP. (2023). *The Human Development Report 2023.* https://hdr.undp.org/towards-2023-human-development-report

Vallejos, C. A. (2019). Exploring a world of a thousand dimensions. *Nature Biotechnology*, *37*(12), 1423–1424. doi:10.1038/s41587-019-0330-9 PMID:31796932

Veretiuk, S. M., & Pilinskyi, V. V. (2016). Determining the priority areas of the digital economy development in Ukraine. *Scientific Notes of the Ukrainian Research Institute of Communications, 2,* 51–58.

Vinyals, O., Blundell, C., Lillicrap, T., & Wierstra, D. (2016). Matching networks for one shot learning. *Advances in Neural Information Processing Systems*, 29.

Voitenko V. O. (2020). Comparative analysis of the level of digitalisation of the economy of Ukraine in international rankings. *The Strategy of Economic Development of Ukraine, 46,* 23-36.

Wadhawan, S., Gupta, N., Kaur, A., & Bhardwaj, A. (2022). Transformational leadership and employee performance amid COVID-19 crisis. *Journal of Information and Optimization. The Sciences*, *43*(6), 1431–1441. doi:10.1080/02522667.2022.2117345

Wang, Z., Draghi, B., Rotalinti, Y., Lunn, D., & Myles, P. (2024). *High-Fidelity Synthetic Data Applications for Data Augmentation*. Academic Press.

Wang, Z., Myles, P., & Tucker, A. (2021). Generating and evaluating cross-sectional synthetic electronic healthcare data: Preserving data utility and patient privacy. *Computational Intelligence*, *37*(2), 819–851. doi:10.1111/coin.12427

Williams, T. R. (2005). Exploring the Impact of Study Abroad on Students' Intercultural Communication Skills: Adaptability and Sensitivity. *Journal of Studies in International Education*, *9*(4), 356–371. doi:10.1177/1028315305277681

Wilson, J. D., Baybay, M., Sankar, R., Stillman, P., & Popa, A. M. (2021). Analysis of population functional connectivity data via multilayer network embeddings. *Network Science*, *9*(1), 99–122. doi:10.1017/nws.2020.39

Wilson, J. D., Cranmer, S., & Lu, Z. L. (2020). A hierarchical latent space network model for population studies of functional connectivity. *Computational Brain & Behavior*, *3*(4), 384–399. doi:10.1007/s42113-020-00080-0

WIPO - World Intellectual Property Organization. (2022). *Global Innovation Index 2022 – Which are the most innovative countries*. Retrieved from: https://www.wipo.int/global_innovation_index/en/2022/

Witvliet, D., Mulcahy, B., Mitchell, J. K., Meirovitch, Y., Berger, D. R., Wu, Y., Liu, Y., Koh, W. X., Parvathala, R., Holmyard, D., Schalek, R. L., Shavit, N., Chisholm, A. D., Lichtman, J. W., Samuel, A. D. T., & Zhen, M. (2021). Connectomes across development reveal principles of brain maturation. *Nature*, *596*(7871), 257–261. doi:10.1038/s41586-021-03778-8 PMID:34349261

World Bank Group. (2018). *The digital agenda of the Eurasian Economic Union until 2025: prospects and recommendations*. EEC.

World Health Organization. (2019). *Burn-out an "occupational phenomenon": International Classification of Diseases*. https://surl.li/avahb

WorldBank. (2022). Retrievedfrom https://data.worldbank.org/country

Wright, I. (2017). *Human Error is Worse in Manufacturing Compared to Other Sectors*. Retrieved from https://www.engineering.com/story/human-error-is-worse-in-manufacturing-compared-to-other-sectors

Xu, Y., Liu, X., Cao, X., Huang, C., Liu, E., Qian, S., & Zhang, J. (2021). Artificial intelligence: A powerful paradigm for scientific research. *Innovation (Cambridge (Mass.))*, *2*(4), 100179. doi:10.1016/j.xinn.2021.100179 PMID:34877560

Yale, A., Dash, S., Dutta, R., Guyon, I., Pavao, A., & Bennett, K. P. (2020). Generation and evaluation of privacy preserving synthetic health data. *Neurocomputing*, *416*, 244–255. doi:10.1016/j.neucom.2019.12.136

Yan, C., Yan, Y., Wan, Z., Zhang, Z., Omberg, L., Guinney, J., & Malin, B. A. (2022). A multifaceted benchmarking of synthetic electronic health record generation models. *Nature Communications*, *13*(1), 7609. doi:10.1038/s41467-022-35295-1 PMID:36494374

Yang, Y., Qiao, S., Sani, O. G., Sedillo, J. I., Ferrentino, B., Pesaran, B., & Shanechi, M. M. (2021). Modelling and prediction of the dynamic responses of large-scale brain networks during direct electrical stimulation. *Nature Biomedical Engineering*, *5*(4), 324–345. doi:10.1038/s41551-020-00666-w PMID:33526909

Yang, Y., Tuong, Z. K., & Yu, D. (2023). Dimensionality reduction under scrutiny. *Nature Computational Science*, *3*(1), 8–9. doi:10.1038/s43588-022-00383-1 PMID:38177957

Yatsina, M.M. (2013). Improvement of energy efficiency of a pneumatic engine on the basis of geometrical parameters of elements of a working chamber. *Transactions of Kremenchuk Mikhail Ostrogradsky National University, 5*(82), 93-97.

Yatsyna, M.M., & Litvinenko, B.Y. (2008). Pneumodyngyon with a circular rotor in mechanotron systems. *Transactions of Kremenchuk Mikhail Ostrogradsky National University*, *2*(49), 68-72.

Yuan, L., Chen, D., Chen, Y. L., Codella, N., Dai, X., Gao, J., & Zhang, P. (2021). Florence: A new foundation model for computer vision. *arXiv preprint arXiv:2111.11432*.

YurchakO. (2018). Retrieved from https://industry4-0-ukraine.com.ua/2017/03/06/industry-4-0-%D1%8F%D0%BA-%D1%83%D0%BD%D0%B8%D0%BA%D0%BD%D1%83%D1%82%D0%B8-%D0%BF%D0%BB%D1%83%D1%82%D0%B0%D0%BD%D0%B8%D0%BD%D0%B8-%D1%82%D0%B0-%D0%BE%D0%B1%D1%94%D0%B4%D0%BD%D0%B0/

Zenkevich, S. LYushchenko, A. S. (2005). *Basics of manipulation robot management*. N. E. Bauman.

Related References

To continue our tradition of advancing information science and technology research, we have compiled a list of recommended IGI Global readings. These references will provide additional information and guidance to further enrich your knowledge and assist you with your own research and future publications.

Aasi, P., Rusu, L., & Vieru, D. (2017). The Role of Culture in IT Governance Five Focus Areas: A Literature Review. *International Journal of IT/Business Alignment and Governance, 8*(2), 42-61. https://doi.org/ doi:10.4018/IJITBAG.2017070103

Abdrabo, A. A. (2018). Egypt's Knowledge-Based Development: Opportunities, Challenges, and Future Possibilities. In A. Alraouf (Ed.), *Knowledge-Based Urban Development in the Middle East* (pp. 80–101). Hershey, PA: IGI Global. doi:10.4018/978-1-5225-3734-2.ch005

Abu Doush, I., & Alhami, I. (2018). Evaluating the Accessibility of Computer Laboratories, Libraries, and Websites in Jordanian Universities and Colleges. *International Journal of Information Systems and Social Change*, *9*(2), 44–60. doi:10.4018/IJISSC.2018040104

Adegbore, A. M., Quadri, M. O., & Oyewo, O. R. (2018). A Theoretical Approach to the Adoption of Electronic Resource Management Systems (ERMS) in Nigerian University Libraries. In A. Tella & T. Kwanya (Eds.), *Handbook of Research on Managing Intellectual Property in Digital Libraries* (pp. 292–311). Hershey, PA: IGI Global. doi:10.4018/978-1-5225-3093-0.ch015

Afolabi, O. A. (2018). Myths and Challenges of Building an Effective Digital Library in Developing Nations: An African Perspective. In A. Tella & T. Kwanya (Eds.), *Handbook of Research on Managing Intellectual Property in Digital Libraries* (pp. 51–79). Hershey, PA: IGI Global. doi:10.4018/978-1-5225-3093-0.ch004

Agarwal, P., Kurian, R., & Gupta, R. K. (2022). Additive Manufacturing Feature Taxonomy and Placement of Parts in AM Enclosure. In S. Salunkhe, H. Hussein, & J. Davim (Eds.), *Applications of Artificial Intelligence in Additive Manufacturing* (pp. 138–176). IGI Global. https://doi.org/10.4018/978-1-7998-8516-0.ch007

Al-Alawi, A. I., Al-Hammam, A. H., Al-Alawi, S. S., & AlAlawi, E. I. (2021). The Adoption of E-Wallets: Current Trends and Future Outlook. In Y. Albastaki, A. Razzaque, & A. Sarea (Eds.), *Innovative Strategies for Implementing FinTech in Banking* (pp. 242–262). IGI Global. https://doi.org/10.4018/978-1-7998-3257-7.ch015

Alsharo, M. (2017). Attitudes Towards Cloud Computing Adoption in Emerging Economies. *International Journal of Cloud Applications and Computing*, *7*(3), 44–58. doi:10.4018/IJCAC.2017070102

Amer, T. S., & Johnson, T. L. (2017). Information Technology Progress Indicators: Research Employing Psychological Frameworks. In A. Mesquita (Ed.), *Research Paradigms and Contemporary Perspectives on Human-Technology Interaction* (pp. 168–186). Hershey, PA: IGI Global. doi:10.4018/978-1-5225-1868-6.ch008

Andreeva, A., & Yolova, G. (2021). Liability in Labor Legislation: New Challenges Related to the Use of Artificial Intelligence. In B. Vassileva & M. Zwilling (Eds.), *Responsible AI and Ethical Issues for Businesses and Governments* (pp. 214–232). IGI Global. https://doi.org/10.4018/978-1-7998-4285-9.ch012

Anohah, E. (2017). Paradigm and Architecture of Computing Augmented Learning Management System for Computer Science Education. *International Journal of Online Pedagogy and Course Design*, *7*(2), 60–70. doi:10.4018/IJOPCD.2017040105

Anohah, E., & Suhonen, J. (2017). Trends of Mobile Learning in Computing Education from 2006 to 2014: A Systematic Review of Research Publications. *International Journal of Mobile and Blended Learning*, *9*(1), 16–33. doi:10.4018/IJMBL.2017010102

Arbaiza, C. S., Huerta, H. V., & Rodriguez, C. R. (2021). Contributions to the Technological Adoption Model for the Peruvian Agro-Export Sector. *International Journal of E-Adoption*, *13*(1), 1–17. https://doi.org/10.4018/IJEA.2021010101

Bailey, E. K. (2017). Applying Learning Theories to Computer Technology Supported Instruction. In M. Grassetti & S. Brookby (Eds.), *Advancing Next-Generation Teacher Education through Digital Tools and Applications* (pp. 61–81). Hershey, PA: IGI Global. doi:10.4018/978-1-5225-0965-3.ch004

Baker, J. D. (2021). Introduction to Machine Learning as a New Methodological Framework for Performance Assessment. In M. Bocarnea, B. Winston, & D. Dean (Eds.), *Handbook of Research on Advancements in Organizational Data Collection and Measurements: Strategies for Addressing Attitudes, Beliefs, and Behaviors* (pp. 326–342). IGI Global. https://doi.org/10.4018/978-1-7998-7665-6.ch021

Banerjee, S., Sing, T. Y., Chowdhury, A. R., & Anwar, H. (2018). Let's Go Green: Towards a Taxonomy of Green Computing Enablers for Business Sustainability. In M. Khosrow-Pour (Ed.), *Green Computing Strategies for Competitive Advantage and Business Sustainability* (pp. 89–109). Hershey, PA: IGI Global. doi:10.4018/978-1-5225-5017-4.ch005

Basham, R. (2018). Information Science and Technology in Crisis Response and Management. In M. Khosrow-Pour, D.B.A. (Ed.), Encyclopedia of Information Science and Technology, Fourth Edition (pp. 1407-1418). Hershey, PA: IGI Global. doi:10.4018/978-1-5225-2255-3.ch121

Batyashe, T., & Iyamu, T. (2018). Architectural Framework for the Implementation of Information Technology Governance in Organisations. In M. Khosrow-Pour, D.B.A. (Ed.), Encyclopedia of Information Science and Technology, Fourth Edition (pp. 810-819). Hershey, PA: IGI Global. doi:10.4018/978-1-5225-2255-3.ch070

Bekleyen, N., & Çelik, S. (2017). Attitudes of Adult EFL Learners towards Preparing for a Language Test via CALL. In D. Tafazoli & M. Romero (Eds.), *Multiculturalism and Technology-Enhanced Language Learning* (pp. 214–229). Hershey, PA: IGI Global. doi:10.4018/978-1-5225-1882-2.ch013

Bergeron, F., Croteau, A., Uwizeyemungu, S., & Raymond, L. (2017). A Framework for Research on Information Technology Governance in SMEs. In S. De Haes & W. Van Grembergen (Eds.), *Strategic IT Governance and Alignment in Business Settings* (pp. 53–81). Hershey, PA: IGI Global. doi:10.4018/978-1-5225-0861-8.ch003

Bhardwaj, M., Shukla, N., & Sharma, A. (2021). Improvement and Reduction of Clustering Overhead in Mobile Ad Hoc Network With Optimum Stable Bunching Algorithm. In S. Kumar, M. Trivedi, P. Ranjan, & A. Punhani (Eds.), *Evolution of Software-Defined Networking Foundations for IoT and 5G Mobile Networks* (pp. 139–158). IGI Global. https://doi.org/10.4018/978-1-7998-4685-7.ch008

Bhatt, G. D., Wang, Z., & Rodger, J. A. (2017). Information Systems Capabilities and Their Effects on Competitive Advantages: A Study of Chinese Companies. *Information Resources Management Journal*, *30*(3), 41–57. doi:10.4018/IRMJ.2017070103

Bhattacharya, A. (2021). Blockchain, Cybersecurity, and Industry 4.0. In A. Tyagi, G. Rekha, & N. Sreenath (Eds.), *Opportunities and Challenges for Blockchain Technology in Autonomous Vehicles* (pp. 210–244). IGI Global. https://doi.org/10.4018/978-1-7998-3295-9.ch013

Bhyan, P., Shrivastava, B., & Kumar, N. (2022). Requisite Sustainable Development Contemplating Buildings: Economic and Environmental Sustainability. In A. Hussain, K. Tiwari, & A. Gupta (Eds.), *Addressing Environmental Challenges Through Spatial Planning* (pp. 269–288). IGI Global. https://doi.org/10.4018/978-1-7998-8331-9.ch014

Boido, C., Davico, P., & Spallone, R. (2021). Digital Tools Aimed to Represent Urban Survey. In M. Khosrow-Pour D.B.A. (Ed.), *Encyclopedia of Information Science and Technology, Fifth Edition* (pp. 1181-1195). IGI Global. https://doi.org/10.4018/978-1-7998-3479-3.ch082

Borkar, P. S., Chanana, P. U., Atwal, S. K., Londe, T. G., & Dalal, Y. D. (2021). The Replacement of HMI (Human-Machine Interface) in Industry Using Single Interface Through IoT. In R. Raut & A. Mihovska (Eds.), *Examining the Impact of Deep Learning and IoT on Multi-Industry Applications* (pp. 195–208). IGI Global. https://doi.org/10.4018/978-1-7998-7511-6.ch011

Brahmane, A. V., & Krishna, C. B. (2021). Rider Chaotic Biography Optimization-driven Deep Stacked Auto-encoder for Big Data Classification Using Spark Architecture: Rider Chaotic Biography Optimization. *International Journal of Web Services Research*, *18*(3), 42–62. https://doi.org/10.4018/ijwsr.2021070103

Burcoff, A., & Shamir, L. (2017). Computer Analysis of Pablo Picasso's Artistic Style. *International Journal of Art, Culture and Design Technologies*, *6*(1), 1–18. doi:10.4018/IJACDT.2017010101

Byker, E. J. (2017). I Play I Learn: Introducing Technological Play Theory. In C. Martin & D. Polly (Eds.), *Handbook of Research on Teacher Education and Professional Development* (pp. 297–306). Hershey, PA: IGI Global. doi:10.4018/978-1-5225-1067-3.ch016

Calongne, C. M., Stricker, A. G., Truman, B., & Arenas, F. J. (2017). Cognitive Apprenticeship and Computer Science Education in Cyberspace: Reimagining the Past. In A. Stricker, C. Calongne, B. Truman, & F. Arenas (Eds.), *Integrating an Awareness of Selfhood and Society into Virtual Learning* (pp. 180–197). Hershey, PA: IGI Global. doi:10.4018/978-1-5225-2182-2.ch013

Carneiro, A. D. (2017). Defending Information Networks in Cyberspace: Some Notes on Security Needs. In M. Dawson, D. Kisku, P. Gupta, J. Sing, & W. Li (Eds.), Developing Next-Generation Countermeasures for Homeland Security Threat Prevention (pp. 354-375). Hershey, PA: IGI Global. https://doi.org/ doi:10.4018/978-1-5225-0703-1.ch016

Carvalho, W. F., & Zarate, L. (2021). Causal Feature Selection. In A. Azevedo & M. Santos (Eds.), *Integration Challenges for Analytics, Business Intelligence, and Data Mining* (pp. 145-160). IGI Global. https://doi.org/10.4018/978-1-7998-5781-5.ch007

Chase, J. P., & Yan, Z. (2017). Affect in Statistics Cognition. In *Assessing and Measuring Statistics Cognition in Higher Education Online Environments: Emerging Research and Opportunities* (pp. 144–187). Hershey, PA: IGI Global. doi:10.4018/978-1-5225-2420-5.ch005

Chatterjee, A., Roy, S., & Shrivastava, R. (2021). A Machine Learning Approach to Prevent Cancer. In G. Rani & P. Tiwari (Eds.), *Handbook of Research on Disease Prediction Through Data Analytics and Machine Learning* (pp. 112–141). IGI Global. https://doi.org/10.4018/978-1-7998-2742-9.ch007

Cifci, M. A. (2021). Optimizing WSNs for CPS Using Machine Learning Techniques. In A. Luhach & A. Elçi (Eds.), *Artificial Intelligence Paradigms for Smart Cyber-Physical Systems* (pp. 204–228). IGI Global. https://doi.org/10.4018/978-1-7998-5101-1.ch010

Cimermanova, I. (2017). Computer-Assisted Learning in Slovakia. In D. Tafazoli & M. Romero (Eds.), *Multiculturalism and Technology-Enhanced Language Learning* (pp. 252–270). Hershey, PA: IGI Global. doi:10.4018/978-1-5225-1882-2.ch015

Cipolla-Ficarra, F. V., & Cipolla-Ficarra, M. (2018). Computer Animation for Ingenious Revival. In F. Cipolla-Ficarra, M. Ficarra, M. Cipolla-Ficarra, A. Quiroga, J. Alma, & J. Carré (Eds.), *Technology-Enhanced Human Interaction in Modern Society* (pp. 159–181). Hershey, PA: IGI Global. doi:10.4018/978-1-5225-3437-2.ch008

Cockrell, S., Damron, T. S., Melton, A. M., & Smith, A. D. (2018). Offshoring IT. In M. Khosrow-Pour, D.B.A. (Ed.), Encyclopedia of Information Science and Technology, Fourth Edition (pp. 5476-5489). Hershey, PA: IGI Global. https://doi.org/ doi:10.4018/978-1-5225-2255-3.ch476

Coffey, J. W. (2018). Logic and Proof in Computer Science: Categories and Limits of Proof Techniques. In J. Horne (Ed.), *Philosophical Perceptions on Logic and Order* (pp. 218–240). Hershey, PA: IGI Global. doi:10.4018/978-1-5225-2443-4.ch007

Dale, M. (2017). Re-Thinking the Challenges of Enterprise Architecture Implementation. In M. Tavana (Ed.), *Enterprise Information Systems and the Digitalization of Business Functions* (pp. 205–221). Hershey, PA: IGI Global. doi:10.4018/978-1-5225-2382-6.ch009

Das, A., & Mohanty, M. N. (2021). An Useful Review on Optical Character Recognition for Smart Era Generation. In A. Tyagi (Ed.), *Multimedia and Sensory Input for Augmented, Mixed, and Virtual Reality* (pp. 1–41). IGI Global. https://doi.org/10.4018/978-1-7998-4703-8.ch001

Dash, A. K., & Mohapatra, P. (2021). A Survey on Prematurity Detection of Diabetic Retinopathy Based on Fundus Images Using Deep Learning Techniques. In S. Saxena & S. Paul (Eds.), *Deep Learning Applications in Medical Imaging* (pp. 140–155). IGI Global. https://doi.org/10.4018/978-1-7998-5071-7.ch006

De Maere, K., De Haes, S., & von Kutzschenbach, M. (2017). CIO Perspectives on Organizational Learning within the Context of IT Governance. *International Journal of IT/Business Alignment and Governance, 8*(1), 32-47. https://doi.org/doi:10.4018/IJITBAG.2017010103

Demir, K., Çaka, C., Yaman, N. D., İslamoğlu, H., & Kuzu, A. (2018). Examining the Current Definitions of Computational Thinking. In H. Ozcinar, G. Wong, & H. Ozturk (Eds.), *Teaching Computational Thinking in Primary Education* (pp. 36–64). Hershey, PA: IGI Global. doi:10.4018/978-1-5225-3200-2.ch003

Deng, X., Hung, Y., & Lin, C. D. (2017). Design and Analysis of Computer Experiments. In S. Saha, A. Mandal, A. Narasimhamurthy, S. V, & S. Sangam (Eds.), Handbook of Research on Applied Cybernetics and Systems Science (pp. 264-279). Hershey, PA: IGI Global. doi:10.4018/978-1-5225-2498-4.ch013

Denner, J., Martinez, J., & Thiry, H. (2017). Strategies for Engaging Hispanic/Latino Youth in the US in Computer Science. In Y. Rankin & J. Thomas (Eds.), *Moving Students of Color from Consumers to Producers of Technology* (pp. 24–48). Hershey, PA: IGI Global. doi:10.4018/978-1-5225-2005-4.ch002

Devi, A. (2017). Cyber Crime and Cyber Security: A Quick Glance. In R. Kumar, P. Pattnaik, & P. Pandey (Eds.), *Detecting and Mitigating Robotic Cyber Security Risks* (pp. 160–171). Hershey, PA: IGI Global. doi:10.4018/978-1-5225-2154-9.ch011

Dhaya, R., & Kanthavel, R. (2022). Futuristic Research Perspectives of IoT Platforms. In D. Jeya Mala (Ed.), *Integrating AI in IoT Analytics on the Cloud for Healthcare Applications* (pp. 258–275). IGI Global. doi:10.4018/978-1-7998-9132-1.ch015

Doyle, D. J., & Fahy, P. J. (2018). Interactivity in Distance Education and Computer-Aided Learning, With Medical Education Examples. In M. Khosrow-Pour, D.B.A. (Ed.), Encyclopedia of Information Science and Technology, Fourth Edition (pp. 5829-5840). Hershey, PA: IGI Global. https://doi.org/ doi:10.4018/978-1-5225-2255-3.ch507

Eklund, P. (2021). Reinforcement Learning in Social Media Marketing. In B. Christiansen & T. Škrinjarić (Eds.), *Handbook of Research on Applied AI for International Business and Marketing Applications* (pp. 30–48). IGI Global. https://doi.org/10.4018/978-1-7998-5077-9.ch003

El Ghandour, N., Benaissa, M., & Lebbah, Y. (2021). An Integer Linear Programming-Based Method for the Extraction of Ontology Alignment. *International Journal of Information Technology and Web Engineering, 16*(2), 25–44. https://doi.org/10.4018/IJITWE.2021040102

Elias, N. I., & Walker, T. W. (2017). Factors that Contribute to Continued Use of E-Training among Healthcare Professionals. In F. Topor (Ed.), *Handbook of Research on Individualism and Identity in the Globalized Digital Age* (pp. 403–429). Hershey, PA: IGI Global. doi:10.4018/978-1-5225-0522-8.ch018

Fisher, R. L. (2018). Computer-Assisted Indian Matrimonial Services. In M. Khosrow-Pour, D.B.A. (Ed.), Encyclopedia of Information Science and Technology, Fourth Edition (pp. 4136-4145). Hershey, PA: IGI Global. doi:10.4018/978-1-5225-2255-3.ch358

Galiautdinov, R. (2021). Nonlinear Filtering in Artificial Neural Network Applications in Business and Engineering. In Q. Do (Ed.), *Artificial Neural Network Applications in Business and Engineering* (pp. 1–23). IGI Global. https://doi.org/10.4018/978-1-7998-3238-6.ch001

Gardner-McCune, C., & Jimenez, Y. (2017). Historical App Developers: Integrating CS into K-12 through Cross-Disciplinary Projects. In Y. Rankin & J. Thomas (Eds.), *Moving Students of Color from Consumers to Producers of Technology* (pp. 85–112). Hershey, PA: IGI Global. doi:10.4018/978-1-5225-2005-4.ch005

Garg, P. K. (2021). The Internet of Things-Based Technologies. In S. Kumar, M. Trivedi, P. Ranjan, & A. Punhani (Eds.), *Evolution of Software-Defined Networking Foundations for IoT and 5G Mobile Networks* (pp. 37–65). IGI Global. https://doi.org/10.4018/978-1-7998-4685-7.ch003

Garg, T., & Bharti, M. (2021). Congestion Control Protocols for UWSNs. In N. Goyal, L. Sapra, & J. Sandhu (Eds.), *Energy-Efficient Underwater Wireless Communications and Networking* (pp. 85–100). IGI Global. https://doi.org/10.4018/978-1-7998-3640-7.ch006

Gauttier, S. (2021). A Primer on Q-Method and the Study of Technology. In M. Khosrow-Pour D.B.A. (Eds.), *Encyclopedia of Information Science and Technology, Fifth Edition* (pp. 1746-1756). IGI Global. https://doi.org/10.4018/978-1-7998-3479-3.ch120

Ghafele, R., & Gibert, B. (2018). Open Growth: The Economic Impact of Open Source Software in the USA. In M. Khosrow-Pour (Ed.), *Optimizing Contemporary Application and Processes in Open Source Software* (pp. 164–197). Hershey, PA: IGI Global. doi:10.4018/978-1-5225-5314-4.ch007

Ghobakhloo, M., & Azar, A. (2018). Information Technology Resources, the Organizational Capability of Lean-Agile Manufacturing, and Business Performance. *Information Resources Management Journal, 31*(2), 47–74. doi:10.4018/IRMJ.2018040103

Gikandi, J. W. (2017). Computer-Supported Collaborative Learning and Assessment: A Strategy for Developing Online Learning Communities in Continuing Education. In J. Keengwe & G. Onchwari (Eds.), *Handbook of Research on Learner-Centered Pedagogy in Teacher Education and Professional Development* (pp. 309–333). Hershey, PA: IGI Global. doi:10.4018/978-1-5225-0892-2.ch017

Gokhale, A. A., & Machina, K. F. (2017). Development of a Scale to Measure Attitudes toward Information Technology. In L. Tomei (Ed.), *Exploring the New Era of Technology-Infused Education* (pp. 49–64). Hershey, PA: IGI Global. doi:10.4018/978-1-5225-1709-2.ch004

Goswami, J. K., Jalal, S., Negi, C. S., & Jalal, A. S. (2022). A Texture Features-Based Robust Facial Expression Recognition. *International Journal of Computer Vision and Image Processing, 12*(1), 1–15. https://doi.org/10.4018/IJCVIP.2022010103

Hafeez-Baig, A., Gururajan, R., & Wickramasinghe, N. (2017). Readiness as a Novel Construct of Readiness Acceptance Model (RAM) for the Wireless Handheld Technology. In N. Wickramasinghe (Ed.), *Handbook of Research on Healthcare Administration and Management* (pp. 578–595). Hershey, PA: IGI Global. doi:10.4018/978-1-5225-0920-2.ch035

Hanafizadeh, P., Ghandchi, S., & Asgarimehr, M. (2017). Impact of Information Technology on Lifestyle: A Literature Review and Classification. *International Journal of Virtual Communities and Social Networking*, *9*(2), 1–23. doi:10.4018/IJVCSN.2017040101

Haseski, H. İ., Ilic, U., & Tuğtekin, U. (2018). Computational Thinking in Educational Digital Games: An Assessment Tool Proposal. In H. Ozcinar, G. Wong, & H. Ozturk (Eds.), *Teaching Computational Thinking in Primary Education* (pp. 256–287). Hershey, PA: IGI Global. doi:10.4018/978-1-5225-3200-2.ch013

Hee, W. J., Jalleh, G., Lai, H., & Lin, C. (2017). E-Commerce and IT Projects: Evaluation and Management Issues in Australian and Taiwanese Hospitals. *International Journal of Public Health Management and Ethics*, *2*(1), 69–90. doi:10.4018/IJPHME.2017010104

Hernandez, A. A. (2017). Green Information Technology Usage: Awareness and Practices of Philippine IT Professionals. *International Journal of Enterprise Information Systems*, *13*(4), 90–103. doi:10.4018/IJEIS.2017100106

Hernandez, M. A., Marin, E. C., Garcia-Rodriguez, J., Azorin-Lopez, J., & Cazorla, M. (2017). Automatic Learning Improves Human-Robot Interaction in Productive Environments: A Review. *International Journal of Computer Vision and Image Processing*, *7*(3), 65–75. doi:10.4018/IJCVIP.2017070106

Hirota, A. (2021). Design of Narrative Creation in Innovation: "Signature Story" and Two Types of Pivots. In T. Ogata & J. Ono (Eds.), *Bridging the Gap Between AI, Cognitive Science, and Narratology With Narrative Generation* (pp. 363–376). IGI Global. https://doi.org/10.4018/978-1-7998-4864-6.ch012

Hond, D., Asgari, H., Jeffery, D., & Newman, M. (2021). An Integrated Process for Verifying Deep Learning Classifiers Using Dataset Dissimilarity Measures. *International Journal of Artificial Intelligence and Machine Learning*, *11*(2), 1–21. https://doi.org/10.4018/IJAIML.289536

Horne-Popp, L. M., Tessone, E. B., & Welker, J. (2018). If You Build It, They Will Come: Creating a Library Statistics Dashboard for Decision-Making. In L. Costello & M. Powers (Eds.), *Developing In-House Digital Tools in Library Spaces* (pp. 177–203). Hershey, PA: IGI Global. doi:10.4018/978-1-5225-2676-6.ch009

Hu, H., Hu, P. J., & Al-Gahtani, S. S. (2017). User Acceptance of Computer Technology at Work in Arabian Culture: A Model Comparison Approach. In M. Khosrow-Pour (Ed.), *Handbook of Research on Technology Adoption, Social Policy, and Global Integration* (pp. 205–228). Hershey, PA: IGI Global. doi:10.4018/978-1-5225-2668-1.ch011

Huang, C., Sun, Y., & Fuh, C. (2022). Vehicle License Plate Recognition With Deep Learning. In C. Chen, W. Yang, & L. Chen (Eds.), *Technologies to Advance Automation in Forensic Science and Criminal Investigation* (pp. 161-219). IGI Global. https://doi.org/10.4018/978-1-7998-8386-9.ch009

Ifinedo, P. (2017). Using an Extended Theory of Planned Behavior to Study Nurses' Adoption of Healthcare Information Systems in Nova Scotia. *International Journal of Technology Diffusion*, *8*(1), 1–17. doi:10.4018/IJTD.2017010101

Ilie, V., & Sneha, S. (2018). A Three Country Study for Understanding Physicians' Engagement With Electronic Information Resources Pre and Post System Implementation. *Journal of Global Information Management*, *26*(2), 48–73. doi:10.4018/JGIM.2018040103

Ilo, P. I., Nkiko, C., Ugwu, C. I., Ekere, J. N., Izuagbe, R., & Fagbohun, M. O. (2021). Prospects and Challenges of Web 3.0 Technologies Application in the Provision of Library Services. In M. Khosrow-Pour D.B.A. (Ed.), *Encyclopedia of Information Science and Technology, Fifth Edition* (pp. 1767-1781). IGI Global. https://doi.org/10.4018/978-1-7998-3479-3.ch122

Inoue-Smith, Y. (2017). Perceived Ease in Using Technology Predicts Teacher Candidates' Preferences for Online Resources. *International Journal of Online Pedagogy and Course Design*, *7*(3), 17–28. doi:10.4018/IJOPCD.2017070102

Islam, A. Y. (2017). Technology Satisfaction in an Academic Context: Moderating Effect of Gender. In A. Mesquita (Ed.), *Research Paradigms and Contemporary Perspectives on Human-Technology Interaction* (pp. 187–211). Hershey, PA: IGI Global. doi:10.4018/978-1-5225-1868-6.ch009

Jagdale, S. C., Hable, A. A., & Chabukswar, A. R. (2021). Protocol Development in Clinical Trials for Healthcare Management. In M. Khosrow-Pour D.B.A. (Ed.), *Encyclopedia of Information Science and Technology, Fifth Edition* (pp. 1797-1814). IGI Global. https://doi.org/10.4018/978-1-7998-3479-3.ch124

Jamil, G. L., & Jamil, C. C. (2017). Information and Knowledge Management Perspective Contributions for Fashion Studies: Observing Logistics and Supply Chain Management Processes. In G. Jamil, A. Soares, & C. Pessoa (Eds.), *Handbook of Research on Information Management for Effective Logistics and Supply Chains* (pp. 199–221). Hershey, PA: IGI Global. doi:10.4018/978-1-5225-0973-8.ch011

Jamil, M. I., & Almunawar, M. N. (2021). Importance of Digital Literacy and Hindrance Brought About by Digital Divide. In M. Khosrow-Pour D.B.A. (Ed.), *Encyclopedia of Information Science and Technology, Fifth Edition* (pp. 1683-1698). IGI Global. https://doi.org/10.4018/978-1-7998-3479-3.ch116

Janakova, M. (2018). Big Data and Simulations for the Solution of Controversies in Small Businesses. In M. Khosrow-Pour, D.B.A. (Ed.), Encyclopedia of Information Science and Technology, Fourth Edition (pp. 6907-6915). Hershey, PA: IGI Global. doi:10.4018/978-1-5225-2255-3.ch598

Jhawar, A., & Garg, S. K. (2018). Logistics Improvement by Investment in Information Technology Using System Dynamics. In A. Azar & S. Vaidyanathan (Eds.), *Advances in System Dynamics and Control* (pp. 528–567). Hershey, PA: IGI Global. doi:10.4018/978-1-5225-4077-9.ch017

Kalelioğlu, F., Gülbahar, Y., & Doğan, D. (2018). Teaching How to Think Like a Programmer: Emerging Insights. In H. Ozcinar, G. Wong, & H. Ozturk (Eds.), *Teaching Computational Thinking in Primary Education* (pp. 18–35). Hershey, PA: IGI Global. doi:10.4018/978-1-5225-3200-2.ch002

Kamberi, S. (2017). A Girls-Only Online Virtual World Environment and its Implications for Game-Based Learning. In A. Stricker, C. Calongne, B. Truman, & F. Arenas (Eds.), *Integrating an Awareness of Selfhood and Society into Virtual Learning* (pp. 74–95). Hershey, PA: IGI Global. doi:10.4018/978-1-5225-2182-2.ch006

Kamel, S., & Rizk, N. (2017). ICT Strategy Development: From Design to Implementation – Case of Egypt. In C. Howard & K. Hargiss (Eds.), *Strategic Information Systems and Technologies in Modern Organizations* (pp. 239–257). Hershey, PA: IGI Global. doi:10.4018/978-1-5225-1680-4.ch010

Kamel, S. H. (2018). The Potential Role of the Software Industry in Supporting Economic Development. In M. Khosrow-Pour, D.B.A. (Ed.), Encyclopedia of Information Science and Technology, Fourth Edition (pp. 7259-7269). Hershey, PA: IGI Global. doi:10.4018/978-1-5225-2255-3.ch631

Kang, H., Kang, Y., & Kim, J. (2022). Improved Fall Detection Model on GRU Using PoseNet. *International Journal of Software Innovation*, *10*(2), 1–11. https://doi.org/10.4018/IJSI.289600

Kankam, P. K. (2021). Employing Case Study and Survey Designs in Information Research. *Journal of Information Technology Research*, *14*(1), 167–177. https://doi.org/10.4018/JITR.2021010110

Karas, V., & Schuller, B. W. (2021). Deep Learning for Sentiment Analysis: An Overview and Perspectives. In F. Pinarbasi & M. Taskiran (Eds.), *Natural Language Processing for Global and Local Business* (pp. 97–132). IGI Global. https://doi.org/10.4018/978-1-7998-4240-8.ch005

Kaufman, L. M. (2022). Reimagining the Magic of the Workshop Model. In T. Driscoll III, (Ed.), *Designing Effective Distance and Blended Learning Environments in K-12* (pp. 89–109). IGI Global. https://doi.org/10.4018/978-1-7998-6829-3.ch007

Kawata, S. (2018). Computer-Assisted Parallel Program Generation. In M. Khosrow-Pour, D.B.A. (Ed.), Encyclopedia of Information Science and Technology, Fourth Edition (pp. 4583-4593). Hershey, PA: IGI Global. doi:10.4018/978-1-5225-2255-3.ch398

Kharb, L., & Singh, P. (2021). Role of Machine Learning in Modern Education and Teaching. In S. Verma & P. Tomar (Ed.), *Impact of AI Technologies on Teaching, Learning, and Research in Higher Education* (pp. 99-123). IGI Global. https://doi.org/10.4018/978-1-7998-4763-2.ch006

Khari, M., Shrivastava, G., Gupta, S., & Gupta, R. (2017). Role of Cyber Security in Today's Scenario. In R. Kumar, P. Pattnaik, & P. Pandey (Eds.), *Detecting and Mitigating Robotic Cyber Security Risks* (pp. 177–191). Hershey, PA: IGI Global. doi:10.4018/978-1-5225-2154-9.ch013

Khekare, G., & Sheikh, S. (2021). Autonomous Navigation Using Deep Reinforcement Learning in ROS. *International Journal of Artificial Intelligence and Machine Learning*, *11*(2), 63–70. https://doi.org/10.4018/IJAIML.20210701.oa4

Khouja, M., Rodriguez, I. B., Ben Halima, Y., & Moalla, S. (2018). IT Governance in Higher Education Institutions: A Systematic Literature Review. *International Journal of Human Capital and Information Technology Professionals*, *9*(2), 52–67. doi:10.4018/IJHCITP.2018040104

Kiourt, C., Pavlidis, G., Koutsoudis, A., & Kalles, D. (2017). Realistic Simulation of Cultural Heritage. *International Journal of Computational Methods in Heritage Science*, *1*(1), 10–40. doi:10.4018/IJCMHS.2017010102

Köse, U. (2017). An Augmented-Reality-Based Intelligent Mobile Application for Open Computer Education. In G. Kurubacak & H. Altinpulluk (Eds.), *Mobile Technologies and Augmented Reality in Open Education* (pp. 154–174). Hershey, PA: IGI Global. doi:10.4018/978-1-5225-2110-5.ch008

Lahmiri, S. (2018). Information Technology Outsourcing Risk Factors and Provider Selection. In M. Gupta, R. Sharman, J. Walp, & P. Mulgund (Eds.), *Information Technology Risk Management and Compliance in Modern Organizations* (pp. 214–228). Hershey, PA: IGI Global. doi:10.4018/978-1-5225-2604-9.ch008

Lakkad, A. K., Bhadaniya, R. D., Shah, V. N., & Lavanya, K. (2021). Complex Events Processing on Live News Events Using Apache Kafka and Clustering Techniques. *International Journal of Intelligent Information Technologies*, *17*(1), 39–52. https://doi.org/10.4018/IJIIT.2021010103

Landriscina, F. (2017). Computer-Supported Imagination: The Interplay Between Computer and Mental Simulation in Understanding Scientific Concepts. In I. Levin & D. Tsybulsky (Eds.), *Digital Tools and Solutions for Inquiry-Based STEM Learning* (pp. 33–60). Hershey, PA: IGI Global. doi:10.4018/978-1-5225-2525-7.ch002

Lara López, G. (2021). Virtual Reality in Object Location. In A. Negrón & M. Muñoz (Eds.), *Latin American Women and Research Contributions to the IT Field* (pp. 307–324). IGI Global. https://doi.org/10.4018/978-1-7998-7552-9.ch014

Lee, W. W. (2018). Ethical Computing Continues From Problem to Solution. In M. Khosrow-Pour, D.B.A. (Ed.), Encyclopedia of Information Science and Technology, Fourth Edition (pp. 4884-4897). Hershey, PA: IGI Global. doi:10.4018/978-1-5225-2255-3.ch423

Lin, S., Chen, S., & Chuang, S. (2017). Perceived Innovation and Quick Response Codes in an Online-to-Offline E-Commerce Service Model. *International Journal of E-Adoption*, *9*(2), 1–16. doi:10.4018/IJEA.2017070101

Liu, M., Wang, Y., Xu, W., & Liu, L. (2017). Automated Scoring of Chinese Engineering Students' English Essays. *International Journal of Distance Education Technologies*, *15*(1), 52–68. doi:10.4018/IJDET.2017010104

Ma, X., Li, X., Zhong, B., Huang, Y., Gu, Y., Wu, M., Liu, Y., & Zhang, M. (2021). A Detector and Evaluation Framework of Abnormal Bidding Behavior Based on Supplier Portrait. *International Journal of Information Technology and Web Engineering*, *16*(2), 58–74. https://doi.org/10.4018/IJITWE.2021040104

Mabe, L. K., & Oladele, O. I. (2017). Application of Information Communication Technologies for Agricultural Development through Extension Services: A Review. In T. Tossy (Ed.), *Information Technology Integration for Socio-Economic Development* (pp. 52–101). Hershey, PA: IGI Global. doi:10.4018/978-1-5225-0539-6.ch003

Mahboub, S. A., Sayed Ali Ahmed, E., & Saeed, R. A. (2021). Smart IDS and IPS for Cyber-Physical Systems. In A. Luhach & A. Elçi (Eds.), *Artificial Intelligence Paradigms for Smart Cyber-Physical Systems* (pp. 109–136). IGI Global. https://doi.org/10.4018/978-1-7998-5101-1.ch006

Manogaran, G., Thota, C., & Lopez, D. (2018). Human-Computer Interaction With Big Data Analytics. In D. Lopez & M. Durai (Eds.), *HCI Challenges and Privacy Preservation in Big Data Security* (pp. 1–22). Hershey, PA: IGI Global. doi:10.4018/978-1-5225-2863-0.ch001

Margolis, J., Goode, J., & Flapan, J. (2017). A Critical Crossroads for Computer Science for All: "Identifying Talent" or "Building Talent," and What Difference Does It Make? In Y. Rankin & J. Thomas (Eds.), *Moving Students of Color from Consumers to Producers of Technology* (pp. 1–23). Hershey, PA: IGI Global. doi:10.4018/978-1-5225-2005-4.ch001

Mazzù, M. F., Benetton, A., Baccelloni, A., & Lavini, L. (2022). A Milk Blockchain-Enabled Supply Chain: Evidence From Leading Italian Farms. In P. De Giovanni (Ed.), *Blockchain Technology Applications in Businesses and Organizations* (pp. 73–98). IGI Global. https://doi.org/10.4018/978-1-7998-8014-1.ch004

Mbale, J. (2018). Computer Centres Resource Cloud Elasticity-Scalability (CRECES): Copperbelt University Case Study. In S. Aljawarneh & M. Malhotra (Eds.), *Critical Research on Scalability and Security Issues in Virtual Cloud Environments* (pp. 48–70). Hershey, PA: IGI Global. doi:10.4018/978-1-5225-3029-9.ch003

McKee, J. (2018). The Right Information: The Key to Effective Business Planning. In *Business Architectures for Risk Assessment and Strategic Planning: Emerging Research and Opportunities* (pp. 38–52). Hershey, PA: IGI Global. doi:10.4018/978-1-5225-3392-4.ch003

Meddah, I. H., Remil, N. E., & Meddah, H. N. (2021). Novel Approach for Mining Patterns. *International Journal of Applied Evolutionary Computation*, *12*(1), 27–42. https://doi.org/10.4018/IJAEC.2021010103

Mensah, I. K., & Mi, J. (2018). Determinants of Intention to Use Local E-Government Services in Ghana: The Perspective of Local Government Workers. *International Journal of Technology Diffusion*, *9*(2), 41–60. doi:10.4018/IJTD.2018040103

Mohamed, J. H. (2018). Scientograph-Based Visualization of Computer Forensics Research Literature. In J. Jeyasekar & P. Saravanan (Eds.), *Innovations in Measuring and Evaluating Scientific Information* (pp. 148–162). Hershey, PA: IGI Global. doi:10.4018/978-1-5225-3457-0.ch010

Montañés-Del Río, M. Á., Cornejo, V. R., Rodríguez, M. R., & Ortiz, J. S. (2021). Gamification of University Subjects: A Case Study for Operations Management. *Journal of Information Technology Research*, *14*(2), 1–29. https://doi.org/10.4018/JITR.2021040101

Moore, R. L., & Johnson, N. (2017). Earning a Seat at the Table: How IT Departments Can Partner in Organizational Change and Innovation. *International Journal of Knowledge-Based Organizations*, *7*(2), 1–12. doi:10.4018/IJKBO.2017040101

Mukul, M. K., & Bhattaharyya, S. (2017). Brain-Machine Interface: Human-Computer Interaction. In E. Noughabi, B. Raahemi, A. Albadvi, & B. Far (Eds.), *Handbook of Research on Data Science for Effective Healthcare Practice and Administration* (pp. 417–443). Hershey, PA: IGI Global. doi:10.4018/978-1-5225-2515-8.ch018

Na, L. (2017). Library and Information Science Education and Graduate Programs in Academic Libraries. In L. Ruan, Q. Zhu, & Y. Ye (Eds.), *Academic Library Development and Administration in China* (pp. 218–229). Hershey, PA: IGI Global. doi:10.4018/978-1-5225-0550-1.ch013

Nagpal, G., Bishnoi, G. K., Dhami, H. S., & Vijayvargia, A. (2021). Use of Data Analytics to Increase the Efficiency of Last Mile Logistics for Ecommerce Deliveries. In B. Patil & M. Vohra (Eds.), *Handbook of Research on Engineering, Business, and Healthcare Applications of Data Science and Analytics* (pp. 167–180). IGI Global. https://doi.org/10.4018/978-1-7998-3053-5.ch009

Nair, S. M., Ramesh, V., & Tyagi, A. K. (2021). Issues and Challenges (Privacy, Security, and Trust) in Blockchain-Based Applications. In A. Tyagi, G. Rekha, & N. Sreenath (Eds.), *Opportunities and Challenges for Blockchain Technology in Autonomous Vehicles* (pp. 196–209). IGI Global. https://doi.org/10.4018/978-1-7998-3295-9.ch012

Naomi, J. F. M., K., & V., S. (2021). Machine and Deep Learning Techniques in IoT and Cloud. In S. Velayutham (Ed.), *Challenges and Opportunities for the Convergence of IoT, Big Data, and Cloud Computing* (pp. 225-247). IGI Global. https://doi.org/10.4018/978-1-7998-3111-2.ch013

Nath, R., & Murthy, V. N. (2018). What Accounts for the Differences in Internet Diffusion Rates Around the World? In M. Khosrow-Pour, D.B.A. (Ed.), Encyclopedia of Information Science and Technology, Fourth Edition (pp. 8095-8104). Hershey, PA: IGI Global. https://doi.org/ doi:10.4018/978-1-5225-2255-3.ch705

Nedelko, Z., & Potocan, V. (2018). The Role of Emerging Information Technologies for Supporting Supply Chain Management. In M. Khosrow-Pour, D.B.A. (Ed.), Encyclopedia of Information Science and Technology, Fourth Edition (pp. 5559-5569). Hershey, PA: IGI Global. doi:10.4018/978-1-5225-2255-3.ch483

Negrini, L., Giang, C., & Bonnet, E. (2022). Designing Tools and Activities for Educational Robotics in Online Learning. In N. Eteokleous & E. Nisiforou (Eds.), *Designing, Constructing, and Programming Robots for Learning* (pp. 202–222). IGI Global. https://doi.org/10.4018/978-1-7998-7443-0.ch010

Ngafeeson, M. N. (2018). User Resistance to Health Information Technology. In M. Khosrow-Pour, D.B.A. (Ed.), Encyclopedia of Information Science and Technology, Fourth Edition (pp. 3816-3825). Hershey, PA: IGI Global. doi:10.4018/978-1-5225-2255-3.ch331

Nguyen, T. T., Giang, N. L., Tran, D. T., Nguyen, T. T., Nguyen, H. Q., Pham, A. V., & Vu, T. D. (2021). A Novel Filter-Wrapper Algorithm on Intuitionistic Fuzzy Set for Attribute Reduction From Decision Tables. *International Journal of Data Warehousing and Mining, 17*(4), 67–100. https://doi.org/10.4018/IJDWM.2021100104

Nigam, A., & Dewani, P. P. (2022). Consumer Engagement Through Conditional Promotions: An Exploratory Study. *Journal of Global Information Management, 30*(5), 1–19. https://doi.org/10.4018/JGIM.290364

Odagiri, K. (2017). Introduction of Individual Technology to Constitute the Current Internet. In *Strategic Policy-Based Network Management in Contemporary Organizations* (pp. 20–96). Hershey, PA: IGI Global. doi:10.4018/978-1-68318-003-6.ch003

Odia, J. O., & Akpata, O. T. (2021). Role of Data Science and Data Analytics in Forensic Accounting and Fraud Detection. In B. Patil & M. Vohra (Eds.), *Handbook of Research on Engineering, Business, and Healthcare Applications of Data Science and Analytics* (pp. 203–227). IGI Global. https://doi.org/10.4018/978-1-7998-3053-5.ch011

Okike, E. U. (2018). Computer Science and Prison Education. In I. Biao (Ed.), *Strategic Learning Ideologies in Prison Education Programs* (pp. 246–264). Hershey, PA: IGI Global. doi:10.4018/978-1-5225-2909-5.ch012

Olelewe, C. J., & Nwafor, I. P. (2017). Level of Computer Appreciation Skills Acquired for Sustainable Development by Secondary School Students in Nsukka LGA of Enugu State, Nigeria. In C. Ayo & V. Mbarika (Eds.), *Sustainable ICT Adoption and Integration for Socio-Economic Development* (pp. 214–233). Hershey, PA: IGI Global. doi:10.4018/978-1-5225-2565-3.ch010

Oliveira, M., Maçada, A. C., Curado, C., & Nodari, F. (2017). Infrastructure Profiles and Knowledge Sharing. *International Journal of Technology and Human Interaction, 13*(3), 1–12. doi:10.4018/IJTHI.2017070101

Otarkhani, A., Shokouhyar, S., & Pour, S. S. (2017). Analyzing the Impact of Governance of Enterprise IT on Hospital Performance: Tehran's (Iran) Hospitals – A Case Study. *International Journal of Healthcare Information Systems and Informatics, 12*(3), 1–20. doi:10.4018/IJHISI.2017070101

Otunla, A. O., & Amuda, C. O. (2018). Nigerian Undergraduate Students' Computer Competencies and Use of Information Technology Tools and Resources for Study Skills and Habits' Enhancement. In M. Khosrow-Pour, D.B.A. (Ed.), Encyclopedia of Information Science and Technology, Fourth Edition (pp. 2303-2313). Hershey, PA: IGI Global. https://doi.org/ doi:10.4018/978-1-5225-2255-3.ch200

Özçınar, H. (2018). A Brief Discussion on Incentives and Barriers to Computational Thinking Education. In H. Ozcinar, G. Wong, & H. Ozturk (Eds.), *Teaching Computational Thinking in Primary Education* (pp. 1–17). Hershey, PA: IGI Global. doi:10.4018/978-1-5225-3200-2.ch001

Pandey, J. M., Garg, S., Mishra, P., & Mishra, B. P. (2017). Computer Based Psychological Interventions: Subject to the Efficacy of Psychological Services. *International Journal of Computers in Clinical Practice, 2*(1), 25–33. doi:10.4018/IJCCP.2017010102

Pandkar, S. D., & Paatil, S. D. (2021). Big Data and Knowledge Resource Centre. In S. Dhamdhere (Ed.), *Big Data Applications for Improving Library Services* (pp. 90–106). IGI Global. https://doi.org/10.4018/978-1-7998-3049-8.ch007

Patro, C. (2017). Impulsion of Information Technology on Human Resource Practices. In P. Ordóñez de Pablos (Ed.), *Managerial Strategies and Solutions for Business Success in Asia* (pp. 231–254). Hershey, PA: IGI Global. doi:10.4018/978-1-5225-1886-0.ch013

Patro, C. S., & Raghunath, K. M. (2017). Information Technology Paraphernalia for Supply Chain Management Decisions. In M. Tavana (Ed.), *Enterprise Information Systems and the Digitalization of Business Functions* (pp. 294–320). Hershey, PA: IGI Global. doi:10.4018/978-1-5225-2382-6.ch014

Paul, P. K. (2018). The Context of IST for Solid Information Retrieval and Infrastructure Building: Study of Developing Country. *International Journal of Information Retrieval Research, 8*(1), 86–100. doi:10.4018/IJIRR.2018010106

Paul, P. K., & Chatterjee, D. (2018). iSchools Promoting "Information Science and Technology" (IST) Domain Towards Community, Business, and Society With Contemporary Worldwide Trend and Emerging Potentialities in India. In M. Khosrow-Pour, D.B.A. (Ed.), Encyclopedia of Information Science and Technology, Fourth Edition (pp. 4723-4735). Hershey, PA: IGI Global. https://doi.org/ doi:10.4018/978-1-5225-2255-3.ch410

Pessoa, C. R., & Marques, M. E. (2017). Information Technology and Communication Management in Supply Chain Management. In G. Jamil, A. Soares, & C. Pessoa (Eds.), *Handbook of Research on Information Management for Effective Logistics and Supply Chains* (pp. 23–33). Hershey, PA: IGI Global. doi:10.4018/978-1-5225-0973-8.ch002

Pineda, R. G. (2018). Remediating Interaction: Towards a Philosophy of Human-Computer Relationship. In M. Khosrow-Pour (Ed.), *Enhancing Art, Culture, and Design With Technological Integration* (pp. 75–98). Hershey, PA: IGI Global. doi:10.4018/978-1-5225-5023-5.ch004

Prabha, V. D., & R., R. (2021). Clinical Decision Support Systems: Decision-Making System for Clinical Data. In G. Rani & P. Tiwari (Eds.), *Handbook of Research on Disease Prediction Through Data Analytics and Machine Learning* (pp. 268-280). IGI Global. https://doi.org/10.4018/978-1-7998-2742-9.ch014

Pushpa, R., & Siddappa, M. (2021). An Optimal Way of VM Placement Strategy in Cloud Computing Platform Using ABCS Algorithm. *International Journal of Ambient Computing and Intelligence*, *12*(3), 16–38. https://doi.org/10.4018/IJACI.2021070102

Qian, Y. (2017). Computer Simulation in Higher Education: Affordances, Opportunities, and Outcomes. In P. Vu, S. Fredrickson, & C. Moore (Eds.), *Handbook of Research on Innovative Pedagogies and Technologies for Online Learning in Higher Education* (pp. 236–262). Hershey, PA: IGI Global. doi:10.4018/978-1-5225-1851-8.ch011

Rahman, N. (2017). Lessons from a Successful Data Warehousing Project Management. *International Journal of Information Technology Project Management*, *8*(4), 30–45. doi:10.4018/IJITPM.2017100103

Rahman, N. (2018). Environmental Sustainability in the Computer Industry for Competitive Advantage. In M. Khosrow-Pour (Ed.), *Green Computing Strategies for Competitive Advantage and Business Sustainability* (pp. 110–130). Hershey, PA: IGI Global. doi:10.4018/978-1-5225-5017-4.ch006

Rajh, A., & Pavetic, T. (2017). Computer Generated Description as the Required Digital Competence in Archival Profession. *International Journal of Digital Literacy and Digital Competence*, *8*(1), 36–49. doi:10.4018/IJDLDC.2017010103

Raman, A., & Goyal, D. P. (2017). Extending IMPLEMENT Framework for Enterprise Information Systems Implementation to Information System Innovation. In M. Tavana (Ed.), *Enterprise Information Systems and the Digitalization of Business Functions* (pp. 137–177). Hershey, PA: IGI Global. doi:10.4018/978-1-5225-2382-6.ch007

Rao, A. P., & Reddy, K. S. (2021). Automated Soil Residue Levels Detecting Device With IoT Interface. In V. Sathiyamoorthi & A. Elci (Eds.), *Challenges and Applications of Data Analytics in Social Perspectives* (Vol. S, pp. 123–135). IGI Global. https://doi.org/10.4018/978-1-7998-2566-1.ch007

Rao, Y. S., Rauta, A. K., Saini, H., & Panda, T. C. (2017). Mathematical Model for Cyber Attack in Computer Network. *International Journal of Business Data Communications and Networking*, *13*(1), 58–65. doi:10.4018/IJBDCN.2017010105

Rapaport, W. J. (2018). Syntactic Semantics and the Proper Treatment of Computationalism. In M. Danesi (Ed.), *Empirical Research on Semiotics and Visual Rhetoric* (pp. 128–176). Hershey, PA: IGI Global. doi:10.4018/978-1-5225-5622-0.ch007

Raut, R., Priyadarshinee, P., & Jha, M. (2017). Understanding the Mediation Effect of Cloud Computing Adoption in Indian Organization: Integrating TAM-TOE- Risk Model. *International Journal of Service Science, Management, Engineering, and Technology*, *8*(3), 40–59. doi:10.4018/IJSSMET.2017070103

Rezaie, S., Mirabedini, S. J., & Abtahi, A. (2018). Designing a Model for Implementation of Business Intelligence in the Banking Industry. *International Journal of Enterprise Information Systems*, *14*(1), 77–103. doi:10.4018/IJEIS.2018010105

Rezende, D. A. (2018). Strategic Digital City Projects: Innovative Information and Public Services Offered by Chicago (USA) and Curitiba (Brazil). In M. Lytras, L. Daniela, & A. Visvizi (Eds.), *Enhancing Knowledge Discovery and Innovation in the Digital Era* (pp. 204–223). Hershey, PA: IGI Global. doi:10.4018/978-1-5225-4191-2.ch012

Rodriguez, A., Rico-Diaz, A. J., Rabuñal, J. R., & Gestal, M. (2017). Fish Tracking with Computer Vision Techniques: An Application to Vertical Slot Fishways. In M. S., & V. V. (Eds.), Multi-Core Computer Vision and Image Processing for Intelligent Applications (pp. 74-104). Hershey, PA: IGI Global. https://doi.org/doi:10.4018/978-1-5225-0889-2.ch003

Romero, J. A. (2018). Sustainable Advantages of Business Value of Information Technology. In M. Khosrow-Pour, D.B.A. (Ed.), Encyclopedia of Information Science and Technology, Fourth Edition (pp. 923-929). Hershey, PA: IGI Global. doi:10.4018/978-1-5225-2255-3.ch079

Romero, J. A. (2018). The Always-On Business Model and Competitive Advantage. In N. Bajgoric (Ed.), *Always-On Enterprise Information Systems for Modern Organizations* (pp. 23–40). Hershey, PA: IGI Global. doi:10.4018/978-1-5225-3704-5.ch002

Rosen, Y. (2018). Computer Agent Technologies in Collaborative Learning and Assessment. In M. Khosrow-Pour, D.B.A. (Ed.), Encyclopedia of Information Science and Technology, Fourth Edition (pp. 2402-2410). Hershey, PA: IGI Global. doi:10.4018/978-1-5225-2255-3.ch209

Roy, D. (2018). Success Factors of Adoption of Mobile Applications in Rural India: Effect of Service Characteristics on Conceptual Model. In M. Khosrow-Pour (Ed.), *Green Computing Strategies for Competitive Advantage and Business Sustainability* (pp. 211–238). Hershey, PA: IGI Global. doi:10.4018/978-1-5225-5017-4.ch010

Ruffin, T. R., & Hawkins, D. P. (2018). Trends in Health Care Information Technology and Informatics. In M. Khosrow-Pour, D.B.A. (Ed.), Encyclopedia of Information Science and Technology, Fourth Edition (pp. 3805-3815). Hershey, PA: IGI Global. doi:10.4018/978-1-5225-2255-3.ch330

Sadasivam, U. M., & Ganesan, N. (2021). Detecting Fake News Using Deep Learning and NLP. In S. Misra, C. Arumugam, S. Jaganathan, & S. S. (Eds.), *Confluence of AI, Machine, and Deep Learning in Cyber Forensics* (pp. 117-133). IGI Global. https://doi.org/10.4018/978-1-7998-4900-1.ch007

Safari, M. R., & Jiang, Q. (2018). The Theory and Practice of IT Governance Maturity and Strategies Alignment: Evidence From Banking Industry. *Journal of Global Information Management, 26*(2), 127–146. doi:10.4018/JGIM.2018040106

Sahin, H. B., & Anagun, S. S. (2018). Educational Computer Games in Math Teaching: A Learning Culture. In E. Toprak & E. Kumtepe (Eds.), *Supporting Multiculturalism in Open and Distance Learning Spaces* (pp. 249–280). Hershey, PA: IGI Global. doi:10.4018/978-1-5225-3076-3.ch013

Sakalle, A., Tomar, P., Bhardwaj, H., & Sharma, U. (2021). Impact and Latest Trends of Intelligent Learning With Artificial Intelligence. In S. Verma & P. Tomar (Eds.), *Impact of AI Technologies on Teaching, Learning, and Research in Higher Education* (pp. 172-189). IGI Global. https://doi.org/10.4018/978-1-7998-4763-2.ch011

Sala, N. (2021). Virtual Reality, Augmented Reality, and Mixed Reality in Education: A Brief Overview. In D. Choi, A. Dailey-Hebert, & J. Estes (Eds.), *Current and Prospective Applications of Virtual Reality in Higher Education* (pp. 48–73). IGI Global. https://doi.org/10.4018/978-1-7998-4960-5.ch003

Salunkhe, S., Kanagachidambaresan, G., Rajkumar, C., & Jayanthi, K. (2022). Online Detection and Prediction of Fused Deposition Modelled Parts Using Artificial Intelligence. In S. Salunkhe, H. Hussein, & J. Davim (Eds.), *Applications of Artificial Intelligence in Additive Manufacturing* (pp. 194–209). IGI Global. https://doi.org/10.4018/978-1-7998-8516-0.ch009

Samy, V. S., Pramanick, K., Thenkanidiyoor, V., & Victor, J. (2021). Data Analysis and Visualization in Python for Polar Meteorological Data. *International Journal of Data Analytics, 2*(1), 32–60. https://doi.org/10.4018/IJDA.2021010102

Sanna, A., & Valpreda, F. (2017). An Assessment of the Impact of a Collaborative Didactic Approach and Students' Background in Teaching Computer Animation. *International Journal of Information and Communication Technology Education, 13*(4), 1–16. doi:10.4018/IJICTE.2017100101

Sarivougioukas, J., & Vagelatos, A. (2022). Fused Contextual Data With Threading Technology to Accelerate Processing in Home UbiHealth. *International Journal of Software Science and Computational Intelligence, 14*(1), 1–14. https://doi.org/10.4018/IJSSCI.285590

Scott, A., Martin, A., & McAlear, F. (2017). Enhancing Participation in Computer Science among Girls of Color: An Examination of a Preparatory AP Computer Science Intervention. In Y. Rankin & J. Thomas (Eds.), *Moving Students of Color from Consumers to Producers of Technology* (pp. 62–84). Hershey, PA: IGI Global. doi:10.4018/978-1-5225-2005-4.ch004

Shanmugam, M., Ibrahim, N., Gorment, N. Z., Sugu, R., Dandarawi, T. N., & Ahmad, N. A. (2022). Towards an Integrated Omni-Channel Strategy Framework for Improved Customer Interaction. In P. Lai (Ed.), *Handbook of Research on Social Impacts of E-Payment and Blockchain Technology* (pp. 409–427). IGI Global. https://doi.org/10.4018/978-1-7998-9035-5.ch022

Sharma, A., & Kumar, S. (2021). Network Slicing and the Role of 5G in IoT Applications. In S. Kumar, M. Trivedi, P. Ranjan, & A. Punhani (Eds.), *Evolution of Software-Defined Networking Foundations for IoT and 5G Mobile Networks* (pp. 172–190). IGI Global. https://doi.org/10.4018/978-1-7998-4685-7.ch010

Siddoo, V., & Wongsai, N. (2017). Factors Influencing the Adoption of ISO/IEC 29110 in Thai Government Projects: A Case Study. *International Journal of Information Technologies and Systems Approach, 10*(1), 22–44. doi:10.4018/IJITSA.2017010102

Silveira, C., Hir, M. E., & Chaves, H. K. (2022). An Approach to Information Management as a Subsidy of Global Health Actions: A Case Study of Big Data in Health for Dengue, Zika, and Chikungunya. In J. Lima de Magalhães, Z. Hartz, G. Jamil, H. Silveira, & L. Jamil (Eds.), *Handbook of Research on Essential Information Approaches to Aiding Global Health in the One Health Context* (pp. 219–234). IGI Global. https://doi.org/10.4018/978-1-7998-8011-0.ch012

Simões, A. (2017). Using Game Frameworks to Teach Computer Programming. In R. Alexandre Peixoto de Queirós & M. Pinto (Eds.), *Gamification-Based E-Learning Strategies for Computer Programming Education* (pp. 221–236). Hershey, PA: IGI Global. doi:10.4018/978-1-5225-1034-5.ch010

Simões de Almeida, R., & da Silva, T. (2022). AI Chatbots in Mental Health: Are We There Yet? In A. Marques & R. Queirós (Eds.), *Digital Therapies in Psychosocial Rehabilitation and Mental Health* (pp. 226–243). IGI Global. https://doi.org/10.4018/978-1-7998-8634-1.ch011

Singh, L. K., Khanna, M., Thawkar, S., & Gopal, J. (2021). Robustness for Authentication of the Human Using Face, Ear, and Gait Multimodal Biometric System. *International Journal of Information System Modeling and Design, 12*(1), 39–72. https://doi.org/10.4018/IJISMD.2021010103

Sllame, A. M. (2017). Integrating LAB Work With Classes in Computer Network Courses. In H. Alphin Jr, R. Chan, & J. Lavine (Eds.), *The Future of Accessibility in International Higher Education* (pp. 253–275). Hershey, PA: IGI Global. doi:10.4018/978-1-5225-2560-8.ch015

Smirnov, A., Ponomarev, A., Shilov, N., Kashevnik, A., & Teslya, N. (2018). Ontology-Based Human-Computer Cloud for Decision Support: Architecture and Applications in Tourism. *International Journal of Embedded and Real-Time Communication Systems, 9*(1), 1–19. doi:10.4018/IJERTCS.2018010101

Smith-Ditizio, A. A., & Smith, A. D. (2018). Computer Fraud Challenges and Its Legal Implications. In M. Khosrow-Pour, D.B.A. (Ed.), Encyclopedia of Information Science and Technology, Fourth Edition (pp. 4837-4848). Hershey, PA: IGI Global. doi:10.4018/978-1-5225-2255-3.ch419

Sosnin, P. (2018). Figuratively Semantic Support of Human-Computer Interactions. In *Experience-Based Human-Computer Interactions: Emerging Research and Opportunities* (pp. 244–272). Hershey, PA: IGI Global. doi:10.4018/978-1-5225-2987-3.ch008

Srilakshmi, R., & Jaya Bhaskar, M. (2021). An Adaptable Secure Scheme in Mobile Ad hoc Network to Protect the Communication Channel From Malicious Behaviours. *International Journal of Information Technology and Web Engineering, 16*(3), 54–73. https://doi.org/10.4018/IJITWE.2021070104

Sukhwani, N., Kagita, V. R., Kumar, V., & Panda, S. K. (2021). Efficient Computation of Top-K Skyline Objects in Data Set With Uncertain Preferences. *International Journal of Data Warehousing and Mining, 17*(3), 68–80. https://doi.org/10.4018/IJDWM.2021070104

Susanto, H., Yie, L. F., Setiana, D., Asih, Y., Yoganingrum, A., Riyanto, S., & Saputra, F. A. (2021). Digital Ecosystem Security Issues for Organizations and Governments: Digital Ethics and Privacy. In Z. Mahmood (Ed.), *Web 2.0 and Cloud Technologies for Implementing Connected Government* (pp. 204–228). IGI Global. https://doi.org/10.4018/978-1-7998-4570-6.ch010

Syväjärvi, A., Leinonen, J., Kivivirta, V., & Kesti, M. (2017). The Latitude of Information Management in Local Government: Views of Local Government Managers. *International Journal of Electronic Government Research, 13*(1), 69–85. doi:10.4018/IJEGR.2017010105

Tanque, M., & Foxwell, H. J. (2018). Big Data and Cloud Computing: A Review of Supply Chain Capabilities and Challenges. In A. Prasad (Ed.), *Exploring the Convergence of Big Data and the Internet of Things* (pp. 1–28). Hershey, PA: IGI Global. doi:10.4018/978-1-5225-2947-7.ch001

Teixeira, A., Gomes, A., & Orvalho, J. G. (2017). Auditory Feedback in a Computer Game for Blind People. In T. Issa, P. Kommers, T. Issa, P. Isaías, & T. Issa (Eds.), *Smart Technology Applications in Business Environments* (pp. 134–158). Hershey, PA: IGI Global. doi:10.4018/978-1-5225-2492-2.ch007

Tewari, P., Tiwari, P., & Goel, R. (2022). Information Technology in Supply Chain Management. In V. Garg & R. Goel (Eds.), *Handbook of Research on Innovative Management Using AI in Industry 5.0* (pp. 165–178). IGI Global. https://doi.org/10.4018/978-1-7998-8497-2.ch011

Thompson, N., McGill, T., & Murray, D. (2018). Affect-Sensitive Computer Systems. In M. Khosrow-Pour, D.B.A. (Ed.), Encyclopedia of Information Science and Technology, Fourth Edition (pp. 4124-4135). Hershey, PA: IGI Global. doi:10.4018/978-1-5225-2255-3.ch357

Triberti, S., Brivio, E., & Galimberti, C. (2018). On Social Presence: Theories, Methodologies, and Guidelines for the Innovative Contexts of Computer-Mediated Learning. In M. Marmon (Ed.), *Enhancing Social Presence in Online Learning Environments* (pp. 20–41). Hershey, PA: IGI Global. doi:10.4018/978-1-5225-3229-3.ch002

Tripathy, B. K. T. R., S., & Mohanty, R. K. (2018). Memetic Algorithms and Their Applications in Computer Science. In S. Dash, B. Tripathy, & A. Rahman (Eds.), Handbook of Research on Modeling, Analysis, and Application of Nature-Inspired Metaheuristic Algorithms (pp. 73-93). Hershey, PA: IGI Global. https://doi.org/ doi:10.4018/978-1-5225-2857-9.ch004

Turulja, L., & Bajgoric, N. (2017). Human Resource Management IT and Global Economy Perspective: Global Human Resource Information Systems. In M. Khosrow-Pour (Ed.), *Handbook of Research on Technology Adoption, Social Policy, and Global Integration* (pp. 377–394). Hershey, PA: IGI Global. doi:10.4018/978-1-5225-2668-1.ch018

Unwin, D. W., Sanzogni, L., & Sandhu, K. (2017). Developing and Measuring the Business Case for Health Information Technology. In K. Moahi, K. Bwalya, & P. Sebina (Eds.), *Health Information Systems and the Advancement of Medical Practice in Developing Countries* (pp. 262–290). Hershey, PA: IGI Global. doi:10.4018/978-1-5225-2262-1.ch015

Usharani, B. (2022). House Plant Leaf Disease Detection and Classification Using Machine Learning. In M. Mundada, S. Seema, S. K.G., & M. Shilpa (Eds.), *Deep Learning Applications for Cyber-Physical Systems* (pp. 17-26). IGI Global. https://doi.org/10.4018/978-1-7998-8161-2.ch002

Vadhanam, B. R. S., M., Sugumaran, V., V., V., & Ramalingam, V. V. (2017). Computer Vision Based Classification on Commercial Videos. In M. S., & V. V. (Eds.), Multi-Core Computer Vision and Image Processing for Intelligent Applications (pp. 105-135). Hershey, PA: IGI Global. https://doi.org/ doi:10.4018/978-1-5225-0889-2.ch004

Vairinho, S. (2022). Innovation Dynamics Through the Encouragement of Knowledge Spin-Off From Touristic Destinations. In C. Ramos, S. Quinteiro, & A. Gonçalves (Eds.), *ICT as Innovator Between Tourism and Culture* (pp. 170–190). IGI Global. https://doi.org/10.4018/978-1-7998-8165-0.ch011

Valverde, R., Torres, B., & Motaghi, H. (2018). A Quantum NeuroIS Data Analytics Architecture for the Usability Evaluation of Learning Management Systems. In S. Bhattacharyya (Ed.), *Quantum-Inspired Intelligent Systems for Multimedia Data Analysis* (pp. 277–299). Hershey, PA: IGI Global. doi:10.4018/978-1-5225-5219-2.ch009

Vassilis, E. (2018). Learning and Teaching Methodology: "1:1 Educational Computing. In K. Koutsopoulos, K. Doukas, & Y. Kotsanis (Eds.), *Handbook of Research on Educational Design and Cloud Computing in Modern Classroom Settings* (pp. 122–155). Hershey, PA: IGI Global. doi:10.4018/978-1-5225-3053-4.ch007

Verma, S., & Jain, A. K. (2022). A Survey on Sentiment Analysis Techniques for Twitter. In B. Gupta, D. Peraković, A. Abd El-Latif, & D. Gupta (Eds.), *Data Mining Approaches for Big Data and Sentiment Analysis in Social Media* (pp. 57–90). IGI Global. https://doi.org/10.4018/978-1-7998-8413-2.ch003

Wang, H., Huang, P., & Chen, X. (2021). Research and Application of a Multidimensional Association Rules Mining Method Based on OLAP. *International Journal of Information Technology and Web Engineering*, *16*(1), 75–94. https://doi.org/10.4018/IJITWE.2021010104

Wexler, B. E. (2017). Computer-Presented and Physical Brain-Training Exercises for School Children: Improving Executive Functions and Learning. In B. Dubbels (Ed.), *Transforming Gaming and Computer Simulation Technologies across Industries* (pp. 206–224). Hershey, PA: IGI Global. doi:10.4018/978-1-5225-1817-4.ch012

Wimble, M., Singh, H., & Phillips, B. (2018). Understanding Cross-Level Interactions of Firm-Level Information Technology and Industry Environment: A Multilevel Model of Business Value. *Information Resources Management Journal*, *31*(1), 1–20. doi:10.4018/IRMJ.2018010101

Wimmer, H., Powell, L., Kilgus, L., & Force, C. (2017). Improving Course Assessment via Web-based Homework. *International Journal of Online Pedagogy and Course Design*, *7*(2), 1–19. doi:10.4018/IJOPCD.2017040101

Wong, S. (2021). Gendering Information and Communication Technologies in Climate Change. In M. Khosrow-Pour D.B.A. (Eds.), *Encyclopedia of Information Science and Technology, Fifth Edition* (pp. 1408-1422). IGI Global. https://doi.org/10.4018/978-1-7998-3479-3.ch096

Wong, Y. L., & Siu, K. W. (2018). Assessing Computer-Aided Design Skills. In M. Khosrow-Pour, D.B.A. (Ed.), Encyclopedia of Information Science and Technology, Fourth Edition (pp. 7382-7391). Hershey, PA: IGI Global. doi:10.4018/978-1-5225-2255-3.ch642

Wongsurawat, W., & Shrestha, V. (2018). Information Technology, Globalization, and Local Conditions: Implications for Entrepreneurs in Southeast Asia. In P. Ordóñez de Pablos (Ed.), *Management Strategies and Technology Fluidity in the Asian Business Sector* (pp. 163–176). Hershey, PA: IGI Global. doi:10.4018/978-1-5225-4056-4.ch010

Yamada, H. (2021). Homogenization of Japanese Industrial Technology From the Perspective of R&D Expenses. *International Journal of Systems and Service-Oriented Engineering*, *11*(2), 24–51. doi:10.4018/IJSSOE.2021070102

Yang, Y., Zhu, X., Jin, C., & Li, J. J. (2018). Reforming Classroom Education Through a QQ Group: A Pilot Experiment at a Primary School in Shanghai. In H. Spires (Ed.), *Digital Transformation and Innovation in Chinese Education* (pp. 211–231). Hershey, PA: IGI Global. doi:10.4018/978-1-5225-2924-8.ch012

Yilmaz, R., Sezgin, A., Kurnaz, S., & Arslan, Y. Z. (2018). Object-Oriented Programming in Computer Science. In M. Khosrow-Pour, D.B.A. (Ed.), Encyclopedia of Information Science and Technology, Fourth Edition (pp. 7470-7480). Hershey, PA: IGI Global. doi:10.4018/978-1-5225-2255-3.ch650

Yu, L. (2018). From Teaching Software Engineering Locally and Globally to Devising an Internationalized Computer Science Curriculum. In S. Dikli, B. Etheridge, & R. Rawls (Eds.), *Curriculum Internationalization and the Future of Education* (pp. 293–320). Hershey, PA: IGI Global. doi:10.4018/978-1-5225-2791-6.ch016

Yuhua, F. (2018). Computer Information Library Clusters. In M. Khosrow-Pour, D.B.A. (Ed.), Encyclopedia of Information Science and Technology, Fourth Edition (pp. 4399-4403). Hershey, PA: IGI Global. doi:10.4018/978-1-5225-2255-3.ch382

Zakaria, R. B., Zainuddin, M. N., & Mohamad, A. H. (2022). Distilling Blockchain: Complexity, Barriers, and Opportunities. In P. Lai (Ed.), *Handbook of Research on Social Impacts of E-Payment and Blockchain Technology* (pp. 89–114). IGI Global. https://doi.org/10.4018/978-1-7998-9035-5.ch007

Zhang, Z., Ma, J., & Cui, X. (2021). Genetic Algorithm With Three-Dimensional Population Dominance Strategy for University Course Timetabling Problem. *International Journal of Grid and High Performance Computing*, *13*(2), 56–69. https://doi.org/10.4018/IJGHPC.2021040104

About the Contributors

Marzena Sobczak-Michalowska is Vice-Rector of International Affairs, University of Economy in Bydgoszcz, Poland and Director of the Europe Direct European Information Point in Toruń. She obtained her Ph.D. in 1992 in the field of pedagogy, Academy of Pedagogical Sciences in Moscow. She has been awarded with acknowledgement letter from the Marshal of the Kuyavian-Pomeranian Voivodeship, Waldemar Achramowicz, for involvement and contribution to the construction of a strategy for social welfare and from the Mayor of Bydgoszcz for presenting a review of the study and for fruitful cooperation with the District Labour Office in Bydgoszcz. She obtained a commemorative medal minted on the occasion of the 95th anniversary of the CSO and medal of the National Education Commission for special merits in the field of education and upbringing. Also she obtained Zhubanov University medal for building international relations. She is involved with more than 15 number of selected scientific and research projects and scientific editor of more than 20 books.

Samarjeet Borah is currently working as Professor in the Department of Computer Applications, SMIT, Sikkim Manipal University (SMU), Sikkim, India. Dr. Borah handles various academics, research and administrative activities such as curriculum development, Board of Studies, Doctoral Research Committee, IT Infrastructure Management etc. inSikkim Manipal University. Dr. Borah is involved with various funded projects from AICTE (Govt. of India), DST-CSRI (Govt. of India)etc. in the capacity of Principal Investigator/Co-principal Investigator. He has organized various national and international conferences such as ISRO Sponsored Training Programme on Remote Sensing & GIS, NCWBCB 2014, NER-WNLP 2014, IC3-2016, IC3-2018, ICDSM-2019, ICAET-2020, IC3-2020 etc. Dr. Borah is involved with various book volumes and journals of repute for Springer, IEEE, Inderscience, IGI Global etc. in the capacity of Editor/Guest Editor/Reviewer.He is editor-in-chief of the book/proceedings series – Research Notes on Computing and Communication Sciences, Apple Academic Press, USA.

Zdzislaw Polkowski is associated with the Department of Humanities and Social Sciences, The Karkonosze University of Applied Sciences in Jelenia Góra, Poland. He holds a PhD degree in Computer Science and Management from Wroclaw University of Technology, Post Graduate degree in Microcomputer Systems in Management from University of Economics in Wroclaw and Post Graduate degree IT in Education from Economics University in Katowice. He obtained his Engineering degree in Industrial Computer Systems from Technical University of Zielona Gora. He has published more than 55 papers in journals, 15 conference proceedings, including more than 8 papers in journals indexed in the Web of Science. He served as a member of Technical Program Committee in many International conferences in Poland, India, China, Iran, Romania and Bulgaria.

Sambit Kumar Mishra is having more than 25 years of teaching experience in different AICTE approved institutions in India. He obtained his Bachelor Degree in Engineering in Computer Engineering from Amravati University, Maharashtra, India in 1991, M.Tech. in Computer Science from Indian School of Mines, Dhanbad(Now IIT, Dhanbad), India in 1998 and Ph.D. in Computer Science and Engineering from Siksha 'O' Anusandhan University, Bhubaneswar, Odisha, India in 2015. He has more than 33 publications in different peer reviewed International Journals and editorial board member of different peer reviewed indexed Journals. Presently he is working as Professor in the Department of Computer Science and Engineering, Gandhi Institute for Education and Technology, Baniatangi, Bhubaneswar, Odisha, India.

* * *

Olena Akilina is a Ph.D. in Economics, Associate Professor of the Department of Management at Borys Grinchenko Kyiv Metropolitan University. She has repeatedly trained in the Czech Republic, Poland and the Baltic States with the focus on the problem of leadership in education. She has twenty-five years of teaching experience. She has been lecturing on the topics of labour and social economics, management, change management. She is an author of more than 80 scientific and methodical papers. Participation in co-project of Kyiv National Economic University, Jean Monnet Fund and Education, Audiovisual and Culture Executive Agency (528395-LLP-1-2012-1- UA-AJM-CH/1), personal contribution: development of the research 'Social identification of EU regions development'. Currently a member of the EU project (Erasmus+ "Peace education for consolidated and human-centered Europe" 101094420 — PeaECH — ERASMUS-JMO-2022-HEI-TCH-RSCH-UA-IBA). Within the framework of this project, she created a content module ("Basic Mediation Skills"), which is part of the course " Peace Education in Management and Business " taught at the second master's level for managers (including educational managers) and civil servants.

Parimal Kumar Giri has over 25 years of academic experience in teaching and research. He received his PhD in Information and Communication Technology from Fakir Mohan University, Balasore, India. His research interests are machine learning techniques, evolutionary optimization, social network analysis and financial engineering problems.

Liudmyla Ilich is a Doctor of Economics, Associate Professor, Mentor, Coach, Emotional intelligence analyst. In 2001 graduated from the State Academy of Statistics, Accounting and Audit, Kiev. Specialty: Economist. In 2006 she defended her PhD thesis 'The Labor Potential of Ukraine and Efficiency of Its Using' specialty 08.09.01 – 'Demography, Labor Economics, Social and Economic Policy'. In 2018 she defended her doctoral thesis 'Structural changes in the transitional labor market: theory and methodology of regulation' specialty 08.09.01 – 'Demography, Labor Economics, Social and Economic Policy'. The overall research and teaching experience – 19 years. Author of more than 100 scientific and methodical publications, including monographs: 'The Formation and Realization of Labor Potential of Ukraine in a Demographic Crisis', 'Reproduction of Labor Potential and Effectiveness of Its Using in Ukraine', collective monograph 'Strategy of Socio-Economic Development: State, Society, Person', 'The New Format of Strategy and Tactic of Social and Economic Development of Ukraine: People, Community, Nation', 'The Way to Leadership - European Choice of Ukraine', 'Joint Stock Model of the Economy of Ukraine', 'Corporate Capitalism: Prerequisites of Formation', 'Socio and Economic Paradigms of Modern Humanism', 'Intellectualization of Human Capital', 'Labor Market and Education: Searching the Interaction', 'Ukrainian Labor Market: Characteristics of and Efficiency of Functioning', 'Socio-economic reforms of the national economy recovery: the experience of Ukraine', ' Structural risks and systemic dynamics of socio-economic development of the national economy: the european vector' and others. She is co-author of the textbook 'Labor Economics and Labor Relations'. During her research activities she participated in 70 international scientific conferences and congresses. Scientific interests: Problems of labour and educational markets, methodological and practical aspects of social monitoring, forecasting skills and labour market needs, supervising of educational quality.She completed an internship in Germany, the Czech Republic, Poland, Slovakia, Croatia, Latvia, Lithuania, Estonia, and Turkey, where she learned about the specifics of the organisation and regulation of the educational systems of the EU countries, tools for implementing the European Qualifications Framework, the possibilities of using a project approach in the management of educational processes, as well as other innovative technologies used in higher education within the Bologna Process. Academic coordinator of the Erasmus+ Jean Monnet Module "Peace education for consolidated and human-centred Europe" (01.10.2022 to 30.09.2025. 101094420

- PeaECH - ERASMUS-JMO-2022-HEI-TCH-RSCH-UA-IBA). Researcher and trainer in the Erasmus+ Jean Monnet Module "European Digital Governance Expertise Brought to Ukraine: tools and effects" (01.10.2023 to 30.09.2026. 101127007- e-DEBUT- ERASMUS-JMO-2023-HEI-TCH-RSCH-UA-IBA).

Olha Ilyash is a Doctor of Economics, Professor. Member of the European Association of Labour Economists (Maastricht, the Netherlands). Member of the Shevchenko Scientific Society in Lviv. Head of the NGO 'Academic Space'. Head of the Section "Economic transformation; demographic changes and well-being of society" of the Expert Council of the Ministry of Education and Science of Ukraine on the examination of projects of scientific works, scientific and technical (experimental) developments of young scientists. Expert of the Horizon 2020 programme, in the area of Education, Audio-Visual and Culture Executive Agency programmes COSME PRESTIGIOUS PRIZES AND AWARDS: State Award, Acknowledgment of the Ministry of Education and Science of Ukraine «For many years of diligent work, a significant contribution to the training of highly qualified specialists and fruitful scientific and pedagogical activity" (2018) Certificate of Merit from the National Technical University of Ukraine "Igor Sikorsky Kyiv Polytechnic Institute" "For a significant personal contribution to the formation of the youth scientific environment and state policy in the field of developing the scientific potential of young scientists" (2017). Certificate of Merit from the National Institute for Strategic Studies under the President of Ukraine "For diligent work at the Institute, exemplary fulfillment of duties, high professionalism and on the occasion of the 25th anniversary of the National Institute for Strategic Studies foundation. Certificates of Merits and Awards of the Central Union of Consumer Associations of Ukraine "For high scientific achievements and diligent work" (2009, 2013) Winner of the Lviv Regional State Administration Award (2010).

Shyamala Devi J. is Assistant Professor at SRM IST, Ramapuram campus, Department of Computer Applications was 25 years of experience. Working on domains like Information Extraction and Machine Learning and presented paper at Internal conference and published paper at more than ten journals

Chandrakant Mallick is a Research Scholar (Engineering) in the Department of Computer Science and Engineering, Biju Patnaik University of Technology, Rourkela, Odisha, India. He is working as an assistant professor at Gandhi Institute of Technological Advancement (GITA) Autonomous College, Bhubaneswar. His experience in academia spans over two decades. His areas of research interest include machine learning, deep learning, online social networks, wireless networks, and cyber security.

Vijayalakshmi N. is an Assistant Professor (Sr.G), Department of BCA, SRMIST, Ramapuram. She completed MCA and completed his Doctorate in 2018. His area of interest is Internet of Things, Machine Learning. He published 15 research articles in reputed journal and conference proceedings.

Agusthiyar R. is currently serving as the Head of Computer Applications (BCA) at SRM Institute of Science and Technology, Chennai with an experience of more than 20 years. He obtained his Ph.D degree in the year 2017 from Anna University in the field of Data Mining. He has published several research papers in peer reviewed reputed Scopus indexed journals in the areas of Machine Learning, Cloud Computing, IOT and Data Analytics. He also the coordinator for ISRO Nodal center.

Sindhu S. received bachelor's degree in BCA Computer Application at Bharathi Women's Arts and Science College, Kallakurichi, 2009. And completed Masters in MCA Computer Applications at Dhanalakshmi Srinivasan College of Arts and Science, Perambalur, 2011. Currently doing a Ph.D in Computer Science. Specialization includes Internet of Things, Image processing and Segmentations, Machine Learning.

Suriya S. is currently serving as an Assistant Professor in the Department of Computer Applications (BCA) at SRM Institute of Science and Technology, Chennai with an experience of more than 4 years. She is Pursuing PhD at SRM Institute of Science and Technology, Chennai. She obtained her MCA degree in the year 2014 from Jerusalem College of Engineering affiliated to Anna University. She has been extensively involved in research works and published more than 10 papers in International/National level conferences and reputed Journals, in the areas of Machine Learning and IoT.

Index

M

N

O

P

R

S

T

U

www.ingramcontent.com/pod-product-compliance
Lightning Source LLC
LaVergne TN
LVHW080642011026
849160LV00014B/1298